A Cultural History
of Modern
Korean Literature

Critical Studies in Korean Literature and Culture in Translation

Series Editors: Hyunjoo Kim, Yonsei University, and Theodore Yoo, Yonsei University

This series will introduce English-language readers to critically acclaimed works written by leading Korean scholars in the arts and humanities. Korean studies is increasing in size and importance around the world—this series intends to support that growth by augmenting the body of English-language work on Korea through the translation of new and important scholarship by South Korean scholars. This includes books produced recently by a new generation of Korean scholars as well as older works that have not previously appeared in English. The studies will appeal to both academics and students interested in Korea and will include substantive introductions, as well as critical and explanatory notes and select bibliographies, by the series board.

Advisory Board

Theodore Hughes, Columbia University
Kelly Jeong, University of California, Riverside
Bodurae Kwon, Korea University
Serk Bae Suh, University of California, Irvine
Yerim Kim, Yonsei University
Steven Chung, Princeton University
Hyeryoung Lee, Sungkyunkwan University

Titles in the Series

A Cultural History of Modern Korean Literature: The Birth of Oppa, by Kyounghoon Lee
Reading Colonial Korea through Fiction: The Ventriloquists, by Kim Chul
The History of the Modern Korean Novel, 1890–1945, by Young Min Kim

A Cultural History of Modern Korean Literature

The Birth of Oppa

Kyounghoon Lee
Translated by John M. Frankl

LEXINGTON BOOKS
Lanham • Boulder • New York • London

Azaleas: A Book of Poems, by Kim Sowŏl, trans. David R. McCann. Copyright ©
2007 New York: Columbia University Press. Reprinted with permission of Columbia
University Press.

Selected Poems of So Chongju in *The Columbia Anthology of Modern Korean Poetry*,
trans. David R. McCann. Copyright © 2004 New York: Columbia University Press.
Reprinted with permission of Columbia University Press.

오빠의 탄생 Copyright © 2003 by Kyounghoon Lee
Originally published in 2003 by Moonji Publishing Co., Ltd.
All rights reserved.

Published by Lexington Books
An imprint of The Rowman & Littlefield Publishing Group, Inc.
4501 Forbes Boulevard, Suite 200, Lanham, Maryland 20706
www.rowman.com

86-90 Paul Street, London EC2A 4NE

Copyright © 2022 by The Rowman & Littlefield Publishing Group, Inc.

British Library Cataloguing in Publication Information Available

Library of Congress Cataloging-in-Publication Data

Names: Yi, Kyŏng-hun, 1962– author. | Frankl, John Mark, translator.
Title: A cultural history of modern Korean literature : the birth of oppa / Kyounghoon
    Lee ; translated by John Frankl.
Other titles: Oppa ŭi t'ansaeng. English
Description: Lanham : Lexington Books, [2022] | Series: Critical studies in Korean
    literature and culture in translation | Translation of: Oppa ŭi t'ansaeng : Han'guk
    kŭndae munhak ŭi p'ungsoksa : Yi Kyŏng-hun pip'yŏngjip. | Includes bibliographical
    references and index.
Identifiers: LCCN 2021053790 (print) | LCCN 2021053791 (ebook) |
    ISBN 9781666906288 (cloth) | ISBN 9781666906301 (paper) |
    ISBN 9781666906295 (ebook)
Subjects: LCSH: Korean fiction—20th century—History and criticism. |
    Korean literature—Social aspects. | Korea—Social life and customs—1910–1945.
Classification: LCC PL967.6 .Y5613 2022 (print) | LCC PL967.6 (ebook) |
    DDC 895.73/309—dc23/eng/20211129
LC record available at https://lccn.loc.gov/2021053790
LC ebook record available at https://lccn.loc.gov/2021053791

Contents

Acknowledgments

I would like to express my profound gratitude to Professor John M. Frankl for his elaborate translation of the book, Yonsei University's College of Liberal Arts for supporting this project with a generous translation fund, and Professor Theodore Jun Yoo for shepherding the manuscript through the publication process with Lexington Books. In addition, I would like to thank Professors Janet Poole, Jin-kyung Lee, Travis Workman, Yoon Sun Yang, and Youngju Ryu for reading this book and providing valuable comments.

Preface

Theodore Jun Yoo

Kyounghoon Lee (Yi Kyŏnghun) is a professor of modern Korean literature in the Korean Language and Literature Department at Yonsei University. Lee was born in Seoul in 1962, graduated from Yonsei University in 1985 where he later earned both his master's degree and doctorate in modern Korean literature. He spent several years abroad, studying at Tokyo University of Foreign Studies in Japan. From 1996 to 1999, he worked as a full-time instructor in the Department of Korean Language and Literature at Seonam University before returning to his alma mater in 2000. Lee is widely regarded as a leading commentator on modernism and colonial literature whose penetrating and incisive insights have garnered attention from a broad audience. His research and teaching interests have focused on everyday life, modernity, mass culture, and urban space, particularly wartime fascism and *chin-il* (pro-Japanese) literary works. A prodigious scholar, Lee is the author of seven critical monographs: *A Study on the Pro-Japanese Literature of Yi Kwangsu* (1998), *A Certain 100 Years, A Pleasurable New Life* (1999), *Yi Sang, The Piercing Rhetoric* (2000), *The Birth of Oppa* (2003), *Dictionary of Manners and Customs in Early Modern Korean Literature* (2006), *Memories of the Waiting Room* (2007), and *The Sunday of History, The Sunday after History: The Modern Literature of Colony* (2018). In addition to editing several important volumes, he has authored numerous articles on the works and lives of colonial writers such as Yi Sang, Pak Taewŏn, and Yŏm Sang-sŏp in top literary journals including *SAI*, *Hyŏndae munhak ŭi yŏn'gu*, *Munhak kwa sahoe*, *Sahoe wa yŏksa*, and *Sanghŏ hakbo*. Lee has also translated Japanese and English works by Karatani Kojin, Takahashi Fujitani, Tomi Suzuki, and Michael Ryan into Korean. He has served as president of International Association for Korean Literary and Cultural Studies and the director of the *Sanghŏ hakhoe* (Association for the Study of Yi T'aejun) and was a member of the editorial committee for the literary journal *Yi Sang Review* from 2000 to 2010.

A distillation of his major works, *A Cultural History of Modern Korean Literature: The Birth of Oppa*, which was selected as an outstanding work in 2004 by the National Academy of Sciences (Republic of Korea), is by any measure a remarkable work. Lee considers a wide range of literary and cultural texts, exploring significant historical moments while critically assessing everyday life, mainly how modernity, colonialism, and total war shaped national and cultural identities. This text also reflects the complex and refractory legacy of Japanese colonialism and modernity, offering surprising new perspectives and astute insights into Korean society and popular culture.

A Cultural History of Modern Korean Literature: The Birth of Oppa covers a broad range of topics in modern Korean literature, history, and culture in ten diverse chapters. The opening chapter, "Nolbu-esque Things" named after the eponymous protagonist from classical literature, explores familiar characters and themes from classical and early modern eras in Korean literature. "The Birth of *Oppa*," from which the book takes its name, offers a genealogy of the term *oppa* (a woman's older brother) and its socio-historic and cultural contexts and relevance in contemporary Korean popular culture. The complex relations between Korea, Japan, and the West are the topic of "'Trademark' of the Colony," which sheds light on the effects of commodity capitalism under colonialism. "The Fashion of *Mujŏng*" analyzes Yi Kwangsu's famous novel to elucidate on the rise of modern customs and fashion. The characteristics of modernity come under scrutiny in "Barbarian of the Laboratory," which considers issues such as suicide, the invention of time, free love, and capitalist fetishism. "Rice Speculation, Hot Springs, English" probes the relationship between the laboratory and the market and modern desire through mundane activities like leisure, luxury, and language. Lee interrogates the influence of the English language, physical activity, and modern technology on Koreans in "English Grammar, Sports, Cyborg." In "The Flesh, Yi Sang's Windowpane," Lee offers a window into the world of the colonial intellectuals through a nuanced reading of the oeuvres of Yi Sang, a modernist writer, artist, and architect. He follows up with "The Humor of an Empty Stomach," which investigates modernist aesthetics through Yi Sang's fictional and poetic explorations of food and drink, hunger and thirst, and modern taste and appetite. The final chapter, "Manchuria and Pro-Japanese Romanticism," engages with the thorny issue of empire and wartime politics, particularly the politically charged atmosphere of the Pacific War and Japan's establishment of a puppet state of Manchukuo.

A Cultural History of Modern Korean Literature: The Birth of Oppa is a significant scholarly achievement that provides a gateway to Korean literature for the Anglophone world. A work of brilliant scholarship and profound erudition, broad in scope and rich in creativity, depth, and originality, Lee delves deeply into the logic of modernity, everyday life, and material reality in colonial Korea. This book offers what Bertolt Brecht calls "the distancing effect" of modern Korean culture, inspiring readers to view what was familiar to them as strange and new.

Introduction

Colonial Modern Literature, Modern Literature as Colony

This book seeks to investigate modern Korean literature and modernity itself through a diversity of colonial customs. Here, customs refer to, as the novelist Kim Namch'ŏn put it, conditions in which "the essence of social organizations" has become "fully incarnate." This can be discussed in several dimensions. To begin with, it evokes the issue of literary material. For instance, as can clearly be seen in both Ch'oe Namsŏn's "*Kyŏngbu ch'ŏlto norae*" (Song of the Seoul-Busan Railway, 1908) and Yi Kwangsu's *Kaech'ŏkcha* (*The Pioneer*, 1917–1918), trains and clocks are objects frequently treated in modern literature. Of course, they are not mere random material. Trains and clocks, by measuring and segmenting time and space according to a new criterion, are involved in the core modern project of neutralizing and demystifying time and space. Moreover, by genuinely routinizing rational planning and the ideology of progress, these objects mediate the themes of enlightenment and civilization. The Buddhist monk and poet Han Yongun's establishing of the Kyŏngsŏng Myŏngjin Surveying Institute, and, furthermore, Im Hwa's writing the following lines of poetry are not unrelated to this.

> The road to that great capital called Hope
> though perhaps not straight as the Seoul-Busan Railroad line,
> Ah! Friends, my eyes
> like sparks, are blazing red over the several places north and south
> to which you have all scattered like stars.
>
> Im Hwa, "*Chido.*" (Map, 1937)

With this in mind, Ch'oe Sŭnggu's essay "Nŏ-rŭl hyŏngmyŏng hara" ("Revolutionize Yourself!," 1915), which asserted that in order to participate in the "university athletic meets" that were being held between each nation

1

and country Koreans must run "with at least ten times more speed," is of profound significance. This is because it specifies the meaning of sporting events such as the marathon or the 100-meter dash. These record competitions verify that, regardless of the various mythological imaginations or actual lived experiences of space and time, 42.195 kilometers and 100 meters can be measured in exactly the same way at any place in the world (or universe), as well as the fact that the speed at which a human being runs those distances can be measured with an identical clock. Having been measured and organized by the same ruler, all time and space are occupied by the modern. Each time a competition is held, the occupation is reconfirmed. This is how the pioneering of a colony begins. History is a human practice that vitalizes and grants diverse substance to sports, which homogenize time and space.

Viewed from this perspective, the famous scene in Yi Kwangsu's *Mujŏng* (*The Heartless*, 1917) that discovers "the violence of nature" in the form of a flood at the Samnangjin railroad junction is symbolic. To the modern person, nature is either an alienated "landscape" (Karatani Kojin) or a "ruins" (Yŏm Sangsŏp "*P'yehŏ-e sŏsŏ*" [Standing at the Ruins, 1920]). In fact, to the urban architect Yi Sang, the bucolic hamlet of Sŏngch'ŏn, lacking even a single telegraph pole, was "a horrifying green." It is in every sense the Other. This suggests the true meaning behind descriptions like the one below.

> From Ilsan all the way to Munsan, the traces of flood damage also appear not insignificant. The leaves of grain are covered in dirt, meaning it really does need to rain. Sand keeps on being washed down from upstream, which raises the water level of the Han River, and doesn't this in turn mean that the danger of flooding on the coastal plains will yearly increase? As for a remedy, afforestation seems the only hope, but I am truly worried.
>
> The scenery when looking from the Taedong River northeast out toward Sŏngsan is simply without rival.
>
> "It's too beautiful," went K's worry. Indeed, that the nature of P'yŏngyang is too beautiful is its flaw.
>
> Both the Ch'ŏngch'ŏn River and the Amnok River are swollen. . . .
>
> Departing Sinŭiju Station by the Amnok River, we set our clocks back one hour.
>
> Yi Kwangsu, "*Manju esŏ.*" (In Manchuria, 1933)

Beginning from the conclusion, what is described in the above quotation is not nature itself. The narrator's eye, in turn, is not the naked eye. The narrator's viewpoint when consecutively depicting the Han River–Taedong River–Ch'ŏngch'ŏn River–Amnok River is in all respects mediated by the train and its speed, which unfurl the "landscape" like a panorama as they hurtle forward. The rivers appear upon the train's window one after the next like scenes from a movie. Moreover, this sequential order is based less on the natural location of the rivers than on the route of the Seoul-Sinŭiju Railroad. In nature, there simply is no spatiotemporal order. Which is to say, the order of Han River–Taedong River–Ch'ŏngch'ŏn River–Amnok River cannot be detached from the teleology of the railroad as it advances northward from Seoul to Sinŭiju. Unless the train derails, or one has sufficient funds to purchase a ticket for beyond the Amnok River, this order and objective will continue to be smoothly confirmed.

Often they are mistaken for the natural locations of these linked spaces. Such confusion and derangement form the modern person's sense of space. As evidenced in the act of setting back the clock or in the mentioning of "afforestation," nature is to the modern person a reconstituted and conquered nature. More than nature, it is at once "national territory" and "the world" developed and imagined as railroads or national parks. What's more, it is a market abstracted and reorganized not only by diverse scientific investigations and technology but also countless exchanges. It is a type of colony. "Landscape" reconciles with and becomes the environment of human beings only as colony. Thus, Yi Sang wrote the following.

The microscope
Beneath it, artificiality developed exactly the same as nature.
Yi Sang, *"Ijōna kagyaku hannō"* (A Strange Reversible Reaction, 1931)

Just as the telescope shows us the macroscopic world of a distant universe invisible to the naked eye, the microscope abstracts the sense of sight to open up an infinitesimal world that would be otherwise unreachable. Through these devices, human beings gradually deepen their understanding and their utilization of nature. But this is grounded in a curious situation. In reality, the nature whose principles are observed and perceived through contrivances such as the telescope or microscope is not nature at all. This is due to the fact that nature already connotes the fact that distant stars and miniscule cells cannot be seen by the human eye. Put another way, the sense of sight alone cannot be abstracted and ideated apart from the organic constitution of the human body, and, as a result, it is precisely the inevitable limitations of that body, such as the inability to observe cells or viruses visually, that represent true nature. As such, the apprehension of nature through science and technology means, in the end, the conquering of nature and of human beings themselves by artificiality. Such operations are naturalized under the names of truth (concepts) and beauty. That being the case, nature is ultimately society.

This is the essential custom of the modern era. Nature and time and space themselves are a sort of custom. On the one hand, this manifests itself in the affective and aesthetic form known as "hometown." Together with the rational forms of "science" and "progress," this represents the modern sentimentalization of nature. The "nation" and "national territory," by artificially synthesizing rationality and sentiment, carry out full-scale mobilization. Now human beings will gladly sacrifice their lives for the country. Though this goes without saying when invading other countries, it is also the case that defending one's hometown from enemy incursions represents a conquest. These natives, by protecting their bodies from all manner of germs and viruses, also come to occupy themselves. They are patriots, people of custom who hygienically martyr themselves to the modern era.

Forming a dyad with this sort of sentimentalism is a hypersensitivity of the sort depicted below.

> On the night before I went to Namp'o, the symptoms were even more serious. Dazzled by the electric light hung high in the straitened room, and though not without apprehension that I might not once again be tormented by the hallucinations should I turn it off, I grew cross and, naked to the waist, bolted up, twisted the switch, and lay back down. But no sooner had the clinking sound faded beyond my door than my thoughts were once again seized by the scalpel of my bewhiskered teacher, the straight razor inside the drawer.
>
> Yŏm Sangsŏp, "*P'yobonsil ŭi ch'ŏnggaeguri*"
> (Green Frog of the Specimen Room, 1921)

What is tormenting the protagonist are his dissection of a frog and the "scalpel" he used to do it. Dissection takes the physical body alone and separates it from the soul or emotions, while through this process an extremely materialistic physical body becomes all the more conceptualized/ideated. Therein lies the cruelty of dissection. Dissection does not simply tear the flesh. Rather it tears the soul from the flesh. Accordingly, abstraction and conceptualization are the underlying causes of sentimentalism and hypersensitivity. This is also the fundamental principle of the electric light turned off by the protagonist. In contrast to candles or oil lamps, electric lights, by minimizing shadows and heat, seek to abstract light alone. That light must neither flicker nor burn. It is dispassionately bright, and nothing other than bright. Indeed, it emblematizes light and the idea of enlightenment. No longer can the protagonist dream. In that sense, his hallucinations and hypersensitivity are not necessarily due solely to darkness. On the contrary, they may even be due to the piercing rays of the electric light.

An analogous aspect is found in the case of Sŏngsun, the female protagonist of Yi Kwangsu's *Kaech'ŏkcha* (*The Pioneer*, 1917–1918), who thinks "after her flesh had ceased to exist, that love alone would spring forth and live on for ever and ever." For her, love is not a concrete and predicative practice. Rather it is a noun and a notion that has been semiotized as "love." Her suicide, in capitulating to precisely that notion, suggests the irony of acquiring the qualification of a modern person: being free from one's parents. Imitating Paul Eluard's poem, we could say that Sŏngsun is a human being born in order to know "love/freedom," in order to name "love/freedom." The following passage by Yi Kwangsu represents an appropriate critique of her conceptualized love.

> Although this may be said of nearly everything, by nature what we call love does not exist by itself. There may be an individual person's love—and that too for a specific person at a particular time, but there is no such thing as just love.
>
> Yi Kwangsu, *Kŭ yŏja ŭi ilsaeng*
> (*That Woman's Life*, 1934)

Modern literature sees through these sorts of customs of colonization. Of course, colonization here refers not only to the political situation of Japanese colonial rule and control. Rather it signifies the universal aspects and activities of modernity, which include the colonial system. In fact, this is the principle of modern literature itself. Figuratively speaking, description in modern fiction bears a resemblance to such things as surveying, dissecting frogs, architecture, and the construction of railroads. The use of the past tense, "*haettal*" (했다), and of "puppet manipulation," theory, both of which were stressed by Kim Tongin, reveal the modern pioneering of the colony known as literature. The modern novel dissects, calculates, designs, and organizes the material known as story, and thereby devises plot and fiction. All the way down to their innermost psychology, the characters suffer occupation at the hands of the author. The rational and teleological description of the novel is like a railroad. Just as tracks are plotted and installed on the ground, the novel experiments with causality based on the story. What progresses is not so much the story but the logic. As such, what Kim Tongin referred to as "a world of one's own creation" is actually a world conquered and reconstructed by the author's reason. Through the principle of the novel itself, the inevitability of the modern era is proclaimed and persuaded.

With regard to this sort of aspect, the case of the modern poem is also no exception. Rhythm is generated by rending selected images from nature's context and then recombining them anew. This recontextualization bears a strong resemblance to chemical research, which also artificially selects and combines natural elements to create new substances. The metaphorical vision revealed by free verse is chemical. At the same time, in that the basis for the metaphors and symbols is an individual speaker, it is also individual. As such, free verse accomplishes the individual. This in turn resembles the features of the modern person, who leaps over the existing context of social status (family origin) to occupy a new social position. Metaphorically speaking, free verse's rhythm is profession. This internalizes the temporality of "growth" and "progress."

Of course, in the sense that it aims for organic structure and existence itself, free verse is also biological and ecological. But the organism itself, so seamlessly posited by the modern person, has in many respects been reconstituted. The modern person imagines the nation-state and the universe as a community without conflict or rupture. And this is repeated as the monophonic and organic structure of free verse. Therefore, free verse belongs to the most proactive system of observing nature and appropriating "landscape." This is another name for civilization.

Thus, modern literature in and of itself is extremely customary. Moreover, it is printed and distributed in large quantities, and then exchanged for money in the market. It is often also utilized for various facets of education and mobilization. Put another way, modern literature is the actual system that activates and naturalizes such various modern discourses and practices as the individual, the ethnonation, the market, society, hometown, and love. Modern literature has been deeply pioneered while taking modern principles and aspects as its own flesh.

In this regard, modern literature is a typical colony. I intended to explore those scenes of literary colonization. The "*Oppa*" used in the title of this book represents one kind of the subject's location that symbolizes this modern activity. It is another name for custom. In short, this book is a report on the colonial customs that, by being colonized, pioneered the colony.

As I complete this book, there are a few individuals to whom I must express my gratitude. Professors Kim Ch'ŏl, Sin Hyŏnggi, and Chŏng Kwari, all at Yonsei University's Department of Korean Language and Literature, come immediately to mind. Professors Kim and Sin selflessly provided keen observations and critiques of, as well as undeserved encouragement for, the various chapters. Because of this, I was able to organize my disordered thoughts and to correct certain errors. Professor Chŏng, through his genial advice and support, made the publication of this book possible. Also deserving mention are the important observations and motivations I received from my seminar group, the "Korean-Japanese Literature Research Society," which met nearly every week for many years. I want to express my heartfelt thanks to the many friends in that seminar who studied together with me over such a sustained period of time. In addition, I would like to thank Munhak kwa chisŏng sa (Literature and Intellect) for publishing this book.

Chapter 1

Nolbu-esque Things

That gracefully flying swallow, at the hands of a cruel human
Its two wings, two legs, all broken
Scrambling to survive, gasping
At last, defeated, simply exhausted

Na Hyesŏk
"Sinsaenghwal e tŭlmyŏnsŏ"
(Upon entering a new life, 1935)

NOLBU'S SWALLOW

To Hŭngbu, "Nolbu's swallow" must have been extremely unfamiliar.[1]
Nolbu, operating under the assumption that he too will receive gourd seeds
filled with treasure, breaks and then mends a swallow's legs. The swallow's
legs are disassembled-reassembled. This is incomprehensible to Hŭngbu. The
swallow is merely an innocent creature. Accordingly, as evidenced below,
Hŭngbu is unable to imagine anything beyond saving the swallow's pitiful
life.

> After chasing it away, he sees it has eaten five of the six baby swallows. One
> remains alone and alive, but in its attempts to fly has caught its foot in a bamboo
> screen and is almost dead. Hŭngbo,[2] seeing this, is shocked, places the baby
> swallow in his hand, and sighs endlessly. "Oh, your pitiful life. Escaping the ser-
> pent, you believed you were safe, but now you must suffer the trials of a broken
> leg. Is it sins in a past life, or just a passing calamity? Among the 300 winged

animals, swallows are the truly innocent. . . . As your appearance is pitiful, I shall do my all to save you."[3]

Hŭngbu, having saved a swallow's life following an attack by a serpent, mends the swallow's legs by "wrapping them in the skin of a kingfish from Ch'ilsan, and binding them with five-colored silk thread." And he grows so close to the swallow that he asks, "Lovely swallow, do you intend to abandon me and depart?" and entreats "When you return next spring, please do visit my home." To Hŭngbu, the swallow represents an opportunity to actualize compassion and benevolence, unchanging truths that pervade the universe. The swallow's broken leg mediates between nidana and the heavens. To Hŭngbu, who attributes "the trials of a broken leg" to things such as "sins in a past life," it is not a mere functional part of a biological life form, not a mere physical appendage made up of bones, muscles, blood vessels, nerves, and cells. The swallow is a sacred object in which form and emptiness simultaneously operate. The act of preserving its existence is a kind of rite. As such, Hŭngbu's receiving the reward of the gourd seeds is predetermined, because the belief that goodwill be rewarded while evil is punished is at once the narrative principle of this sort of world and a necessity of this sort of worldview.

Nolbu's behavior below, however, stands in fundamental contrast.

Nolbo[4] had failed and, worried that he might lose his opportunity if he waited for a leg to break on its own, vowed to make it cry in order to console it. He jammed his hand into the swallows' nest, pulled out a baby swallow, snapped its two fragile legs over his knee, hurriedly placed it on the floor, then, feigning ignorance, coolly clasped his hands behind his back and paced while reciting poetry in a loud voice. . . .

   And when that no good Nolbo went to mend the swallow's legs, in an attempt to outdo Hŭngbo, he used three overlapping layers of great croaker skin, and, saying that silk thread was too thin, he tightly bound them with eight-stranded silk cord from a purse before returning it to the nest. . . . "Look here, swallow, since by my skill you were returned from near death to life, although you are a mere animal, surely you will not forget my virtue in saving you. The swallow that repaid Hŭngbo's kindness gave him three gourd seeds, so be a nice bird and more than double that, bringing me six, no, ten gourd seeds."[5]

To Nolbu, the swallow's legs are mere flesh. Not concerning himself with such trivialities as divine retribution, with his act of "snapping" them, they become simple physical organs. In order to make them heal better, he uses great croaker skin and eight-stranded silk cord in place of kingfish skin and five-colored silk thread; Nolbu only performs a surgical operation. Rather than expressing the sympathy and devotion evidenced in saying, "As your appearance is pitiful, I shall do my all to save you," he searches for and calculates efficiency in physical and medical methods to expedite the body's repair. With this, the swallow is deprived of any transcendental elements that might allow it to mediate with the heavens. Even before the comparison, "Whether the body of a man or the body of an animal, they are all like machines that make warmth"[6] appeared, Nolbu was viewing the swallow's body as a type of machine. Nolbu is the precursor for Yi Kwangsu's descriptions such as, "He was suddenly aware of an emptiness as if he had lost a few crucial parts of his internal organs."[7] And he also resembles Kim Tongin's protagonist who, after performing a surgery in which he, "after opening the abdomen, takes out some thing or the other, places some sort of metal inside, and sews it back together," muses "I'm pretty sure that my mind is not inside my body." In that same vein, the protagonist below, who intends to dissect a crow in order to eliminate the superstitious anxiety and fear of a woman suffering from tuberculosis, is also a descendent of Nolbu.

> He soon returned to his room, and later ordered the groundskeeper to hang that dead crow by its neck from a tree branch. And when the young woman appeared he vowed to dissect like a skilled surgeon its black corpse and prove that in the belly of this crow, just like other flying creatures, there were only the simple organs of a bird, and absolutely nothing like a talisman, a knife, or a blue flame.[8]

Of course, in terms of having only organs inside its belly, the swallow's case is no different. In a word, Nolbu the "dissector" discovered the physical body.

THE SWALLOW AND THE CROW

As seen above, Hŭngbu's treatment and Nolbu's treatment are fundamentally different acts. Hŭngbu's act, arising from a kind heart (ethos), has something in common with Sim Ch'ŏng's[9] martyrly act, which stems from extreme filial piety (ethos), of casting her "living body" (pathos) into the Indang Sea. Nolbu's act, however, is different from Sim Ch'ŏng's prayer: "Oh please take my father's darkened eyes and soon open them brightly so that he may see the world." It rather brings to mind the anatomical imagination and wisdom (logos) of Rabbit in *T'obyŏl-ga*[10] who says, "I have a hole in my backside from which, if I tighten my stomach, my liver comes out, and if I put it in my mouth and swallow it returns again." Rabbit, who preserves his life by convincing others that there is no liver in his body, mocks the stupidity of Turtle and the Dragon King as follows:

Hey you damn Turtle, if we discuss your crime, you are disgraceful enough to deserve death. If the Dragon King had a mind intelligent as mine, and if I didn't have my eloquence and were as stupid as the Dragon King, this body would end up a vengeful ghost of the waters. In the book *Tongnae pakŭi* it says the stupidity of animals is the same for those in water and those on land, but it appears those with scales are stupider than those with fur. How could I offer up my liver when it part of my innards?[11]

Nolbu's saying "(S)ince by my skill you were returned from near death to life, although you are a mere animal, surely you will not forget my virtue in saving you" is similar to this. Nolbu's attitude in discussing "skill" as he toys with the swallow is comparable to Rabbit's "intelligence" in mocking the stupidity of the Dragon King and Turtle. And both Nolbu and Rabbit understood the physical body as a kind of machine that could be taken apart and put back together. They stripped living creatures down to their anatomy. They eliminated the words, stories, myths, and rituality associated with the existence of living creatures.[12]

But this act of teleologically dissecting/organizing/appropriating the object (nature) resembles the activity of the rational intellect. The ulterior motive "to make it cry in order to console it" is related to this rational intellect. In his treatment Nolbu used higher better quality materials than Hŭngbu, thus he demands more seeds in return. Nolbu's logic of calculation/investment/exchange in not begrudging the expenses incurred on the swallow actualizes this rationality. To the swallow, Hŭngbu says "When you return next spring, please do visit my home." Hŭngbu's affection cannot be separated from the cycle of the seasons. Nolbu, however, when he says "How nice it would be if you didn't delay till March, but returned as soon as the new year comes, before two weeks have passed, so as not to vex me with waiting" plans a period of profit production with no relation to the seasons.

Accordingly, Nolbu's act, which simultaneously resembles both surgeon and industrialist, possesses an extremely modern character. By way of comparison, it has acquired a perspective through a windowpane[13] on the other side of which the frog is dissected in the specimen room.[14] In a broad sense, this is related to the perspective of Benjamin, who counterposed the surgeon who, at the decisive moment, abandons treating the patient as human and the cameraman.[15] Nolbu pointed the camera at the swallow. He founded the "institution of the other." And this perspective developed as follows:

Again with nickel colored forceps he clamped the flesh parted by the scalpel and opened it left and right. He selected and clamped blood vessels, and then scraped and soaked the periosteum, after which he then took up a saw and cut the leg bone. . . .

Doctors seemed to be people who had only eyes and hands, while nurses seemed to have only ears and eyes. At a single glance or word from a doctor, they moved here, moved there, like a well-oiled machine.

"No mistakes. Quickly."

Aside from these, they had no other thoughts.

"Thud."

With this strange sound, Chŏngsŏn's leg dropped. The leg was still warm, still supple. The nurse, as if lifting a piece of wood, took the fallen leg and placed it atop something that looked like a large metal plate. . . .

The doctor took his forceps and returned the displaced flesh and skin to cover the severed bone, then quickly sewed it up using a crescent moon shaped needle and white silk thread.[16]

The heavens respond to both Hŭngbu, who bestowed love without discrimination upon both humans and swallows, and Sim Ch'ŏng, who actualized extreme filial piety by offering up her own body. And, in accordance with this, the punishing of evil and rewarding of good is expected as a restoration and reaffirmation of values that operate identically upon the whole of creation. A fortune is granted as compensation for a rite. By contrast, Nolbu, viewing the swallow's body with an instrumental rationality that moves "like a well-oiled machine" and through the windowpane of profit production (trafficking in human organs would be the most extreme example of this), historicizes a causality of exchange that is divorced from the heavens. Following this, the causality that allows Sim Chŏng's filial piety to grant sight to her father can no longer exist. When viewed in terms of a rational causality (society/history) that is logically interpreted/planned/composed, the act of miraculous treatment through sacrifice is not merely impossible but even superstitious. As the history of modern literature shows us, along with the new Nolbu-esque "God" of "bodily pleasure" and of the "method by which a nervous system makes connections," trifling things such as "the soul" have already become "outdated terms." Humans no longer make offerings to the heavens. The market is the only place where contracts are made. The following scene illustrates this well.

"My single body's pleasure!" This was a new philosophy called God—the philosophy closest to scientific truth, while both his true parents and himself were unaware, had regulated not his soul (This is an outdated term.) but the method by which his nervous system makes connections.[17]

Of course, this sort of perspective will eventually transform into sociology. This applies to expressions such as "This old woman had consumed all the oil that should have been underneath her skin, and had probably consumed the oil that should have been in her internal organs and bones, and was left barely clinging to life with nothing but her hide."[18] The modern body can no longer mediate conclusions that reward good and punish evil, that unite heaven and man. Hŭngbu, who is "always working for others and unable to earn a cent," will never become a rich man. The short story "*Unsu choŭn nal* (A lucky day, 1923)"[19] proves that such things as "luck" do not exist, and Hŭngbu in modern society would be fortunate if he can merely keep his wife from starving to death.

This being the case, the reason behind Nolbu's ruin is self-evident. Nolbu fell because, by imitating Hŭngbu, he arbitrarily set foot in a world to which he had no connection. Nolbu had committed all of the following abuses and more: "selling a village's mountain," "stealing a carpenter's plane," "stripping off a tenant's clothing and evicting him just after the harvest," "welching on his debts at a bar," and "thieving an acupuncturist's needles." But these misdeeds, far from leading to Nolbu's downfall, actually served to increase his wealth. In a word, Nolbu could have gone on living as a wealthy man in a world unconnected to cosmic and human morality.

Despite this, however, Nolbu chose to capture the swallow. This was a decisive error. In so doing, he ensnared himself in a world (–rites and gifts) where divine retribution is realized. What's more, his imitating of Hŭngbu neither adhered to his own world (contracts and exchanges) nor truly followed the principles of the heavens. It was no more than a kind of parody. As evidenced in the various puns regarding his obsession below, Nolbu had deviated from his path.

Nolbu is lovesick over the swallow: among the furred animals he loves only the swallow weasel; for dishes he purchases only swallow bowls; for food he eats only swallow noodles and swallow soup; when he sees paper he folds it into swallows; and when he gets mad he swallows so hard he breaks his own neck![20]

Nolbu hovered between the world of the crow (dissection and surgery) and the world of the swallow (compassion and sympathy). By projecting the entirely physical principle of the crow onto the world of Hŭngbu, it was Nolbu's leg that wound up with a limp. Accordingly, once Nolbu had lost property and originality, it was also perfectly natural that he lost his fortune. This suggests Nolbu's true desire. He intended to possess at once the riches of both worlds, that is, both worlds themselves. He was a crow who set foot in the swallow's playground. But this was impossible for Nolbu. For it was he above all who endeavored to distinguish between Hŭngbu and himself, swallows (the heavens) and humans, as well as the spirit and the flesh.

THE SWALLOW'S LEG AND ONGNYŎN'S LEG

The swallow, however, was not the only one with an injured leg. Ongnyŏn, the protagonist of *Hyŏl ŭi nu* (*Tears of blood*, 1906), also injured her leg.

On the day she had fled, Ongnyŏn, not knowing where her parents had gone, had stood beneath Peony Peak, calling for her mother and crying her heart out. A stray bullet flew over and pierced her left leg. She fell down, and only just clung onto life that night on the mountainside.

The next day a Japanese Red Cross nurse found her and had her taken to a field hospital. When the Medical Officer saw her, he said that it was not a serious wound. The bullet had gone right through her leg. If she had been hit by a Chinese bullet—Chinese bullets had poison on them—he said, since it was last night she had been hit, the poison would have spread through her body. However, he said, the bullet which had hit her had been a Japanese one, and treatment would be very easy. Sure enough, within three weeks she was back to normal.[21]

What we can first discuss in relation to the above is the historical meaning carried by Ongnyŏn's injury. Unlike the reason behind the swallow's broken leg, her leg is hit by a bullet due to the Sino-Japanese War (1894–1895), an actual historical event. It was an injury that from the beginning had no connection to either the heavens or nature. In addition, she is injured at the same time she is separated from her parents. This is symbolic. It suggests that she has been removed from the world of filial piety as represented in the following passage from the *Book of Filial Duty*: "Our bodies—to every hair and bit of skin—are received by us from our parents, and we must not presume to injure or wound them. This is the beginning of filial piety." [22]

The line "Our bodies—to every hair and bit of skin—are received by us from our parents," uses the human body to unite the heavens (nature) and humans, parents and children. As such, humans may not do as they please with their bodies, which have been granted them by the heavens and their parents. Their existence itself is a manifestation of sanctity and spirit. Maintaining their bodies intact is not a matter of mere hygiene or health, rather it is a type of rite. And this is not only for humans; it also applies equally to all living things. It realizes humans and the totality of all that dwell in the universe, as well as nature in the traditional sense of the word. This is why the heavens can be revealed through a single trifling swallow's leg. It is also the reason the ordinance forcing men to cut their hair, which later mutated into both policing long hair (fashion–hygiene–mobilization–surveillance) and exporting wigs (fashion–exchange–growth), contained such historical significance.[23]

In separating from her parents and having her leg hit by a bullet, Ongnyŏn departs from the world of "Our bodies—to every hair and bit of skin—are received by us from our parents." Just as Chŏngsŏn, who has her leg amputated in the novel *The Soil*, takes her "rubber leg" and departs from the environment of her father, Ongnyŏn is cut off from the order of the heavens. Not only is the country housing the "son of heaven" criticized for putting poison in its bullets[24] but it also loses in a war with the country that now has the "emperor of heaven."[25] Through history, the sky has ceased to exist. With the war and international law, the sky above "Independence Gate"[26] lost its absoluteness and transformed into mere "mushy vapor." Kim Kwangjin, a character in *Kŭ yŏja ŭi ilsaeng* (That woman's life, 1934), says the following:

> What we call the sky is merely blue rays reflecting off of dust and water droplets, and thus not scary in the least, however.[27]

In this sense, Ongnyŏn's wound is critical. It produces a fissure that divides sky from man, parent from child, and flesh from spirit. Sim Ch'ŏng meets her father again, and Ch'unhyang is reunited with Yi Toryŏng.[28] Even Nolbu promises brotherly love in front of the "swallow-chinned"[29] Zhang Fei.[30] As late as the dawn of the early modern period, the elder brother in Yi Haejo's "*Ujung haengin (Wayfarer in the rain*, 1913)" decides to meet with his younger brother again after overcoming his doubts concerning the relationship of his wife and younger brother. But, in contrast to this, and more like the eternally separated brothers in Kim Tongin's "*Paettaragi (The seaman's chant*, 1921)," Ongnyŏn separates from all preexisting relationships. This is when the true wound occurs. It gives birth to a separate existence. By becoming a physical body, a lump of flesh that is not united with the spirits, the heavens, or even his own mind, man becomes a genuine individual as mediated by modern relationships. The scene below from Natsume Sōseki's *Kōjin* (*The wayfarer*, 1913), in addition to the subtle situations between elder and younger brother surrounding the elder's wife, also alludes to the position as physical body of modern man who has internalized all sorts of separations.

> Blessed is Mallarmé, whose peace of mind was disturbed by such a thing as the loss of his chair. I for one have lost almost all. Even this body—even these limbs—the little that is left in my possession, betrays me mercilessly.[31]

In accordance with the above, unlike Sim Ch'ŏng, Ongnyŏn does not make an offering to the heavens in order to actualize her filial piety. She is simply a young individual, an injured singular body. As such, Ongnyŏn's departing for Japan or America is natural. This is because the spiritual contents to fill her body, now mere flesh cut off from the heavens, will not come from the *Book of Filial Duty* or *Elementary Education*,³² which stress filial piety, but rather from the modern knowledge she will acquire through study abroad. And that knowledge will in turn give birth to a child based on Yi Kwangsu's "theory of the primacy of children,"³³ which privileges membership in society and *minjok* (ethnonation) over family.

Another thing that must be discussed is the issue of Major Inoue, the Japanese military doctor, and his sympathy for Ongnyŏn. Through him, we are able to discover a structure embedded in *Hyŏl ŭi nu* that resembles that of *Hŭngbu-chŏn*. Major Inoue, who, after treating her leg, with no thought of repayment, adopts and educates Ongnyŏn, is an existence equal to Hŭngbu. The relationship between Ongnyŏn and Inoue corresponds to that of the swallow and Hŭngbu. That being the case, the modern knowledge she will receive while studying abroad corresponds to the seeds brought back by the swallow. Just as the swallow returns to Hŭngbu's house carrying the seeds in its beak, Ongnyŏn will return to Chosŏn carrying modern knowledge in her heart.

This, however, is no more than a single aspect of the work. Inoue, who on the surface appears Hŭngbu-esque, is actually prosecuting a war as a member of the Japanese imperialist forces. As the subject in a Nolbu-esque struggle for control of Chosŏn, he will perform a surgical operation on a wound incurred in battle. In fact, Ongnyŏn's injury is due to the war, and, like Nolbu, Inoue himself is responsible for both injuring and treating her. When viewed from this perspective, the relationship between Ongnyŏn and Inoue corresponds to that between the swallow and Nolbu. Ongnyŏn is the object of a surgical operation performed by Inoue. This is Ongnyŏn's true historical location. The Sino-Japanese War was also fought on her body.

This suggests the abstract optimism of the ideology of "civilization and enlightenment." Things such as falling prey to psychoneurosis while conjuring up images of a frog in a specimen room had yet to be experienced. Inoue looked like Hŭngbu. But he performed surgery. Even adopting Ongnyŏn as his daughter was a kind of surgical operation. And this later tied into things such as the "Greater East Asia Co-Prosperity Sphere." Nolbu disguised as compassion his calculations to possess both the world of exchange and the order of the heavens. In like fashion, Japan wrapped its imperialist aggression and desire for markets in the rhetoric of family with slogans such as "universal benevolence," while also loudly proclaiming "moral principles" for "the world" and a "divine war." Imperialist Japan's policy was indeed Nolbu-esque. As such, "overcoming modernity" may actually be the rationalization/theorization of this Nolbu-esque aspect.

The problem that arises here, however, is that there are no longer gourd seeds to visit divine retribution on this new Nolbu. On the one hand, the celestial world that granted the seeds has already vanished, while, on the other hand, the foreign countries that will provide modern knowledge in place of these seeds possess the ill nature of Nolbu. Even Ongnyŏn herself departed for study abroad upon legs treated by Nolbu. Nature too, as one great body granted by the heavens, should not have been harmed. But Nolbu did violence to nature while constructing new legs (trains and steamships), upon which Ongnyŏn accessed a similarly Nolbu-esque modern knowledge and history. In the end, she set foot on that same knowledge and history that would redefine the swallow as follows:

> Oh, loveable little bird
> long have you been lauded
> as symbol of peace and love.
> But those poems
> sung not of your full value.
>   . . . .
> Only the swallow's peace and love
> leave such poems to the maidens in their chambers
> I wish to extol the swallow's battle for living
> to sing the song of this tiny warrior.
> . . . Ah, hundreds of thousands of swallows
> gulping down the oceans
> overwhelming the heavens
> intermingling their wings like a black cloud.
> Oh, bracing will
> neither eating nor sleeping
> stopping nor resting
> such is the dread figure of the Air Force![34]

WALK OF "THE CRIPPLE"

Through study abroad, Ongnyŏn begins a great walk that imagines a map of the world and the *minjok*. Within that walk, nature is both damaged and developed. As an object for man, it loses Heaven (天) and becomes "landscape."[35] In addition, it is newly appropriated (occupied) either as a social/historical territory of the world or of a country (ethnonation), or as a "hometown" onto which those convoluted relationships are sentimentally inscribed. Accordingly, Ongnyŏn's journey, which sets these operations in motion, is a walk upon a very different map than the swallow's flight south of the river, which signifies both eternal and noumenal circulation of nature. Ongnyŏn's study abroad is a journey taken upon the train of civilization and enlightenment. It is a sort of spirit of the age that organizes landscape as it propels history. These are the true coordinates of Ku Wansŏ, who says to Ongnyŏn just before she departs America for Korea, "Tomorrow, since you will take a boat across the Pacific Ocean, let us say our goodbyes tomorrow at the edge of the Pacific Ocean."[36] The position of modern man, who "rushes against the cold winds of Siberia" or "fights at sea under the blistering rays of the Equator,"[37] that is to say the perspective that draws maps of the world and bird's-eye views, came to replace the celestial world.

But this "landscape" that is reappropriated by such things as the world, the nation, and the hometown also stands in opposition to the individual and his interiority. This suggests the disability that constitutes the modern subject in general. By way of comparison, it is only through her crippled leg, the injury that gives rise to her separation from her family and from the heavens, that Ongnyŏn becomes a modern person. With each and every step, she must newly rearrange herself within the landscape. Just like her mother tongue, a harmonious and eternal environment (fate) that is granted a priori is nowhere to be found. As can be discerned from the case of Ok Kwinam, one's position by destiny is nothing more than a "false accusation carried deep in one's bones."[38] She is born "the lowly daughter of a brawler," "the lowly daughter of a loose bar wench." Kwinam therefore strives hard and becomes a "nurse." Rosa in Cho Myŏnghŭi's "*Nakdong-kang (The Nakdong river*, 1927)," by becoming a teacher, escapes from the "outcast" status she inherited from her father. Ongnyŏn differs from Hŭngbu as well, who is no more than Nolbu's nice younger brother and lacks any social status. By learning and speaking foreign languages, and thus inscribing her position into social and historical relationships, she both discovers and organizes her subjectivity. This is suggested by the fact that Ongnyŏn first becomes a student of Japan and later becomes a student of America. It is then that the era of "becoming" has dawned.

Thus nature and landscape are thoroughly exterior, and, as a result, Ongnyŏn is thoroughly interior, but in order to acquire the consistent contents of this interior, one way or another, she must conquer and possess the exterior. Ongnyŏn is reunited with her father due to the newspaper article documenting her graduation. It is only through the social position gained by learning a foreign language that she is able to meet her parents who taught her her mother tongue. This defines the modern person. The modern person must endlessly become something. In the competitive arena of the modern era, which is led by "rate of economic growth" or "technological innovation," the modern person, who is a wayfarer, cannot exist unless s/he constantly moves forward. Just as a bicycle that stands still falls over, Ongnyŏn, in spite of her injured leg—no, because of her injured leg—has no choice but to walk continuously. The modern age, with development and progress as its essence, is the history of "the cripple." If, as the protagonist of Sōseki's *Sorekara* (*And then*, 1909) thinks, "only the lowly walked with a purpose,"[39] then modernity is the era of the lowly. A newspaper piece titled "*Chŏryŏng sinhwa* (New tale of cutting the hat string),"[40] for example, calls for an actualization of this modern "becoming." The quotation below, by satirizing those "good sirs" who wish to occupy high social positions based solely on the excellence of their family backgrounds, attempts to institutionalize this "becoming."

> The ministers, vice ministers, secretaries, and governors living in Pukch'on, how did they rise to such prominence? They were able to do so by playing the son, or elder brother, or grandson of Chillyŏnggun,[41] once powerful enough to lift the heavens and move the earth. The lords, undersecretaries, directors, and magistrates, how did they rise to such prominence? They were able to do so by playing the son, or elder brother, or grandson of the fabled Suryŏn of Samch'ŏng-dong. So, good sirs, you too should find such a benefactor and act as son, older brother, or grandson. Forgetting all shame, close your eyes just this once.[42]

This is the true meaning contained in the arguments of Yi Kwangsu who, while urging all people to gain specialized knowledge or skill and gain employment,[43] asserted that unemployment is "the root of all evil, the root of all misfortune."[44] This walk of "the cripple," which begins in earnest with employment, symbolizes the life and existence of the modern person. Now "evil" or base refers not to Nolbu's nature but to Hŭngbu's state of joblessness. Employment mediates and institutionalizes modern "becoming" (school) and "exchanging" (market). And this supplants status based on family (bloodline, inheritance) and rite (memorial ceremonies, ancestors).

As a result, the novelist Kubo's resolution—"Now I shall get a life"[45]—and Yi Sang's lumpen protagonist's self-deprecation—"He is base. His existence is utterly ridiculous"[46]—are only natural. They must externalize themselves to the world of employment. If they fail to do so, just like Bunzo in *Ukigumo* (*The drifting cloud*, 1897), they will lose love. Hazama Kan'ichi in *Konjiki yasha* (*The Gold Demon*, 1897) and Yi Suil in *Changhanmong* (*A long and sorrowful dream*, 1913) becoming loan sharks are also related to this. They gain employment due to the "diamond" of Tomiyama and Kim Chungbae, respectively. And their social activities are mediated by the respective betrayals of Mia and Sim Sunae. This applies as well to the case of Sin Ponggu, the protagonist of Yi Kwangsu's *Chaesaeng* (*Rebirth*, 1924), who, having been wounded by Sunyŏng's betrayal, falls into "rice speculation, which he had formerly considered no different from thievery." All of the above suggest the various contractual relationships (the promise of marriage, the promise of debt servicing) that organize (divide) modern society, as well as their fundamentally crippled nature. Modernity, which thoroughly performs the equation "fixed property=a constant mind," might define Hŭngbu, who lives in full communion with the heavens and without knowing this modern wound, by such terms as disabled, evil, abnormal, and criminal. For example, Cho Chunghwan's 1912 work *Pyŏngja samin* (*The three invalids*), commonly considered the first work of modern drama in Korea, uses modern occupations to fill its modern roles. Here, in contrast to their wives who work as a doctor, a school principal, and a school teacher, the male characters have lost their jobs, retain only the "occupation of husband," and eventually wind up as invalids—deaf, dumb, and blind, respectively. This in turn leads to their being branded "criminals," and put in danger of being rounded up by the assistants to the military police.

The above informs us of the fact that in the modern world—where not only is there no celestial realm to aid Hŭngbu and punish Nolbu but where only the cold principles of "survival of the fittest" and "the strong prey upon the weak" operate—the existence of the individual is no more than a societal role (relationship, contract). In society, which now stands in for nature, all existence is forced to walk; however, this also makes one constantly conscious of the borders (injuries) and of the Other. No, it is in fact the borders and the Other that constitute the origin of the modern walk. What we call "inner rhythm"[47] is just another name for an alienated walk. Ongnyŏn was thus punished by inner rhythm. Accordingly, as "grass that has lost its roots,"[48] she has no choice but to scatter "azaleas."[49] The mutually distinct rhythms in operation between individuals gave birth to those who would depart and those who would hold on. In front of a departing lover (horizontal), flowers fall (vertical). Horizontal movement and vertical movement compete. When flowers are stepped upon, horizontal transforms into vertical. It is thus that the lover is held. In the end, the lover's legs will be crippled.

In a fashion similar to the above parting, the modern person will separate things (images) from their original contexts. Just as Kim Sŏngjae, the chemist in Yi Kwangsu's *Kaech'ŏkcha* (*The pioneer*, 1917–1918), newly combines natural materials and dreams of inventions, the "lover," as he departs a woman who sheds "not a single tear," shall also liberate metaphor from the constraints of nature and of conventional figures of speech. And the modern person, as he both betrays and newly appropriates the Other, shall arrive at free verse. Accordingly, the abstruseness of modern poetry is a kind of sentimentalism that actively presents and institutionalizes this crippled modern walk.

NOLBU AND "X"

In light of the above, we may be able to read Yi Sang's protagonist's becoming a "cripple" on the "*t'orok'o* (mine cart)" rails of a Sakhalin coal mine as a metaphor for all of these situations. The following is the scene of the accident.

> "Hey X, jump out. You're gonna die. . . ."
> "The 'cart' behind you is empty. Jump out!"
> . . . .
> At the very moment I was going to step from my own arrow-like "cart," it was already too late. The ownerless "cart" that had been gaining ground from behind, its hatred for me running curiously deep, crashed into my "cart" with an enormous sound like the final gasp of a wild beast exerting every last ounce of energy. At that moment, all events and things were no longer within my mental realm, so much so that I can report that the universe ceased to exist for me, and there was only a continuous state of prolonged nothingness.
> . . . .
> "I don't think he'll be able to avoid becoming a cripple."[50]

It is necessary, however, to analyze in detail X's becoming a "permanent cripple," because this work also has a structure similar to *Hŭngbu-chŏn*. The character known as Ŏp[51] has an uncle—his father's older brother—who brings back a large fortune from Japan. This uncle corresponds to Nolbu, while Ŏp's father, T, who is unemployed and lives off the generosity of X's friend M, corresponds to Hŭngbu.

It is also interesting, however, to note those aspects that have changed. X, who is in the position of Nolbu, injures his leg and becomes a "cripple." By selflessly ministering to a bedridden innkeeper, however, he inherits a fortune. He performs the roles of both the swallow and Hŭngbu. First, in gaining wealth through acting like Hŭngbu, X resolves the "good/evil" binary opposition embodied by Hŭngbu and Nolbu. X is both Hŭngbu-esque and Nolbu-esque; however, he is neither purely one nor the other. (As such, X appears to be an "X" that crosses out or negates both of these aspects. And, accordingly, this is finally the sign for Nolbu. This is because Nolbu is less a name for evil than the "negation" itself that mediates relations with the Other). Therefore, even his Hŭngbu-esque acts cannot be totally positive. For example, regarding the enormous fortune controlled by X, the gentleman he meets on the train displays "an air of sarcasm and derision." X's good deeds, which showed a devotion worthy of the inheritance he would receive, are not acknowledged. Furthermore, X is suspicious and skeptical of himself, as witnessed in the scene below.

> Someone else's things, for free—Did I not simply take someone else's things for free?—Even if he died and is no longer of this world—His will—Even if it grants permission for this—Even if he and I were so close that I may take

possession of it all without the slightest qualms—Had I not just taken possession of his enormous fortune in its entirety? Someone else's things.[52]

X, who has taken possession of a fortune that should have been donated to "social programs," compares himself to a "respectable pickpocket." Evident here is the fact that the world of values (quality), as suggested by social programs, and the logic of exchange (quantity) cause an internal conflict in X. But X does not donate his fortune to social programs. A similar phenomenon arises in the case of T. Unlike Hŭngbu, who unhesitatingly observes filial piety, T anxiously awaits orders from the "arrogant and dissipated" unfilial son Ŏp, all the while apologizing for his own incompetence. It is not a matter of merely failing to treat a swallow's leg; he goes so far as to set fire to the hospital built with his brother's money. T is not only an incompetent character but also one who burns with the desire for revenge.

On the one hand, Ŏp wanders the dark streets in search of that "feint pleasure of the skin," while on the other he complains, "Father, why couldn't you have earned more money like other fathers?" Furthermore, with respect to his rich uncle, with his own death he carries out a "revenge held deep in his bones." Ŏp, who knows neither filial gratitude nor filial piety, is neither the swallow nor Sim Ch'ŏng. To him, his father and uncle are no more than a poor man and a rich man. The moving story of the swallow is extinct. The good and evil that divided Hŭngbu and Nolbu have also disappeared, which brings to mind the following lines: "Evil? Why? Where on earth are there good people? Everyone's more or less the same."[53] Thus, secondly, that X injures his leg is important. He was also the swallow. This also suggests the modern logic by which not only swallows but also human beings themselves become the objects of producing profits. In place of the vanished story of Hŭngbu and the swallow, a new Nolbu, who breaks his own leg and plays multiple roles, is born. With this, the "Hŭngbu–Nolbu–Swallow" structure became completely meaningless. In short, with its comments on "inheritance" and "social programs," and, going further, with its demands for the father's money, Yi Sang's *12 wŏl 12 il* strongly suggests the extinction of "giving." To "take someone else's things for free" is now impossible—even if that "someone else" is father or uncle. Of course, what leads society in place of "giving" is "exchanging." This signifies society (the market) has replaced family as the site of human activity.

It is at this precise moment that the "doctor in charge" and "laboratory animal" of which Yi Sang spoke take on an important meaning. This is because they deny not only the obvious "Hŭngbu–Nolbu–Swallow" structure but even the "sacrifice" of Sim Ch'ŏng. Just as receiving money from one's father has disappeared, things such as sacrifices that gain heavenly recompense are even more impossible. The doctor in charge simply makes the laboratory animal into an "aggrieved skeleton appearing in an academic paper."[54] To Sŏngsun, the protagonist of *Kaech'ŏkcha* who dissected her lover's body in her mind's eye, Sim Ch'ŏng's sacrifice is a benighted old tale. This is also related to the "heartlessness" of Yi Kwangsu's *Mujŏng* (*The heartless*, 1917). Yŏngch'ae becomes a *kisaeng* in order to look after her imprisoned father and brothers; however, because of that fact her father and brothers commit suicide. Of course Sim Ch'ŏng is gone, but her father, Blindman Sim, is gone as well. And with them has disappeared the sublime nature of sacrifice. The operating table replaced the altar, while upon it laboratory animals were torn apart by the scalpel of the doctor in charge. In addition, the crippled "X" himself was a doctor. If Hŭngbu and the swallow, who had been separate existences, became united and praised for a single shared value through treatment based on compassion, X, simultaneously doctor in charge and laboratory animal, is ridiculed below for performing surgery on himself.

"Certainly bizarre when it's the doctor's leg that hurts!"
"Yeah, he thought his shit don't stink!"[55]

THE BOB: NOLBU'S FASHION

This sort of situation suggests that two pairs of Nolbu-esque genres arose to supplant the literary tradition of rewarding good and punishing evil. Ritual sacrifice was rent into the couplets "suicide–hygiene" and "exchange–fashion." Suicide and hygiene express the "self-sustaining" of a separate body, as well as its social relationships. The modern subject who invented the microscope (germ theory) rejects the intervention of an exterior (the celestial realm, nature) that has been corrupted by germs and infection. Additionally, by ending his own life, he bears witness to the exclusive ownership of the flesh (market) and a time plan (history). This is the proclamation of a modern logic that stands in opposition to the ethics of "(o)ur bodies—to every hair and bit of skin—are received by us from our parents," which demands "reimbursement of costs for serum" even from "skeletons in the grave."[56] Now the behavior and familial logic of Advisor Cho,[57] who bequeathed his estate to his grandson rather than his son in order to ensure the continuance of proper ancestral memorial ceremonies, have become outdated tales.

Meanwhile, the modern person, instead of mediating prayer and sacredness with rites and offerings, exchanges wage labor for money by means of contractual relations. Moreover, he sensuously adorns himself and communicates socially using capitalistic trends and fashions in place of seasonal cycles. But he also frequently displays the features of a "skeleton whose knees are above its ears." In fact, Yi Sang's protagonist, who in an "alley" unknown to his parents has learned "only letters that they cannot recognize,"[58] upon hearing the "report" of "a severed foot,"[59] had his leg crippled in the opposite direction from that of Ongnyŏn. In a word, the infirm (hygiene) protagonist of "*Nalgae* (Wings, 1936)," who owns only "a single corduroy suit" (fashion), by sleeping in the room of his "wife" after giving her five *wŏn* (exchange), turns himself into a "stuffed specimen" (suicide).

As a result, what most befits this new Nolbu is "the bob"—a hairstyle that takes "cut hair" and "buries it in the ground."[60] Yi Sang's lumpen protagonists, who rolled their bodies through the "turbid" streets, inscribed "suicide–hygiene" and "exchange–fashion" until they finally arrived at the character Tokduong, or Bald-headed Old Man.[61] The structure of Yi's existence as an unfilial son was forever "*chagi*"—the single pronunciation for three homophones meaning self-abandonment, self, and self-deception.[62] A laboratory animal, he put up in place of Sim Ch'ŏng's sacrifice the "irony" and "paradox" of "binging on the food he most hates."

In addition, he conducted a visual investigation that placed mass-produced wrapping paper and the duplicate fashion of the department store uniform in a position superior to skin. This is also related to anatomical and X-ray photographic (as in Yi's poem "*Ogamdo* [Crow's eye view, 1931]") descriptions such as the following: "SS emerged carrying his young daughter in the space between his bouldery chest and stomach—inside his body this would correspond to the area around his diaphragm."[63] It implies the operation of a modern perspective bereft of aura. And it is this post-aural perspective that discovers the "*kisaeng* in the city—their sort of beauty would not have been approved of by our forefathers—wrapped in 'josette' skirts, svelte as 'Westminster' cigarettes."[64] This gaze indulges in mass-produced goods (Westminster cigarettes = *kisaeng* = prostitution) devoid of originality ("approved by our forefathers" = "Our bodies—to every hair and bit of skin—are received by us from our parents"). Now sacrifices upon the altar are replaced by exchanges in the market. The sublimity of rites yields its place to the sentimentalism of the streets. Of course, no exceptions were made for Nolbu's partners, the daughters of respectable families. As evidenced below, they too cut their hair.

> In a holding cell, the daughter of a respectable family, stripped of everything right down to the string that held up her drawers, requested a pair of scissors from a policeman.
> "I am producing a weapon."
> In short order, the woman's hair, cut into a bob.[65]

In light of the above, this woman who cavalierly treats her body, her "every hair and bit of skin," is not the "daughter of a respectable family." Rather, she is a "genius of deception." She is completely distinct from Sim Ch'ŏng who prayed "with the heavens looking down" for her father's eyes to be opened. Of course, the background for this change may be found in the custom of "specialized" and "business-like love."

> Even the love they spoke of was completely different from the "divine love" of ten years ago. The love they were concerned with was removed from all anti-quated rites and decorum; it was a straightforward love that treated as process things such as a handshake, embrace, kiss, rendezvous, cohabitation, or separa-tion. In fact, it was a scientific and business-like love.
>
> . . . .
>
> She got a taste of good manners from this man, a whiff of dynamic attitude from that man, appreciated the physical beauty of yet another man, and finally sought financial assistance with buying a car or buying dinner from still another man. Such was the specialized and divided way she looked to several men in order sought to satisfy herself with regard to the opposite sex. There were also many men who did the same.[66]

Yi Sang's crow-eyed protagonist's discovery of these "shapeless modern boys" was also due to the above customs. At this point, the sense of sight (doc-tor in charge), through an endless nullification of the distance from its object (laboratory animal), transforms into the sense of touch. Amid these countless specialized relationships and introspections, and with the "sense of touch's diagramming these emotional landscapes,"[67] the modern perspective that con-structed world maps and bird's eye views is lost. Having lost the location of the perspective from which doctor in charge and laboratory animal gazed at one another, each came to grope the "glass=mirror" border.[68] This being the case, "crow's eye view" represents the rhetoric of modern blindness, which stands in fundamental contrast to the sight of Blindman Sim in the following passage.

> Blindman Sim is astonished. "If my daughter has returned alive, though my eyes remained closed I have no regrets. Do not die. Do not die." He rolls his eyes once, then again, at which his two eyes are suddenly bright. Blindman Sim had recognized her voice, but had no way of recognizing her face. His eyes unexpectedly opened, he finds himself seated beside a lady resembling a magnificent empress. Again astonished, he turns and moves away, only to turn back and return to his seat. "I must be dreaming." The Empress grabs hold of him. "Father, don't you know me? I am Sim Ch'ŏng, back from the dead and returned as an empress."[69]

The "magnificent empress" Blindman Sim gazes up at glimmers with a halo of the enchanting aura emitted by this incarnation of filial piety, and with an unrepeatable and inimitable exalted inspiration. That light, which expresses the sublime order of the celestial realm, proves overwhelmingly strong and sacred to Blindman Sim who has spent his entire life in darkness. This is not something that relates only to the operation of the sense of sight. Thus, Blindman Sim has no choice but to turn and move away even from Sim Ch'ŏng, his own daughter, before returning to his seat. Perhaps he truly "must be dreaming."

As such, Blindman Sim failed to arrive at the modern opening of the eyes (blindness) pushed to the extreme in the descriptions of Yi Sang. He never witnessed the "daughter of a respectable family" with a bob. To Blindman Sim, eyes just opened, this "weapon"-like bob that adorned "those ever so many wives in whom he could not find the slightest difference from his own wife"[70] was nowhere to be found. He did not know Nolbu's fashion, mass-produced with arbitrary and specialized scissoring. This is because Sim Ch'ŏng in fact never sold herself for 300 bags of rice. She merely sacrificed herself, which is why she was reborn an "empress." But, in complete contrast to this, perhaps in order to exact revenge upon parents who force "prostitution on daughters no older than 14,"[71] Yi Sang's "daughters of respectable families" flaunt their "weapons" while raising "swallows." "Swallows" of the following type:

> Her friends too usually had one or more so-called "swallows" attached to them. Yŏngsuk's current husband had previously been the "swallow" of one of her friends.[72]

To Blindman Sim, this "swallow" is invisible. This is because the "genius of deception" is not Sim Ch'ŏng. Nor is the Dragon King a "swallow." In this respect, Blindman Sim, even after rolling his eyes, remained Blindman Sim. He opened his eyes only upon the premodern.

On the other hand, this "swallow" is far more unfamiliar to Hŭngbu than was "Nolbu's swallow." Hŭngbu cannot treat the leg of this "swallow." Nor, obviously, can he receive gourd seeds. Instead, he will turn rewarding good and punishing evil on its head. While dreaming of revolution, he may even kill Nolbu. In a manner different from before, Hŭngbu will reconcile with his older brother.

NOTES

1. The original version assumes all readers will be familiar with *Hŭngbu-chŏn* (*The tale of Hŭngbu*). Although there are slight differences in the details among the different versions of the work, the basic story remains consistent. Nolbu and Hŭngbu are brothers. Nolbu, the elder of the two, lives in affluence while his younger brother

barely survives in abject poverty. Despite Hŭngbu's requests for succor, the greedy and miserly Nolbu flatly refuses to provide any relief. One day, Hŭngbu discovers a badly injured baby swallow and nurses it back to health, of course, with no ulterior motive. Later in the story, the swallow returns with gourd seeds as a reward for his kindness. Hŭngbu plants them, they grow, and when he cuts open the gourds, they are filled with treasure. Nolbu, hearing of this, captures a swallow, deliberately injures it, nurses it back to health, and then sends it away with a request for treasure. This swallow too returns with gourd seeds, which Nolbu plants and harvests. But out of these gourds come not riches but thieves and goblins who beat Nolbu and relieve him of his fortune. Their roles and fortunes now reversed, Nolbu goes to Hŭngbu for aid. The younger brother, completely overlooking his older brother's past misdeeds, responds with proper fraternal affection and assistance.—Trans.

2. Although the formal names of the two protagonist brothers are Hŭngbu and Nolbu, certain versions of the tale alternately render them Hŭngbo and Nolbo.—Trans.

3. Sin Chaehyo, *Han'guk p'ansori chŏnjip* (*Anthology of Korean p'ansori*) (Seoul: Sŏmundang, 1979), 174–75.

4. See footnote above regarding the alternate spellings of the protagonists' names.—Trans.

5. Sin Chaehyo, *Han'guk p'ansori chŏnjip*, 198–89.

6. Pin T'on, "*Saram mada almyŏn chyohŭl il*" (Things everyone should know), in *Tae Chyosyŏn tongnip hyŏbhoe hoebo* 4 *ho*, January 1896, 9.

7. Yi Kwangsu, "*Kaech'ŏkcha* (*Pioneer*)," in *Yi Kwangsu ŭi chŏnjip* 1 (Seoul: Samjungdang, 1962), 468.

8. Yi T'aejun, "*Kkamagwi* (The crow)," in *Chogwang*, January 1936, 78.

9. Sim Ch'ŏng is the eponymous protagonist of *Sim Ch'ŏng-chŏn* (*The tale of Sim Ch'ŏng*), an exemplary tale of filial piety in which she sacrifices her very life to restore the sight of her blind father.—Trans.

10. This tale is also known as *Sugung-ga* (lit., *Song of the underwater palace*), in which the Dragon King requires a rabbit's liver to cure his disease. Turtle is sent from under the sea to trick Rabbit into returning to the Dragon Palace to be killed. Rabbit, however, discovering this, in turn tricks the king and returns safely.—Trans.

11. Sin Chaehyo, Han'guk p'ansori chŏnjip, 154.

12. Michel Foucault, *The Order of Things*, trans. Yi Kwangrae (Seoul: Minŭmsa, 1987), 169.

13. For a discussion of the modern meaning of the windowpane, see chapter 4, "The Fashion of *Mujŏng*."

14. This is a reference to Yŏm Sangsŏp's 1921 short story "*P'yobonsil ŭi ch'ŏnggaeguri*," whose title literally means "green frog of the specimen room." The comparison alludes to the separation of man and nature, to man's placing a real or metaphorical "windowpane" between himself and the natural world, which he is now no longer a part of but rather observes, researches, and experiments upon from an "objective" distance.—Trans.

15. Walter Benjamin, "The Work of Art in the Age of Mechanical Reproduction," in *Palt'ŏ Penyamin ŭi munye iron* (*The literary theory of Walter Benjamin*), trans. Pan Sŏngwan (Seoul: Minŭmsa, 1983), 220.

16. Yi Kwangsu, "*Hŭlk* (The soil)," in *Yi Kwangsu chŏnjip* 6 (Seoul: Samjungdang, 1962), 318–19.

17. Yi Kwangsu, "*Hyŏngmyŏngga ŭi anae* (A revolutionary's wife)," in Yi Kwangsu chŏnjip 2 (Seoul: Samjungdang, 1962), 361.

18. Yi Kwangsu, *Hŭlk*, 101.

19. This is Hyŏn Chin'gŏn's best known short story, and chronicles the dilemma of a rickshaw man who, due to grinding poverty, must leave his wife in order to work despite her critical illness.—Trans.

20. The Korean word for swallow is *chebi* (제비). All of the puns in the original contain the word *chebi*, although in them it does not actually mean swallow. In order to preserve the pun engendered by the homophones in Korean, however, I chose to use the word "swallow" in English. It is not an ideal solution, but without it the entire passage is next to meaningless.—Trans.

21. Yi Injik, "*Hyŏl ŭi nu (Tears of blood)*," in *Sinsosŏl, Pŏnan (yŏk) sosŏl che-1 kwŏn (New novels, adapted (translated) novels, volume 1)* (Seoul: Asea munhwasa, 1978), 34–35. The English translation is taken from W. E. Skillend's *Tears of Blood*, in *Korean Classical Literature: An Anthology*, ed. Chung Chong-wha (London: Keegan Paul International, 1989), 181.

22. The original title is *XiaoJing* (孝經), and it is alternatively translated as the *Classic of Filial Piety*. The English translation is taken from the following source: http://www.chinapage.com/confucius/xiaojing-be.html

23. This is a reference to the infamous "*tanballyŏng* (斷髮令)," announced on December 31, 1895, as part of the Kabo Reforms, which mandated that all Korean adult men cut off their topknots. The topknot was a symbol not only of adult manhood but also of Confucian tradition. The conservative *yangban* Ch'oe Ikhyŏn is most famously remembered for declaring he would sooner have his head cut off than his hair.

Much later, in the late 1960s and early 1970s, Park Chung-hee also forced young Korean men to cut their hair, albeit this time for nearly the opposite reasons: they were viewed as not conservative enough, and too open to pernicious foreign, which is to say Western, influences. The author also points out the irony of South Korea's simultaneously exporting all of this cut hair as wigs in order to bolster its then quite fragile economy.—Trans.

24. The narrator of *Hyŏl ŭi nu* informs readers that Ongnyŏn was actually fortunate to have been hit in the leg by a Japanese bullet. Had it been a Chinese bullet, he continues, which were laced with poison, she surely would have died.—Trans.

25. The original includes Chinese characters, which make the reversal of traditional hierarchies in the early modern period much more apparent. China's emperor was traditionally designated 天子 or "son of heaven." Japan, following the restoration of its own emperor in 1868, referred to him as 天皇 or the "heavenly emperor." This was cause for much alarm not only in China but in Korea as well. Other countries could have kings, but only China could have an emperor. Less than thirty years later, in 1894–1895, Japan defeated China in the Sino-Japanese War, effectively bringing an end to the traditional East Asian world order.

26. Independence Gate was erected on the site where Yŏngŭn-mun, the gate at which Chinese envoys were welcomed into Seoul, had formerly stood. It was

modeled after the Arc de Triomphe in Paris, and construction began the year after the Sino-Japanese War ended.—Trans.

27. Yi Kwangsu, *"Kŭ yŏja ŭi ilsaeng* (That woman's life)," in *Yi Kwangsu chŏnjip* 7 (Seoul: Samjungdang, 1966), 263.

28. Ch'unhyang is the eponymous protagonist of *Ch'unhyang-chŏn* (*The tale of Ch'unhyang*). If Sim Ch'ŏng is the exemplar of a filial daughter, Ch'unhyang is that of a chaste woman. She endures many trials to maintain her chastity, and, in the end, she is rewarded by being reunited with her lover.—Trans.

29. The original is *chebi t'ŏk*, which actually means "double chin." The author, in keeping with the tradition of the *Hŭngbu-chŏn*, has used it here because it is a homophone for "swallow chin."—Trans.

30. Zhang Fei is a famed Chinese general from the *Romance of the Three Kingdoms*. Premodern Korean literature knew no strict national boundaries, and in fact drew freely from Chinese literature, as well as from myth, history, and geography, for enrichment.—Trans.

31. Natsume Sōseki, *Kōjin* (*The wayfarer*, 1913), trans. Beongcheon Yu (Detroit: Wayne State University Press, 1967), 297.

32. This is the common English translation for the work *Xiao xue* (小學), written by the Neo-Confucian philosopher Zhuzi, perhaps better known in Western scholarship as Chu Hsi (朱子, 1130–1200).—Trans.

33. See Yi Kwangsu, *"Chanyŏ chungsimnon* (On the centrality of children)," in *Yi Kwangsu chŏnjip* 17 (Seoul: Samjungdang, 1962), 40–47.

34. Kim Yongje, *"Chebi* (Swallow)," in *Tongyang chi kwang*, September 1939, 96–98. (The original is in Japanese. This excerpt was translated into Korean by the author.)

35. For a more detailed discussion of this process, see Karatani Kōjin, *Nihon kindai bungaku no kigen* (*The origins of modern Japanese literature*) (Tokyo: Kodansha, 1983), 7–43.

36. Yi Injik, *"Moranbong* (Peony peak)," in *Han'guk sinsosŏl chŏnjip* (Seoul: Ŭlyu munhwasa, 1968), 62. (This is the sequel to *Hyŏl ŭi nu*, and chronicles the protagonists' return to and adventures in Korea.)—Trans.

37. Ch'oe Namsŏn, *"Uri ŭi undongjang* (Our playing field)," in *Sonyŏn*, December 1908, 33.

38. Yi Kwangsu, *"Sarang ŭi tagakhyŏng* (The polygon of love)," in *Yi Kwangsu chŏnjip* 7 (Seoul: Samjungdang, 1962), 388.

39. Natsume Sōseki, *Sorekara* (*And then*, 1909), trans. Norma Field (Ann Arbor: Center for Japanese Studies, The University of Michigan, 1997), 129.

40. The original title is *Chŏryŏng sinhwa* (絕纓新話). The first two characters, which literally mean to cut the string that keeps one's hat or crown on, connote a removal of the traditional Korean hat, symbol of *yangban* status and official rank, both of which were legally abolished with the Kabo Reforms of 1894–1895, but echoes of which obviously lingered well into the twentieth century. The author's pseudonym, Paekch'isaeng (白痴生), or "Master Idiot," is also an obvious pun.—Trans.

41. An extremely influential shaman patronized by the Empress Myŏngsŏng (r. 1866–1895).—Trans.

42. Paekch'isaeng, "*Chŏryŏng sinhwa*," in *Taehan minbo*, November 23, 1909.
43. See the essay "*Minjok kaejoron* (On national reconstruction)."
44. Yi Kwangsu, "*Nongch'on kyebal* (Rural development)," in *Yi Kwangsu chŏnjip* 17 (Seoul: Samjungdang, 1963), 89.
45. This is a reference to the eponymous protagonist of Pak T'aewŏn's 1934 novella *Sosŏlga Kubo Ssi ŭi ilil* (*A day in the life of the novelist Kubo*).—Trans.
46. Yi Sang, "*Chiju hoesi* (Two spiders meet a pig)," in *Yi Sang munhak chŏnjip* 2, ed. Kim Yunsik (Seoul: Munhak sasangsa), 208.
47. The word in the original is *naejaeyul* (内在律) and refers to the inner rhythm or cadence of free verse poetry in Korean.—Trans.
48. Yi Kwangsu, *Hŭlk*, 11.
49. This is a reference to Kim Sowŏl's 1925 poem "*Chindallaekkot* (Azaleas)." The following English translation is from Kim Sowŏl, *Azaleas: A Book of Poems*, trans. David R. McCann (New York: Columbia University Press, 2007).

> When you turn away from seeing me
> and go,
> gently, without a word, I shall send you away.
> From Mount Yak in Yongbyon,
> azaleas
> I shall gather an armful and scatter them on your way.
> Step after step away
> on those flowers placed
> before you, press deep, step lightly, and go.
> When you turn away from seeing me
> and go,
> though I die, no, not a single tear shall fall.

50. Yi Sang, *12 wŏl 12 il* (*December 12*), in *Yi Sang munhak chŏnjip 2*, ed. Yi Sŭnghun (Seoul: Munhak sasangsa, 1989), 231.
51. The name Ŏp (業) is itself something of a morbid pun. The modern usage of the character is most often for either "industry" or "occupation," as in the mining industry and occupation that lead to X's accident. From much earlier, however, the character was/is also used in Buddhism to translate the term and concept of karma.—Trans.
52. Yi Sang, *12 wŏl 12 il*, 71.
53. Yi Kwangsu, "*Kŭ yŏja ŭi ilsaeng*," 231.
54. Yi Sang, "*Kŭmje* (Taboo)," in *Yi Sang munhak chŏnjip* 1, ed. Yi Sŭnghun (Seoul: Munhak sasangsa, 1989), 75.
55. Yi Sang, *12 wŏl 12 il*, 81.
56. Yi Sang, "*Munbŏl* (Pedigree)," in *Yi Sang munhak chŏnjip* 1, ed. Yi, 83.
57. Advisor Cho is the patriarch of the family depicted in Yŏm Sangsŏp's *Samdae* (*Three Generations*), a 1931 novel that chronicles the often tense relations among the members of an extended family struggling with the balance between tradition and modernity.—Trans.
58. Yi Sang, "*Sŭlp'ŭn iyagi* (A sad story)," in *Yi Sang munhak chŏnjip* 3, ed. Kim Yunsik (Seoul: Munhak sasangsa, 1993), 63.

59. Yi Sang, "*1931 nyŏn* (1931)," in *Yi Sang munhak chŏnjip* 1, ed. Kim, 238.

60. Yi Sang, "*Chakp'um che 3 bŏn* (The 3rd work)," in *Yi Sang munhak chŏnjip* 2, ed. Kim Yunsik (Seoul: Munhak sasangsa, 1993), 323.

61. Ibid. The protagonist's name is rendered in Chinese characters: 禿頭翁.—Trans.

62. 自棄, 自己, and 自欺, respectively.—Trans.

63. Yi Sang, "*Hyuŏp kwa sajŏng* (Closures and circumstances)," in *Yi Sang munhak chŏnjip* 2, ed. Kim, 154.

64. Yi Sang, "*Sanch'on yŏjŏng* (Lingering Impressions of a Mountain Village)," in *Azalea: Journal of Korean Literature & Culture*, Volume 2, trans. John M. Frankl, Harvard University, 2008, 331–45.

65. Yi Sang, "*Chakp'um che 3 bŏn*," 323.

66. Yi Kwangsu, "*Chaesaeng* (Rebirth)," in *Yi Kwangsu chŏnjip* 2 (Seoul: Samjungdang, 1962), 166–67.

67. Yi Sang, "*Tonghae* (Child's Skeleton)," in *Yi Sang munhak chŏnjip* 2, ed. Kim, 259.

68. For a more in-depth discussion of this phenomenon, see chapter 8, "The Flesh, Yi Sang's Windowpane."

69. Sin Chaehyo, Han'guk p'ansori chŏnjip, 114.

70. Yi Sang, "*Chiju hoesi*," 305.

71. Yi Sang, "*Chongsaenggi* (Record of a life)," in *Yi Sang munhak chŏnjip* 2, ed. Kim, 388.

72. Kim Tongin, "*Munŭngja ŭi anhae* (The incompetent's wife)," in *Kim Tongin chŏnjip* 2 (Seoul: Chosŏn ilbosa, 1988), 225.

Chapter 2

The Birth of *Oppa*

Tracks of Colonial Period Youth

THE SISTER COMPLEX AND REJECTING THE PARENTS

It is a widely known[1] fact that "sister" possesses an important meaning in the poems of Im Hwa. The "*oppa*-sister structure"[2] apparent in poems such as "*Negŏri ŭi Suni* (Suni at the crossroads, 1929)" and "*Uri oppa wa hwaro* (My *oppa* and the brazier, 1929)" constitutes the crux of Im's poetry. This is also seen in the novel *Ch'oehu ŭi myŏnhoein* (*The final visitor*, 1927). Accordingly, Kim Yunsik has pointed out Im Hwa's "sister complex." He discusses this "sister orientation" as a condition of "seeking the mother"[3] that stands in opposition to "seeking the father," which represents the fascistic will to power. This represents a sense of balance that enabled him to neutralize and negotiate the "bias toward KAPF's organizational structure as the will to power."[4] As evidenced in the quotations below, "Mother" and "Suni at the Crossroads" do in fact display a similar poetic structure and sentiment.

This, my beloved mother, do you not also know it well
Yes! Mother!
Mother, this unfilial son, for what, for whom
roaming about and whispering with Oksun's[5] Sunbong day and night,
Mother, even amidst your love, worrying for your child, did you not know this well!
But that boy has died!
Thinking of his aged mother's travails, always going about wearing only a black shirt
That kindhearted boy, whether mother knew it or h_ted it, has ___ fallen
Mother!

Oksun rested from ___* for a full two days, did not eat, and merely cried, and cried, and cried.[6]

Suni in the heart of Chongno, wretched city of biting snow and wind!
You and I, in the flowers of last spring, lost our beloved mother amidst tearful poverty!
Thus, you have worried for this unreliable, pale-faced oppa, and oppa was concerned for you even in days vexed with poverty
Oh, Suni!
You had a reliable youth of this land in whom to entrust your heart
My beloved comrade. . . .
The youth's lover, a laboring girl, he had you.[7]

However I will approach the sister complex from a perspective different from that of Kim Yunsik. Far more important than seeking the mother in opposition to seeking the father is the fact that in Im Hwa's poetry there is essentially no mother (or father). This is the reason behind the phrase "lost our beloved mother amidst tearful poverty!" In addition, Im also wrote a poem that reads in part:

Mother in the countryside
wept each night beside my bed
but, to the end, I never returned to my hometown.[8]

In the consciousness of the poetic narrator who recited "cutting power lines and lying atop railroad tracks / the lamentable superstitions of elders in the past,"[9] his mother was already dead.

And in the place of that absent mother, Suni makes her appearance. Parents disappear, and the sister appears as the new interlocutor. What is important at this point is that Suni is not solely the younger sister of her *oppa*. She is also the lover of "(t)hat kindhearted boy" "always going about wearing only a black shirt." She is "(t)he youth's lover." That is to say, the relationship between *oppa* and younger sister mediates the youth, as evidenced in the lines below:

Oppa, a while ago the rest of your young friends came to visit
They brought tearful news of my *oppa* and comrades
They were lovable and courageous youths
They were the greatest youths in all the world.[10]

In the above quotation, there is no space for a mother or father to enter. This is because they are not "youth," the "young painters of a new map."[11] As such, the sister complex possesses a meaning different from seeking the mother. It mediated a new relationship distinct from familial relationships; rather, it was "rejecting the parents."

Of course, "rejecting the parents" and the "*oppa*-sister structure" were not unique to Im Hwa. These are universally observable conditions of colonial period literature. Accordingly, this chapter, rather than limiting discussion to Im Hwa, will use this issue as a framework with which to explain the entirety of modern Korean literary history.

OPPA, THE FORM OF YOUTH

Only after separating from her parents does young Ongnyŏn embark upon her journey of study abroad and civilization and enlightenment. This also corresponds to the position as orphans of Yi Kwangsu and Yi Hyŏngsik, his autobiographical protagonist in *Mujŏng*. It is also in *Mujŏng* that Pyŏnguk poses the following questions to Yŏngch'ae: "Was it you who decided to give your heart to Mr. Lee (Hyŏngsik)? . . . Or did a single word from your father decide for you?"[12] Pyŏnguk goes on to label the "three obediences"[13] an "accursed two words,"[14] thereby tearing down the context of the father, which has theretofore regulated and decided Yŏngch'ae's actions and existence.

This also represents the core issue raised by Yi's short story "*Sonyŏn ŭi piae* (The sorrows of a boy, 1917)." Munho, the "cousin *oppa*," loves his "younger sister cousin"[15] Nansu, who shows promise as a fellow poet. He says to her, "Hey, come with me to Seoul. Let's flee on a train tonight. I'll make it so you can study there." While trying to persuade her, he is also attempting to protect their world from their parents' generation. In response, her obstinate father (his uncle) merely puts forth outmoded *yangban* standards: "What use is study to a girl!" In the end, she acquiesces, and at the age of sixteen marries a fifteen-year-old imbecile from a rich family.

In early modern Korean literature, this vertical hierarchy between parents and children that stressed submission to the will of the parents (father) faces direct and fundamental challenges. An extreme example of this is Yi Kwangsu's *Chaesaeng*, in which Kim Kyŏnghun, the young male protagonist, in order to provide 100,000 *wŏn* in operating funds to a patriotic organization that has come in from Shanghai, kills his rich rice speculator father with a "six gun." While in Han Sŏlya's *Maŭm ŭi hyangch'on* (Country village of the heart, 1939), Ch'ohyang thinks that Sanggi, her *oppa*, is "better than five fathers."[16]

In this context, the titles *Sonyŏn* (*The boys*) and *Ch'ŏngch'un* (*The youth*), early magazines published by Ch'oe Namsŏn, are of a profound significance. They indicate the horizon of a new solidarity and new relationships removed from the established order that placed the relationship between parent and child at its center. Kim Ilyŏp's writing "I absolutely cannot sacrifice my entire life for filial love"[17] is also relevant here. This announces the appearance of the executors of enlightenment, both students and teachers, who took the schools as their primary sites of practice. This eloquently proclaims "the birth of youth."[18] For example, *Sonyŏn* ran serial columns with titles such as "*Hyŏndae sonyŏn ŭi sinhohŭp* (The new breath of the modern boy)" and "*Sinsidae ch'ŏngnyŏn ŭi sinhohŭp* (The new breath of youth of the new generation)," while also introducing pieces such as Fukuzawa Yukichi's *Shūshin yōryō* (*Moral code*, 1900), "*Amerik'a hapjungguk ŭl kŏnsŏlhan chayu sonyŏn Wŏsingt'ŏn ŭi chwaumyŏng* (The motto of Washington, free boy who designed the United States of America)," and "*Amerik'a myŏngin P'ŭraengk'ŭllin chwaumyŏng* (The motto of Franklin, the renowned American)." It also translated and ran James Montgomery's "Aspirations of Youth" under the title "*Ch'ŏngnyŏn ŭi sowŏn*." The retranslation of a portion of the rather liberal Korean version goes as follows:

> Deeply, deeply, deep deeply dig the mines of knowledge
> The exquisite principles governing all things and the treasures of encyclopedic knowledge
> In mountains and fields pheasants and rabbits, from storehouses gold and silk
> As if hunting, as if pulling them out, we shall obtain these in school
> We youth, as one who gathers coral
> Picking up various pieces from the bottom of the deep sea
> Finer that the jewels adorning a crown
> We shall find the beads of knowledge and polish and grind and cut them.[19,20]

As evidenced above, "the birth of youth" is the decisive scene in modern Korean literary history. "*Ch'ŏngnyŏn* (youth[s] as a person)," "*ch'ŏngch'un* (youth as a concept)," and "*sonyŏn* (boy[s])" are the forms of the subjects who take a dim view of their parents' generation as stubbornly premodern, while leading the way to the modern era. In fact, the inaugural issue of the magazine *Sonyŏn* demanded "Make our Korea a boys' country," while *Ch'ŏngch'un* exhorted "Let us all learn together. Learning more, let us learn still more," thereby establishing youth as "comrades in learning."[21] The phrase "comrades in learning" suggests an arena for the subject in place of the premodern family. The subject, having left the home either for a foreign country (study abroad) or the crossroads (society), is no longer someone's son or daughter but rather someone's friend (classmate, comrade, colleague). One expression of this may be seen in the excerpt below.

> The 5th Youth: Are you saying that what is my parents' is also mine? Then doesn't that mean we belong to our parents? If the father and son are of one

mind, there is no reason to distinguish between the things of the parents and those of the children, but when that is not the case, it is right to treat the father and son as separate individuals![22]

The father and son are no longer "of one mind." The moment that difference is apprehended, youth is born. Thus begins the opposition between old things and new. It makes us aware of the importance of Yi Hyongsik's choosing to study biology in *Mujŏng*. This is because it implies that the very establishment of the youth as separate from parents is mediated by the theory of evolution. Father and son will be reunited not in genealogical records but in history, through the macro subject of *minjok* (Jap. *minzoku* [ethnonation]), which is pioneered by the youth.[23] Moreover, the youth, as the sprouts of both the individual and society, will mediate civil society as they differentiate into diverse economic, political, and emotional locations. As such, the victory of youth is inevitable. In relation to this, the following excerpt appeared in the journal *Hak chi kwang* (*The Light of Learning*).

Today, amidst the silently decaying old ideas and spirit, that a new spirit and new thought arises is certainly an expression of the great power of unceasing and ever-flowing life, so that I may confidently proclaim the following: in the clash between new and old, victory, when all is said and done, is in the hands of the youth. Thus, what I wish of my father and my elders is that they not needlessly criticize the words and deeds of the youth according to their own standards, that they not cause the youth to fall into infinite anguish, but rather that they listen to the youth and express respect for their behavior, thereby allowing society to create a completely new appearance in accordance with the spirit of the times. To reiterate, I say that it is possible to believe in the youth, and to entrust the future to them.[24]

The journal *Sinch'ŏngnyŏn* (*New youth*),[25] based around the *Kyŏngsŏng ch'ŏngnyŏn kurakbu* (Seoul youth club) and launched slightly earlier than the better known *Ch'angjo* (*Creation*), also lies within this context. Of course, the emergence of youth is not a phenomenon limited to colonial Korea. For just one example, the bilingually titled magazine *Xinqingnian La Jeunesse*[26] was published in China. In Japan, the terms *seinen* (Kor. *ch'ŏngnyŏn*) and *seishun* (Kor. *ch'ŏngch'un*) were also quite modish.[27] *Seinen* was used by Mori Ōgai as the title for one of his novels, while Sōseki even contemplated adopting it as the title of the work that eventually became known as *Sanshiro*.[28] The various youth organizations that sprung up in Meiji Japan labeled themselves either "youth clubs (*seinenkai*)" or "boys' clubs (*shonenkai*)," while their club journals also used these terms on their mastheads.[29] In relation to this, one Japanese scholar made the following observation: "This trend, to which

Kitamura Tōkoku granted substance, Tokutomi Soho attached a name, and which Kunikida Doppo actualized, was predominant in Japan from the fin de siècle through the outset of the twentieth century."[30]

In reality, the "seinen" of Japan was created by Tokutomi Soho, the founder of *Kokumin no tomo* (*The people's friend*), Japan's first general news magazine, as an existence that could represent the *kokumin*.[31,32] Tokutomi proclaimed, "I too am one who has joined the ranks of *seinen* society."[33] He established "*seinen*" while excluding "*sōshi* (壯士)," whom he viewed as teaching through their poor examples and as a "negative image of the Other." These so-called *sōshi*, or ex-samurai thugs, held athletic meets, which were actually political rallies, or, in righteous indignation, challenged cabinet members to duels. *Kokumin no tomo*, while defining these "*sōshi*" as representing the "old Japanese order" in the second decade of Meiji, criticized these utterly destructive fellows as "evildoers" who "integrate a pitiful history of violence, failure, and anguish" with a politics of "complaint, disturbance, disappointment, and resentment."[34] It continued, "They have no employment, and as a matter of course have no stable income. They have no art, no education, and as a matter of course do almost nothing beyond drinking liquor and wasting energy." In this manner, *Kokumin no tomo* treated the *sōshi* of the previous era as the emblem of "a group with no capital, no employment, and no property." Before long, this led to statutes such as the Ordinance to Control the *Sōshi*, relegating them to the status of a group of petty offenders or delinquents, and differentiating them from the *seinen*. At the time, the key quality differentiating the *seinen* from the *sōshi* was education. One Japanese scholar put it as follows:

> At this time, the important element distinguishing the new "*seinen*" from the "*wakamono* (young men)" who displayed old abuses was the presence or absence of education. As seen in the case of Chiba, the "*seinen*" used the dissemination of print media, or academic speeches and magic lantern shows in the firm belief that obtaining knowledge qua enlightenment using these means would lead to the creation of a subject compatible with the "*seinen*." At times, at the center of this change were the children of rural elites who had formerly studied in Tokyo or other large cities.[35]

Particularly important in the above quotation are the forms of media such as print, speeches, and magic lanterns. These brought attention to a *seinen* style praxis that was different from that of the *sōshi*. It was expressed through activities such as speeches, meetings, and journal publication. In fact, when the government-sponsored students from Chosŏn arrived at Tokyo's Shinbashi station on May 1, 1895, the very first thing they encountered was a speech given by Fukuzawa Yukichi at the Mita Enzetsukan (Mita

Auditorium). It was following that when Korean students abroad began to engage in speeches, debates, lectures, mock assemblies, and other "oral speech activities."[36] These led to the sound of applause, which was quite different from the "plaintive sound of the curfew bell," which was lamented by one author as having "rung the same so many hundreds of thousands of times over the last 500 years."[37] This became the sound that symbolized the modern age. The following scene relates to this.

> Someone among the people assembled clapped. All eyes turned in the direction of this strange sound of clapping. Seeing this, the person who had been clapping quickly arose and said, "Ladies and gentlemen, originally one should clap when the president's speech ends. So let us clap," after which he began clapping again. The others also began to clap. Some of the bystanders also began to clap. The missionaries too, grinning, began to clap.
>
> Ch'a Chinsa (Mr. Cha) waited for the clapping to end, then said, "Ladies and gentlemen! Just as there are guide ropes at the edge of a fishing net, an assembly must have a president. We shall first nominate three people then take a vote."[38]

This brings to mind Sŏ Chaep'il's leading of debates in the *Hyŏpsŏnghoe* (founded in 1895, this was the student organization of the pioneering Western-style educational institution, *Paejae hakdang*) and the *Tongnip hyŏphoe* (Independence club), in which he taught not only motions, seconding, and amending but also how to clap.[39] Accordingly, the "sound of clapping" seems almost a response to the line from the Introduction of *Mujŏng* that reads "Sound—sound—we thirst for a true sound, long for that sound."[40] The sound of a "paddleboat steamer going round"[41] or the sound of clapping for a speech, these are what will raise Yi Hyŏngsik from the boy of the past who "wore a white pigtail ribbon in his hair and toddled with feet wrapped in strips of cloth" in to "Mister Lee."[42] And Yŏngch'ae will become a *"reidi* (lady)." In this respect, these are the "true sound(s)" Yi Kwangsu spoke of. This also suggests a structure of youth operating on a deep level in works such as An Kuksŏn's *Kŭmsu hoeŭirok* (*Record of a meeting of birds and beasts*, 1908), Kim P'ilsu's *Kyŏngsejong* (*Bell to awaken the world*, 1910), and the satirical *Pyŏngin kanch'inhoerok* (*Record of a social meeting among invalids*, 1909).[43] It denotes the beginning of the formation of political masses and assemblies. Even if we do not make reference to the Japanese discussion that links the greatest characteristic of the Meiji period *seinen* organizational activities to the publication of journals, it is quite clear that in the Korean case "print media activities" such as the publication of newspapers and journals are also inextricably related to the formation of the youth.

The above discussions all combine to push us toward a rereading of *"Taegu esŏ* (From Daegu)." In this work, Yi Kwangsu criticizes the "burglary case" caused by "those who organized a friendly gathering in Daegu with the aim to improve the progressiveness of Daegu youth,"[44] while also arguing that "since we have newspapers and journals and books and social institutions such as this good youth organization, if we take every opportunity to imbue them with new knowledge, they will never again engage in this sort of reckless-ness."[45] This bears a resemblance to the Tokutomi-esque stance on the *seinen*, which criticized the *sōshi*. Yi Kwangsu, following their first meeting in 1916 in Busan, either talked directly with Tokutomi at places such as *Kokumin sin-bosha*, Minyusha (the publishing company established by Tokutomi in 1887) in the Ginza, and Sanno sodo (Tokutomi's personal residence from 1924 to 1943), or they corresponded by letter.[46] In addition, Yi received requests and advice from Tokutomi such as "Please become my Korean son,"[47] "Please don't do anything that will land you in jail," and "You should live your life by the pen."[48] With these facts alone we may surmise that Tokutomi's thought exerted a certain influence on the discussion in *"Taegu esŏ."* In *"Nongch'on kyebal* (Rural development, 1916–17)" for example, the opening of "newspa-per clubs" or the "magic lantern shows" are archetypal youth activities that replace the recklessness of the *sōshi*. Yi Kwangsu expressed this as follows:

> For the magic lantern show, of course the youth but also the elderly and children gathered, and even the womenfolk wanted to watch. But because the room was small and could not fit them all, they decided to divide it into day one, day two, and day three, and to have the youth, the elderly, and then the women and chil-dren view it in turns. On this day, it was decided to let the youth enter.
>
> The pictures projected on this day were primarily of the lives of civilized people. They showed luxuriant forests, orderly farmlands and irrigation, levees, cultivation in America using steam engines, actual scenes of stock farming, beautiful scenes of rural villages, the magnificent and prosperous cities of Britain and America, as well as the amazing pictures of sericulture and spinning. They also showed armies and warships and vessels docked in ports, and, at the end, they showed an artist's impression of this village in the future.[49]

Yi Kwangsu's modern project as seen in works such as *"Kŭmil aHan ch'ŏngnyŏn kwa chŏngyuk* (Our Korean youth today and emotional rearing, 1910)," *"Minjok kaejoron* (On national reconstruction, 1922)," and *"Chanyŏ chungsimnon* (On the primacy of children, 1918)" defined a praxis of youth that established as Other not only the previous generation and its formal and heartless feudal familial relationships but also the haphazard and violent *sōshi*. Of course, a similar way of thinking is generally apparent in many of the pieces published in the journal *Hak chi kwang*. One example of this may be found in the above-quoted *"Yuhaksaeng ŭi sŏngjŏk ŭl tŭrŏ puhyŏng ŭige kohanora."* It criticizes the "dissipated heroism" of the Koreans studying in Tokyo who "label as spiritless" anyone who does not study "politics" or "law," while in its place encouraging a "graceful gentlemanliness" that "studies a field related to industry" and "does not fall into idle reverie but rather thinks of matters in a 'reliable' and orderly fashion."[50] This shares much in common with Yi Kwangsu's emphasis on education and employment.

The youth of Yi Kwangsu, however, as expressed in pieces such as "*Minjokchŏk kyŏngnyun* (National administration and knowledge, 1924)" and "*Sonyŏn ege* (To the boys, 1922)," were primarily enlightening and patriotic subjects.[51] With the institutionalization of the educational and legal systems, or of cultural institutions such as the press and publishers, however, they began to rely more heavily on print media than patriotic speeches. The aspects apparent in literary men such as Kim Tongin are an example of the latter. On the other hand, full-scale modern industry and employment will mediate the proletariat youth and the avant-garde: the former being class-based and organized activists—distinct from such categories as *sōshi*, patriots, and literary men—who "deliberate in the back alleys, and ___ in the factories."[52] And the commercial city of the neon sign shall give birth to the "formless modern boys" of writers such as Yi Sang and Pak T'aewŏn. The youth are the origin of all these modern subjects. This is pointed out in the quotation below.

> It was the undercurrent known as the popularization of youth that brought about the rise of Marxism and the flourishing of the proletariat literary movement, and not the other way around. Revolution too is no more than one derivation of youth.[53]

The *oppa*-sister structure is the indicator that decisively points to the location of youth described above. As implied by terms such as *puhyŏng* (father and elder [brother]) and *hakbuhyŏng* (school parent[s]), which may refer to "parents" but only contain the actual Chinese characters for "father" and "elder brother," there is a danger of fraternal relations among men being reduced to a Confucian vertical hierarchy based on the paternal line and centered upon the eldest son. In place of this, the relationship among "brothers" and "sisters" who might belong to different families is able to promote a connection among youth that is relatively more equal and horizontal. In fact, the very act of sons and daughters communicating from a position of equality is already beyond the logic of parents and families that cleave to a patriarchal order of primogeniture.[54] As a result, the falling out between brothers in "*Paettaragi*" is symbolic. Unlike *Hŭngbu-chŏn* in which, through the involvement of the swallow, the brothers' a priori relationship and universal order are reconfirmed, the brothers in this Kim Tongin story, through the intrusion of a mouse, will experience a fatal parting and new relationship. Departing forever from the cramped quarters that gave rise to misunderstanding and conflict, they shall gather amid the thundering sound of speeches in the square of brothers and sisters.

As seen in the works of Im Hwa, the *oppa*-sister structure also allows for the strong establishment of relationships among friends (comrades). The youth are not only friends of the *oppa* but also lovers of the sister. Now amid this new context defining human relationships, the youth shall freely expand their territory and actualize themselves. And it is there that modern temporality newly occurs. In place of a patrimonial time based on genealogy (social status), it will launch social relationships formed in the homogenous modern space of capital and science and racing trains, as well as a progressive time mediated by that space. This is implied by the lives' of Sŏngjae and Sŏngsun, the brother and sister protagonists of Yi Kwangsu's *Kaech'ŏkcha*, strictly revolving around thoroughgoing time plans all in the name of invention. And in Im Sŏn'gyu's "*Sarang e sokko ton e ulgo* (Deceived by Love and Crying over Money),"[55] Hongdo and her *oppa* both sentimentalize and popularize this modern condition.

It is in this way that brother and sister become a sort of spirit of the age. As a result, Han Int'aek's female protagonist asks, "Since I trust *oppa* (you) limitlessly, should I not follow *oppa* (you)?",[56] making her rejection of the marriage offer from "such a trifling place" a matter of course. This is also the reason Chŏn Yŏngt'aek's female protagonist says, "I will spend my whole life unmarried, and take care of, help, and comfort *oppa* (you), and live as a virgin." Not only were Hyŏndŏk and her *oppa* "together wherever they went" and unaware of "the passage of time as they sat facing each other and talking" but also since they ate "meals together at the same table," were scolded by their own mother: "I know you two like each other as brother and sister, but you like each other too much." "There aren't even married couples like you two."[57]

In light of all this, it becomes understandable that Tuhwan, the protagonist of Ch'oe Sŏhae's *Hooe sidae* (Age of the extra), was more "jealous of Ch'anhyŏng for having two younger sisters than for being the son of a wealthy man."[58] Brothers and sisters behaving "as if they were lovers" did not stop at the level of simple and accidental sibling affection. In the face of family opposition, the one and only character who supported Hyŏndŏk's studying was her *oppa*. This expresses a connection among youth that rejects the ancient regime. Therefore the category of youth in and of itself contains ample politicity. Kim Tongni describes the "age of passion," which gave birth to the youth, as follows:

> And thus in that "age of passion" that once set ablaze the hearts of all young people, in that year, at only eighteen years of age, did Chinsuk set out following her *oppa*. After that, in only a few months, they, together with nearly all the friends who shared their vision, had unawares become an imprisoned body.[59]

The relationship between brother and sister forms the heart described in poetry as follows:

A road to the great capital known as hope
Even if you are not as complete as the railroad from Seoul to Busan, Ah!
Friends, in my eyes
You are scattered like stars
Over several places north and south, like sparks burning bright.[60]

The above is, in turn, the device that mediates "Its home left behind distant / Its road ahead long / My youthful heart."[61] This is the key form of the youth, who were composed of students, patriots, writers, activists, and "modern boys." Seen here in one embodiment in an Im Hwa poem, it was at once the powerful impetus for modern Korean literary history and the essential structure of modern Korean literature. As Chŏng Chiyong put it in a poem, to the modern people who had gained "independence" from premodern parents and feudal families, "my youth and my fatherland"[62] were one.

THE CUSTOM OF SWORN BROTHERS AND SISTERS

Thus, when viewed in relation to the birth of the youth, Kim Tongin's founding of the journal *Ch'angjo* (*Creation*, February 1919) is deeply significant. Even as it carried on the tradition started by *Sonyŏn* and *Ch'ŏngch'un*, *Ch'angjo* differed from them in more concretely mediating through literature and art "the irrepressible demands that well up within us."[63] At this point, together with the linguistic construction "literary youth," art and literature are fixed as activities of the youth. Moreover, by subdividing activities in this way, literary coterie magazines both justify and fully establish the youth. This occurred in tandem with the declaration that "with my specialty in precious art, I cannot become the spokesman for those virtuous moralists of eternally-scowling countenance," and, as witnessed below, the subject's organizing and specializing of a new psychology and sentiment.

> Come all those of lonely mind. We shall cry together with them. Come all those of aching heart. We aim to share their troubles, share their pains. Come all those of joyous temperament. We intend to dance and sing with them. Come all those stifled over their own lives. Together let us knock upon those doors of the soul that remain unopened.
>
> At any rate, it is our pleasure to see this magazine overcome all obstacles and reach publication. All that we ask is for you to have a look at the path we travel.[64]

The crux of the above quotation is the oft-repeated "we."[65] Or it is the emotions and sentiments expressed by terms such as loneliness, aching heart, joy, stifling, and pleasure. Even while these are related to the "comrades in learning" stressed by Ch'oe Namsŏn, they also activate a distinct emotional connection among writers. Just as the postal system produced not only emotions of love but also youth networks (akin to the internet or cellular phones today), literary coterie magazines did more than just translate and express the preexisting emotions—"happiness, anger, sadness, pleasure, love, hate, and desire"[66]—in a modern literary language. Rather, they literarily organized and produced the youth's emotions and sensations themselves. In addition, as an institutional sphere for the consumption and circulation of youthful emotion, they also created a new material medium based on publication laws and sold in the marketplace. Of course, these two processes by which the youth were "created" occurred simultaneously. This constructed "emotion=medium," along with the actual organization of social movement groups, would come to regulate human thought and behavior. This, in distinction to the "comrades in learning" who had schools as their origin, is the condition for "members (of a literary coterie)" and "writers." In this way, the fatherland of youth and its citizens were established through the coterie magazines. Accordingly, the following words of Namgung Pyŏk reveal the essence of the situation: "In the world at large, many make various comments upon our journal *P'yehŏ* (*The ruins*), and those comments appear more or less critical. However, regarding the irresponsible criticisms from this uncritical and unsympathetic society of ours, we, for now, have no choice but to observe the virtue of silence." More than Namgung Pyŏk as an individual, the objective process of "*P'yehŏ*" and "*P'yehŏ*'s members" become the issue.[67]

At the time, among the most important sentiments sparking criticism of the members was the new concept of love appearing first through translated works. As evidenced by many of the works published in the journal, the main factor giving rise to loneliness, heartache, joy, stifling, and pleasure is love, or male-female relationships. This is one characteristic of the youth involved in literary magazines. They are not "decent." This is quite clear in the poems below by Hwang Sŏku and No Chayŏng, respectively.

Oh, my love, now is the very time for you to come.

Even brushing against the thin shadows of reed flowers
my heart may ache, may cry
I now cry, oh, my breast wells up as again I cry.
With tears hot as candle wax melting
Amidst my eyes preventing you from coming, me from going
I made a tiny, tiny shortcut.

Inside my eyes, inside my eyes, come my love.

Oh, like a butterfly on a spring evening
On the fire-flushed flower petals of my lover
Irremovable even if seized and rent with tongs
My heart joyously, profoundly secured
Warmed by such large, overwhelming eyes
Cries, my love Master of my entire existence, my love[68]

The heavens were formed and the earth was formed
And to me there is you. . . .

Oh, my beloved, do you thirst?
Then I shall briefly lend you the knife in my breast!
Stab my heart until content
And with its surging crimson blood
Shall I slake your thirst. . . .[69]

As seen above, the youth cried and cried with aching hearts while entrusting their entire existences to their lovers. Or they wrote poems about quenching their lovers' thirst with blood from their own hearts. It was likely this excessively emotional "self" and "world created by the self" of Kim Tongin that led Yi Kwangsu to criticize the youth in his essay "*Munsa wa suyang* (The writer and cultivation, 1921)." Yi was criticizing the fact that the term writer had come to mean "a person possessing the following qualities: 'has not graduated from school,' 'of course craves alcohol, strong red alcohol,' 'must publicly discuss love affairs,' 'sports a rakish hairstyle and attire,' 'has a nervous and anemic appearance,' and 'engages in an irregular and irrational lifestyle.'"[70] What deserves particular attention here is the phrase "publicly discuss love affairs." To Yi, who wrote, "Because, following my decision to live according to the Bible, I have continuously maintained the thought that young women are my (younger) sisters, at this point it has simply become a habit,"[71] this is no different from those men at church who sit "always close to the ladies' seats" or have "their eyes always on the ladies' seats." Contrary to Yi's thoughts, however, the church custom of "going on about brothers and sisters" was not from the beginning completely unrelated to "love affairs."

Taebong never once talked about the church, what its truths were, going to Heaven after death, none of it.
    "Hey, Kilson. Let's go to the congregation this next Sunday."
    He threw this out, and in reply received the question,
    "What's to do there?", which he immediately followed with,

"You don't want to have a look at the new wives and young ladies? You get to sing praise together, offer prayers, and go on about brothers and sisters. It's fun."

He (Kilson) at first responded to this sarcasm with,

"You son of a bitch."

And then punched him on the shoulder and turned away. But on Sunday morning, he ate breakfast early and came around asking,

"Is Taebong home?"[72]

In any case, from Yi Kwangsu's perspective, an important factor in the conversion of the youth from patriots to writers was the *nanpa*-style love affair.[73] Of course, criticism of love affairs was not limited to Yi. As one example, Yi Kiyŏng satirically reveals a secret letter in which an *oppa* loudly proclaims "The youth can love one another!"

Oh my dear, beautiful as an angel! I long to see you. If I cannot see you, I cannot live in this world. You are the goddess of my life! Whether you kill me or save me, I entrust my life to only you. Shall I jump from the bridge over the Han River? Shall I hang myself in the pine forest at Ch'ŏngnyang-ni?[74]

But this also brings to mind the situation in which the letter from Maria's *oppa* gained widespread popularity for No Chayŏng's collection of love epistles. No wrote an article titled "*Yŏsŏng undongŭi cheilinja Ellen Kei* (Ellen Kay, leader of the women's movement)," which appeared in the journal *Kaebyŏk* (*The dawn of civilization*) in February and March of 1921, in which she also included an example of a love letter. In response, Paek Ch'ŏl pointed out "the fact that Ch'unsŏng's (No Chayŏng's pen name) girlish pamphlet in praise of love, *Sarang ŭi pulkkot* (The fireworks of love), swayed the minds of a generation and was widely read by large numbers of young men and women," while also raising the issue of the "level of the writing of young authors at that time." He criticized their "way of writing as merely selecting and stringing together beautiful modifiers in order to affect elegant prose."[75] This is also likely related to the 1920s custom, following the publication of *Sarang ŭi pulkkot*, of (male) students' all possessing a romantic novel or volume of "popular songs," even when they did not have a textbook or study guide, while in their drawers they all kept "flowered envelopes and flowered notepads to write letters to female students."[76]

Yi Kwangsu heckled this "love" as being "like the candy strewn all over town," while it also acted as the backdrop for introducing writer and artist Kim Ch'anghyŏn as a character in his fiction. Comparing love to the candy sold in markets at the time gets right to the heart of the matter. This is because love vitalizes the market. For example, as can be seen in the case of Ŏp in

Yi Sang's *12-wŏl 12-il*, who is in conflict with his uncle over buying beach accoutrements for his date with Nurse C, or of Such'ŏl in Kim Tongin's "*Kudu* (Dress Shoes, 1930)," who has a pair of white dress shoes made as a gift for Miss K in order to prevail over her other suitors, from the very beginning, love and consumption went hand in hand. Love, that is to say modern dating, usually took place in urban spaces such as movie theaters, parks, cafes, and restaurants, as well as at hot springs, while it was also closely connected with the giving and receiving of presents purchased at department stores. Emotion was not the only thing exchanged. Therefore, it may only be natural that "love," the "pride" of youth, became something like "candy."[77] It is symbolic that No Chayŏng's collection of love letters sold well against the backdrop of the advent of publication capital. With respect to the market as well, *sarang* (love) and *sat'ang* (candy) were a minimal pair.

As a result, Yi Kwangsu writes that "dedicating one's life to Korea has become a childish dream from days past," and "love and money, these things have become the religion that rules their minds."[78] He continues, writing this love "is completely different from love of ten years ago, which was held sacred," and is now a "direct," and "scientific and businesslike love." This is the mid-1920s custom as understood by Yi. Of course, as seen below, this custom is also related to the matter of *oppa* and younger sisters.

> Thus, when he thought that if by chance Sunyŏng had gone to Tongnae Hot Springs with her second *oppa* there was no doubt that some rich brat would have gone with them, upon the sea of Ponggu's heart, which had for a brief moment grown calm, waves again began to rise. One more thing that agonized Ponggu about the word "*oppa*" was the fact that there were many young men Sunyŏng called *oppa*. He found particularly distasteful that among them Sunyŏng was on the friendliest terms with Kim Ch'anghyŏn, who carried around a violin, wrote fiction, and had a fair complexion and long hair.[79]

Ponggu agonizes over the term "*oppa*." More than anything, this is due to Sunyŏng's actual elder brother, Sun'gi. In order to raise funds for a business venture, he intends to give Sunyŏng as a concubine to the wealthy Paek Yunhŭi. Sun'gi is an *oppa* with a disposition exactly the opposite of that shown by Sambong.[80] Not only does Sambong oppose his sister Ŭlsun's being given as a concubine to Mr. No, who is a man of means, a public official, and also a notorious lecher, but is also dragged off to prison for assaulting Mr. No during his attempted rape of Ŭlsun. But Sun'gi is quite different. In a different sense than Maria's wanting to take out a newspaper ad that reads "My good-looking *oppa* is a sex maniac. My *oppa* is dog shit wrapped in nice blue cloth. Friends! Do not be fooled by handsome men!,[81] Sun'gi mediates a negative image of *oppa*. He is equal to Pak Yong in Han Sŏrya's

Ch'ŏngch'un'gi (Record of youth, 1937). This carries an important meaning
in that the Paek Yunhŭi–Sun'gi–Sunyŏng relationship replaces the Ponggu–
Sunhŭng–Sunyŏng relationship, which corresponds to Im Hwa's original
"comrade–*oppa*–younger sister" formulation. As such, Ponggu's wariness
concerning Sun'gi is quite natural. The latter (Ponggu–Sunhŭng–Sunyŏng)
relationship is of the following type.

> It was in February of 1919, about four or five days before the onset of the inde-
> pendence movement that swept over the entire nation. When they were trying
> to form a coalition of students from each school (Each school does not mean
> every school, but this is how it was phrased), it just so happened that Ponggu
> was tasked with the boys' schools while Sunyŏng took responsibility for the
> girls' schools, which afforded them the opportunity to meet quite often. Prior
> to that, as Sunyŏng's third *oppa* was two years ahead of him in school, Ponggu
> had visited their house and met her a few times. From then he had thought to
> himself that she was a beautiful girl, but he had no particular feelings for her. It
> was in fact through her third *oppa*, Sunhŭng, that the two gained the opportunity
> to meet frequently in order to work for the country.[82]

In Yi Kwangsu's opinion, the problem in the mid-1920s lay in the facts
that the *oppa*-younger sister relationship between Sunhŭng and Sunyŏng who
had devoted themselves to social movements had ceased to exist, and that a
new relationship in which Sun'gi would willingly conspire to make Sunyŏng
a "mistress for money" had arisen. Of course, this sort of change also arises in
Ponggu following his release from prison. Ponggu has thrown away "the eyes
he viewed the world with four years ago," and, filled with a thirst for personal
revenge in place of "thoughts of what he would do for the country, or do for
the world," falls into "rice speculation, which he formerly considered no different from thievery."[83] The youth have been corrupted, and solidarity has
been broken. Yi Kwangsu describes this situation as follows.

> "Love and money," these are the religion that rules their spirits. But this is true
> not only of girls. Their elder brothers have become no different. As the months
> and years passed, their brothers' minds grew slack until all had become selfish
> individualists. They engaged in rice speculation, drank alcohol, and stayed up
> all night in *kisaeng* houses, so that their younger sisters had no choice but to
> wander in the wakes of rich husbands. This is how the sons and daughters of
> Korea came to forget Korea a bit more each day, and to search only for money
> and pleasure.[84]

But this is not such a strange occurrence. From the start, *ch'ŏngch'un* and
ch'ŏngnyŏn were "synonymous with the rise and expansion of the bourgeois

class" and "the worldwide spread of industrial capitalism." "The light and shadow of youth were, in fact, no different from the light and shadow of capitalism."[85] The elegant prose of No Chayŏng moved the hearts of the youth and sold well. This implies something about the true essence of the modern individual. Above all, the capitalistic individual is the subject of equal contracts and of possession. As one example of this, in *Kaech'ŏkcha*, Yi Kwangsu writes that "a large lawsuit will arise over the issue of Sŏngsun's ownership," while also posing the question of "whether it belongs to Sŏngsun's mother and *oppa*, or whether it belongs to Sŏngsun." In addition, he narrates that true love is established based on "an understanding of each other's individuality," and also that "in all matters and all operations 'we two' have been the nominative case."[86]

But in the end, the "I" and "you" independent from parents who comprise "we two" suggest the relationship of subjects in a contractual agreement free from the interference of others and from traditional social status. That is to say, "(m)arriage is a contractual act voluntarily undertaken by adult males and females."[87] The problem with the custom of early marriage is that the subject of the contract is the parents (particularly the father). In early marriages, the premodern family, which is not distinguished from the actual person getting married, carries out the contract. But market contracts are not concluded in this manner. The family, nuclear or extended, cannot be the subject of a liberalistic contract. Moreover, contracts have nothing to do with premodern social status. Therefore, the matter of Sŏngsun's ownership is related not with her family or status but rather with the custom of free love and the order of the market. In this way, free love and the market seem to be in collusion. What the promise of love in the quotation below suggests is the structure of a contract undertaken by an equal and independent first person and second person.

"Yes, and then what do you intend to do?"
"I will follow you."
For the first time, Sŏngsun used the second person pronoun with Min.
"Where to?"
"Anywhere!"[88]

Sunyŏng's betrayal (or Sim Sunae's betrayal) displays the process of moving from one contract (a promise of love) to another (an exchange in the market). Mediated by the breakdown of love, the essential location of the first person and the second person became the market. At the risk of a slight leap, love was a mechanism for universalizing and romanticizing the market system. In that respect, Sun'gi's actions can be evaluated as an exposure of the market contracts hidden behind pledges of love.

Although Sun'gi is the one who makes plain the market (exchange) contract, there are still countless other *oppa* out there who equally vex Ponggu. Apart from her actual elder brothers Sunhŭng and Sun'gi, Sunyŏng uses the term *oppa* toward several different men. This attitude, at first sight, may be viewed as akin to Yi Kwangsu's "puritanical" custom of "viewing young women as sisters," and, seen from that perspective, it may appear that Ponggu has no particular reason to anguish.

The problem, however, is that the practice of viewing young women as sisters and that of viewing young men as *oppa* come together in a sense quite different from Yi's intentions. In fact, even the passage below, which suggests the destruction of traditional social class order, is difficult to read as purely puritanical.

> "Kyehyang, your face is as red as if you were drunk!", he said. Wondering whether Hyŏngsik knew she hesitated because she didn't know what to call him, Kyehang's face flushed even more.
>   "Oppa's face also . . . ," she said as she shyly bowed her head even further, unable to finish the sentence. Kyehyang thought of Hyŏngsik's saying "She is my younger sister." a bit earlier. What Hyŏngsik wanted to hear from Kyehyang was this word "oppa." But when he did hear her say "Oppa's face also . . . ," he undoubtedly felt embarrassed. Hyŏngsik had a real younger sister and two or three female younger cousins. . . . The real reason he used to go home during school vacations was to hear these young cousins call him "oppa." Kyehyang's simple phrase, "Oppa's face also . . . ," brought him infinite happiness.[89]

Thus, unrelated to Yi Kwangsu's intentions, "*oppa*" indirectly expresses the sexual attraction of young women toward young men. This is expressed when Yŏngsun says "Your *oppa* looks good. Manly," to which Maria responds, "Well then, why don't you call him *oppa* too!", while also raising the issue of "sworn brothers and sisters."[90] Mediated both by his close relationship with a girl's real elder brother and by their sphere of activity, an "*oppa*" often forms a powerful analogous relationship to the actual *oppa*. At the same time, however, an "*oppa*" is distinguished of course from the actual *oppa*, as well as from the comrade who represents the solidarity of youth. And *oppa* obviously also operates as a symbol articulating love affairs between men and women. No matter how much a woman vows "I will spend my whole life unmarried, and take care of, help, and comfort *oppa* (real elder brother), and live as a virgin," a real elder brother is different from an "*oppa*." The passage below is an example of this.

> "So what if he's a boy. I'll just meet him as an oppa. . . ." This was as far as the "thought" developed.

"Oppa! That's right. These days everyone's trying so hard to find sworn brothers and sisters. . . ."

In her mind, Sunmo pictured Sangch'ŏl's gentle eyes and towering physique, which she wanted to climb and dangle from like a tree. Then that towering physique suddenly appeared before her and spread its arms. All at once, Sunmo's arms and legs trembled making her quickly want to take a step back.

But when she collided with the thought "Hey, I have and oppa at home. . . ," for some reason it was not so enjoyable. Only a few days earlier she had said to Tŏgin, "I don't like people like Sangch'ŏl. I like people like my oppa." But, as if she had lied to herself, her emotions at that moment rather made her feel more uncomfortable toward her real elder brother.

No matter how much she liked the elder brother at home, if she called out to him, "Oppa?", she could find nothing particularly new or pleasant. If she began a letter with "Dear Elder Brother," there would be nothing to write other than the family and I are well. And neither of these would offer the slightest bit of comfort from her present loneliness.

By contrast, if she could be close to Sangch'ŏl and call out "Oppa?", like some sort of delicious dish it seemed that word would impart a beautiful feeling to her lips. And if she could take up the brush with the words "Dear Elder Brother" for him, it seemed she could produce a great mountain of words she desired to write, none of which needed to be about the family.[91]

In short, Yi Kwangsu, who was in the habit of viewing young women as younger sisters, was also not completely removed from the above custom of sworn brothers and sisters. Yi's habit goes together with Ch'anhyŏng's painful decision: "No! Never! I shall forever love her as a younger sister!"[92] It is precisely this attitude of trying to view young women as sisters that proves an interest in them as members of the opposite sex.

This is yet another core of the *oppa*-younger sister structure. That is why the scene in which Hyegyŏng goes to her lover who is about to be released from prison and says, "From now on let's just be comrades. Get rid of words like lover or whatever"[93] is so interesting. Just as market contracts and love were intimately entangled, this speaks eloquently to the fact that "movements" also were not separate from love. In fact, Ponggu thinks "I love Korea because it gave birth to and raised Sunyŏng," so much so that he has "forgotten for what reason I even started this movement." Ponggu was Sunyŏng's "*oppa*." At this juncture, Hyŏn Chin'gŏn's writing that "'*Oppa*' would not have been so foreign to their ears. They also became comrades. They became fathers and daughters. And they became brothers and sisters"[94] really hits the mark.

Accordingly, in a different sense than the anguish caused by her second *oppa* Sun'gi, Ponggu could not help but be burdened by "the fact that there were many young men Sunyŏng called *oppa*." This was because "*oppa*" could be another term for lover, while the contract of sworn brothers and sisters could be carried out several times.

THE SWALLOW AND THE *KISAENG'S* BROTHER

As discussed above, the work *Chaesaeng* suggests aspects of the good *oppa* (Sunhŭng the activist) and the bad *oppa* (Sun'gi the *kisaeng*'s brother). And both of these actual *oppa* yield their places to an "*oppa*" who is actually a lover. In this respect, Sin Ponggu and Paek Yunhŭi may not be such different characters. Despite the fact that they represent, respectively, a promise of love and a monetary contract, the two correspond in that they are both Sunyŏng's "*oppa*."

In light of this, in the Hyŏn Chin'gŏn work *Chŏkdo* (*The equator*, 1933), it is symbolic when Yŏngae goes to visit Yŏhae as he gets out of prison and says, "Yŏhae, let's become brother and sister!" "Please be my *oppa*. Huh, *oppa*!" In response to this, Yŏngae's husband, Pak Pyŏngil, counters her saying, "Is it so easy to make a former lover into a brother?" But, in the end, he bows to her will and tries to consider Yŏhae, once his rival in love, as his "younger brother-in-law."

The above forms a pair with both the pure emotions of Hyŏndŏk, who was as affectionate toward her real "*oppa*" as if he were a lover, and with the unspoken but "sacred(?) promise" that bound Chin'gu and Chinsuk. Between the latter two, actual brother and sister, a "peculiar spiritual relationship" in which "for the rest of their lives neither would get married or even date, but rather live and die together in loneliness and solitude"[95] was in operation. The reason Chinsuk severed this relationship and began dating Yunsik was that Chin'gu, her *oppa*, by meeting Chŏnghŭi, another woman, had broken their bond, which had been "a reality more solemn and immaculate than any sort of love or familial ethics." In a word, she meets Yunsik in order to "retaliate" for her *oppa*'s "betrayal."

What made possible Yŏngae's idea that she could reduce a lover to an *oppa* is related to this sort of atmosphere at the time. If an *oppa* can replace a lover, it stands to reason that a lover may also be reduced to an *oppa*. Through all of these processes, however, the *oppa*-younger sister structure comes to lose its role and significance. Just as Yŏngae got married, her *oppa* also marries. As a result, those younger sisters who were left alone must have come to think something like the passage below.

"After marriage, oppa became useless. It's different from before."
To the question of what this meant and the reasons behind it, Hyŏndŏk continued,

"After oppa got married last spring, he has become so different. It began a little after he got engaged last year, but after he got married he really changed. After you went to prison, even though oppa once loved me so much and I was right beside him, he completely ignored me and only thought of you and wept. It's the same even now. He calls me over here, but how much does he really think of me? He thinks only of you."[96]

The scene above announces the end of a complex *oppa*-younger sister relationship that could contain both romance and camaraderie. The tender relationship in which "(u)ntil last year, Nansu had dangled from Munho's hand, but from this year, when he touched her hand, her face grew red and she retreated"[97] has already grown childish. The lonely *oppa* who naturally commits suicide following the suicide of a lonely younger sister (Ch'oe Sŏhae, "*Nui tongsaeng ŭl ttara* (Following the younger sister)," 1930) has become extinct. This is an ineluctable outcome of individual maturation. By way of comparison Kyŏngho, who is unable to meet with his twin younger sister, simply looks at his own reflection in the mirror in order to paint a picture of the "sister he misses" (Hyŏn Kyŏngjun, "*Maŭm ŭi t'aeyang* (Sun of the heart)," 1934). In addition, Kyŏngsun, having been reunited with Kyŏngho following all of the happenings and problems, informs him "I have no reason at all to be called sister by you," before going on to finish with "I have no recollection of ever having an *oppa* like you." Following the "distant, youthful byways / of throat-tight longing," the "(f)lower, like my sister returning / to stand before the mirror"[98] has fallen. The *oppa* and younger sister, now adults, have parted ways.

At this point, individual maturation as represented by marriage acts as a metaphor for the complexity of the advancement of and relationships in modern society. Just as an *oppa* and younger sister each go on to form different families, the youth's ideology and sphere of activity, both of which used the *oppa*-younger sister relationship to reject premodern parents, gradually have their epochal significance stripped or curtailed. Now all that remains are individuals as the subjects of contracts and divided into the first person and the second person. This was an inevitable consequence. Just as with love, and quite separate from their blood ties, the "sacred promise" and "peculiar spiritual relationship" between an *oppa* and younger sister were also from the very beginning not completely separate from the contracts of the market.

As a result of the above, the Ch'ae Mansik protagonist, Yun Yŏngsŏp, who finds his younger sister involved in a world he cannot abide says to her, "You and I are no longer siblings!" Of course, in terms of not being able to accept the other party, the café waitress "Helen," who sarcastically addresses this same *oppa*, who is a school teacher, as "Sir Upright Gentleman!" is also the same. Following the demise of the solidarity of youth, this *oppa* and younger sister use money originating from two different worlds (markets). This is the true origin of their conflict. The conflict originates from the interaction between ties based on blood (the family), which are no more than an empty shell, and contractual ties (the market), which are the practical substance of life. The following scene shows the eruption of the conflict between Hyeryŏn ("Helen") and Yŏngsŏp.

> "What? Who the hell are you calling dirty with that hole of yours?"
> Helen had already leisurely wiped her hands with a towel, found and donned her hat, and was sitting at the edge of the veranda lacing up her dress shoes.
> "Why? What's wrong with me? . . . I'm a café waitress. I'm a whore. . . . So what? Am I plotting a rebellion? Am I cheating on a husband? . . . I'm fine with it, and that's all that matters.!"
> "No, you! What the hell are you saying?"
> "Why don't you go right out front to the street and whisper the question in any passing girl's ear? Just see if ten out of ten girls among them who are hungry, ragged, and suffering don't say they envy the lot of a kisaeng waitress!"[99]

So falls the *oppa*-younger sister structure that once constituted the youths' ideologically or emotionally unified sphere. Save for its brief resurrection by Yi Kwangsu in a passionate pair of Japanese and Korean elder brothers and younger sisters who devoted themselves to the ideals of Greater East Asia Co-Prosperity,[100] the *oppa*-younger sister structure fractures into later works such as Yi Pŏmsŏn's "*Obalt'an* (A stray bullet, 1959)" and Son Ch'angsŏp's "*Pi onŭn nal* (A rainy day, 1953)." That the married Yŏngae had thought to take her ex-lover as an *oppa* testifies that this sort of breakdown(?) had already begun.

In addition, against the backdrop of such a situation, *oppa* and lover become interchangeable terms in a very different sense from before. This is no longer mediated by the ideology of the youth. Meeting a friend of your *oppa* through your *oppa* and taking him as your lover, and through that friend of your *oppa* making a new *oppa*-younger sister relationship not based on blood ties—these activities of the youth came to an end. Now "*oppa*" becomes a word that conceals sexual relationships with men, as well as the lustful feelings they arouse. This implies a custom at the time worthy of being called the "*oppa* phenomenon." The society was overflowing with innumerable exchangeable "*oppa*" and their "younger sisters." The passage below represents one aspect of this.

> "See here. From now on do not call that person oppa! Oppa, what sort of oppa is he supposed to be? Is that person a relative of yours? I hate the sound of that word!"

. . . .

"No. No. What's your problem? Why can't I call him oppa? Why can't I love him as an oppa? Are you going to break my freedom just like that? I won't have it. I won't!"

She resolutely shook her head, threatening to send her chignoned hair tumbling. It was as if a rebellious air were permeating the room. Lawyer Yun, as if disgusted, gazed upon Sŏnju with the eyes of a parent scolding a child.

"You love your brother, too? Do you think love is just some word to be bandied about? Is it like that with all women these days? They love their husbands, and they love their oppa as well. . . ."

. . . .

"Why can't they? There is a separate love for a husband, as well as a separate love for an oppa. Right, men can get a good wife for their family register, get a kisaeng for a mistress, or, taking a second wife when they already have one, get married to a virgin—they can have two or three women and no one minds. So why is it so horrible if a woman chastely, truly chastely, loves an oppa with a "platonic love"? Isn't that right?"[101]

The comment in *Chŏkdo* that "*oppa* back then and *oppa* today are exactly the same word," but "it is just that in terms of actual meaning they came to be extremely different"[102] is related to the "custom of *oppa*" above. Yŏngae's attitude in intending to taker her former lover as *oppa*, her putting forth "platonic love" to counter married men's taking *kisaeng* mistresses, has as its backdrop the popularization of using *oppa* to justify married women's lovers. This implies the exchange and market logic that had begun to rule the society. It shows that *oppa* and lover could now be exchanged. In addition, such exchange could occur multiple times. Regardless of Ch'ohyang`s (Sŏnyŏng`s) sincerity as she endlessly respected and waited for her stepbrother *oppa* who was in Shanghai, in accordance with the changing times, *kisaeng* came, "in front of other people, to call *oppa* those men, usually called something like lovers or paramours, who, having run out of money and having only feelings remaining, commonly chased after them saying the day you die will be the day I die."[103] This announces the onset of the demise of free love, which had been accepted as both an ideology of the youth and as a plan for modern enlightenment. Accordingly, the lines below by Kim Tongin are significant.

Her comrades as well almost all kept one, or several, of these so-called "swallows." Yŏngsuk's present husband had once been the "swallow" of one of her friends.[104]

A "comrade" had become a "swallow." No, actually from the beginning the youth were simultaneously comrades and swallows. And younger sisters also become *kisaeng*. Thus, it is precisely at this point that the literary-historical meaning embodied by Kim Namch'ŏn's works such as "*Sonyŏnhaeng* (A boy's stroll, 1937)," "*Nammae* (Brothers and sisters, 1937)," "*Mujari* (The lowly, 1938)," and "*Nuna ŭi sagŏn* (Elder sister's affair, 1938)" becomes clear.[105] Kim, in setting up the dandy-*kisaeng* relationship, was reflecting on a time "after" *Maŭm ŭi hyangch'on* the "young dreams of ten years ago"[106] and the "powerful wave of youths that surged along these streets"[107] had already vanished without a trace. In "*Nammae*," at one time Kyehyang, "despite being beaten by her father and struck by her mother, liked the impoverished Yun Chaesu, and to the last would not give her body to another man," however, "in the end because of money" she offers up her body. Seeing this, her younger brother Ponggŭn, to whom people sarcastically ask "Do you have a dozen brothers-in-law? Or two dozen?", thinks, "The sublime and sacred are nowhere to be found in this world."[108] Ponggŭn also reminisces that "my elder sister didn't used to be the kind of girl who would worship Pak Pyŏnggŏl, who, after carelessly going to and fro in the name of socialism, has become a mining broker"[109] like the heavens, and try to work him for the capital to start a bar.

At this point, the *oppa*-younger sister structure had vanished. The "sound of applause" of the youths too could no longer be heard. In a situation where only "great enterprises" were emphasized, and that relegated such things as "humanitarian righteous indignation" over the plight of laborers to "youthful sentimentality," they were, "without a single word of impassioned speech to spark a fire in the heart,"[110] to take up their picks and hoes and till the earth.

In this way, Kim Namch'ŏn, through Ponggŭn's elder sister Kyehyang, recalls the Kyehyang of old who called Yi Hyŏngsik *oppa* in *Mujŏng*. Through the eyes of a *kisaeng*'s brother, he recollected the passionate structure of the youth and of *oppa* and sisters, a structure that had been popularized then destroyed through a process of so many exchanges and substitutions. This also represents one of the consciousnesses in Kim's *Taeha* (*Great River*, 1939), a novel that depicts a youth's coming of age during the Korean Enlightenment Period, as well as forming the core of Han Sŏrya's *Ch'ŏngch'un'gi*. T'aeho believes that Ch'ŏlsu, a friend he misses so much he even has a dream has died in Moscow, will definitely return. Not only does he attempt, however, to deny the fact that Ŭnhŭi is the younger sister of the untrustworthy Pak Yong but also calls her by a name of his own choosing, "Ch'ŏlchu," imagining her to be the younger sister of the "strong willed" Ch'ŏlsu. Thus "*Ch'ŏngch'un'gi*" attempts to defend the world of "Ch'ŏlsu–Ch'ŏlchu–T'aeho," which is being seriously challenged by the world of "Pak Yong–Ŭnhŭi–Myŏnghak." It is an attempt to resurrect the structure of "youth."

When viewing fiction written at the end of the Japanese Colonial Period with this situation in mind, the following passage becomes complicatedly symbolic.

God summoned his right hand, who had theretofore been expelled by God and been slovenly wallowing in worthless works. Thinking he must go at once, God's expelled right hand scrambled and prostrated himself before God's throne. God is now finally ready to forgive my sins, the right hand thought. When He saw his beautiful and powerful right hand at His knee, God did think about forgiving his right hand. However, He soon thought again of the past, and, without even turning His face in that direction, gave the following order. "Go down to the ground. In the exact form of the humans you have seen, and so that I may properly observe you, you shall stand completely naked atop a mountain." Perhaps because the story was difficult for him, Ch'angi soon closes his eyes. But I mumble a bit more to myself.

"If you want to do that, as soon as you get to the ground, go to where there is any young woman and say this, whispering quietly in her ear, 'I want to live.'"[111]

The position of the father gazing upon his son who has fallen asleep while listening to the story brings to mind Munho and Munbae's stroking their beards while saying "It looks like the heaven for boys is gone forever."[112] The father can no longer be in the position of even a dandy or *kisaeng*'s brother. That is the reason the protagonist says, "I want to live." In spite of this, however, he intends to say these words only to a "young woman." This is in accordance with the fact that the quotation above is "a letter to his elder sister." In brief, the protagonist was still endeavoring to be a "young *oppa*." But, at the same time, he prostrated himself before "God." In the end, it was the father who was resurrected.

NOTES

1. The term *oppa* literally refers to a woman's older brother. In practice, however, it is used by women to refer to elder male cousins, friends, and even lovers.—Trans.

2. Son Chŏngsu, "'*Oppa-nui*' *kujo ŭi yŏnwŏn* (The origin of the '*oppa*-sister' structure)," in *Ch'oe Sŏhae munhak ŭi chaejomyŏng* (Seoul: Saemi, 2002), 303.

3. Kim Yunsik, *Im Hwa yŏn'gu (A study of Im Hwa)* (Seoul: Munhak sasangsa, 1989), 191–92.

4. Ibid, 191.

5. Oksun is the given name of the younger sister of Im's poetic narrator. In the original, he adds a suffix to denote familiarity/intimacy, writing it "Oksuni." In certain places, this is again altered, shortened simply to "Suni."—Trans.

6. Im Hwa, "*Ŏmŏni* (Mother)," in *Chosŏn chi kwang*, April 1929, 124.

The underscores represent letters or words elided from the original text by censors.

7. Im Hwa, "*Negŏri ŭi Suni* (Suni at the crossroads)," in *K'apŭ siinjip* (Seoul: Chipdansa, 1931), 54–55.

8. Im Hwa, "*Hwangmuji* (Wasteland)," in *Hyŏnhaet'an* (Seoul: Tonggwangdang sŏjŏm, 1939), 156.

9. Ibid.

10. Im Hwa, "*Uri oppa wa hwaro* (My *oppa* and the brazier)," in *K'apŭ siinjip*, 64–65.

11. Im Hwa, "*Chido* (Map)," in *Hyŏnhaet'an*, 171.

12. Yi Kwangsu, *Mujŏng* (Seoul: Hoedong sŏgwan, 1925), (sixth printing), 399.

13. The three obediences (*samjong*) stipulated that prior to marriage the woman was to obey her father; after marriage she was to obey her husband; and, if her husband passed away, she was to obey her son. Taken literally, according to this Confucian doctrine, a woman was dependent upon and subordinate to men throughout her life.—Trans.

14. This particular translation ("accursed two words") is taken verbatim from Ann Lee's English translation of *Mujŏng*. Even when, as above, original translations are used, reference is most often made to Lee's seminal work.—Trans.

See Ann Sung-Hi Lee, *Yi Kwang-Su and Modern Korean Literature* (Ithaca: Cornell East Asia Series, 2005), 272.

15. Although somewhat awkward, these terms have been translated literally to display a concrete case of the "*oppa*-(younger) sister" structure in a literary work.—Trans.

16. Han Sŏrya, "*Maŭm ŭi hyangch'on* (Hometown of the heart)," in *Sinmun yŏnjae sosŏl chŏnjip* 2, 2nd ed. (Seoul: Kip'ŭnsaem, 1999), 454.

17. Kim Ilyŏp, "*Chagak* (Awakening)," in *Tonga ilbo*, 1926, in *Chaetbit chŏksam e sarang ŭl mutgo*, ed. Kim Sangbae (Seoul: Solmoe, 1982), 153–54.

18. I borrow this concept from the title of a book by Kimura Naoe.

Kimura Naoe, *Seinen no tanjō* (*The birth of youth*) (Tokyo: Shinyōsha, 1998).

19. The translation appeared in the journal *Sonyŏn* (*Boys*) Year 2, Vol. 3, March 1909, 2.

20. The much terser corresponding portion of the original reads as follows:
Deeper, deeper let us toil
In the mines of knowledge;
Nature's wealth and learning's spoil
Win from school and college;
Delve we there for richer gems
Than the stars of diadems.—Trans.

21. *Ch'ŏngch'un* (*Youth*), Inaugural Issue, October 1914, 5.

22. Song Saeng, "*Salgi wihayŏ* (In order to live)," in *Ch'angjo* Vol. 5, March 1920, 81.

23. For more on this, see my conference presentation: Lee Kyounghoon, "*Ch'ŏngnyŏn kwa minjok:* Hak chi kwang *chungsim ŭro* (Youth and the ethnonation as seen in *Hak chi kwang*)," in *Kŭndae chŏnhwan'gi ŏnŏ chilsŏ ŭi pyŏndong kwa kŭndaejŏk maech'e tŭngjang ŭi sanggwansŏng* (Seoul: Taedong munhwa yŏn'guwŏn chungjŏm kwaje haksul palp'yohoe, June 20, 2003).

24. P'yŏnjibin (Editor), *"Yuhaksaeng ŭi sŏngjŏk ŭl tŭrŏ puhyŏng ŭige kohanora* (A declaration to fathers and elders regarding the grades of students abroad)," in *Hak chi kwang*, Vol. 10, September 1916, 10.

25. See Han Kihyŏng, *"Chapji* Sinch'ŏngnyŏn *sojae kŭndae munhak sinjaryo* (1) (*New materials for the study of modern literature in the journal* Sinch'ŏngnyŏn [1])," in Sŏnggyun'gwan daehakkyo tongasia haksulwŏn taedong munhwa yon'guwŏn, December 2002, and *"Kŭndae chapji* Sinch'ŏngnyŏn *kwa Kyŏngsŏng kurakbu* (The Modern Magazine Sinch'ŏngnyŏn and the Seoul Club)," in *Sŏji hakbo*, Spring 2003.

26. When first published it was titled merely *Qingnian zazhi (Youth Magazine)*.

27. Although perhaps not immediately apparent in English translation, the terms in Korean, Chinese, and Japanese are merely different pronunciations of the same characters: (新)青年.—Trans.

28. Miura Masashi, *Seishun no shūen (The end of youth)*, 6th ed. (Tokyo:Kodansha, 2002), 37.

29. Kimura Naoe, *Seinen no tanjō*, 162.

30. Miura Masashi, *Seishun no shūen*, 39.

31. Kimura Naoe, *Seinen no tanjō*, 43.

32. Although translated here as "people," *kokumin* (Kor. *kungmin*) literally means the people of a nation. As such, according to context, it can mean nation, people, the public, or citizen. In all cases, however, it stood as a new and unifying concept, in contrast to earlier and divisive regional and class-based loyalties and identities.—Trans.

33. Tokutomi Soho, *"Shin Nippon no seinen oyobi shin Nippon no seiji* (The youth of new Japan and the politics of new Japan)," in *Kokumin no tomo*, September 1887, 17.

34. Kimura Naoe, *Seinen no tanjō*, 47.

35. Ibid, 145.

36. Ch'a Paekŭn, Kaehwagi Ilbon yuhaksaengdŭl ŭi ŏllon ch'ulp'an hwaltong yŏn'gu (1) (A study of the press and publication activities of Korean students in Japan during the enlightenment period [1]) (Seoul: Sŏuldae ch'ulp'anbu, 2000), 62.

37. Yi Kwangsu, *"Sŏndoja* (The leader)," in *Yi Kwangsu chŏnjip* 4 (Seoul: Samjungdang, 1962), 419.

38. Ibid, 391.

39. Kim Yŏngu, Han'guk kŭndae t'oron ŭŭ sajŏk yŏn'gu (A historical study of modern Korean debate) (Seoul: Iljisa, 1991), 102.

40. Yi Kwangsu, *Mujŏng*, 1 (These words were written by Han Saem, one of Ch'oe Namsŏn's pennames.)

41. Ibid, 280.

42. The words in the original are *taenggi* and *kambal*, both distinctly premodern articles of Korean clothing, while the modern, English *"Misŭt'ŏ Ri* (Mister Lee)" is how Yi Hyŏngsik is first addressed in *Mujŏng*.—Trans.

43. The author of the final work opted for a pen name, Kwengosaeng (轟笑生), or "Mr. Uproarious Laughter."—Trans.

44. Yi Kwangsu, *"Taegu esŏ* (From Daegu)," in *Yi Kwangsu chŏnjip* 18 (Seoul: Samjungdang, 1962), 206.

45. Ibid, 209.
46. Yi Kwangsu, "Tokutomi Soho *sŏnsaeng kwa mannan iyagi* (Tales of my meetings with Mr. Tokutomi Soho," in *Tongp'o e koham* (*Informing my countrymen*), eds. Kim Wŏnmo and Lee Kyounghoon (Seoul: Ch'ŏrhak kwa hyŏnsilsa, 1997), 281–83.

Of course, the students abroad of the previous generation who published *Ch'inmokhoe hoebo* would also have been influenced by Tokutomi's thoughts on youth. This is because *Kokumin no tomo* and *Jyogaku zasshi* (Journal of Women's Studies) were being donated to and read by the members of *Tae Chosŏnin Ilbon yuhaksaeng ch'inmokhoe*, the group that published the *Ch'inmokhoe hoebo* from February 15, 1896. Interestingly, however, is that according to the donated book records of the *Ch'inmokhoe*, the person who donated both *Kokumin no tomo* and *Kattei zasshi* (*Journal of family*) was the critic and businessman Hitomi Ichitaro (1865–1924).

See Cha Paegŭn, op. cit., appendix.
47. Yi Kwangsu, "Tokutomi Soho *sŏnsaeng kwa mannan iyagi*," 257.
48. Ibid, 258.
49. Yi Kwangsu, "Nongch'on kyebal," in *Yi Kwangsu chŏnjip* 17 (Seoul: Samjungdang, 1962), 94.
50. P'yŏnjibin, *Hak chi kwang*, Vol. 10, September 1916, p. 7.
51. For more on this, see Sŏ Yŏngch'ae, "*Han'guk kŭndae sosŏl e nat'anan sarang ŭi yangsang kwa ŭimi e kwanhan yŏn'gu* (A study of the meaning of the types and meanings of love appearing in early modern Korean fiction)," PhD diss. (Seoul National University, 2002).
52. Im Hwa, "*Negŏri ŭi Suni* (Suni at the crossroads)," in *Chosŏn chi kwang*, January 1929, 137.
53. Miura Masashi, *Seishun no shūen*, 57.
54. As a result, this is quite different from the brother-sister relationships embodied in the *hyangga* "*Chemangmae-ka*" or in the Greek drama(s) *Electra*. In both of these works, brother and sister as individuals are merely devices for reconfirming that the origin of individuals lies in the patriarchal family. That is, rather than a connection as youth between brother and sister, their consanguinity is emphasized.
55. Im Sŏn'gyu, "*Sarang e sokko ton e ulgo* (Deceived by love and crying over money)." This is a play that was premiered at the Tongyang kŭkchang in July 1936.
56. Han Int'aek, "*Oppa* (Older brother)," in *Sindonga*, May, 1936, 321.
57. Chŏn Yŏngt'aek, "*Nammae* (Brother and sister)," in *Munjang*, November 1939, 21.
58. Ch'oe Sŏhae, *Hooe sidae* (*Age of the extra*) (Seoul: Munhak kwa chisŏngsa, 1994), 82.
59. Kim Tongni, "*Onui* (Brother and sister)," in *Kim Tongni chŏnjip* 1 (Seoul: Minŭmsa, 1995), 319.
60. Im Hwa, "*Chido*," 171–72.
61. Im Hwa, "*Haengbok ŭn ŏdi issŏtnŭnya?* (Where was Happiness?)," in ibid, 239.

62. Chŏng Chiyong, "*Haehyŏp* (The straight)," in *Chŏng Chiyong chŏnjip* 1, 2nd ed. (Seoul: Minŭmsa, 1992), 98.

63. Kim Tongin, "*Namŭn mal* (Words left over)," in *Ch'angjo*, February 1919, 80.

64. Ibid, 81.

65. It should be noted here that in the Korean original, not only "we" but also "us" and "our" share the same word, "*uri*."—Trans.

66. This is a literal translation of a Sino-Korean list in the original: 喜怒哀樂愛惡欲.—Trans.

67. Namgung Pyŏk, "P'yehŏ *chapki* (Miscellaneous writings on *P'yehŏ*)," in *P'yehŏ*, Volume 2, January 1921, 151.

68. Hwang Sŏku (Sangat'ap), "*Nun ŭro aein a onŏra* (Come my lover with the snow)," in *Ch'angjo*, Volume 6, May 1920, 44.

69. No Chayŏng, "*Aein ŭl wihayŏ* (For my lover)," in *Nae honi pult'al ttae* (Seoul: Ch'ŏngjosa, 1928).

70. Yi Kwangsu, "*Munsa wa suyang* (The writer and cultivation)," in *Ch'angjo*, Volume 8, January 1921, 14.

71. Yi Kwangsu, "*Kŭ ŭi chasŏjŏn* (His autobiography)," in *Yi Kwangsu chŏnjip* 9 (Seoul: Samjungdang, 1962), 293.

72. Kim Namch'ŏn, *Taeha* (*The great river*) (Seoul: Inmunsa, 1939), 254.

73. *Nanpa* (軟派) in the Japanese, and by extension the Korean, literature of the time referred to a "soft type" of masculinity characterized by womanizing and selfish pursuits, as contrasted to the *kōha* (硬派) or more traditional "hard type," which was characterized by machismo and discipline.—Trans.

74. Yi Kiyŏng, "*Oppa ŭi pimil p'yŏnji* (*Oppa*'s secret letter)," in *Kaebyŏk*, July 1924, 148.

75. Paek Ch'ŏl, *Sinmunhak sajosa* (*History of new literary trends*) (Seoul: Sin'gumunhwasa, 1980), 230.

76. For more on this phenomenon, see Kwŏn Podŭrae, "*Yŏnae ŭi hyŏngsŏng kwa toksŏ* (Reading and the formation of love)," in *Yŏksa munje yŏn'gu*, Volume 7, 2001, 101–30, and Yi Kihun, "*Kŭndaejŏk toksŏ ŭi t'ansaeng* (The birth of modern reading)," in *Yŏksa pip'yŏng*, Volume 62, 2003, 341–56.

77. Although largely lost in translation, it is worth noting here that the point made by the original sentence is strengthened by the visual and phonetic similarity of the three words in quotation marks: *charang* (자랑), *sarang* (사랑), and *sat'ang* (사탕). Linguistically, *sarang* forms a minimal pair with both *charang* and *sat'ang*.—Trans.

78. Yi Kwangsu, *Chaesaeng*, 260.

79. Ibid., 12

80. Sambong is the eponymous protagonist of the novel *Sambongi ne chip* (*Sambong's house*), a novel written by Yi Kwangsu and serialized in the *Tonga ilbo* from November 29, 1930, to April 24, 1931.

81. Yi Kiyŏng, "*Oppa ŭi pimil p'yŏnji*," 150.

82. Yi Kwangsu, *Chaesaeng*, 19.

83. For more on this, see chapter 6 "Rice Speculation, Hot Springs, English."

84. Yi Kwangsu, *Chaesaeng*, 260.

85. Miura Masashi, *Seishun no shūen*, 10.

86. Yi Kwangsu, *Kaech'ŏkcha*, 469.

87. Yi Kwangsu, "*Honinnon* (On marriage)," in *Yi Kwangsu chŏnjip* 17 (Seoul: Samjungdang, 1962), 141.

88. Yi Kwangsu, *Kaech'ŏkcha*, 428.

89. Yi Kwangsu, *Mujŏng*, 276–77.

90. Yi Kiyŏng, "*Oppa ŭi pimil p'yŏnji*," 142.

91. Yi T'aejun, "*Sŏngmo* (The Virgin Mary)," in *Sinmun yŏnjae sosŏl chŏnjip* 4, 2nd ed. (Seoul: Kip'ŭnsaem, 1999), 177–78.

92. Ch'oe Sŏhae, *Hooe sidae*, 232.

93. Hyŏn Chin'gŏn, "*Yŏnae ŭi ch'ŏngsan* (The liquidation of love)," in *Chosŏn ŭi ŏlgul* (Seoul: Munhak kwa pip'yŏngsa, 1988), 17.

94. Hyŏn Chin'gŏn, *Chŏkdo* (*The equator*) (Seoul: Munhak kwa pip'yŏngsa, 1988), 17.

95. Kim Tongni, "*Onui*," 324.

96. Chŏn Yŏngt'aek, "*Nammae*," 31.

97. Yi Kwangsu, "*Sonyŏn ŭi piae* (The sorrows of a boy)," in *Yi Kwangsu chŏnjip* 14 (Seoul: Samjungdang, 1962), 12.

98. Sŏ Chŏngju, "*Kukhwa yŏp esŏ* (Beside a chrysanthemum)," in *Selected Poems of Sŏ Chŏngju*, trans. David R. McCann (New York: Columbia University Press, 1989), 20.

99. Ch'ae Mansik, "*Irŏn nammae* (This type of brother and sister)," in *Ch'ae Mansik chŏnjip* 7 (Seoul: Ch'angjak kwa pip'yŏngsa, 1987), 467.

100. Yi Kwangsu, "*Chinjŏng maŭm i manna sŏya mallo* (Only by a true meeting of the hearts)," in *Nokki*, March-July 1940.

101. Yi Kwangsu, *Chaesaeng*, 45–46.

102. Hyŏn Chin'gŏn, *Chŏkdo*, 117.

103. Han Sŏrya, *Maŭm ŭi hyangch'on*, 438.

104. Kim Tongin, "*Munŭngja ŭi anhae* (The incompetent's wife)," in *Kim Tongin chŏnjip* 2 (Seoul: Chosŏn ilbosa, 1988), 225.

105. For more on this, see my article "*Ch'ŏngnyŏn ŭi chwajŏl, sonyŏn ŭi chugŭm* (The frustration of the youth, the death of the boys)," in *Munye yŏn'gu*, Volume 22, September 1999, 83–102.

106. Kim Namch'ŏn, "*Odŭi* (Mulberry)," in *Munjang*, April 1944, 119.

107. Im Hwa, "*Tasi negŏri esŏ* (Again at the crossroads)," in *Hyŏnhaet'an* (Seoul: Tonggwangdang, 1939), 75.

108. Kim Namch'ŏn, "*Nammae* (Brother and sister)," in *Sonyŏnhaeng* (Seoul: Hagyesa, 1939), 32.

109. Ibid, 58.

110. An Sugil, *Mokch'ukki* (*A record of stock farming*), in *An Sugil* (Seoul: Pyŏkho, 1993), 73.

111. Kim Namch'ŏn, "*Tŭngbul* (Lamplight)," in *Kungmin munhak*, March 1942, 124–25.

112. Yi Kwangsu, "*Sonyŏn ŭi piae*," 22.

Chapter 3

"Trademark" of the Colony

THE CUSTOM OF *HAKURAI*

Myŏngu,[1] who plays the "role of cook" at the restaurant Hwawŏnjang[2] in the Han Sŏrya short story *"T'aeyang ŭn pyŏng tŭlda* (The sun grows ill, 1940)," possesses an outstanding talent for "making (Western-style) liquor."[3] He buys up a bunch of cheap liquors, blends different ones together, and creates a taste that is actually like imported liquor. Accordingly, it is only natural that Tanaka, who manages a particularly large restaurant in "Port W,"[4] displays a marked interest in him. The situation is depicted below.

> But liquor is expensive. And the hakurai stuff is hopelessly expensive. That's why people make arguments for using domestic, but this stuff tastes totally different.
> "Bring me the hakurai. The hakurai. . . . I don't care how much it costs. Enough with the cheap swill."
> There are some young men who yell this way when they're drunk.
> And there are some others who reprimand,
> "The liquor here is all wrong. It's 50 chŏn a shot for absinthe, but I can drink five doubles and still not feel a thing. There's no fun in drinking liquor like this."
> But Mr. Tanaka is unable even to conceive of using hakurai. Unable, in a word, means he cannot sever his attachment to that pleasing domestic liquor of which he can buy a bottle for just over 10 wŏn then sell it for nearly 200.[5]

But the reason Tanaka's customers drink this liquor, about which they really know nothing, is that it is what the "Western big-noses" drink. These customers, "the Romantics of the harbor," consider it a "shame for youth" "not to know popular songs, not to know how to waltz, not to know the taste of imported liquor, and not to know the taste of black tea."[6] Like Mun Ch'imyŏng in Yi Sangch'un's "*Kiro* (Crossroads, 1917)," they have been influenced by the "hairy teacher." The "hairy teacher" refers to the fact that "due to the energy of their sound mind and fighting spirit, those who invented such elusive contrivances as the telegraph and telephone are all Westerners."[7]

After Ongnyŏn drank "*burande*" (brandy) in Yi Injik's *Moran-bong* (*Peony peak*, 1913), and Sim Sunae drinks "*samp'anju*" (champagne) in Cho Ilchae's *Changhanmong* (*A long and sorrowful dream*, 1913), Western liquor and Western goods in general came to function also as symbols of modernity. Yŏm Sangsŏp's young neurotic on a train feels the modern sensations of the train and of hygiene together with inebriation from Western liquor. Yŏm described it as "the power of strong 'whiskey' coupled with severe agitated resistance, the rumbling creaking sound, the speed hurtling through the darkness, and the shoulder pain where he had been injected."[8] In a broad sense, this corresponds with certain Yi Sang`s descriptions such as "that sound of water like popping champagne"[9] or statements like "alcohol shines inside my body like perfume."[10]

In short, *hakurai*, more than anything else, promotes and leads the drinking of liquor. Colonial period liquor is produced not so much by distilleries as by the overall trade that produced the ideology of civilization and enlightenment and "*hakurai*." The sensation and intoxication of liquor that "warms you to the groin"[11] originates from the fierce movement and violent stimulus of a market that, following the fire from warships, wound up exporting whiskey or "*apsan*" (absinthe) to even the smaller ports of the colony. For example, in Kim Tongin's "*Maŭm i yŏt'ŭn chayŏ* (Oh, ye with faint hearts, 1919–1920)," we discover an American "Singer Company dealer" has established itself in a small village in the Diamond Mountains, but this is not so surprising. As early as February 22, 1886, in an advertisement by the company *Sech'ang yanghaeng* (Sech'ang Western goods) in the weekly paper *Hansŏng chubo*, we find Western sewing needles along with such items as Western belts, Western lamps, and Western silk. In addition, in the April 7, 1896, inaugural issue of the *Tongnip sinmun* (*Independence newspaper*), which championed "independence," advertisements such as the following appeared.

> The Anch'ang Company, Chŏng-dong, Seoul: We sell both Western and Chinese goods, with plenty of high quality Western liquor and all types of cigarettes in stock.[12]

> K. Kameya GENERAL STORE KEEPER CHONGDONG, SEOUL; Fresh California Butter, Cheese, Ham, Bacon, Canned Fruits, Vegetables &c.&c., Just arrived[13]

Particularly noteworthy in the quotations above is the phrase "plenty of high quality Western liquor and all types of cigarettes." This is because it is related to a statement that, in the olden days prior to the Japanese' establishing the "Monopoly Bureau" through the Government General, "Chemulpo Tobaco co., known in Korean as the 'British and American Tobacco Corporation,' supplied smokers with various brands such as 'Coral,' 'Drum,' and 'Knife.'"[14] It also helps us gain a clearer understanding of the line below from Yi Sang.

> That my—no! my wife's name card, no bigger than a Knife brand label cut into quarters, is stuck off to one side above the sliding door of my room must also be seen as following this custom.[15]

The "Knife brand" that appears in the quotation is a nickname for "Pirate," a brand of cigarette sold by the British and American Tobacco Corporation. This same Knife brand appears in many other works. In Yang Kŏnsik's "*Sŭlp'ŭn mosun* (A sad contradiction, 1918)" we read that "he got angry if he saw a rickshaw driver pull out the Knife brand"; in *Mujŏng* the old woman who runs the *kisaeng* house, when sending Yŏngch'ae off to P'yŏngyang, "generously buys her a second class ticket, something to eat for lunch, and even Knife brand cigarettes";[16] and in Chŏn Yŏngt'aek's "*K wa kŭ ŏmŏni ŭi chugŭm* (K and his mother's death, 1921)," "S leisurely twirled his silver tipped walking cane, and, while puffing his Knife brands, was staring into the glowing stove and thinking of something."[17] Therefore, the meaning of the quotation from Yi Sang is that his wife's calling card was small, only one-quarter the size of a pack of Knife brand cigarettes, or, in Yi Kiyŏng's words a "thimble-sized calling card."[18] As witnessed by his younger sister Kim Okhŭi, not only did the young Kim Haegyŏng (Yi Sang's birth name) draw a picture so amazingly identical to the actual design of Knife brand that his mother held on to it for many years but Yi himself also used it metaphorically. As such, the "Chemulpo Tobaco co." may also be the source of the descriptions below from Yi's essay "*Sanch'on yŏjŏng* (Lingering impressions of a mountain village, 1935)."

> I have a brief dream in which a young city girl appears; she looks like the "Paramount" Pictures logo.[19]
>
> I reminisce about the actual kisaeng in the city—their sort of beauty would not have been approved of by our forefathers—wrapped in "josette" skirts, svelte as "Westminster" cigarettes.[20]

Accordingly, modern literature was not concerned only about things such as civilization and enlightenment, the individual, love affairs, the nation-state, and revolution. Of course through its contents, and through things like the forms of texts' production and metaphors, modern literature also expressed the market order into which the colony was incorporated. Modern literature in and of itself was an excellent example of "*hakurai*."

BOILERMAKERS AND HYBRIDS

Along with the importation of such commodities as liquor, cigarettes, and butter, the systems, practices, behaviors, sensations, desires, languages, and discourses of consuming those things or their images were imported as well. For example, when Sŏnju is in a room complete with "expensive and delicious looking cookies," "fragrant Ch'ŏngjiyŏn (The 'Three Castles')" cigarettes, a 10-pack of which cost a full 40 *chŏn*," and "bottles of wine and brandy from the West," his invitation to Sunyŏng—"Miss Sunyŏng, tonight let us go together to a ball"[21]—is quite natural. In addition, scenes such as Kang Hanyŏng, the "high collar young man" of Ch'oe Ch'ansik's novel *Ch'uwŏlsaek* (*Autumn moon colors*, 1912), rushing at Chŏngim saying "the people of civilized countries often greet each other by shaking hands . . . and they also often do so by kissing,"[22] or Sŏngsun in Yi Kwangu's *Kaech'ŏkcha* thinking "If I meet M tomorrow I should speak a bit more affectionately. How nice would it be to shake his hand in the Western style. Or a kiss. . . . Oh, why am I having such thoughts?,"[23] are related to the point made above. Free love is difficult to distinguish from behavior such as buying "ham and bread because you said you were going to make a sandwich, and a tin of cocoa because *oppa* liked it."[24] What gave rise to Yi Sang's deathbed desire for and sensation of "French-style coupé breads"[25] and a "melon from Sembikiya"[26] were precisely that: French-style coupé breads and melons from Sembikiya. It is also the reason he wrote in the poem "*Muje* (Untitled)," "the size of my heart is no bigger than the length of a cigarette."[27] These newly appeared Western goods form an equivalent relationship with Sŏngsun's "such thoughts" as wanting to shake hands with or kiss the man she loves. No, it may even be that the Western goods themselves are the origin of the desire for love. Of course, this is related not only to free love. And this leads to a peculiar reading of the Yi Yuksa poem "*Ch'ŏng p'odo* (Blue grapes, 1939)."

July in my hometown
Is the season of the ripening, deep blue grapes.

Legends cluster thick about the village,
And each day the sky descends in a dream, pressing deep
into each fruit.

Beneath the blue sky the green sea unlocks its heart,
And a boat comes gliding, its white sail spread.

As I hear that my weary guest has come,
Tired body draped in a robe of deep blue,

In welcoming him, if I pluck these blue grapes,
What does it matter if my two hands are drenched?

There, child, on our low table's silver platter,
Set out the white linen cloths.[28]

When we consider that grapes are a fruit that really began being cultivated in Korea after French priests brought them in for use in Catholic Mass, the "legends . . . about the village," which are remembered along with the blue grapes, provide an interesting issue. Blue grapes may be a fruit that was not originally "in my hometown." And the "boat . . . its white sail spread" and the "table" with "silver platter" atop it are also more at home in a Western landscape. A small cabriole tray with earthenware pot atop it would be much more familiar in a Korean hometown.

Saying that, however, does not of course mean that this poem cannot be evaluated with respect to ethnonational consciousness. This is due to the fact that, just as Yi Kwangsu's expression "*kimch'i* is national spirit (*minjok chŏngsin*) among food"[29] elucidates the deeply rooted translation process at work in "*minjok chŏngsin*," modern national consciousness itself contains an aspect of imported Western goods. The modern age not only drives Chang Siyŏng, the protagonist of Yu Chino's novel *Hwasangbo (Mellifluous score,* 1938), to collect specimens and do research on the distribution of Korean herbaceous plants[30] but also makes society import foreign plants in earnest. As described in *Taeha*, enlightenment began together with things like the "matches in a box," lamps, and "Pine brand oil from New York, U.S.A." in the Nakanishi Store.[31]

Of course, these modern phenomena also display diverse and complicated aspects that cannot be contained one-sidedly. Occasionally, they even make directly opposing expressions. Below are scenes from two full-length novels: Yi Kwangsu's *Hŭlk* (1932–1933) and Yi Hyosŏk's *Pyŏkgong muhan* (*Endless Blue Sky,* 1939).

Okay, tell him to bring some cups and whiskey. Let's drink like men, and forget the great sorrow of an ill-timed hero. Isn't that right. The others are blabbering about stuff like international federations and reducing military preparations, but we'll just drink. Nothing else to do.[32]

Ŭnp'a put the boiled tea on the table and poured a bit of whiskey into each cup.

For Hun, this was a different kind of tea. The fragrance of the whiskey in the hot tea seemed to seep warmly into his entire body. This was the tastiest cup of tea he had ever had.[33]

The whiskeys in the two quotations seem to give rise to totally different feelings. But the two situations, which appear externally to be completely unrelated, are interconnected. Both suggest the position of the colony, which became nearly unilaterally the object of capital and of exchange. One laments the hero's fall, while the other enjoys the "flavor" of tea spiked with whiskey, but in the end the origin of both these types of sentimentalism is the market. This is intimately related with the position of the colonized as importers of whiskey. The importation of liquor reveals the position—whether resistant nationalism or exotic tastes—of the colony (and colonized) placed inside the world market. Simultaneous with the importation of liquor, social and national positions that import the liquor are also imported. "Arrayed atop the table / an exhibition / of national language and national language and national language and national language"[34] has literally opened. In that sense, whiskey might even be the origin of national consciousness.

Accordingly, attempts to forget things like national resentment by drinking whiskey are likely doomed to failure. Intoxication brings to mind the nation's oppression. At the same time, the consumption of whiskey further strengthens a world order of international federations and reducing military preparations in which the colonized cannot participate. In fact, what capital wants is for people self-deprecatingly to say "we'll just drink. Nothing else to do" while drinking whiskey "like men." Furthermore, the market within Korea, which carries out the violence of capital upon the colony, is even a bit more cunning and complicated. Far from adding to the flavor of tea, imported liquor in the colony could lead to a result very different from the opinion that "imported liquor is truly noble among alcohols" and "never gives you a headache."[35] This is because the colony's liquor is the fake "*hakurai*" that Myŏngu made by mixing this and that. It is precisely this mongrel "*hakurai*" that symbolizes what Hyŏn Chin'gŏn expressed in his short story "*Sul kwŏnhanŭn sahoe* (A society that drives you to drink, 1921)" as "society as a poisonous state."[36] The poem below is also related to this aspect of colonial society.

Boy! Boy!
I don't want *soju*!
Take away the "whiskey" too . . .
Something a bit stronger . . . stronger!
Bring me the "social"cohol.
Hurry up and bring me the "communi"liquor
I am a "citizen of the world"!
Hey you damn boy, Boy![37]

In all of these senses, colonial society is from the outset "a society that drives you to drink." Unrelated to the "ire" of the protagonist who torments his wife—no, by further amplifying his wrath—capital, which circulates having "hitched a ride on the swift horse of alcohol,"[38] stimulates consumption. The protagonist unable to restrain his anger is the finest citizen in a society that drives you to drink. The revolution too may very well be consuming a liquor called "communiliquor." For a revolution is a "feast for the glorious new age" with "a glass of wine red as flame"[39] raised high.

In this paradoxical situation, capital reveals an essence rivaling the menace of warships. Together with fake "*hakurai*," capital expands tremendously. As such, that Yŏhae, who is at once "a character seething with such passion" he could commit rape, and also "the equator line of life,"[40] takes a bomb in his mouth and commits suicide is symbolic. This is because Yŏhae's being wrongly imprisoned as a "member of XX," an overseas secret society, or dying as an "ex-convict" forms a pair with the following portrait of Pyŏngil, the colonial "young entrepreneur" who stews himself in boilermakers.

> Pyŏngil, who had kicked away the pillow, mat, and blanket to roll about and sleep on the bare floor, was awakened by the fresh air. Perhaps because at the main building of Myŏngwŏlgwan he had drunk beers with shots of whiskey in them, as soon as his eyes opened he felt a burning thirst.[41]

After the frustration of the modern project that asked "under the blistering rays of the Equator / who shall engage in naval battles?,"[42] the passion of the "Equator" came to manifest itself as the thirst of boilermakers. Thus, the "hybrid *hakurai*" boilermakers that set Pyŏngil rolling about symbolize colonial identity. Not only was modernity imported into the colony but it is also a mongrel. The mongrel expresses the predicative identity mediated by the total relationship between importation and trade. Accordingly, when viewed from the position that stresses the stable existence and singularity of the purebred, the "hybrid *hakurai*" is already exploded (deconstructed). This is the real meaning of fake liquor. The sea as mediated by the nationalism of Ch'oe

Namsŏn's 1908 poem "*Hae egesŏ sonyŏn ege* (From the sea to the boys)" gave birth to a daily life in which surged waves of Western liquor, Western goods, Western dresses, Western suits, Western lamps, Western candles, Western houses, Western food, Western socks, Western steel, Western medicine, Western measurements, Western pigs,[43] and Western dogs. In the hall of "an exhibition / of national language and national language and national language and national language," the colonized always drank boilermakers. Or, as expressed by Kim Namch'ŏn, "upstairs they ate Western food, but when they came downstairs it was *kkakdugi* (spicy pickled radish) with chopsticks."[44] This is the reason Yi Sang's narrator thought that on the restaurant's "menu there were only the names of a few dishes" but they "resembled the names of my childhood friends."[45] In this regard, the newspaper article below is significant.

> What comes of a relationship between a donkey and a horse is a mule. Some point to this and call it "*t'ŭk*" (also *t'ŭgi*, mongrel). This is not only true of animals but of people as well; in Japanese they call a child born of different ethnicities "*ainoko*." "*T'ŭk*," "*ainoko*." If we mix *takuan* with sweet sticky rice this is "*t'ŭk ŭmsik*" (mongrel food). . . . At a certain public bathhouse, a young man wearing a *yukata* is reading the *Tonga ilbo*. He is undeniably a member of our 20 million. But his clothing reflects the practices he learned after crossing the Korea Strait. Regardless of whether it is right or not, this is one of the "*t'ŭk*" now in fashion. "*T'ŭk*" has already been in fashion for some time now. At a minimum, from the time Korea began its enlightenment the "modern *t'ŭk*" appears to have been circulating.[46]

AJINOMOTO, THE CIVILIZED SEASONING

Now let us contemplate yet another issue in relation to the discussion above. It is the issue of chemistry, which early on had been evaluated as having "a utility so broad and large as to be nearly unfathomable," while there was "nothing better than it for researching the knowledge of the world."[47] In modern literary history this theme has produced such works as Yi Kwangsu's *Kaech'ŏkcha*, which depicts Sŏngjae's experiments and failures, and Kim Tongin's "*K paksa ŭi yŏn'gu* (Doctor K's research, 1929)," which describes the development of "the newest, best food made solely from well-digested products such as cheese, starch, and fat, all extracted from feces."[48] This implies the scientific worldview upon which modern literature was predicated. Returning to liquor, it brings to mind the issue of Western science. This applies equally to commodities such as cosmetics and pharmaceuticals. It is true of liquor, and much more so of cosmetics and pharmaceuticals, that these things represent an indicator in customs that simultaneously expresses and institutionalizes both science and the market. In this regard, such things are extremely modern. The reason Sŏngjae's and Doctor K's researches could not succeed was that their experiments and inventions were unable to attain a modern everydayness predicated on the intervention of capital.

This everydayness functions as a general system that manifests science and the market in life. As one example, Mun Ch'imyŏng, who studied "methods for making dyes" in applied chemistry, predicts that "since dyes have become extremely expensive due to the World War I, if we take this opportunity to set up a factory and produce dyes, we stand to make large profits."[49] This general system that commodities produce and circulate in earnest will allow for the various conditions of modernity to communicate. Advertisements are its explicit and regular channel. The following are advertisements for "Lion Tooth Powder" and "Ajinomoto" that appeared in the February 25 and 26, 1920, editions of the daily *Maeil sinbo*.

> Lion Tooth Powder, large size, is the most efficacious and profitable tooth powder for your esteemed family.
> Lion Tooth Powder, as a tooth powder possessing the standard conditions of hygienic effects, is a world-class product with an honorable recent history of having been granted a certificate by a hygienic testing center in London.[50]

"The Shortcut to Delicious Cooking" "The Civilized Seasoning, Ajinomoto"

What deserves our attention here are the expression "world-class product" that has been granted a certificate by a hygienic testing center in London, and the phrase "civilized seasoning." Tooth powders and seasonings are not mere inanimate objects. Tooth powders and seasonings express cutting-edge science. In addition, in that they circulate various elements aside from themselves such as hygiene, testing, certification, and "the world," they are in all respects commodities. As such, that a certain youth whom Kubo observed could "have taken an immature pride in something so trifling as the fact that he was carrying a single container of *Jintan*[51] (Kor. *Indan*) and some Rohto eye drops"[52] is completely understandable. This is because the cosmetic known as "Rohto Medicinal Cream" was advertised in the May 1940 edition of the journal *Yŏsŏng* (*Women*) as a "highest level medicinal cream invented with the awesome power of the 20th century's newest science" that had "applied the purity of medicinal science, pharmacology, and chemistry" to make "the number one cosmetic in the world."

And what integrates all of these aspects is the modifier for *Ajinomoto*: "civilized." Adding to this is the fact that Ikeda Kikunae (1864–1936), who in 1908 invented *Ajinomoto*, a "seasoning with monosodium glutamate as its main ingredient," was a chemist who had studied in Germany.[53] "Ajinomoto" has its origins in the *bunmei kaika* (civilization and enlightenment) ideology of Meiji Japan. As such, the taste of the food created by this seasoning must be of a completely different sensation than the taste longed for in the following poem.

> Ah, what welcome thing is this
> What whitish, tender, pleasantly plain, mild thing is this
> On a winter's night, I like the ice-cracking sour brine of pickled radish, I like burning crushed red pepper, and I like the meat of fresh wild pheasant
> And liking the *arŭgut*[54] boiling hot in a reed mat room thick and dense with the smell of tobacco, the smell of vinegar, and the smell of boiling beef broth, what is this
>
> What is this caring and closeness to this quiet village and its dignified residents
> What infinitely elegant yet rustic thing is this[55]

The "whitish, tender, pleasantly plain, mild" taste in the poem above cannot of course be separated from the various "smells," but neither can it be from the "*arŭgut* boiling hot" and the "quiet village." It is the memory of play, legend, ritual, and community. This is a complete world expressed in verse as "White rice and sole and I / It seems that we could talk about anything."[56] Compared to this, the taste that "civilized seasoning" provides is an analytical flavor mediated by science and society. Unlike Paek Sŏk's taste, which, as seen in the line "what welcome thing is this," can only be expressed, what "civilized seasoning" creates is a rational taste that can be measured, explained, predicted, exchanged, and sold. Like the "taste of fragrant MJB" that Yi Sang lauds in "*Sanch'on yŏjŏng*," this is a flavor that can be represented by a brand. Or, rather, this is a form of alienation.

In this way, commodities and brands integrate modern processes and rational causality such as modern learning through study in the West and the application of that learning, the production and selling of commodities, and the system of disciplining national citizens. Therefore, the following scene from Yi Kwangsu's novel *Kaech'ŏkcha*, in which "Lion Tooth Powder" is specifically mentioned, corresponds to his essay "*Minjok kaejoron*," in which he consistently emphasized such things as education, hygiene, and a well-regulated life. Enlightenment, by making exchange and brand part of daily life, constructed the modern system.

> Due to excessive worry and inadequate sleep, Sŏngsun was dizzy and his head ached. For a moment he languidly propped himself against the wall, then folded

his blankets before taking Lion Tooth Powder, a cup with a toothbrush in it, and a towel and exiting the room.[57]

What must also be considered here is the fact that the production process of "Lion Tooth Powder" stands in contrast to the experiments of Sŏngjae. That these ingenuous experiments are also contrasted with Myŏngu's "talent" for making fake "*hakurai*" demands attention as well. Although as a modern person he was thoroughly punctual and lived according to a plan, Sŏngjae, who spent his time locked up in a laboratory, fell because he lacked "talent." Excluded from capital, Sŏngjae, in failing to pay off his debts within the allotted period, which is the core time constraint of the modern age, had his house seized and lost his family.

When compared, however, with "Lion Tooth Powder" or "Ajinomoto," Sŏngjae's experiments and Myŏngu's "talent" have something in common. From the perspective that just as Sŏngjae lacked money Myŏngu could not employ science, both of them failed to create an original brand that combined science and capital. As a result, Sŏngjae's fall into debtor status and Myŏngu's being selected by Tanaka to make fake liquor are no different. Both Sŏngjae, who knows nothing of the "firm handshake between factory and store,"[58] and Myŏngu himself, by making fake "*hakurai*," are merely imitating modern civilization. As a result, in a beef soup restaurant like a "large-scale garbage can," "it makes no difference at all if the damn scum beneath fingernails and sleep from eyes were just now used in place of Ajinomoto."[59]

Of course, this imitation does not apply only to production. In fact, the essence of consumption carried out by the colonized is also a kind of imitation. For example, what an advertisement in the November 1939 issue of *Yŏsŏng* for the "Aihon Beautiful Eye Device," which makes a double eyelid through a "physical orthopedic effect," emphasizes is the fact that it is a "world-class great invention" "regularly used by all the high-society women and movie stars in the *naichi*."[60] Modern consumption begins from the imitation of civilized people.

Imitation, however, guarantees neither a genuine understanding of modernity nor a sharing in its material and spiritual benefits. On the contrary, it may even promote misunderstanding, which would lead to the frequent occurrence of scenes like the following.

Ongnyŏn and her mother were showing signs of physical discomfort at the tedious time, so Sŏ Sukcha brought in a gramophone and turned it on. Since Kim Kwanil and his wife were hearing a gramophone for the first time, they weren't sure if this was human magic or a ghost in a machine, but, saying "It's strange. It's mysterious. It's fun.", time passed without their knowing as they listened.[61]

The principle behind the gramophone is incomprehensible to the colonized. It is thought of as the mischief of ghosts. In addition, as narrated in a work by Kim Tongin, the gramophone is also mistaken for "the study of music."[62] This unfamiliar and amazing contraption leads to the mystification of modern civilization. The colony is completed together with this ghost-resurrecting misunderstanding. This also gives birth to the colonial custom that causes the department store employee Myŏngja, called "a single, silent flower that bloomed inside the glass display cases of the department," to take a whole 5 *wŏn* from her paltry monthly paycheck and "use it at any cost to dress herself up."[63] This in turn brings about the "somehow anxious psychology of Korean women" that "requires them, even though they come out of a dilapidated, tiny thatch-roofed house, once they are on the street, to sport the clothing worn by the women coming and going in Paris, France or Manhattan, New York."[64] As pointed out by Kim Kirim, "as the modern technology of highly developed production became merely a legend or anecdote," modernity in the colony "was, like a 'show window,' displayed fragmentarily in the area of consumer life."[65] As a result, this suggests the social meaning of "Coty made in Paris building a White House on their (Korean women's) flat noses."[66] In short, the custom of "the Oriental autumn" met by "Coty perfume that had set sail from Marseilles in spring"[67] expressed the blindness that was colonial misunderstanding and imitation.

T'ŬRADE MALK'Ŭ AND ADALIN

When viewed in light of these sorts of colonial customs, the following lines from Yang Chudong's *Munju pansaenggi* (*Record of half a life spent on literature and liquor*, 1959) take on a symbolic meaning.

> The very first time I saw Western writing was a bit before that. I believe it was printed on something like a box of matches, but I definitely remember it was the letters "TRADE MARK." I really wanted to know what on earth these strange horizontal letters were and what they meant. I visited the admirer of Chu Hsi's theory and enlightenment intellectual Mr. C and asked him, to which he replied that they were English letters, taught me that they were pronounced "*t'ŭrade malk'ŭ*," but informed me the meaning was unknown.[68]

The above quotation, more than anything else, is interesting for its account of the simultaneous experience of brands and Western letters. Foreign languages too were exchange and trade. But the unfamiliar foreign word "TRADE MARK" was untranslatable and undecipherable even to the enlightenment intellectual "Mr. C." This is because it was a language of the market, which he had yet to learn, or, to use a Kim Kirim expression, it was because it was jargon of the "business establishments wearing the battle helmets of Caesar."[69] Kim followed up with the lines below.

Before long, the sound of a whistle . . .
Bicycles dash. Athletes dash. But, later on, only trademarks dash.

Atop the venue of the moving commercial exhibition
Boggled minds stand in a row. Hesitate. Decide.
"This company seems to be a bit more accelerative"
"No, that firm is out in front"
"Next time I'll have to buy my cotton cloth from that store"[70]

In the modern world, where, in place of humans, only "trademarks" dash about, a "hybrid *hakurai*" knowledge of foreign languages that can go no further than a parsing of English letters gives rise to lack of understanding and delusion that rival the misunderstanding of the gramophone. In a way different from Sŏngsun's mistakenly naming her spotted cat "Puppy" in *Kaech'ŏkcha*, "TRADE MARK" is read "*t'ŭrade malk'ŭ*." Despite the fact that some "went into a watch store and bought a platinum-plated 'Longines,' and went into a hat shop and bought a 'Borsalino,'"[71] and also despite the fact that others finally chose, "after hesitating a while, the knickerbockers, a new style of clothes recommended by the employee,"[72] in the end the colonized always consumed a "*t'ŭrade malk'ŭ*" whose "meaning was unknown." This "*t'ŭrade malk'ŭ*" phenomenon expresses the essence of colonial modernity.

This is the reason that as the protagonist of "*Nalgae*" takes Adalin he also actualizes the "irony of gorging oneself on the food one hates most."[73] In so doing, he pointed out that in colonial society aspirin and Adalin, like fake "*hakurai*," are continually confused. He showed that in the "boggled minds" of the colonized, which could not keep up with the "acceleration" of trademarks, aspirin and Adalin were popular as "*t'ŭrade malk'ŭ*," the true meaning(s) and principle(s) of which were difficult to grasp and differentiate.

This powerfully metaphorically expresses market consumption, which manifests not use value but exchange value. People mistakenly believe they are taking aspirin (use value) to treat their colds. But in reality they are forever taking Adalin (exchange value) and merely becoming stupefied. Through consumption, people are not fulfilling their needs but rather vitalizing the market. They are consumers. This corresponds to the delusion of the protagonist concerning aspirin: "I shall keep taking them to bolster my health."[74] This is because, just as aspirin is not a tonic, modern society, which emphasizes hygiene, operates less like a tonic and more like a poison (pharmacon) that kills and eliminates germs.

In light of the above, giving the protagonist Adalin in place of aspirin is not an individual and random incident plotted by Kŭmhong. Rather it symbolizes the essence of the neon sign-flashing social order. Kŭmhong was merely a single chance that presented the society's essence. Realizing this, the protagonist takes the ludicrous-tasting Adalin of his own accord. Just as he slept in his own wife's room for the first time after giving her five *wŏn*, he voluntarily entrusted his body not to his house but to the streets. The streets were another name for the market, while his location was no more than a single point within the market. His environment was neither "the streets outside the house" nor "the house outside the streets" but "the streets outside the streets."[75]

The meaning of his house, Number 33 that resembles a brothel, of course, and of the rooftop of the Mitsukoshi Department Store that the protagonist wanders on to are also related to this. This is because the department store, which drove the colonized to "in place of the blue ocean / in order to look at crumpled clouds / on the 'elevator' / go up to the fifth floor,"[76] is above all else the temple of exchange value. It synthesizes the "relationships" and principles of the "streets," which never fail to "seep through the walls" "regardless of whether I close up all the doors to my room, and lay in there for a full 12 months of the year without shaving."[77] It continually asks "What is your worth in currency?" No one can be free from this question, as evidenced below.

> As the chastity badge affixed to the collar of my traditional overcoat came into view, she says I can go in. The woman who said I could go in then says since I have a certain distinct chastity how about it. It means she is asking me what is your worth in currency.[78]

Amid this sort of street bargaining, the act of taking Adalin became the ironical actualization of the colonized who expressed through their bodies the essence of a society dyed in the operations of exchange value and exclusion. Moving beyond misunderstanding and imitation, for the first time he began to employ paradox and humor toward both himself and society.

Thus, Adalin was the latest "*t'ŭrade malk'ŭ*" this colonial "genius" lumpen gloomily produced. Through Yi Sang's Adalin, "*t'ŭrade malk'ŭ*" became a humorous trademark genuinely invented by "hybrid *hakurai*."

NOTES

1. This chapter is the first half of the chapter "Yobo, Mobo, Kubo" in the Yŏnse kukhak yŏn'guwŏn (Yonsei University Institute for Korean Studies) monograph *Ilche*

ŭi singmin chibae wa ilsang saenghwal (*Japanese colonial rule and daily life*) (Seoul: Hyean, 2004).

2. *Hakurai* (舶来) literally means "to arrive by boat." As Japan is composed of islands, this is synonymous with "import(ed)." As such, it is also synonymous with the Sino-Korean *suip* (輸入). In order to represent their distinct usage both in this book and in the quotations from literary works, *suip* will be translated as "import(ed)," while *hakurai* will simply be transliterated.—Trans.

3. Although translated here simply as "liquor," the term in the original text is *yangju* (洋酒), which is already marked as "Western" by the Chinese characters. As such, the discussion here is all about Western-style liquor, but the crux is whether it is produced domestically or imported from the West. Unless otherwise noted, in this text "liquor" will denote *yangju*.—Trans.

4. This is not an atypical way to refer to the city of Wŏnsan, a then bustling port on the east coast of what is now North Korea. Even in fictional works otherwise completely rendered in (Sino-)Korean, the names of cities, schools, and people were often represented by the upper case letter from the Roman alphabet that most closely corresponded with their initial letter in Korean.

5. Han Sŏrya, "*T'aeyang ŭn pyŏng tŭlda* (The sun grows ill)," in *Han Sŏrya tanp'yŏn sŏnjip* 2 *Kwihyang*, ed. Kim Oegŏn (Seoul: T'aehaksa, 1989), 235.

6. Ibid., 34.

7. Yi Sangch'un, "*Kiro* (Crossroads)," in *Ch'ŏngch'un*, Volume 11, November 1917, 41.

8. Yŏm Sangsŏp, "*P'yobonsil ŭi ch'ŏnggaeguri* (Green frog of the specimen room)," in *Yŏm Sangsŏp chŏnjip* 9 (Seoul: Minŭmsa, 1987), 14.

9. Yi Sang, "*Ch'ŏtpŏntchae pangnang* (The first wandering)," in *Yi Sang munhak chŏnjip* 3, ed. Kim Yunsik (Seoul: Munhak sasangsa, 1993), 169.

10. Song Minho and Yun Taeyŏng, *Chŏlmang ŭn kigyo rŭl natko* (*Despair gave rise to virtuosity*) (Seoul: Kyohaksa, 1968), 27.

11. Han Sŏrya, "T'aeyang ŭn pyŏng tŭlda," 234.

12. The original advertisement is in Korean.

13. This is the original advertisement. It appeared in English.

14. Ko Il, *Inch'ŏn kŭmgo* (*Incheon present and past*) (Kyŏnggi munyesa, 1955), 5.

15. Yi Sang, "*Nalgae* (Wings)," in *Yi Sang munhak chŏnjip* 2, ed. Kim Yunsik (Seoul: Munhak sasangsa, 1991), 320.

16. Yi Kwangsu, *Mujŏng* (*The heartless*), in *Yi Kwangsu chŏnjip* 1 (Seoul: Samjungdang, 1962), 129.

17. Chŏn Yŏngt'aek, "*K wa kŭ ŏmŏni ŭi chugŭm* (K and his mother's death)," in *Ch'angjo* Volume 9, May 1921, 17.

18. Yi Kiyŏng, *In'gan suŏp* (*Human lessons*) (Seoul: Munu ch'ulp'ansa, 1948), 101.

19. Yi Sang, tr. John M. Frankl, "*Sanch'on yŏjŏng* (Lingering Impressions of a Mountain Village)," in *Azaleas: Journal of Korean Literature and Culture*, Volume 2, Harvard University, 2008, 334.

20. Ibid, 336.

21. Yi Kwangsu, *Chaesaeng* (*Rebirth*), in Yi Kwangsu chŏnjip 2 (Seoul: Samjungdang, 1962), 259.

22. Ch'oe Ch'ansik, "*Ch'uwŏlsaek* (Autumn moon colors)," in *Han'guk sinsosŏl chŏnjip* 4 (Seoul: Ŭlyu munhwasa, 1968), 15.

23. Yi Kwangsu, *Kaech'ŏkcha* (*The pioneer*), in *Yi Kwangsu chŏnjip* 1 (Seoul: Samjungdang, 1962), 382.

24. Yi Kwangsu, "*Kŭ yŏja ŭi ilsaeng* (That woman's life)," in *Yi Kwangsu chŏnjip* 7 (Seoul: Samjungdang, 1962), 88.

25. Kim Soun, *Hanŭl kkŭt e sarado* (*Even living at the edge of the sky*) (Tonghwa ch'ulp'an kongsa, 1968), 299.

26. Kim Hyangan, "*Ije Yi Sang ŭi chinsil ŭl alligo sipta* (Now I want to tell the truth about Yi Sang)," in *Munhak sasang*, May 1986, 62.

Kim Hyangan is the name taken by Yi Sang's wife, Pyŏn Tongnim, when she remarried.

Sembikiya is, by its own description, a "venerable fruit shop" operating in Nihonbashi, Tokyo, since 1834. It modeled itself after fruit shops in Europe and sold imported as well as domestic fruits.

27. Yi Sang, "*Muje* (Untitled)," in *Yi Sang munhak chŏnjip* 1, ed. Yi Sŭnghun (Seoul: Munhak sasangsa, 1989), 211.

28. Yi Yuksa, "*Ch'ŏng p'odo* (Blue grapes)," trans. David R. McCann, in *The Columbia Anthology of Modern Korean Poetry* (New York: Columbia University, 2004), 40.

29. Yi Kwangsu, *Hŭlk* (*The Soil*), in *Yi Kwangsu chŏnjip* 6 (Samjungdang, 1962), 27.

Although not completely clear in English translation, the crux of the statement by Yi is that he used a Korean transliteration of the English words national spirit, "*nasyŏnal sŭp'irit'ŭ*," to make his point. The actual Korean translation, *minjok chŏngsin*, was put in only parenthetically. He employed a similar tactic in his essay "*Munhak iran hao*? (What is literature?)," in which he began with a Korean transliteration of the word literature, only after which did he introduce the then neologistic Sino-Korean term "*munhak*."

30. Yu Chino, *Hwasangbo* (*Mellifluous score*), in *Sinmun yŏnjae sosŏl chŏnjip* 3, 2nd ed. (Seoul: Kip'ŭnsaem, 1999), 272.

31. Kim Namch'ŏn, *Taeha* (*The great river*) (Seoul: Inmunsa, 1939), 272.

32. Yi Kwangsu, *Hŭlk*, 225.

33. Yi Hyosŏk, *Pyŏkkong muhan* (*Endless blue sky*) (Seoul: Ch'unjosa, 1959), 399–400.

The translation is from Steven D. Capener, "*Yi Hyosŏk ŭi changp'yŏn sosŏl* Pyŏkkong muhan *ŭi yŏngyŏk kwa chakp'um yŏn'gu*" (An English translation and study of Yi Hyosŏk's *Endless blue sky*, PhD diss. (Yonsei University, 2007), 251.

34. Kim Kirim, "*Ssinema p'unggyŏng hot'el* (Cinema view hotel)," in *Kim Kirim chŏnjip* 1 (Seoul: Simsŏldang, 1988), 83.

35. Han Sŏrya, "*Yujŏn* (Vicissitudes)," in *Han Sŏrya tanp'yŏn sŏnjip* 3 sukmyŏng, ed. Kim Oegŏn (Seoul: T'aehaksa, 1989), 129.

36. Hyŏn Chin'gŏn, *"Sul kwŏnhanŭn sahoe* (A society that drives you to drink)," in *Hyŏn Chin'gŏn chŏnjip* 4 (Seoul: Munhak kwa pip'yŏngsa, 1988), 66.

37. Kim Hyŏngwŏn, *"Chujŏnggun* (A bad drunk)," in *Kaebyŏk*, March 1922, 17.

38. Hyŏn Chin'gŏn, *Chŏkdo* (*Equator*), in *Hyŏn Chin'gŏn chŏnjip* 1 *chŏkdo* (Seoul: Munhak kwa pip'yŏngsa, 1988), 74.

39. Im Hwa, *"Han chan p'odoju rŭl* (A glass of wine)," in *Ch'an'ga* (Seoul: Paegyangdang, 1947), 131.

40. Hyŏn Chin'gŏn, *Chŏkdo*, 288.

41. Ibid., 54.

42. Ch'oe Namsŏn, *"Uri ŭi undongjang* (Our playing field)," in *Sonyŏn*, December 1908, 33.

43. The original is *yangdoeji*, literally "Western pig." But it also has the figurative meaning of a fat, greedy person.—Trans.

44. Kim Namch'ŏn, *"Maek* (Barley)," in *Maek* (Seoul: Ŭryumunhwasa, 1947), 228.

45. Yi Sang *"Nalgae* (Wings)," trans. Walter K. Lew and Youngju Ryu, in *Modern Korean Fiction: An Anthology*, eds. Bruce Fulton and Youngmin Kwon (New York: Columbia University Press, 2005), 79.

46. Tonga ilbo, August 8, 1926, quoted from Kim Yŏnggŭn, Ilche ha ilsang saenghwal ŭi pyŏnhwa wa kŭ sŏnggyŏk e kwanhan yŏn'gu (A study on the changes in daily life under Japanese colonial occupation and its character), PhD diss. (Yonsei University, 1999), 175–76.

47. Yu Kilchun, *Sŏyu kyŏnmun* (*Things seen and heard in the West*), trans. Hŏ Kyŏngjin (Seoul: Hanyang ch'ulp'an, 1995), 306.

48. Kim Tongin, *"K paksa ŭi yŏn'gu* (Doctor K's research)," in *Kim Tongin chŏnjip* 2 (Seoul: Chosŏn ilbosa, 1988), 74.

49. Yi Sangch'un, *"Kiro,"* 53.

50. http://www.ndl.go.jp/scenery/e/data/78/l.html

51. http://en.wikipedia.org/wiki/Jintan_(Japanese_medicine)

52. Pak T'aewŏn, *"Sosŏlga Kubo-ssi ŭi iril* (A day in the life of the novelist Kubo)," in *Sosŏlga Kubo-ssi ŭi iril* (Seoul: Munjangsa, 1938), 267.
      http://en.wikipedia.org/wiki/Rohto_Pharmaceutical_Co

53. Komori Yōichi, *Sōseki o yominosu* (*Rereading Natsume Sōseki*) (Tokyo: Chikuma shōbō, 1995), 71–72.

54. This is another word for *araenmok*, the warmest portion of an *ondol* floor.—Trans.

55. Paek Sŏk, *"Kuksu* (Noodles)," in *Paek Sŏk chŏnjip*, ed. Kim Chaeyong (Seoul: Silch'ŏn munhaksa, 1997), 126.

56. Paek Sŏk, *"Sŏnusa* (Poem of good friends)," in ibid., 71.

57. Yi Kwangsu, *Kaech'ŏkcha*, 405.

58. Kim Kirim, *"Sanggong undonghoe* (The sports meet of commerce and industry)," in *Kim Kirim chŏnjip* 1 (Seoul: Simsŏldang, 1988), 123.

59. Ch'ae Mansik, *"Kŭm ŭi chŏngyŏl* (The passion of gold)," in *Ch'ae Mansik chŏnjip* 3 (Seoul: Ch'angjak kwa pip'yŏngsa, 1987), 213.

60. *Yŏsŏng* (*Women*), November 1939.
      The *naichi* refers to Japan proper, as opposed to the colonies, or *gaichi*.—Trans.

61. Yi Injik, "*Moranbong* (Peony peak, 1913)," in *Han'guk sinsosŏl chŏnjip* 1 (Seoul: Ŭryu munhwasa, 1968), 95.

62. Kim Tongin, "*Ŭmak kongbu* (The study of music)," in *Ch'angjo*, January 1921, 76.

63. Yi Sŏnhŭi, "*Yŏin myŏngnyŏng* (The female command)," in *Sinmun yŏnjae sosŏl chŏnjip* 4 (Seoul: Kip'ŭnsaem, 1999), 342.

64. An Sŏgyŏng, "*Modŏn kkŏl* (Modern girl)," in *Chogwang*, May 1937, 234.

65. Kim Kirim, "*Chosŏn munhak e ŭi pansŏng* (Reflections on Korean literature)," in *Inmun p'yŏngnon*, October 1940, 43.

66. An Sŏgyŏng, "*Ch'ŏn'gukhaeng chiokhaeng ŭi pamyŏlch'a rŭl t'agosŏ* (Riding a night train to heaven and hell)," in *Chosŏn ilbo*, July 1, 1934, 3.

67. Yi Sang, "*au magasin de nouveautes* (at the department store of novelties)," in *Yi Sang munhak chŏnjip* 1, ed. Yi Sŭnghun, 167.

68. Yang Chudong, *Munju pansaenggi* (*Record of half a life spent on literature and liquor*), reprint (Seoul: Sint'aeyangsa ch'ulp'an'guk, 1962), 26.

69. Kim Kirim, "*Sanggong undonghoe*," 122.

70. Ibid., 123.

71. Kim Namch'ŏn, "*T ilbosa* (The T daily news)," in *Inmun p'yŏngnon*, November 1939, 148.

72. Pak T'aewŏn, *Ch'ŏnbyŏn p'unggyŏng* (*Streamside scenes*) (Seoul: Pangmun ch'ulp'ansa, 1947), 158.

73. Yi Sang, "*Nalgae*," 318.

74. Ibid, 338.

75. Although not completely clear in translation, in the original there are three homophones, each pronounced "*kaoega*" and composed using different combinations of the same three (or two) Chinese characters: 家外街; 街外家; and街外街, respectively.—Trans.

76. Kim Kirim, "*Pada ŭi hyangsu* (Longing for the ocean)," in *Kim Kirim chŏnjip* 1, 343.

77. Yi Sang, "*Chiju hoesi* (Two spiders meet a pig)," in *Yi Sang munhak chŏnjip* 2, ed. Kim Yunsik, 312.

78. Yi Sang, "*Paekchu* (Broad daylight)," in *Yi Sang munhak chŏnjip* 1, ed. Yi Sŭnghun, 82.

Chapter 4

The Fashion of *Mujŏng*

The aim of this chapter lies in attaining a more vivid and concrete understanding of *Mujŏng* through a contemplation of the modern customs appearing therein. To this end, it will first present the important aspects of the customs described in *Mujŏng*, then through them will construct, in relation to other literary works, those portions of the work's meaning and structure that have gone heretofore little noticed and relatively unanalyzed. This should also suggest one model for textual analysis.

All of these operations, however, presuppose the viewpoint that "the essence of social organizations is completely incarnated only after it reaches the status of custom."[1] It is the position of this chapter that, in terms of their literary meanings, the customs described in a work are not ancillary and coincidental, but rather central and essential. Its point of departure is a recognition of the negotiations between science and literature, in which "theoretical morals," the "rational core of the theories held by science," appear "through the psyche, through ethics, and through personality as customs."[2]

The word "fashion" as used in this chapter's title corresponds to this point of view. It does not mean merely modern costume. Rather it metaphorically expresses the various devices and phenomena that sensitize, embody, and symbolize the essence of social organizations. For example, "*ŏnmun ilch'i* (Jp., *genbun itchi*)," or the correspondence between spoken and written language, too is a fashion. It is not the transparent recording of existing spoken language. On the contrary, it was the oral expression of the (written language) of the national and/or *minjok* (Jp., *minzoku*, ethnonational) languages that were created together with the modern nation-state.[3] It is a fashion that imagines the *minjok*, and, as a result, modern literature, which proactively intervened in this imaginary behavior, is also highly fashionable. And *Mujŏng* led the way for this modern fashion. The one consistent core of *Mujŏng* is Hyŏngsik's obsession with "high collar" women who attend school, that is to say the fashion called "free love."

That being the case, it may also very well be that the viewpoint of this chapter, which pays attention to this phenomenon, must also be fashionable. It is precisely the extremely superficial-seeming microscopic phenomena themselves causing the core of social structures and ideologies to open itself up for inspection that corresponds to the fashion of *Mujŏng* and constitutes the design of this chapter. Accordingly, above all else, just as one chooses which clothes to wear, this chapter will arrange various selected materials in order to place them in the position where they produce important meanings within the whole. Certain limitations notwithstanding, the reason for this approach is the belief that the act itself of doing this represents one method of physically arriving at the meaning of *Mujŏng*.

PRIVATE TUTORS AND GLASS DOORS

Mujŏng begins with the following well-known and monumental scene. And through it, in a single sentence, Yi Kwangsu comments upon such things as the modern education system, time discipline, and Christianity.

> Yi Hyŏngsik, an English teacher at the Kyŏngsŏng School, having finished his two o'clock elementary English class, sweat beneath the June sunshine as he made his way toward Elder Kim's house in An-dong.[4]

Yi Hyŏngsik clearly exists in modern time and space. Ongnyŏn, the female protagonist of *Hyŏl ui nu*, first appears within the Sino-Japanese War (1894–1895), an actual historical event, then goes on to study abroad and thereby actualize a world map that connects Korea, Japan, and America. Quite different from this, the behavior of Yi Hyŏngsik, who has just "finished his two o'clock elementary English class" and is on his way to Elder Kim's house for a three o'clock private tutor class, is based upon a modernly segmented and compartmentalized time plan. The primary existential coordinate of Hyŏngsik, who, despite his sweating beneath "the June sunshine," pushes through the heat and continues walking, is undoubtedly a single point between two and three in the afternoon. When compared to modern time, the heat, which represents the power of the seasons, is relegated to the position of something accidental and therefore unable to participate meaningfully in Hyŏngsik's social actions. In order to find Yŏngch'ae, he sends a telegram to the P'yŏngyang Police Station. And in Installment 55[5] he reassures "the old woman who still had yet to utilize the power of the telegram or the power of the police station" (삼중당 전집 144). On the other hand, spring always comes "without sending so much as a telegram."[6]

Thus, it is not only the heat of the summer Yi Hyŏngsik is feeling. His face reddening and "flames rising up" in his breast are actually more related to his thoughts below.

That was that, but what about the teaching method. He had been thinking about it from the time he received Elder Kim's request yesterday until now, but no particularly excellent method came to mind. Shall I put a desk between us and teach as we sit facing each other? But then our breath would commingle. Her *hisashi-gami*[7] might even brush against my forehead. Beneath the desk, knee and knee would also lightly touch. With such thoughts, Hyŏngsik's face reddened as he smiled to himself.[8]

The "flames" in his breast, unlike the heat of the "June sunshine," carry an important modern literary meaning. It is related to the collapse of the premodern spatial partition expressed by the Confucian dictum that "boys and girls shall not sit together after they have reached the age of seven." It also corresponds with the meaning of the train in *Hyŏl ŭi nu*, which allowed Ku Wansŏ and Ongnyŏn to meet coincidentally and thereby launch a new narrative. Ch'oe Namsŏn's "Song of the Seoul-Busan Railway" contains the following lyrics:

Old people and young people, sat mixed together
Our people and foreigners, rode together, but
since men and women, friend and stranger, all together, got along well
a tiny new world, the railroad did achieve.[9]

As can be seen in the lyrics, new means of transportation such as the streetcar and the train provided a "new world" in which existed a space where "men and women, friend and stranger" were "all together." This is the origin of the scene below.

The men's gazes occasionally made their way over to Elizabeth. That they looked at her from the corners of their eyes in order to go undetected, Elizabeth was well aware of this, too. Every time the men looked at her, Elizabeth wanted to return a look in their direction. To the last, however, she failed to do so.

While all of this was happening, the streetcar stopped in front of S hospital. Elizabeth, harboring thoughts of regret, got off the streetcar.[10]

Of course, in the case of private tutor Yi Hyŏngsik, it was not only that their breath would commingle and that the hairs of her "*hisashi-gami*" would brush against him but also that he would find himself in a more private space where he envisioned even the possibility of knees touching one another. Boys and girls were literally sitting together in the same room. This reveals the true meaning of Hyŏngsik's musings after he received the private tutor offer. His worries, which are at first glance not only ridiculous but also have nothing at all to do with "teaching method," are actually immensely significant. These worries regarding "teaching method" are of course related to modern knowledge as represented by English, as well as to the possibility of contact with the legs of the women seated across from him, which also finally originates from modernity. Not only studying English but also the very act itself of men and women sitting across from each other in the same room appear to be civilization and enlightenment. Kim Tongin described this modern scene as follows.

> While we spoke, a war of the knees broke out several times. I softly placed my knee against hers. A *je ne sais quoi* tingle! From my knee to her lightly quivering knee, then back from her to me. A bit later, she furtively removed her knee. When I didn't put mine on hers for a while, her knee quietly came to mine. While our mouths were engaged in totally unrelated speech, we two people's knees played out this advance and retreat. Well, this is a satirical scene that wouldn't have happened if it weren't the twentieth century.[11]

Thus, the "flame" in Hyŏngsik's breast as he anticipates a scene like the one above will come to be decisively divided from the heat of the "June sunshine." It is a modern fever distinct both from the nature that pours down "June sunshine" and from the premodern dictum regarding the separation of boys and girls. It appears to be sensitizing and physicalizing the passion of the ideologies of study abroad (civilization and enlightenment) and free love. This fever, which is related to the partitioning of modern space, is clearly expressed in the following passage.

> "He asks that you please come in," said a maidservant, at which, his heart pounding anew, he passed through the inner gate and up to the main hall. In the past there was no way an outside visitor could venture beyond the inner gate; this alone represented a large change from the old customs. The main hall was done in a semi-Western style with glass doors, a table with patterned cloth cover and four or five chairs upholstered in red felt in the middle, and, covering the northern wall, bookshelves piled with works new and old.[12]

The crux of the above quotation is "the inner gate." In traditional society, an "outside visitor" was not permitted to pass through the inner gate and into the space reserved for women and children. But now Yi Hyŏngsik, having just prior been hailed by a friend using the "English" title "*Misŭt'ŏ Ri* (Mister Lee)," passes beyond the inner gate while thinking "this alone represented a large change from the old customs." The following situation from *Hyŏl ŭi nu,* which expresses the conflict arising between the inner courtyard that refused admittance to male outsiders and the modern postal system and its consciousness of space that required the accurate delivery of letters to divided addresses, is already a thing of the past.

> "Who d'you think you are, peeping without so much as a by-your-leave in to the inner court of someone's house? The master's not even here. What sort of a fellow are you, peeping into the inner court of a gentleman's residence?"
>
> "Who are you calling fellow? D'you think a postman's nothing at all? Let me get a word in. Come out here! The only thing I've done wrong is to try and deliver a letter."[13]

One important thing in addition to the spatiotemporal location of *Mujŏng* is the glass doors, which are presented together with such items as the table-cloth, table, chairs, bookshelves, works (books), a doorbell, a glass bowl, and Western-style spoons. As a boy, Hyŏngsik had once been astonished by "the sight of the enormous glass windows on the streets of Taedong-mun" (Installment 63), and this also carries over into a later description: "Reflecting the evening sun, the windows of the Chong-hyŏn Catholic church's pointed tower blazed like fire" (Installment 78). This brings to mind the following lines from "*Ch'ŏnch'i? ch'ŏnjae?*"

> The school, which the principal boasted had been repaired at a cost of 80 *wŏn* now giving us excellent facilities, was only two and a half rooms, and that included the one room the teachers slept in at night, while having a single bro-ken glass window was the most new style thing about it.[14]

As implied by the term "new style," the "glass window" is associated with modern architecture. And Western buildings composed of "windows, which are made of translucent glass, and doors, which are made of substantial wood,"[15] were objects of envy. In fact, Kim Ch'angŏk,[16] imitating Western architecture, builds a "three-story house," while Doctor O,[17] who has returned home after becoming a world-famous vocalist, is tempted by a woman who boasts that her house is "French-style." The school in the above quotation was reconstructed with these sorts of situations as background. The school building would have been an eclectic "semi-Western-style house" that also functioned as in the scene below.

> Whether she had fallen for that guy T's semi-Western-style house, or whether she actually thought of T affectionately, using the excuse that her former fiancé's family suffered from some hereditary disease passed down for generations, she intended to go to T, however.[18]

One important thing in addition to all of this is glass. Glass, which was used in the fabrication of such diverse items as eyeglasses, microscopes, telescopes, clocks, windshields, mirrors, show windows, aquariums, and museums, metaphorically represents the modern perspective. It is the crucial material for explaining modernity. Glass, through the organizations and systems above, provides such modern points of view as the correction and disciplining of sight, the penetration and dissecting of the microscopic world, the expansion of the visual field and adventure, landscape and speed, introspection, the exhibition of commodities, and the display of the past. The following is one example of this.

> Flickering before my eyes even to this day are the countless houses and numerous shop signs and billboards disappearing into the distance amidst the black smoke coming from the train's smokestack and the sound of the train's wheels rubbing against the tracks. These totally new things, through the glass of the train's windows, played a motion picture before my eyes.[19]

Of course, the perspective above does not derive solely from glass. It is produced by the interaction between the glass and the linear movement and speed of the train. The quotation below argues that the glass and the speed of the train perform essentially identical functions.

> He (the traveler) was removed from that "total space" which combined proximity and distance: he became separated from the landscape he saw by what Richard Lucae, speaking of ferro-vitreous architecture, has called an "almost immaterial barrier." The glass separated the interior space of the Crystal Palace from the natural space outside without actually changing the atmospheric quality of the latter in any visible manner, just as the train's speed separated the traveler from the space he had previously been a part of.[20]

The train's speed and glass share in common that they both sever gaze from object of observation. This, in the sense that it makes inevitable a distance between the eye and the object of observation, physically realizes the modern principle by which the subject and the Other are constructed. No

matter how transparent it may appear, observation through glass is different from the sight of the naked eye. Observation with the naked eye, unlike
a journey on a train, means going into the landscape on foot and is akin to
becoming a part of it. Glass, on the other hand, by blocking off what is on
the other side, rather candidly opens up the place and displays it. Think of
how a show window closes off physical contact even as it openly displays
an interior. This is the true meaning of expressions such as "I know what's
going on inside Cho Pyŏnggwŏn as clearly as if I stuck a piece of glass to
him and looked right in,"[21] and "As far as what's going inside Kyŏngho and
his sister's guts, it's like I'm looking in through a piece of glass, but . . . ."[22]
At this juncture, in the sense that it is simultaneously obstructed (excluded)
and completely exposed by the glass window, the object of observation is
thoroughly Otherized.

As a result, that the poet Chŏng Chiyong wrote of a "cold and sad thing" or
of an "oh so cold kiss" was not due simply to the tactile sensation of a glass
window.[23] As symbolized by the expression "distant flower,"[24] the cold also
originates in the distance from the object, that is to say in the coldhearted
objectivity of the gaze that Otherizes the object from the other side of the
glass. That being the case, these "heartless eyes" (Installment 13), as evident
in Yi Sang's anatomically penetrating description "SS emerged carrying his
young daughter in the space between his bouldery chest and stomach—inside
his body this would correspond to the area around his diaphragm,"[25] will con-
clude as a complete visual appropriation.[26] Not only is the object unable to
cross over to the other side of the glass but it is also unable to conceal itself.
By contrast, the gaze, without ever touching or assimilating into the object,
will be free merely to observe coldly. In this manner, glass thoroughly separates subject and object, while, on the other hand, through aspects such as its
transparency, magnification (lenses), and speed, it abstracts sight alone from
the subject of observation. The following passages present this abstraction
effect in a humorous fashion.

> At first, when I first saw this telescope, my old man really pulled the wool over
> my eyes. He asked me if it wasn't just like those things in the distance were right
> in front of my eyes, to which I replied, "Yes, it is." My old man then said that
> after looking through the telescope if I put it up to my ear right away that I could
> even hear what they were saying, so that I should try that.[27]

> Oh, is that so? In any case, they say that these sorts of double eyeglasses are not
> so common even in the West. During the festival at Yasukuni Shrine I can see
> the fireworks quite clearly. Every time I see them I am struck by the thought of
> how nice it would be if I could also hear people talking in the same way. You
> see, they seem so close that it were as if I could hear their sound as well.[28]

Through sensory experiences like those above, gaze and object are genuinely manipulated. And the gaze thus constituted functions as if it were self-evident and natural. That is, it takes on ideological attributes. Concerning this, Yi Sang wrote the following.

> The microscope
> Beneath it, artificiality too appeared just like nature[29]

The meaning of glass is precisely this. Here, glass is not simply a material. It is the structure of the modern gaze, armed with rationality and exclusion, and, by extension, the logic of constitution. In addition to being a private English tutor, Hyŏngsik was standing in front of this glass. Accordingly, Hyŏngsik's location goes well with the following description.

> The train sounded a long whistle as it came around a bend in the mountain. Coal smoke from the engine flew by Yŏngch'ae, depositing a speck of dust in her right eye. Yŏngch'ae closed her eyes, and quickly pulled her head back inside the train. She then dabbed her eye with the silk handkerchief she was holding. But the coal dust wouldn't come out, and only tears flowed forth. Her eye hurt quite badly.[30]

Thus, *Mujŏng*'s basic descriptive principle is passing through (seeing through) glass. The expression "To Hyŏngsik, what he had done over the past month appeared as clearly as if seen through a microscope"[31] symbolizes this. And pursuing objective description in this manner is a type of stylistic ideology that corresponds with the ideologies of civilization and enlightenment, and of the modern nation-state. Additionally, it shares something in common with Kim Tongin's attitude in saying "We realized that if we used existing methods the distinction between subject and object could not be made clear. Thus we boldly rejected them."[32] This is because it is precisely the use of the past tense, "*haetta* (했다)," to express the rupture between the subject and object of the narration that constitutes the "heartless eyes." This was the modern glass placed into the window frame of Korean fiction.

THE AFFECTION OF HIGH COLLAR YOUNG WOMEN

What can be discovered from the discussion above is a modern "shall not sit together" that is different from the traditional "boys and girls shall not sit together after they have reached the age of seven." All individual entities always exist with respect to one another on the other side of "glass=past tense." This is the structure of the modern subject. "The fire that burns in the soul" is not "of the same essential nature as the stars."[33] The "flames" in Hyŏngsik's heart and the "June sunshine" are completely different types of heat.

As such, this new "shall not sit together" indicates a principle of difference and exclusion that engages the entirety of modern society. It also metaphorically presents the social relations expressed in things such as monetary exchange and the market, the colony and imperialism. Figuratively speaking, regardless of the fact that he travels the same road while running ahead of his passenger, the rickshaw man Kim Ch'ŏmji can never reach the position of his fat passenger Master Yun.[34] The "new world" provided by the train is divided into first class, second class, and other class cars.[35] Pongnyŏ of Kim Tongin's "*Kamja* (Potatoes, 1925)" and the protagonists of Yi Hyosŏk's "*Tosi wa yuryŏng* (The city and the ghost, 1928)" belong only to "outside the Seven Star Gate" of P'yŏngyang and beyond the Great East Gate of Seoul.[36] Comparing herself to Yi Kyŏnghŭi, who in order to secure 150,000 *wŏn*, "must merely have dinner at the Chosŏn Hotel" with her father, the head of the Taehŭng Group, "Hyŏnsun, who in order to purchase a single new pair of shoes must continually go over it in her head for two or three months," feels "like a strange foreigner."[37] In this regard, it is only natural for Hyŏngsik to agonize before stepping inside Elder Kim's glass doors.

> In fact, Hyŏngsik lacked any of the power it took to win the affection of a modish high collar young woman. Thinking this, Hyŏngsik was naturally disheartened and sorrowful.[38]

What is this "high collar" that cast Hyŏngsik into anguish? The term "*haikara*," which was popular in Japan from the mid-Meiji period (1868–1912), like the early-Showa (1926–1989) term "*modan* (modern)," was a buzzword used to refer contemptuously to those people who frivolously imitated Western customs. In addition, the word "*bankara*," or "barbarian collar," was in vogue around the same time and used to refer to unrefined dress.[39] Naomi, the protagonist of Tanizaki Junichiro's *Chijin no ai* (*A fool's love*, 1924–1925), is a well-known example of a high collar woman.

The "high collar young women" of whom Hyŏnsik dreams, however, has of course no relation to this pejorative sense of the word. The "high collar young women" from whom he seeks affection signify, above all else, new women who have received modern education. Just as "*bankara*" was the original antonym of "*haikara*," "high collar" implies, at least to Hyŏngsik, the knowledge and civilization that confronted barbarism. In relation to this, Yi Kwangsu wrote the following.

As the student life of students at The First High School represents student life in all of Japan, I will briefly describe it here. The opposite of *haik'alla* (high collar) is *pangk'alla* (barbarian collar), and high school students are actually the epitome of *pangk'alla*. They wear hats with the backs blown out and clogs with broad straps, while carrying thick, knotted cherry wood canes . . . they are actually more like clubs that they drag around quickly flashing backward glances, and they swing their arms and rampantly swagger as if the world were too cramped. These are the high school students who will become future graduates, and the female students' ideal spouses.[40]

It is precisely the "female students" who appear in the quotation who are Yi Hyŏngsik's "ideal spouses." Hyŏngsik's wishes also have something in common with his desires, which were expressed in ways such as "never once did the thought of a 'clean house and a wife who had graduated school' leave his impoverished head."[41] This is how Hyŏngsik's definition of "high collar" relates to modern education. This attitude that idealizes modern knowledge is also presented in the line "He believed that if the old woman were to receive fifteen or sixteen years of education as had he, she would become just like him."[42] The arrogant *pangk'alla* of The First High School students paradoxically expresses this attitude. In short, Hyŏngsik desires "in the Western custom to embrace and kiss" a modernly enlightened woman. Accordingly, he cannot marry Yŏngch'ae. This is because, unlike Sŏnhyong, who graduated from Chŏngsin Girls' School at the top of her class, Yŏngch'ae received only a modicum of education, after which she has only been a *kisaeng*. "She wore her hair in the style of a female student,"[43] but Yŏngch'ae is still a *kisaeng*. As a result, Hyŏngsik undergoes the following mental conflict regarding Yŏngch'ae.

Ah, what shall I do if Yŏngch'ae is quite ignorant? Could I make a happy family with such an ignorant Yŏngch'ae? Ah, what if Yŏngch'ae is ignorant?[44]

At this point, the appearance of Yŏngch'ae is a novelistic event corresponding to the emergence of the "past tense" ("*haetta*"), which represents the modern gaze that looks through the windowpane. Yŏngch'ae is not only his former fiancé but also the "past tense=difference" on which the modern novel is predicated. This in turn implies the ideology of progress (future=difference) symbolized by study abroad. This, combined with Yŏngch'ae's transformation from *kisaeng* to student, mediates history. This is an important theme raised by *Mujŏng*.

On the other hand, however, "high collar" is also related to the phrase "men in Western suits," which appears numerous times in modern literature. "In the uproar to encourage the wearing of color, anyone, whether man or woman, young or old, who dared put on white clothes was doused with black ink."⁴⁵ Soon after this began, the "men in Western suits" began to appear as in the passages below.

In rural areas, the might of the men in Western suits was imposing. The old woman, perhaps mistakenly thinking Injun was a detective, shudderingly told him what she knew.⁴⁶

A few men wearing Western suits could be seen being swept up by the young and old of the village and going into this house and that. It was assumed that they had come from the township office or county office to conduct some sort of survey.⁴⁷

Accordingly, on the other hand, he also had a decently high collar (if a bit moth-eaten) Western suit. But it was a little hot and uncomfortable, so he didn't sport that sucker. He came out wearing those Korean clothes that made him look completely undignified. After only one night they were blackened by the soot and sweat of the train car, and, losing their starch, were already all twisted up and wrinkled. In the end, when facing these types of situations, he was endlessly dejected due to his shabby appearance. When he thought of these things he could not help but feel extremely unpleasant and regretful.⁴⁸

In fact, Ŭnju, when facing the Western-attired Kyŏnghi [*sic*], repeatedly discovered a part of herself that felt a sense of being overpowered, the source of which remained a mystery, as well as the inability to put words together in an orderly fashion. But when Kyŏnghi [*sic*] wore, as she did now, Korean clothes—a navy *ch'ima* with a yellow *chŏgori* and white *pŏsŏn*⁴⁹—she already felt like nothing more than a young child to Ŭnju.⁵⁰

Just as Kim Tongin's "Country Mr. Hwang" "has never seen any men in Western suits save for military policemen, patrol officers, and survey technicians,"⁵¹ and as is dramatically implied in the scene from Yŏm Sangsŏp's novella *Mansejŏn* (*On the eve of the uprising*, 1922) in which "Advisor Kim, clad in his ramie *turumagi*, is being guarded by two men in Western suits,"⁵² "men in Western suits" primarily symbolized the modern civilization and its systems that were in conflict with the premodern "ramie *turumagi*." As such, this forcefully demands an interest in the "semiotics of men in Western suits" that operates in Korean literary history. Below is one example.

"Goodness no! Getting a haircut in the countryside is more troublesome and, in fact, costs more money. . . . What's more, if I do cut my hair then, like you fellows, I have to know how to speak Japanese and have modern knowledge as well. If you just get a haircut and then meet a Japanese person but you can't answer him properly, like when you go to a government office or run into a police officer, there're a lot of times when it's more trouble than it's worth. If I just wear this here manggŭn, because I'm a 'yobo' they pretty much overlook all but the biggest mistakes. Isn't that alone reason enough not to cut it?"

He guffawed as he spoke these words.

"But, just as you get treated differently even among fellow Koreans if you wear a Western suit, won't you also be looked down upon less by those people if you at least cut your hair? Just how long do you intend to carelessly take things as they come, to cringe and bow and be known only as 'yobo'?"[53]

That Koreans who wore Western suits were treated well while the "*yobo*" who wore traditional clothes were "looked down upon" is due to the fact that costume operates as one standard for citizens and subjects. Just as the ability to speak Japanese and Western suits are conflated in the quotation above, and as nation-state and national language are deeply connected, "high collar" or "men in Western suits" constitute a type of signifiant that is combined with the system, which represents the signifié. The Western suit is yet another écriture that ranks with national language. This makes the following scene from Hyŏn Chin'gŏn's "*Kohyang* (Hometown, 1926)," in which a man appears who is wearing clothes from Korea, China, and Japan, as well as speaking a smattering of Korean, Chinese, and Japanese, quite interesting.

He wrapped his *kimono* in a *turumagi* with a *chŏgori* of white cotton visible inside them, while on his lower half he wore Chinese-style pants. These, like the ones those people often wear, were made of a shiny dark brown fabric resembling oil paper. On his feet he wore *kambal* and covered them with *chipsin*, yet no hat sat atop his sheaf-cropped hair.[54] He was decked out in an odd combination that occasionally coincidentally comes together. In the train car we sat down in, as luck would have it, people gathered from all three countries, with a Chinese person reclining beside me. In front of him sat a Japanese person. The man, as reward for being wrapped in garments from all three countries, spoke gushingly in Japanese, and he didn't appear to be too shabby at Chinese either.[55]

Roland Barthes once semiotically analyzed the fashion system, and, when viewed in a similar way, the costume worn by the protagonist of "*Kohyang*" resembles a strange sentence in which selection and combination fail to be appropriately mediated. Accordingly, this costume, an "odd combination" that brings to mind the contiguity disorder of Roman Jacobsen, semiotically expresses the protagonist's marginalized position. In addition, it shares something in common with the "copying" of Gogol's Akaky Akakyevich who paid no attention at all to clothes. Akakyevich's lack of interest in costume corresponds to his obsession with copying the writings of others rather than creating his own sentences.

(A)ll he had to do was to alter the title at the top of the document and change some of the verbs from the first to the third person singular. This, however, gave him so much trouble that he was bathed in perspiration and kept mopping his forehead until at last he said, "No, I can't do it. You'd better give me something to copy." Since then they let him carry on with his copying for ever [sic]. Outside this copying nothing seemed to exist for him. He never gave a thought to his clothes: his uniform was no longer green, but of some non-descript rusty white.[56]

Akakyevich's appearance above, as does his eventually becoming a ghost, metaphorically expresses his dispossessed subjectivity. In like fashion, the costume of the protagonist of "Kohyang" signifies the position of the Other who has been excluded from the process of modernization in many different layers. His strange costume corresponds to the folksong lyrics—"Those friends who can speak a few words go off to prison"—that appear at the close of the story, while it expresses not the subject's coherent utterance but rather the failure thereof. The costume depicted in the quotation below also indicates the position of an individual who was been thoroughly Otherized through things such as incarceration or violation/rape.

Among them all, what hurt Yŏngch'ae's heart the most were the hideous clothes dyed with ocher mud. When she arrived outside the prison gate, she saw figures in these hideous ocher-stained clothes, wearing strange hats of plaited straw, and dragging thick iron chains behind them while carrying on their backs some sort of round containers that reeked of dung. She trembled when she first saw this scene; it was as if she were seeing the demons and ghosts she had feared as a child.[57]

Hyŏngsik stood up tall and, seeing that the ribbon of her blouse was completely undone, and her clothes had fallen down to expose a span of her fair waste, was struck by a new sorrow. He thought "Is this really Pak Yŏngch'ae?" and then "I hope it isn't Pak Yŏngch'ae." He then looked at her clothes, followed by her hair. Of course, she was not wearing a ramie skirt nor was her hair in a Western chignon. Hyŏngsik could tell her skirt was made of some sort of silk, though he did not know what kind.[58]

As seen above, the costume is the sentence. "High collar" and "men in Western suits" are highly connotative signifiers. Accordingly, it is only natural that Hyŏl ŭi nu's Ku Wansŏ "was wearing a Western suit, however, he appeared awkward like a person wearing a Western suit for the first time."[59] His sloppy "high collar" costume is well suited to his position vis-à-vis modernity in that he is merely now departing for study in America. He has yet to become "a youth who has finely adorned his body with good character and abundant knowledge."[60] At this juncture, the passage below reads quite significantly.

> The day I departed for Shanghai the new moon wind of the first month of the lunar new year blew fiercely. Setting out in my new newly tailored suit and newly purchased shoes, I was pleased at looking quite the Western-style gentleman. In addition, the feeling of riding in a rickshaw for the first time in my life and rushing like the wind along the slick broad road of Yŏngdae was a considerable luxury to a bumpkin like me. But when on the road I met a real Western man, the "pride"[61] I had theretofore held suddenly wilted, a cold sweat ran down my spine, and unawares I bowed my head. The Western man's clothes were not necessarily better than mine, nor was the figure I cut necessarily less fine than his. The Western man, however, naturally possessed a spirit of wealth, whereas I seemed to possess the spirit of a pitiful man, cold and poor and shivering in an attempt to imitate Western men. I was appropriately overcome with a feeling of shame.[62]

What is the reason Yi understood his appearance wearing a Western suit as that of "a pitiful man, cold and poor and shivering in an attempt to imitate Western men," and why did he feel shame? It is because, in Orientalist fashion, he idealizes "high collar" and "men in Western suits." To Yi, the Western suit emblematizes modern (imperialistic) activities such as "commercial inspections," "geographical historical expeditions," "social climate and cultural inspections," "political inspections," "military scouting," and "poetry and fiction material collection," as well as the "ability," "knowledge," and "insight" these activities connote. To Yi, however, such activities still feel foreign and distant. This is because he is one of the colonized. In short, low self-esteem at the inability to be truly "high collar," as well as the anxiety that he might never be able to move beyond what Yi Sang termed a "shapeless modern boy"[63] constitute the source of Yi's shame. This yearning for a truly modern "shape" is expressed in the following scene from *Mujŏng*.

> Civilization is a collective term for such things as science, philosophy, religion, art, politics, economics, industry, and social systems. To say one understands Western civilization is to say one understands all the contents mentioned above, so how could Elder Kim have known the West. The Western missionaries are well aware of this. Thus they refer to Elder Kim as a person who imitates the West. This is in no way meant to malign Elder Kim, rather it is a statement of

Elder Kim's true condition. If wearing Western clothes, building a Western-style house, and following Western customs while unaware of the contents of Western people's civilization is not imitation then what shall we call it?[64]

This criticism of Elder Kim reveals the "civilization and enlightenment" will to achieve a universal level of modernity at which a Western suit would look fitting. (This contrasts well with the eponymous protagonist of Ch'ae Mansik's *"Misŭt'ŏ Pang* [Mister Pang, 1948]" who buys a Western suit, becomes an interpreter for the U.S. Army, and thereby paves the way for his success.) It is also one connotation of the words Hyŏngsik "lacked any of the power it took to win the affection of a high collar young woman." Thus, the sense of shame felt by Yi Kwangsu is no different from his frustration regarding the train in the passage below.

"The sound of a whistle!
A train approaches.
I too must get ready to go to the station."
"Crazy fool! Where do you think you're going?
You've got no place to go.
And what would you do there?
You've got nothing to do."
"Oh, train, abandon me and go!
The next train as well, and the train after that as well
Pay no mind and pass on by
I have nothing to do
A living corpse
Tumbling down and rolling about
Shall I try to count the sounds of the whistles?"[65]

The crux of the poem above is the desire to ride "the train called modernity." The speaker, however, is frustrated because he is unable to ride the train. With nothing to do and nowhere to go, he has no reason to ride the train. Just as with Western suits, the train emblematizes truly modern activities (things to do and places to go). This brings to mind Yi Kwangsu's own stance that "ruination is the wages received by he who is not busy."[66]

One minute or one hour of civilized people is worth more than ten years or twenty years of uncivilized people. In like fashion, the former, competing at every minute and every second, on the one hand endeavor to complete the business of their own families, while on the other hand they work to expand the civilization and welfare of their society and country. Thus the right to use such conveniences as the telegraph, telephone, train, and steam ship actually only exists for them.

For people like me it makes no difference if it takes a full ten days to go from Seoul to Ŭiju; it makes no difference if it takes 100 days; and it makes no difference if I don't go at all. Even had I never been born and did not exist in this world there would not be the slightest loss to society or country, so for people like me—daring to use these benefits of civilization is actually presumptuous and deplorable.[67]

Thus, one will of *Mujŏng* is to overcome the passage below in which the mere act of traveling by train or steamship is seen as synonymous with "enlightenment."

(Ch'oe) "Well, what a surprise. You're coming is certainly unexpected. Women have a difficult time traveling even ten li, so how did you manage a journey of 1,500 li all by yourself?"

(Daughter) "A young girl like Ongnyŏn has gone more than 60,000 li to America, and you think I can't make it to a place this close. I went down to Chinnamp'o and took a steam ship from there. Father, I've been enlightened."[68]

Of course, in spite of the distinction between the comparatively simple perspective of Ongnyŏn'g mother and the will of Yi Kwangsu, the important events and causal relations in *Mujŏng* such as Yŏngch'ae's rape and subsequent travel to P'yŏngyang, the meeting of Yŏngch'ae and Pyŏnguk, the benefit concert at Samnyangjin, and study abroad all rely upon the rails of trains and streetcars or the seaways of steamships. Just as Hyesŏn's suicide[69] takes place on the bridge over the Han River, which is beyond the streetcar's final stop (=life's final stop=the story's conclusion), a place where there is no place else to go, Yŏnch'ae's rape takes place in the pine forest of Hongnŭng, beyond the final streetcar stop at Ch'ŏngnyangni. Moreover, events such as Hyŏnsik's mistakenly getting on a streetcar bound for the Great West Gate rather than the Great East Gate and the "infrequent" time intervals of the streetcar bound for Ch'ŏngnyangni are what afford Kim Hyŏnsu and Pae Myŏngsik the time necessary to carry out their rape of Yŏngch'ae.

As is eloquently attested to by the serialization of "*K'wae sonyŏn segye chuyu sibo* (Current news of a vigorous boy's trip around the world)" in Ch'ae Namsŏn's *Sonyŏn*, the ideology of study abroad and civilization came into being along with the modern imagination of foreign places through things such as the seaways of steamships, the Seoul-Busan Railroad, and the Trans-Siberian Railroad, as well as the geographies connected to them. Therefore, these causal relationships that were entrusted to railroads and foreign countries also share something in common with Hyŏngsik's psychology in attempting to become "high collar" by relying on the "affection of a high collar young woman." If receiving the "affection of a high collar young woman" corresponds to railroads (foreign countries), then becoming truly "high collar" on one's own corresponds to modern novelistic causal relations and plots. Even as the "affection of a high collar young woman" means the modern desire to ride on trains and steamships, it simultaneously symbolizes events and causal relations that rely on trains, streetcars, steamships, and foreign countries. Against the backdrop of an ideology of study abroad that was at once modern and extremely abstract and optimistic, the "affection of a high collar young woman" was a device that simultaneously embodied these modern desires and causal relations.

Viewed in this light, works had yet to attain a full-scale dialectics that played out between the subject and the object. The enormous objectivity of modern civilization that has laid the Trans-Siberian Railroad overwhelms the subject who is only now just beginning to learn English. Accordingly, the subject cannot yet adequately stand and face that objectivity. What this subject who feels "presumptuous and deplorable" for merely using the conveniences of civilization can do is sing the praises of the object while abstractly screaming out the ideals of civilization and enlightenment. Naturally, the plot cannot help but be weak. Causal relations that rely on trains are inevitable. *Mujŏng*, which had only just begun to dream of the "development of commerce and industry," failed in so many respects to reach either the position of the chairman of the Taehŭng Group that developed Manchuria, or the sophisticated fashion constituted by his daughter, Yi Kyŏnghŭi.

"It would be perfect for early winter, but it would also be nice for late fall and spring, oh, and I bet it would be okay inside an overcoat in winter. Very nice would be if you wore it under a between-seasons overcoat, that would look best. What color was your between-seasons overcoat again?"

In these words from Hyŏnsun, Kyŏnghi [sic] replied is a subdued voice,

"Cobalt blue dots against a grey background"

"Well then it does go well with the colors of your overcoat"

. . .

"Yes and it would be really great if you combine it with a beret or a toque and some black pumps," interjected the meddling "Madame."[70]

THE PERSPECTIVE OF THE SHOW WINDOW

Slightly different from Hyŏngsik's longing for the "affection of a high collar young woman," the following scene appears in Yŏm Sangsŏp's *"Ttong p'ari wa kŭ ŭi anhae"* (Shit fly and his wife, 1929).

"As a matter of fact, she says it's her wish to try living with something like a man in a Western suit!"

"A man in a Western suit is a man in a Western suit. What the heck's something like a man in a Western suit, someone who wears only Western underpants and a jacket? Ha, ha. . . ."

The women of the village all sat together and when anyone mentioned Shit Fly's wife they made fun of her.[71]

Yi Hyŏngsik, who genuinely wanted to ride a train, and Shit Fly, who was incarcerated for the crime of "obstruction of traffic" after placing a rock on the rails of the Seoul-Wŏnsan line, contrast sharply. Shit Fly's wife, whose "wish" was "to try living with something like a man in a Western suit," is also different from Hyŏngsik. This is because to Shit Fly's wife "men in Western suits" are related solely to worldly self-interest. This is also connected to the perspective of An Hoenam's "*Kigye*" (Machine, 1939), which describes its protagonist, Mr. Kim, as "always going about dressed in a Western suit, dangling a pocket watch from a long chain that may have been pure gold or may have just been gold-plated, and showily brandishing a walking stick."[72] Naturally, "men in Western suits" symbolized not only modern civilization and systems but also the modern wealth (possession=property=capitalist identity) to which they gave rise. Both Im Hwa's poetic question "Isn't a single soiled necktie all that we have left?"[73] and the impoverished political convert[74] Minu's "thrusting a single book in the pocket of his threadbare overcoat before hastily going outside"[75] in search of a job are also related to this. The following passage from *Mujŏng* also addresses this issue.

If Hyŏngsik had arrived wearing a fine Western suit complete with pink necktie, drunk, and brandishing a walking stick while saying "You there," the old woman would have hastily put down her pipe, dashed out into the courtyard, and responded with a forced smile, "Oh goodness, welcome sir." But someone like Hyŏngsik, who wore a *turumagi* of coarse ramie and a flyspecked straw hat, was not drunk, brandished no walking stick, and did not say "You there," appeared to the old woman extremely lower class.[76]

Mujŏng, through this "fine Western suit," is discovering the modern snob. Like two sides of the same coin, this snobbery operates in concert with the enlightenment consciousness expressed in the following line: "Scholar Park immediately cut his hair, put on black clothes, and made both of his sons do the same."[77] This means that yet another modern fashion—one that formed a pair with the ideology of civilization and enlightenment—had been born. This is also implied by the words of the director of sales who in 1927 advised

Kim Insu, a "salesperson for a life insurance company," "you'll never sell anything in that Western suit. Have a new one made, and get some gold-rimmed glasses while you're at it."[78] Thus, the desire of Shit Fly's wife is directed toward the "men in Western suits" as constituted below.

> At first he maintained the appearance of being a *yangban* and a gentleman. But as the *turumagi*, *t'anggŏn*,[79] and leather shoes necessary to affect this appearance disappeared, the pretense of being a *yangban* and a gentleman disappeared along with them. That villain had fallen to where he cared about nothing but making money by any means necessary, and drinking.[80]

Of course, this snobbish tendency can also be applied to Yi Hyŏngsik. He appears to have no connection whatsoever to snobbery. Yi, who not only gives money to impoverished students but also agonizes, "(I)f I want to save Yŏngch'ae" "I would need 1,000 *wŏn*. But I do not have 1,000 *wŏn*,"[81] seems to be the very incarnation of altruism. What merits attention at this juncture, however, is the fact that his anxiety over "where will I come up with 1,000 *wŏn*," which is not only justified but also comes to possess excellent moral value through his dealings with Yŏngch'ae, forms a pair with the following passage.

> "That's right. We must do it. Here lies the reason we are going to study. Who is giving us the fare to ride this train, and the tuition to go and study? Korea is giving it to us. Why? So that we may go and bring back power. Bring back knowledge. Bring back civilization. . . . And in so doing build a strong foundation for life atop this new civilization. . . . Isn't this the reason?" While saying this he pulled his wallet from his vest pocket, produced a blue train ticket, and continued,
>
> "Within this ticket are contained drops of sweat from all those shivering people over there and also from that young man before! They are asking us never to allow them to suffer such pathetic circumstances again!" Hyŏngsik exclaimed, shaking his body and head as if resolving himself anew.[82]

"1,000 *wŏn*" is not merely the sum necessary to save Yŏngch'ae. As can be prognostically glimpsed through the passage's mentioning of the tuition and train fare necessary for study abroad, in fact the words "where will I come up with 1,000 *wŏn*" also expressed Yi Hyŏngsik's personal desire to study abroad. "From among his monthly salary of 35 *wŏn*, he sent five *wŏn* to a bookstore in Tokyo as payment for a set of Plato's collected works, divided ten *wŏn* up among his students, gave eight *wŏn* to his old landlady for board, and all that was presently left in his wallet were a single five-*wŏn* note and a few silver coins."[83] Yi Hyŏngsik is a pauper.

What is even more important is the fact that Hyŏngsik's train fare and tuition come out of Elder Kim's "wallet." Hyŏnsik obscures this fact in the name of the nation when he says that Korea has given him train fare and tuition. What has actually alleviated his poverty, however, is the "affection of a high collar young woman" (or, more accurately, a high collar young woman's father). This is why Usŏn teases him, saying things like "What could the son-in-law of a wealthy family have to worry about?" or "You really hit the jackpot" (Installment 77). This, together with the line "The worries of people nowadays are almost always due to lack of money," is yet another core of "high collar." At this point, Yŏngch'ae, the incarnation of tradition who resembles Sim Ch'ŏng in selling her body to save her father, is completely counterposed to Sŏnhyŏng, the new woman with *hisashi-gami*. Sŏnhyŏng is a high collar woman reminiscent of those in Yi Kwangsu's "*Chanyŏ chung-simnon* (On the Primacy of children, 1918)." Not only does she not sacrifice herself for her father but also burdens him with her spouse's tuition. The case of Pyŏnguk, another "high collar" woman, is the same as well. She not only takes it upon herself to enlighten Yŏngch'ae, a total stranger, and bring her home but also to pay for her study abroad. This suggests both the secret desire of *Mujŏng* and the true meaning of "where will I come up with 1,000 *wŏn*." Through the cases of Sunae, Yŏngch'ae, and Hyŏngsik alike, his concern over the 1,000 *wŏn* reveals the desire to receive financial support.

In fact, such financial support was actually attempted. When Yi Kwangsu left for Beijing, Abe Mitsuie wrote him letters of introduction. He also proposed to Governor General Saito that permission be granted to Ch'oe Namsŏn to publish his journal *Tongmyŏng* (*Light of the East*) in order to forestall the exacerbation of the thought of Korean intellectual circles, while simultaneously suggesting he subsidize the tuition of students such as Yi Kwangsu and Chin Hangmun.[84] On the other hand, on March 19, 1919, October 21, 1923, and September 26, 1924, Yoshino Sakujo, a theorist of Taishō democracy, met with Ch'oe Sŭngman,[85] the editor of *Hak chi kwang* (*Light of learning*) and founding member of *Ch'angjo* (*Creation*), and offered to provide a tuition stipend of 40 *wŏn* per month, but was rebuffed.[86] And, of course, there is the famous instance of Yi Kwangsu's leaving for his second round of study abroad with the help of Kim Sŏngsu.

It follows from the above that this desire, which also shares something in common with the reliant causal relations of *Mujŏng*, represents an important meaning connoted by the "affection of a high collar young woman." The "high collar woman" Sŏnhyŏng is indispensable as one vertex to form the triangle of desire to gain Elder Kim's money. When Hyŏngsik thought about "'going to study in America with money from my wife's family'" he became even more ashamed, and felt as if the entire world were mocking his ugliness" (Installment 97). Even though he agonized over this, after he heard that he was to be engaged to Sŏnhyŏng he "even thought that it was fortunate that Yŏngch'ae had died just in time" (Installment 76). As seen below, to Hyŏngsik, Sŏnhyŏng is "someone he could not do without."

> But to Hyŏngsik as well, Sŏnhyŏng was someone he could not do without. In his mind, it was as if his entire life depended on the person of Sŏnhyŏng. Even if she were to say to him "I don't want to see you anymore. Go away," or to spit in his face and kick him, he would have no choice but to cling to the hem of her skirt.[87]

When seen from this perspective, his criticism of Elder Kim as a "half enlightened fellow," and his contempt for modern snobs in the line "beastly people who have '1,000 *wŏn*' are lurking everywhere" (Installment 25), may be defense mechanisms against this financial dependence. (It just so happens that his criticisms of Elder Kim fully materialize in Installment 79, just following his engagement in Installments 76 and 77.) In addition, this is also related to the opening of the benefit concert for the flood victims at Samnangjin. This may have been no more than the sentimental behavior of a child or hypocrisy. This is due to the fact that Hyŏngsik's essential position is not one of giving money to the flood victims but rather of receiving money from Elder Kim. It is here we come to realize the meaning connoted by the fashion sense of *Mujŏng*, which is presented several times in the passages below.

> Hyŏngsik, thinking of his lot and that of his younger sister, again looked at Sunae's face. Her clothes and hair were done exactly like Sŏnhyŏng's, so it was possible to recognize the friendly feelings between the two girls.[88]

> Hyŏngsik looked at the wide jade-colored ribbons in the Western chignons that adorned the black hair of the two young women's bowed heads. He then looked at the two young girls' fingers upon their desks.[89]

> Wŏlhyang too had four or five P'yŏngyang gentlemen who used to visit her. They all wore shiny Western suits, conversed in Japanese about when they had attended universities in Tokyo, and were extremely arrogant in their pretenses at being gentlemen.[90]

> She looked at his yellowed straw hat and wondered what he did for a living, what kind of a person he was. . . . But, seeing that he wore shabby clothes, she came to the conclusion that he must be a poor person. She next looked at Hyŏnsik's wrinkled *turumagi*. Kyehyang said, "Ah, it got wrinkled in the

train last night. Why didn't you take it off and hang it up?" Then she looked at
Hyŏngsik's feet, and said, "Ah, you have new shoes!"[91]
A young woman in Japanese clothes took up a washcloth and said, "Come sit
over here. Did you get coal dust in your eye?" . . .

As she walked down the aisle, she received a washcloth and some soap from
a boy in a Western suit who had been sitting with her near the middle of the car.
A man in a Western suit who sat across from them and had been reading a book
sat up tall to have a look, then resumed his reading.[92]

The only people in the car were an old Western man who appeared to be a missionary, a portly official sporting two gold cords, and two or three people in
Japanese clothes. They all turned their gazes toward the second-class passengers
in their white clothes as if they thought them strange.[93]

To begin with the conclusion, through these quotations, the "glass doors"
of *Mujŏng* are turned into a show window. This is concentrated into two
issues. The first is the issue of desire. In that it has been mediated by the glass
of modern "shall not sit together," the modern subject is already a structure
of deficiency and desire. The cold gaze and distance (difference) provided
by glass paradoxically gives birth to a powerful desire. For Lacan, linguistic
signs were something that emptied existence and filled desire. In similar
fashion, glass, by preventing approach, gives rise to an endless directivity
toward the object on its other side. The entire world transforms into a show
window. Inside that show window of survival struggle and class conflict are
either every kind of "high collar" and infinite "men in Western suits," or
"men in topknots" and the white clothes of "*yobo*." This, in and of itself, is
the past tense (*haetta*), while simultaneously also meaning the advent of the
constitutive will to plug the interstices between past and future, this side and
that side to which this "*haetta*" gives rise. The train (study abroad) qua reliant
causal relations (constitution) implies the beginning of this novelistic journey
to overcome this distance and difference.

Just as the modern people on a train cannot go into the landscape, however,
the fashions on the other side of the windowpane are projected upon a plane
(social arena) that resembles a train window. Accordingly, the second issue is
that the show window of modernity in the end gives birth to a "perspective"
that foregrounds "high collar" and "men in Western suits." This perspective
embodied by glass does not describe nature itself. On the one hand, it presents
constituted nature, while on the other, it formalizes the modern "shall not sit
together" of social and historical hierarchical order. This is the meaning of
the perspective the show window provides, what Yi Kwangsu referred to as
"heartless eyes." Metaphorically speaking, "men in Western suits" are walking sociology, while screaming "Isn't a single soiled necktie all that we have

left?" is the class struggle at the "crossroads." "Clad in a 'one-piece' of black 'wool,' sporting a 'bolero' of the same color, and wearing a black winged hat"[94]—the extravagant yet sophisticated fashion of Yi Kyŏnghŭi, daughter of the Taehŭng Group's chairman, is related to this issue as well. It is also symbolized by Kim Kwangse, the protagonist of Kim Namch'ŏn's "*T ilbo sa* (The T daily newspaper company)" who proclaims "From today I rule the great city of Seoul," and then proceeds to purchase such items as "enamel dress shoes," a "tuxedo," deep-indigo "double-breasted," "camel overcoat," "underwear," "dress shirt," "necktie," "handkerchief," "leather gloves," "fancy socks," "walking stick," "platinum-plated Longines," "platinum signet ring," "Borsalino" hat, "cufflinks made of gold," and a "green jade necktie pin."[95] Hyŏngsik agonizes in front of Elder Kim's house due to this show-window aspect of society. No matter how closely they may sit, knees brushing against each other, Kim Sŏnhyŏng, daughter of a rich family, and Yi Hyŏngsik, pauper, cannot escape this modern "shall not sit together." The moment one looks out upon that unattainable other side of the windowpane, the gaze of desire and, along with it, the show window come to be created. It is precisely that perspective (or perspectival glimpse) of the desire that discovers the other side imagined to be attainable by train and steamship that is the true origin of *Mujŏng*'s fashion sense. Or, rather, it is the perspective itself, which draws the distant and dazzling "high collar" and "men in Western suits" upon the show window, that constitutes *Mujŏng*'s fashion.

As is the case, however, with Pyŏnguk's hope to start a "sericulture company" with his father's money (Installment 100), *Mujŏng*, composed as it is of the appearances of benefactors and entrusted causal relations, merely discovers and presents this perspective, but does not thoroughly implement it. Just as Hyŏngsik's relationship with Sŏnhyŏng mediates Elder Kim's money, free love, one of the work's major themes, abolishes the cold social perspective that is prioritized around money. Free love gave birth to the "son-in-law of a wealthy family." What Hyŏngsik required to become the son-in-law of a wealthy family was the modern knowledge known as "English." English mediates Hyŏngsik and Sŏnhyŏng. Hyŏngsik approaches Sŏnghyŏng through modern knowledge, while through her he draws near to Elder Kim's money. And Elder Kim's money once again mediates modern knowledge (study abroad).

As evidenced above, *Mujŏng* is cyclically composed. The former student abroad Hyŏngsik's again departing for study abroad as well as all the protagonists' who departed with him returning to Korea are related to this. This cycle creates tense relations against the endless perspectival differences of modern society contained within the work. As for Elder Kim, he approaches Hyŏngsik through his daughter, while also projecting his own modern desires onto the couple's engagement and study abroad. Through this entire process, it is as if Hyŏngsik and Elder Kim are deriving a certain common ground.

Accordingly, in this respect as well, free love and modern knowledge are Yi Hyŏngsik's only weapons in overcoming the modern "shall not sit together." At this juncture, Yi Hyŏngsik's social position becomes clear. He brings to mind a child in the modern sense: in exchange for being exempted from labor and production, supported by social investment, he receives the benefits of such things as mandatory education. Yi Hyŏngsik, who once exclaimed "I skipped over my childhood!" (Installment 67), by becoming engaged to Sŏnhyŏng, the daughter of a rich family, became a child. He was thus reborn to confirm the primacy of children.[96] He had reclaimed "one right of life" that had been stolen from him.

FREE LOVE AND EUGENICS

In addition to the discussion above, free love carries yet another important meaning. Let us first examine the quotation below.

> Hyŏngsik too did not think his appearance could attract Sŏnhyŏng's heart. Following their engagement, Hyŏngsik stood alone facing the mirror, examining his face. He imagined changing it, just has Sŏnhyŏng had, thinking about whether Sŏnhyŏng would like this part here or dislike that part there. . . . He also wondered why he lacked an appearance and presence that women would find intoxicating, as well as why he did not have the wealth and status and honor so envied by the world.[97]

Due to thoughts like those above, Yi Hyŏngsik imagines himself as the "young master of a wealthy family" or as a "luxurious and handsome young man." First of all, this expresses Hyŏngsik's desire to be chosen by women. This is also related to Yun Kwangho's suicide (although, of course, the object of Yun Kwangho's affection is the man P).[98] Going further, however, this also suggests the free competitive order that operates in the selection of the object of love. What we call free love is a type of struggle for survival carried out over the opposite sex. In fact, free love genuinely appeared together with capitalism and colonialism. In this sense as well, to Hyŏngsik free love itself is an actualization of modern life.

Yet another foundation of free love is presented together with such medical metaphors as the "poison germ known as jealousy" or the "poison germ known as love" (Installment 117) and alluded to in the lines below.

> Because there is a pox of the mind, there can also be a small pox of the mind. Whether it is love, or jealousy, disappointment, dejection, sadness, treachery,

cunning, brutality, obscenity, happiness, joy, or success, all the phenomena of life are a type of mental pox.[99]

The quotation equates love and jealousy with "mental pox." Ultimately, this raises the issue of public health and hygiene in relation to free love. On the one hand, *Mujŏng* describes Hyŏngsik's picking maggots out of his bean paste stew, while on the other it presents sentences like the one below.

The one sad thing is that Kyehyang, who accompanied Hyŏngsik out to Ch'ilsŏngmun when he visited P'yŏngyang, having become the concubine of the debauched scion of a wealthy family, contracted syphilis. On top of this, her husband went so far as to throw her out, so that she suffers in utter desolation.[100]

This quotation expresses the core of *Mujŏng*. If free love with the female student Sŏnhyŏng corresponds to hygiene, then keeping a *kisaeng* concubine corresponds to "syphilis." Hyŏngsik says he will study abroad and major in biology, and this not only points out that Kyehyang has contracted syphilis but also pairs well with the mention of a "primitive love that has yet to undergo evolution" (Installment 107). Furthermore, when we reach the passage "to an uncivilized *minjok*, love means only carnal desire, but in Hyŏngsik's love there were many spiritual elements" (Installment 107), we also have our eyes opened to the importance of the words "My goodness! Just look at me. The foreigners must have been laughing" (Installment 109).

Looking at their faces, they did not seem to have any sort of wisdom. They all looked dull and imperceptive. All they did was till the soil with the almost worthless knowledge they had of farming. Doing so, if God left them alone for a few years, they could gather a few rotten sacks of rice until the waters came again and washed them all away. Therefore, without ever becoming any richer, they gradually grew poorer. Therefore, their bodies gradually grew weaker, and their minds gradually grew duller. If left to their own devices, it seemed that in the end they would wind up a strain no different than the "Ainu" of Hokkaido.[101]

The passage above, which mentions "a strain no different than the 'Ainu' people of Hokkaido," brings to mind the position later taken by Yi in his essay "*Sonyŏn ege* (To the boys, 1921)," in which he wrote "the Korean *minjok* could very well become like the Ainu of Hokkaido."[102] This reveals the essence of the free love ideology. These words, which form a pair with the Orientalist attitude conscious of the gaze of "foreigners," suggest yet another perspective at work in *Mujŏng*. Yi Kwangsu, while comparing writers to doctors, labeled both tuberculosis germs and syphilis germs as the "enemy of the *minjok*." He either championed "reconstruction of the *minjok*," or emphasized writers' cultivation as a prerequisite for the "generation of a new *minjok*."[103] In addition, in works such as "*Honin e taehan kwan'gyŏn* (Personal views on marriage, 1917)," Yi discussed the "ethnonational losses" arising from "marriages without love." As such, combined with these other discussions, what *Mujŏng*'s free love raises is the perspective of eugenics, which mediates such things as the ethnonational struggle for survival, evolution, modern hygiene, and the medical system.

For example, "sacred love," one of the discourses of China's May Fourth Movement, was indivisible from eugenics thought. Here the new family model was one with one husband, one wife, and few children in a marriage based on love, a "marriage in accordance with eugenics." This was to carry out the "liberation of women as reproductive machines," while also being considered capable of "bequeathing to the future an improved and superior healthy nation by emphasizing quality over quantity." This shows that the discourse of the Confucian family was being converted to a discourse and culture of nation-state.[104] Indeed, love was something to "unite the family and strengthen the nation."[105] This brings to mind the position of Ellen Key, which was introduced by students returning from abroad.[106]

> The Women's Association Is Born. With Kim Suksŏng, Kim Chŏnghwa, Kim P'illye, Ch'oe Sukcha, and others as founding members, on April 30th a women's society meeting was held at the home of Kim Chŏngsik. They organized the group, named it the Women's Association, and elected Miss Kim P'illye as president. We sincerely hope that they engage not only in socializing but also provide future hope for females by creating what "Ellen Key" referred to as the life of an ideal woman.[107]

> Ellen Key, as I have previously stated, is a lover of life, an admirer of life. And she believed that the improvement and progress of life is naturally realized only during the enjoyment of the happiness of absolutely individual love. This is because she also believed that there are many cases in which the happiness of a separate individual love simultaneously attains the improvement of the race.[108]

As can be seen from the perspective of Ellen Key, who related the "happiness of love" to the "improvement of the race," free love (or rather the freedom to love) was ultimately a system to produce an excellent "race" generation after generation by improving the "strain" through things such as choosing one's spouse or hygiene policies. This was an individual and national project to survive without being culled in the competition of modern society and imperialism. That Yi Kwangsu wrote "today, when the competition among countries has reached maximum intensity, each country considers its geniuses as important as life itself"[109] is related to this. This also gives birth to the thought of Posan that "the fatso SS's brain must be immensely bad," while, as a result, "if we leave this social retard as he is, he will become a canker on humanity," and thus "we should rather encourage SS to commit suicide."[110] For instance, Article 1 of the "National Eugenics Law" enacted on July 1, 1941, makes clear the goal of "preventing the increase of those possessing a predisposition for undesirable genetic disorders, while simultaneously promoting the increase of those possessing healthy predispositions, and thereby contributing to the improvement of the national predisposition."[111] This eugenic perspective is at work in the appearance of characters such as SS or Hwang Sugŏn in Yi T'aejun's *"Talbam* (Moonlit night, 1933)." It is also the social context that causes Ch'ilsŏng to be described as follows.

> Taken aback, when I looked carefully a child it seemed I had seen somewhere before was panting heavily as he stared at me. His face was round and pale, the whites of his eyes were quite large, and the way his face beamed looked somehow strange.[112]

Chŏn Yŏngt'aek understood "geniuses to be of a single heredity,"[113] and the case was the same for "idiots." Ch'ilsŏng, who greeted people with an idiotic face and smile, "with his mouth open stupidly," or broke their fountain pens and watches, was born to a father who "fell seriously ill and eventually lost his life due to the lingering deleterious effects of wine and women." That is, Ch'ilsŏng's novelistic appearance has deep-rooted connections with the assertions of Hŏ Yŏngsuk, who would later become the wife of Yi Kwangsu, in her *"Hwaryupyŏngja ŭi honin ŭl kŭmhal il* (Forbidding the marriage of those with social diseases)," which appeared in the May 10, 1920, edition of the *Tonga ilbo*.

This ultimately means that the modern subject, in both his interior and exterior, deep-rootedly presumes the colony. For example, just as the biologist Elie Metchnikoff emphasized the improvement of daily living in order to ensure long life, coining the term "Orthobiosis,"[114] and, taking this even further, the Japanese colonial hygiene police system made lack of hygiene a crime,[115] all modern people must subjugate (overcome) the Ch'ilsŏng and SS inside of them. By brushing their teeth and getting vaccines, modern people cultivate the colony. The modern order, which puts the past tense (*haetta*) everywhere and inserts windowpanes into it, is repeated through the formation of the subject. This is one connotation of the "cultivation" to which Yi Kwangsu referred. Moreover, it is also one meaning of "hygiene." This suggests the principle of *minjok*. It is closer to a pharmakon than a tonic. This is because the body of a modern person (the *minjok*) endlessly sustains (medicine) itself by killing (poison) germs (the Other). This also allows *Mujŏng* to take notice of the numerous *kisaeng* who have been killed in a variety of ways. Kyehyang contracted syphilis, and Wŏrhwa committed suicide, while Sŏnhyŏng's mother, Puyong, became the lawful wife of Elder Kim. Kye Wŏrhyang becomes the student abroad, Yŏngch'ae. *Kisaeng* are an emblem of barbarity ("primitive love"), which must be overcome and eradicated by whatever means necessary. This is also related to the change in Sin Usŏn depicted below.

> From then on, Sin Usŏn completely stopped visiting the demimonde, and has devoted all his energies to cultivating himself and to his writing. His literary fame has spread throughout the land, while, moreover, his recently published *The Future of Korea* went into its fourth printing less than two weeks after it was first released. . . . Now he has doffed his famous straw hat, and sports a snow-white Panama, while under his nose has grown a fine Kaiser mustache.[116]

Thus, when viewed in relation to all the points above, Hyŏngsik's imagining himself as the "young master of a wealthy family" or a "luxurious and handsome young man" shares a common thread with planning an imperialist modern state by means of a eugenics perspective. That would also have been the consciousness that dominated the following passage from "*Chanyŏ chungsimnon*," a work that advocated a "new race."

> We must consider ourselves people without ancestors, people without parents (in certain respects), a new race descended from heaven onto our land on this very day, this very hour. Thus we must do our utmost in this life and then bequeath what we have gained to our healthy offspring who will come in future generations.[117]

"High collar" and free love were a kind of social Darwinist desire standing before the show window of the law of the jungle and survival of the fittest. Accordingly, the heartlessness of *Mujŏng* (*The Heartless*) applies not only to the fact that Hyŏngsik abandoned Yŏngch'ae. Despite its being replete with tales of love, the reason *Mujŏng* cannot help but be heartless to the end is that free love itself is heartless. Paradoxically, "heartless" is another name for free love.

HEARTLESS FASHION: IN LIEU OF A CONCLUSION

In the pages above, we considered "the fashion of *Mujŏng*." It was comprised of such things as high collar, men in Western suits, show windows, trains, private tutors, study abroad, free love, eugenics, money, and perspective—all sorts of costumes visible on the other side of the windowpane. What *Mujŏng* took notice of were the core scenes of modernity that generated distant places extremely closely. As a result, despite easily becoming the son-in-law of a rich family or gaining new knowledge through study abroad, the fashion of *Mujŏng* was essentially heartless. This is due to the fact the modern desires and methods themselves embodied in the work were facing glass. That fact would set into motion numerous differences and relations, as well as history. Such is the extent to which *Mujŏng* was a modern novel. Put another way, *Mujŏng* was fashionable.

NOTES

1. Kim Namch'ŏn, "*Ilsinsang ŭi chilli wa moral*" (Personal truth and morals), in *Chosŏn ilbo*, April 22, 1938, quoted from *Kim Namch'ŏn chŏnjip* 1, ed. Chŏng Houng (Seoul: Pagijŏng, 2000), 359.

2. Kim Namch'ŏn, "*Set'ae p'ungsok myosa kit'a*" (The description etc. of social conditions and customs), in ibid., 362–67.

3. Karatani Kōjin, "*Ek'ŭrit'uirŭ wa naesyŏnŏrijŭm* (Écriture and nationalism)," trans. Yi Kyŏnghun, in *Yumŏ rosŏ ŭi yumullon* (Seoul: Munhwa kwahaksa, 2002), 61–84.

4. Yi Kwangsu, *Mujŏng* (*The Heartless*) (Seoul: Sinmun'gwan, 1918), 1.

*All ensuing quotations from *Mujŏng* will simply list a page or installment number following the quoted passage.

5. *Mujŏng* was first serialized in 126 separate installments in the daily *Maeil sinbo*. For very brief quotations, the installment number is often provided in lieu of an exact page number. This will also be helpful to researchers due to the sheer number of different versions of *Mujŏng*; their paginations are all different, but the installment numbers remain consistent.—Trans.

6. Kim Kirim, "*Pom ŭn chŏnbo to an ch'igo* (Spring, without sending so much as a telegram)," in *T'aeyang ŭi p'ungsok* (Seoul: Hagyesa: 1939), 63.

7. *Hisashi-gami*, literally meaning "eaves-hair" for the way it projected outward, was a Meiji Japan version of a Western hairstyle. After the actress Kawakami Sadayakko (1872–1946) began sporting it in 1904, it soon became popular among schoolgirls in both Japan and Korea. In *Mujŏng*, Yi does not translate but merely transliterates the Japanese term into Korean.—Trans.

8. Yi Kwangsu, *Mujŏng*, 2.

9. Ch'oe Namsŏn, *Kyŏngbu ch'yŏlto norae* (Song of the Seoul-Busan railway) (Seoul: Sinmungwan, 1908), 1.

10. Kim Tongin, "*Yakhanja ŭi sŭlp'ŭm* (Sadness of the weak)," in *Ch'angjo*, Volume 1, February 1919, 69.

11. Kim Tongin, "*Maŭm i yŏt'ŭn chayŏ* (Oh, ye with faint hearts)," *Ch'angjo*, Volume 3, December 1919, 40.

12. Yi Kwangsu, *Mujŏng*, 8.

13. Yi Injik, *Hyŏl ŭi nu* (*Tears of blood*) in *Kaehwagi sosŏl* (Seoul: T'aegŭk ch'ulpansa, 1985), 175. The English translation is taken from *Tears of Blood*, trans. W. E. Skillend, in *Korean Classical Literature: An Anthology*, ed. Chung Chong-wha (London: Keegan Paul International, 1989), 218.

14. Chŏn Yŏngt'aek, "*Ch'ŏnch'i? ch'ŏnjae?* (Idiot? genius?)," in *Ch'angjo*, Volume 2, March 1919, 23.

15. Yu Kilchun, *Sŏyu kyŏnmun* (*Things seen and heard in the west*) (Tokyo: Kōjyunsha, 1895), 419.

16. Yŏm Sangsŏp, "*P'yobonsil ŭi ch'ŏnggaeguri* (Green frog of the specimen room)," in *Yŏm Sangsŏp chŏnjip* 9 (Seoul: Minŭmsa, 1987), 19.

17. No Chayŏng, "*Insaeng t'ŭkkŭp* (Life special express)," in *Sinmun yŏnjae sosŏl chŏnjip* 4 (Seoul: Kip'ŭnsaem, 1999), 316.

18. Kim Tongin, "*Маɯм i yŏt'ŭn chayŏ*," 25.

19. Kim Yŏp, "*Kangho esŏ Tongjŏngho kkaji* (From Edo to Dongting Lake)," in *Ch'angjo*, Volume 3, December 1919, 67.

20. Wolfgang Schivelbusch, *The Railway Journey: The Industrialization and Perception of Time and Space in the 19th Century* (Berkeley: The University of California Press, 1986), 63.

This is a translation into English of the 1977 German original: *Geschichte der Eisenbahnreise*. It appears to have been translated by the author, as no separate translator is listed. The quotation in the Korean version was taken from the following translation: *Ch'ŏlto yŏhaeng ŭi yŏksa*, trans. Pak Chinhŭi (Seoul: Kungni, 1999), 85.—Trans.

21. Cho Ilchae, Changhanmong (A long and sorrowful dream), in Han'guk sinsosŏl chŏnjip (Seoul: Ŭryu munhwasa, 1968), 67.

22. Sim Hun, "*Yŏngwŏn ŭi miso* (Eternal smile)," in *Han'guk munhak chŏnjip* 17 (Seoul: Minjung sŏgwan, 1959), 390.

23. The lines are taken from the poems "*Yurich'ang* 1" (Windowpane 1) and "*Yurich'ang* 2" (Windowpane 2), respectively. See Chŏng Chiyong, *Chŏng Chiyong chŏnjip* 1 (Seoul: Minŭmsa, 1988), 73, 85.

24. This also comes from "*Yurich'ang* 2."

25. Yi Sang, "*Hyuŏp kwa sajŏng* (Closures and circumstances)," in *Yi Sang munhak chŏnjip* 2, ed. Kim Yunsik (Seoul: Munhak sasangsa, 1991), 154.

26. This again brings to mind the perspective of Walter Benjamin, mentioned in chapter 1, who counterposed the surgeon, who at the decisive moment abandons treating the patient as human, and the cameraman.

27. Cho Chunghwan, Changhanmong (A long and sorrowful dream), in Han'guk sinsosŏl chŏnjip 9 (Seoul: Ŭryu munhwasa, 1968), 97.

28. Ozaki Kōyō, *Konjiki yasha* (*The Gold Demon* [*Kŭmsaek yach'a*]), trans. Sŏ Sŏgyŏn (Seoul: Pŏmusa, 1992), 106.

29. Yi Sang, "*Ijō na kagyaku hannō* (A strange reversible reaction)," in *Chosen to kenchiku*, July 1931, 15.

30. Yi Kwangsu, *Mujŏng*, 431.

31. Ibid., 532.

32. Kim Tongin, "*Chosŏn kŭndae sosŏlgo* (A study of modern Korean fiction)," in *Kim Tongin chŏnjip* 16 (Seoul: Chosŏn ilbosa), 30.

33. Georg Lukacs, *The Theory of the Novel*, trans. Anna Bostock (Cambridge: The MIT Press, 1987), 29.

34. The impoverished rickshaw man Kim Ch'ŏmji is the protagonist of Hyŏn Chin'gŏn's ironically titled short story "*Unsu choŭn nal* (A lucky day, 1924)," while Master Yun is the portly, avaricious protagonist of Ch'ae Mansik's satirical novel *T'aep'yŏng ch'ŏnha* (*Peace under heaven*, 1937). In the opening scene of the latter work, following a long and arduous ride, Master Yun bilks a poor rickshaw man out of his fare.—Trans.

35. On the trains at this time, "second class" did not possess any of the pejorative connotations it has today in terms such as "second class citizen." Rather, it was closer to "business class" on today's airplanes: below first class, but still quite luxurious.—Trans.

36. The gates marked the boundaries of the cities proper. Outside and beyond the gates represent geographical distinctions that translated into markers of social difference in similar ways to the train cars above.—Trans.

37. Kim Namch'ŏn, *Sarang ŭi sujokkwan* (*Aquarium of love*) (Seoul: Inmunsa, 1940), 341.

38. Yi Kwangsu, *Mujŏng*, 7.

39. Nihon fūzokusi gakkai, *Nihon fūzokusi jiten* (Dictionary of the history of Japanese customs) (Tokyo: Kōbundō. 1980), 501.

40. Yi Kwangsu, "*Tonggyŏng chapsin* (Miscellaneous correspondence from Tokyo)," in *Yi Kwangsu chŏnjip* 17 (Seoul: Samjungdang, 1962), 476.

41. Kim Tongin, "*P'igo* (The defendant)," in *Kim Tongin chŏnjip* 1 (Seoul: Chosŏn ilbosa, 1987), 294.

42. Yi Kwangsu, *Mujŏng*, 268.

43. Ibid., 18.

44. Ibid., 56.

45. An Hoenam, "*Kich'a* (The train)," in *An Hoenam tanp'yŏnjip* (Seoul: Hagyesa, 1939), 38–39.

46. Kim Tongin, "*Sup'yŏngsŏn nŏmŏro* (Over the horizon)," in *Kim Tongin chŏnjip* 7 (Seoul: Chosŏn ilbosa, 1988), 193.

47. An Hoenam, "*Kich'a*," 37.

48. Ch'ae Mansik, "*Kŭm ŭi chŏngyŏl* (The passion of gold)," in *Ch'ae Mansik chŏnjip* 3 (Seoul: Ch'angjak kwa pip'yŏngsa, 1987), 315.

49. The italicized Korean words mean traditional Korean skirt, blouse, and socks, respectively. They were left in Korean in order to approximate the difference felt by the characters themselves when viewing/wearing them.—Trans.

50. Kim Namch'ŏn, *Sarang ŭi sujokkwan*, 400.

51. Kim Tongin, "*Sigol Hwang sŏbang* (Country Mr. Hwang)," in *Kim Tongin chŏnjip* 1 (Seoul: Chosŏn ilbosa, 1987), 393.

52. Yŏm Sangsŏp, *Mansejŏn* (On the eve of the uprising), in *Yŏm Sangsŏp chŏnjip 1* (Seoul: Minŭmsa, 1987, 74.

Turumagi is a traditional Korean men's overcoat.—Trans.

53. Yŏm, *Mansejŏn*, 77–78.

Manggŭn is a variation in this dialogue of *manggŏn*, a traditional headband woven from horsehair and used to tie up Korean men's traditionally long hair into a topknot. *Yobo* is a derogatory Japanese term for Koreans.—Trans.

54. The original sentence includes a variety of traditional Korean garments that were already becoming less common on the trains of the 1920s. In order to preserve the effect of the original sentence, these have been transliterated. The italicized Korean words mean an overcoat, a jacket, cotton wrappings in place of socks, and shoes of plaited rice straw, respectively.—Trans.

55. Hyŏn Chin'gŏn, "*Kohyang* (Hometown)," in *Han'guk sosŏl munhak taegye* 7 (Seoul: Tusan donga, 1997), 508.

56. Nicolai V. Gogol, "The Overcoat," in *The Overcoat and Other Tales of Good and Evil*, trans. David Magarshack (New York: W. W. Norton, 1957), 237.

57. Yi Kwangsu, *Mujŏng*, 61–62.

58. Yi, *Mujŏng*, 193.

59. Yi Injik, *Hyŏl ŭi nu*, 164.

60. Pang In'gŭn, "*Nun onŭn pam* (A snowy evening)," in *Ch'angjo*, Volume 6, May 1920, 62.

61. In the original, Yi uses "*p'ŭraidŭ*," a transliteration of the English word.—Trans.

62. Yi Kwangsu, "*Haech'amwi rosŏ* (To Vladivostok)," in *Ch'ŏngch'ŭn*, Volume 6, March 1915, 79.

63. Yi Sang, "*Tonghae* (Child's skeleton)," in *Yi Sang munhak chŏnjip* 2, ed. Kim Yunsik (Seoul: Munhak sasangsa, 1991), 259.

64. Yi Kwangsu, *Mujŏng*, 395.

65. Yi Kwangsu, "*Kich'a* (Train)," in *Chosŏn mundan*, March 1925, 99.

66. Yi Kwangsu, "*Tonggyŏng chapsin*," 488.

67. Ibid., 487–88.

68. Yi Injik, *Hyŏl ŭi nu*, 179. The scene depicted here does not appear in Skillend's abridged translation.—Trans.

69. Chŏn Yŏngt'aek, "*Hyesŏn ŭi sa* (The death of Hyesŏn)," in *Ch'angjo*, February 1919, 52.

70. Kim Namch'ŏn, *Sarang ŭi sujokkwan*, 183–84.

71. Yŏm Sangsŏp's "*Ttong p'ari wa kŭ ŭi anhae* (Shit fly and his wife)," in *Yŏm Sangsŏp chŏnjip* 9 (Seoul: Minŭmsa, 1987), 318.

72. An Hoenam, "*Kigye* (Machine)," in *An Hoenam tanp'yŏnjip* (Seoul: Hagyesa, 1939), 133.

73. Im Hwa "*Negŏri ŭi Suni* (Suni at the crossroads)," in *Hyŏnhaet'an* (Seoul: Tonggwangdang sŏjŏm, 1939), 6.

74. The word in the original is *chŏnhyangja* (轉向者, Jp. *tenkosha*), which was used at the time specifically to refer to those former Marxists who had renounced their beliefs, often under government coercion.—Trans.

75. Han Sŏrya, "*Inyŏng* (Mire)," in *Munjang*, May 1939, 25.

76. Yi Kwangsu, *Mujŏng*, 177.

77. Ibid., 23.

78. Yi Kiyŏng, "*Oegyowŏn kwa chŏndo puin* (The salesman and the missionary woman)," in *Minch'on* (Seoul: Kŏnsŏl ch'ulp'ansa, 1946), 83.

79. A horsehair skullcap formerly worn by officials under their hats.—Trans.

80. Yi Kwangsu, *Mujŏng*, 51.

81. Ibid., 117.

82. Ibid., 610.

83. Ibid., 119.

84. Kim Yunsik, *Yŏm Sangsŏp yŏn'gu* (*A study of Yŏm Sangsŏp*) (Seoul: Sŏul taehakkyo ch'ulp'anbu, 1989), 248–49.

85. Matsuo Takayoshi, "*Yoshino Sakujō to Chōsen* (Yoshino Sakujō and Korea)," in *Chōsenshi kenkyūkai ronbunsyū*, Volume 35, October 1997, 8.

86. Ch'oe Sŭngman, *Na ŭi hoegorok* (*My memoirs*) (Inchŏn: Inha taehakkyo ch'ulp'anbu, 1985), 61–62.

87. Yi Kwangsu, *Mujŏng*, 535.

88. Ibid., 14.

89. Ibid., 129.

90. Ibid., 186.

91. Ibid., 303–04.

92. Ibid., 432–34.

93. Ibid., 507–08.

94. Kim Namch'ŏn, *Sarang ŭi sujokkwan*, 242.

95. Kim Namch'ŏn, "*T ilbo sa* (The T daily newspaper company)," in *Inmun p'yŏngnon*, November 1939, 148–49.

96. Although somewhat difficult to reproduce in translation, the original sentence deftly incorporates the titles of two of Yi's works, the novel *Chaesaeng* (*Rebirth*, 1924) and the essay "*Chanyŏ chungsimnon*" (On the primacy of children, 1918).—Trans.

97. Yi Kwangsu, *Mujŏng*, 477–78.

98. Yun Kwangho is the eponymous protagonist of Yi Kwangsu's 1917 short story "Yun Kwangho." He is a model student at "K University" in Tokyo. He confesses his love to a fellow student known only as "P," but it goes unrequited. He falls into depression and finally commits suicide. It is only at the work's close, when his friend Chunwŏn (Yi Kwangsu's pen name) writes a poem at his grave, that we find out P is a man.

99. Yi Kwangsu, *Mujŏng*, 578.

100. Ibid., 621.

101. Ibid., 606.

102. Yi Kwangsu, "*Sonyŏn ege* (To the boys)," in *Yi Kwangsu chŏnjip* 17 (Seoul: Samjungdang, 1962, 238.

103. See Yi's essays "*Minjok kaejoron* (On national reconstruction)," in *Kaebyŏk* 23, May 1922, 18–72, and "*Munsa wa suyang* (The writer and cultivation)," in *Ch'angjo*, 8, January 1921, 9–18.

104. Sakamoto Hiroko, *Renai shinsei to minzoku kairyō no 'kagaku'* (Sacred love and the 'science' of improving the *minzoku*)," in *Shisō*, December, 1998, 4–34.

105. Yanabu Akira, Honyakugo seiritsu jijyō (Circustances of establishing translated language) (Tokyo: Iwanami shoten, 1998), 98.

106. For more on this, see Ku Inmo, "Mujŏng *kwa usaenghakchŏk yŏnaeron* (*Mujŏng* and the eugenics theory of love)," in *Pigyo munhak*, Volume 28, 2002, 179–98.

107. "*Uri sosik* (Our news)," in *Hak chi kwang*, Volume 5, May 1915, 64.

108. No Chayŏng, "*Yŏsŏng undong ŭi cheil inja* Ellen K'ei (Ellen Key, the leader of the women's movement)," in *Kaebyŏk*, February 1921, 51.

109. Yi Kwangsu, "*Ch'ŏnjaeya! ch'ŏnjaeya!* (Oh, genius! oh, genius!)," in *Yi Kwangsu chŏnjip* 17 (Seoul: Samjungdang, 1962), 51.

110. Yi Sang, "*Hyuŏp kwa sajŏng*," 149–63.

111. Cho Hyŏnggŭn, et al., *Kŭndae chuch'e wa singminji kyuyul kwŏllyŏk* (The modern subject and colonial disciplinary power) (Seoul: Munhwa kwahaksa, 1997), 213–14.

112. Chŏn Yŏngt'aek, "*Ch'ŏnch'i? ch'ŏnjae?*," 24.

113. Chŏn Yŏngt'aek, "*Togŏrok* (Record of a monologue)," in *Hak chi kwang*, Volume 10, May 1916, 39.

114. Rene Dubois, *The Mirage of Health; Utopias, Progress, and Biological Change* (New Brunswick: Rutgers University Press, 1987 [first published in 1959 by Harpers & Brothers, New York]), 168.

115. Cho Hyŏnggŭn, et al., *Kŭndae chuch'e wa singminji kyuyul kwŏllyŏk*, 200–05.

116. Yi Kwangsu, *Mujŏng*, 620.

117. Yi Kwangsu, "*Chanyŏ chungsimnon* (On the primacy of children)," in *Ch'ŏngch'un*, Volume 15, September 1918, 17.

Chapter 5

Barbarian of the Laboratory

SUICIDE AND INVENTION

Yi Kwangsu's *Kaech'ŏkcha* (*The pioneer*, 1917–1918) ends with the suicide of Kim Sŏngsun. Not unlike the *kisaeng* Hwasŏn in Kim Tongin's short story "*Nun ŭl kyŏu ttŭl ttae* (When eyes barely open, 1923)," who dies after ingesting the rat poison *Neko irazu* (cat not necessary), Sŏngsun, the younger sister of the chemist Kim Sŏngjae, commits suicide with "sulfuric acid" from her brother's laboratory.

In terms of ending a fictional work with the suicide of a female protagonist, Chŏn Yŏngt'aek's "*Hyesŏn ŭi sa* (The death of Hyesŏn, 1919)" is also the same. If Sŏngsun commits suicide due to an unsuccessful love affair with her brother's friend Min, Hyesŏn leaps from the bridge over the Han River owing to her student-abroad husband's love affair with another woman.

Of course, a protagonist's attempting suicide over failed love is also seen in Yi Kwangsu's Japanese-language short story "*Aika* (Is it love?, 1909)." This is not a tale of love between members of the opposite sex, but rather of the pubescent homoerotic feelings that a Korean male student, Mun'gil, harbors for a Japanese classmate, Misao. Eventually wounded by the Misao's coldness, Mun'gil attempts to kill himself on the railroad tracks. For reasons completely different from those in the Im Hwa poem "*Chido* (Map, 1937)"—"Cutting the telegraph lines and lying atop the tracks / The sad superstitions of grownups of old"—Mun'gil lays his head upon the rails and waits for a train to come.

Ah, I want to die. I no longer want to be in this world. The Tamagawa streetcar rails. I see them. Still an early eleven o'clock—the streetcars have already

113

stopped. Fine, there are trains. Once the sound of a train comes rattling by, I will already be gone from this world.

    . . .

He hurried his steps toward the Shibuya railroad crossing. Amidst the dark, a sharp steam whistle sounded. Things are working out, he thought, but no sooner had he begun to run than a black figure appeared and stopped his progress. This is serious. Even when it's time to die ghosts follow me around to interfere. The train indifferently rumbled past. He went along the train tracks for about another six yards then lay his head upon the east-facing rail. While waiting for the next train to come, wondering whether it was coming now or later, he stared up at the starlight flowing out from between the clouds. Ah, this is my last. . . . Why isn't the train coming? Why doesn't it quickly come and crush this head of mine? Hot tears flowed without end.[1]

The above quotation is interesting in that Mun'gil's suicide is continually put off due to the circumstances of the streetcars and the trains. Mun'gil, owing to the close of operations of the streetcar and the control of the railroad crossing, is late for his own suicide. As a result, he is left waiting for "the next train" while wondering "Why isn't the train coming?" This brings to mind Yi Injik's *Hyŏl ui nu* (*Tears of blood*, 1906) in which Ongnyŏn's mother attempted suicide by throwing herself into the Taedong River. Separated from her family, she lamented "If I live on alone, my whole life will be tribulation. If I were to die, I would not know this tribulation"[2] before jumping into the water. Regrettably, however, things turned out as below.

If she had jumped from a high bank, whether the water had been deep or shallow, she could hardly have survived, but she had jumped into the water from a sandbank where the water was no more than a foot or two deep. With the water being so shallow, she had not drowned. But since her purpose in throwing herself in had been to kill herself, she remained determined to die even though the water was shallow. She had lain in the water, still alive, and had come floating down until she had been rescued by the men in the boat.[3]

Just as the streetcars or trains that would "crush" Mun'gil's head had to run according to schedules to accomplish his suicide, Ongnyŏn's mother required deep water or a "high bank." She lacks, however, the planning of suicide and the investigation of its methods expressed in works such as "*Hyesŏn ŭi sa*": "In the newspaper the other day it said someone drowned in the Han River, so I went out on a stroll with some friends. I wanted to see if there were any good places to die."[4] Perhaps because her motivation for suicide was not the failure of a love affair but rather the separation of a traditional family, from the outset she had no information regarding the times at which streetcars or trains passed, and not even a "Han River Footbridge" or "Han River Train Bridge" was provided for her. Of course, it is natural that Ongnyŏn's mother, who lived in P'yŏngyang during the Sino-Japanese War (1894–1895), knew nothing of the bridges in Seoul that fiction called the "Han River Rail Bridge of life,"[5] and poems depicted as follows.

"Stop" . . .
This is the final destination at the harbor.
At times ownerless hats hang from the balustrades
"Good-bye to life," in the wind
They flutter.
Thus, at the base of the piles, for the young women
Lies a huge dustpan for tears.[6]
That's right. I mean the Han River Rail Bridge. Why isn't there a sign posted saying "*Chotto matte kudasai*"? I mean over there.[7]

As a result, Ongnyŏn's mother's impulsive and unplanned suicide attempt lies in sharp contrast to Yi Sang who "thought about suicide every time I washed my face over a period of ten long years," "recited the names of all types of popular medicines," or harkened back to venues such as the "footbridge, electricity substation, rooftop of the Hwasin Department Store, Seoul-Wŏnsan train line."[8] Yi Sang complained that in the remote village of Sŏngch'ŏn, where "buses" don't even come, he was unable to find so much as "a clue of suicide." Modern suicide is usually achieved through things like the chemical reactions of pharmaceuticals, the speed, weight, and arrival time of trains, or the height and depth of bridges over the Han River and tall buildings. No matter how much hot tears flow without end, as long as the train doesn't come, Mun'gil has no way to die. The phrase "even though I want to die, I am in a situation where I cannot die because I have no money to buy arsenic"[9] is actually quite convincing.

The sulfuric acid drunk by Sŏngsun, however, set the trend for a genealogy of committing suicide by taking poison that went on to include the "opium prepared in Harbin" that R and his female student (wife) intended to take in Yi Kwangsu's *Yujŏng* (Kindheartedness, 1933), the thirty-six tablets of Allonal taken by Songgun in Yi Sang's "*Hwansigi* (Phantom illusion, 1936)," the twenty Calmotin pills Ch'un'gyŏng swallowed in Yŏm Sangsŏp's *Isim* (Two hearts, 1928), and the sixty Phenobarbitol and five Secobarbitol sodium that Pak Unsam popped into his mouth in Kim Tongni's "*Miltawŏn sidae* (The age of the sweet tea garden, 1933)." Accordingly, suicide is replete with modern meanings. This is because the information implicit in various pharmaceuticals, trains, bridges, tall buildings as well as the methods of suicide (ingesting poison, jumping from high places, lying atop rails, and, going even further, the "six gun" that Ch'oe Sŏk considered in Yi Kwangsu's *Yujŏng*) all derive from society's modern constitution and the products thereof. In Yi Sang's "*Hyuŏp kwa sajŏng* (Closures and circumstances, 1932)," Posan defines "the fatso SS," who does not improve his brain, as a "social retard," and considers recommending suicide. This way of thinking and also the ideology of suicide, which so often concluded failure in free love with death, connote a modern significance related to things such as hygiene or private ownership of existence (the individual). Against the backdrop of a concept of hygiene as defending 'the national borders of the body' from germs, suicide bears witness to modern individual entities as bodies. In fact, Yi Kwangsu's *Kaech'ŏkcha* poses the questions "Does Sŏngsun belong to her mother and elder brother? Or does Sŏngsun belong to herself?" while also predicting that "a large lawsuit will be brought to decide the matter of Sŏngsun's ownership."[10] In regard to this, Sŏngsun makes the following resolution.

> Doing things for oneself is doing things for the new era one represents, so the new era that will be endlessly long and the descendants who will endlessly flourish in the future are more important than the parents. No, they are more important than the past in its entirety. The morals that consider children the possessions of parents will never desirable to teach in the new era. As Min said, in place of the old era centered on parents and the past, we must establish a new era centered on children and on the future. In order to do so, we must first destroy the old era, and in order to destroy it we need people, and in order for there to be people, there must be a single person who will destroy it. As Min said, we must become that first person. We must become the first bullet and the first sacrifice in a large war. (*Kaech'ŏkcha*, 404–5)

These thoughts, which bring to mind Yi's essay "*Chanyŏ chungsimnon* (On the primacy of children, 1918)," match well with the fact that the sulfuric acid Sŏngsun took came from a "chemistry laboratory" that dreamed of new inventions. Sŏngsun overcomes the state of "uncertainty regarding the judgment that I am solely my possession," and, through suicide, rejects the marriage her mother and brother demand. Accordingly, Sŏngsun's suicide represents the "first sacrifice" in the fight against the old era that emphasizes the traditional values embodied in the dictum from the *Book of Filial Duty*: "Our bodies—to every hair and bit of skin—are received by us from our parents, and we must not presume to injure or wound them. This is the beginning of filial piety."[11] Ultimately, her suicide is an act equivalent to the experiments of Sŏngjae, who attempts to create new substances by applying scientific analysis and operations to nature. For instance, Sŏngjae, standing before his younger sister's corpse, while thinking about "coating the dead body with chemicals and making a mummy that would never decompose," never fails to maintain the attitude befitting a chemist. Not to be outdone by her older brother, however, Sŏngsun took her hypothesis, centered upon rational intellect and individual will, that she was a self-possessive modern subject and verified it through suicide and chemical compounds. That is to say, suicide was the experiment with which Sŏngsun simultaneously proved the chemical reactions of compounds and the modern subject. In that sense, Sŏngsun too belongs to the genealogy of *Mujŏng*'s Yi Hyŏngsik who exclaimed, "More than anything else, to the people of Korea we must first give science." Beginning with Yu Kilchun, who emphasized the meaning of chemistry as modern knowledge, and used water as an example in discussing the "analysis" and "combining" of elements,[12] the genealogy of science and experiment was formed and continued on to the making of "XX cakes" in the Kim Tongin short story *"K paksa ŭi yŏn'gu* (Dr. K's research, 1929)."

I'm relying on what the doctor said, but inside shit there are "indigestible substances" like fiber, "connective tissue," horn, the non-essential parts of "intestinal canal secretions," that is to say cholaic acid, D-serine, and gallbladder mucin, in addition to which there are also products of decomposition such as skatole, indole, and fatty acids, together with which there are still a large amount of casein and starch and fats left over. He said that it differs depending on the person and on time, but that somewhere between 30 and 70 percent of the digestible substances remain intact and just come out the anus. And nobody pays any attention to those nutrients that just remain in the feces so that they wastefully rot away, but if there were only some method by which they could be extracted, wouldn't it be great news for humanity now threatened by the problem of feeding itself? So I think he said that after much research he discovered a method, something like the complete combustion of coal, so he has planned out and succeeded in the complete digestion of nutrients. In short, he analyzed feces, got out the 30 or 70 percent of nutrients still remaining, and is proposing that we re-eat them.[13]

Just like Dr. K, Sŏngsun is a modern person who carries out "analysis" and "synthesis." With "extremely cold eyes," she "dissects one by one each line of Min's face, each point, his shoulders and chest, legs, arms, hands, and every other part, then she arranges each part to remake the body, after which she closely inspects the whole for balance, *symmetry*, color, and *harmony*"[14] (*Kaech'ŏkcha*, 402). This shares a common thread with both the perspectival point of view of Min, a Western painter who believes "his learning of art is intended to give one more blessed eye to the Korean people," and with the activities of the "surveyors from the Land Research Bureau" (*Kaech'ŏkcha*, 415).

Much like the "dissection" and "investigation" carried out by Sŏngsun, suicide is a historical act that wholly mediates the modern individual and the ideology of free love, as well as the scientific method and experimental spirit. This is the reason Sŏngsun stipulates "what I am intending to do now is also a kind of adventure," while asserting "our strength is our destiny." Thus, the novel replaces the failure of Sŏngjae's experiments with the success of Sŏngsun's suicide. As a result, the two passages below share a deep resonance.

> "Science! Science!" screamed Hyŏnsik alone as he returned to the inn and sat down. The three young women looked at Hyŏngsik.
> "To the people of Korea, more than anything else, we must first give science. We must give knowledge."[15]
> "Sŏngsun, pull yourself together," he said.
> Sŏngsun again softly closed her eyes and bowed her head. Then, as if babbling, said, "Death! Death!" (*Kaech'ŏkcha*, 466)

Sŏngsun's suicide was a sort of scientific attempt. It was also a form of pathetic will to convince herself and others that her relationship with Min was "sacred" free love. (When viewed in this way, Sŏngsun's suicide could also be compared with Phaedra's disingenuous attempt to convince others of her innocence.) What she did was not a "grave crime immediately punishable by death" (*Kaech'ŏkcha*, 449), but rather "love," which "carried out a revolution of human spirit and body," and "pioneered a new stage in taste and imagination." It was "*love*," which "makes heroes and worthies," and also "unites the family and strengthens the nation."[16] In short, Sŏngsun conceptualized free love while thinking "After her flesh had ceased to exist, that love alone would spring forth and live on for ever and ever" (*Kaech'ŏkcha*, 454).

Due to the above, Sŏngsun stands in complete opposition to the *kisaeng* Suhyang who asks "What are you doing heating up that glass container?" Sŏngsun is close to the "ideal woman" or "self-satisfied woman" spoken of by Na Hyesŏk.[17] Sŏngsun's suicide, which caused Sŏngjae to feel that she "wasn't the young child he had imagined thus far," was a kind of invention realized in the gigantic laboratory known as modern society. Her suicide also gave birth to the modern individual and the modern woman (who negates the sacrifice of Sim Ch'ŏng), while it ideologized and institutionalized free love. This is the true significance of the suicide pioneered by Sŏngsun in place of Sŏngjae's attempts at invention. In fact, in 1916, reporting Fujimura Misao's, a student of Natsume Sōseki's, leaping to his death from the Kegon Falls in Nikko on May 22, 1903,[18] as well as other accounts of the suicides of students at Tokyo's First High School, Yi Kwangsu mentioned as below.[19]

In Korea, those who commit suicide are rare, but we should not pride ourselves on this. We should feel ashamed of the low level of thought, since in those inferior categories below human there is no anguish, no suicide.[20]

ONTOLOGY OF THE CLOCK

Yet another core of *Kaech'ŏkcha* is the issue of modern time. In this regard, the scene below is quite impressive.

The hour hand of the octagonal clock was between four and five, and the minute hand was between six and seven. Sŏngsun thought to herself, "It's five minutes past four-thirty." Four-thirty was the time at which Sŏngjae stopped his experiments and for thirty minutes took a stroll or talked with Sŏngsun; for the past three years this had been an unwavering family rule. If four-thirty passed, Sŏngsun habitually visited the laboratory, and, if Sŏngjae still didn't realize the time, she softly tapped on his left shoulder with the index finger of her right hand saying, "*Oppa*, ten minutes have passed." Then Sŏngjae would turn his head and look at Sŏngsun for a moment, after which he would look at the octagonal clock, put up the test tube, put out the alcohol lamp, get up from his chair, and take Sŏngsun's hand saying, "Ah, another day with no results." Following that he would either say, "I'm going to take a stroll. Give me my hat," or, if he didn't feel like a stroll, "Bring that chair over here and take a seat," and then perhaps have a talk with Sŏngsun. When the octagonal clock chimed five times, he would say, "Well then, let's have dinner," and follow Sŏngsun to enter the living room he had left at eight in the morning for the first time in nine hours. (*Kaech'ŏkcha*, 323)

As evident in the quotation above, the actions and lives of this *oppa* and younger sister completely follow the time of the clock. In addition, the line "The ability of Sŏngsun, who was born to the chiming of the clock, to assimilate the new thought was that much greater than that of Sŏngjae, who was born to the chiming of the Chongno curfew bell,"[21] goes so far as to identify the clock with "the new thought" (*Kaech'ŏkcha*, 388). In that regard, they are the admirable successors of the punctual Kim Kwanil in Yi Injik's *Moranbong* (*Peony peak*, 1913). These sorts of aspects arise persistently throughout the entirety of the novel. Below is only a portion of the numerous examples that can be given.

(1) Around eight o'clock her *oppa* leaves and she cleans his room. After sitting for some time, when the hour hand of the octagonal wooden clock points to nine, she begins to wonder where Min is. At around one or two

in the afternoon, after she sees Min off at the front gate, she has thoughts
that are once a bit sad and a bit lonely. (*Kaech'ŏkcha*, 371)

(2) The store across the street that sells side dishes closed at eight sharp,
and from inside could be heard the sound of laughter and chatter.
(*Kaech'ŏkcha*, 376)

(3) My M! Do I miss M this much? He was here earlier, and has been
gone for no more than three hours, but it feels like it's been ten years.
(*Kaech'ŏkcha*, 382)

(4) The engagement of Pyŏn and Sŏngsun was concluded. Her mother,
Sŏngjae, and Pyŏn, these three people sat together in Sŏngjae's room,
and the outcome was reached in only an hour. (*Kaech'ŏkcha*, 387)

(5) When he thought "I will meet face to face with Sŏngsun and discuss
everything," and looked at the clock, the door opened and Sŏngsun's face
appeared. (*Kaech'ŏkcha*, 426)

(6) The time when Sŏngsun took out a small pocket watch and looked at it
saying, "'Now I must go,'" then stood up, barely managed to screw up
her courage, and shook his hand. (*Kaech'ŏkcha*, 425)

(7) She waited a full ten minutes. It was already nine-forty! The clock struck
ten. (*Kaech'ŏkcha*, 452)

(8) Sŏngjae returned home in disappointment after eleven o'clock, sat down
without a word beside his mother's pillow, when suddenly the sound of
screaming was heard outside the main gate. (*Kaech'ŏkcha*, 458)

Clock time, along with modern surveying, through the neutralization and
demystification of time and space, is a powerful system that also measures
and plans time and space. This in turn implies the constitutive principle of
Kaech'ŏkcha. Its basic form is to make timetables that, through the "seg-
mentation of time," "force specific activities or actions to correspond to
segmented time."[22] This making of timetables is also observed without
exception in relation to suicide as in the following sentences: "I drank this.
I drank a whole bowlful. Now I won't last another hour" (*Kaech'ŏkcha*,
459); "Mother, my life now has no more than a few tens of minutes left!"
(*Kaech'ŏkcha*, 461); and "Even her mother, who had said let's go in front of
your father's grave and die together, was using any means necessary to try
to extend Sŏngsun's life even one minute longer" (*Kaech'ŏkcha*, 464). Or
rather it is precisely suicide that powerfully actualizes this making of timetables. Not only does it most impressively and actively dramatize the material
and temporal inevitability of death at work in human existence but also, by
capturing it within the time plan of the person committing suicide, converts
it into something artificial.

As a result of the above, the suicides or deaths that appear in modern fiction, rather than being connected to the next world or reincarnation, usually

mean the complete end of both the story and of life. By way of comparison, plans are comprised of a beginning, a middle, and an end. And, in this respect, they genuinely express the disposability of modern life. (This is also related to the novelistic form of *Kaech'ŏkcha* in which Sŏngsun's death coincides with the end of the work.) A related point of view is presented in the following scene.

> "Well, after viewing that spectacle, it was as if he weren't alive. After applying artificial resuscitation for some time but seeing it was ineffective, I got up and softly placed my hand on my chest—. To see if my heart was still beating."
> "And was it still beating?"
> It was Pyŏn's question.
> "Yeah, it was still beating."
> "So were you relieved?"
> "How could I be relieved? How long will this keep on beating, won't it stop right now . . . like when you drop a watch on the ground and it just stops? What if it stops like that? And what will happen after that? Whether there is another world or we just fall down dead. . . . I had such thoughts. And then my body would begin to pour sweat." (*Kaech'ŏkcha*, 352)

This disposable life, together with the individual exclusivity of space occupation and the anatomical completion of the structure of the human body, takes a single existence and makes it into a spatiotemporal unit. A modern being, which possesses autonomous physical organs, does not (should not) overlap with other beings (parents, the heavens, spirits, parasites, germs, viruses, etc.), while simultaneously enduring only for a fixed period, and only one time. Like a train that moves linearly from departure to arrival, it is composed of a start and a finish. Each individual life is but a single train journey that runs along only one track. This is the reason Sŏngsun once criticized her friends Myŏngun, Sŏn'gyŏng, Kyŏngun, and Sunmyŏng, and in the past "wore a Swiss watch and summoned them at any hour or minute, day or night" (*Kaech'ŏkcha*, 421), but now likens her life to riding on "the worn-out track of outmoded tradition."

Thus, this at once quantitative and coincidental human life, in so far as it is not spatiotemporally boundless or eternal, rather takes on an absolute meaning. Suicide is a paradoxical act that verifies this fact. The modern being that commits suicide both develops and asserts things such as the independence and freedom of the individual, the sanctity of human rights, and the necessity of health, while simultaneously resolutely pursuing methods and goals. Just as the method of suicide must be planned, the methods and goals of life and being also must be acquired. Modern people, who live disposable and unilinear lives as individual entities, cannot simply exist having entrusted themselves to a transcendental fate and cosmic nidana that are removed from their anatomical bodies. Freed from fate, by actively forming relationships between themselves and others, they must rationally and teleologically plan and adjust within society their coincidental locations cut off from nature and the universe. Quality and value are pursued anew.

This suggests the meaning of the temporal obsession apparent in *Kaech'ŏkcha*. With the advent of clock time, only calculation and measurement were possible. It is the same as all types of modern praxis that convert a completely empty beginning and end that no longer contains shades of transcendental fate and nidana with the advent of clock time by which only calculation and measurement come to be possible, into the logical processes and planned contents of cause and effect. The verb that represents this sort of practice is "*toeda* (되다)" ("to become"). Lines such as "That is the pain of growing up. If the *soul* is to grow, pain is required. That is to say, you feel that way because you're becoming an adult" (*Kaech'ŏkcha*, 377) evoke the verb "*toeda*." The quotation below elucidates this point.

> Do all of you think it meaningless when babies lie atop their blankets and carelessly wave their four limbs? And do you think it meaningless play when babies pull their mothers' hair, and punch holes in paper-covered windows and doors? And do you think it meaningless play when they draw various pictures making lines horizontally and vertically with the tips of their tiny fingers in the soft earth of the yard? That is not the case. Amidst their seemingly meaningless play, they are developing their abilities to act as future adults. Those carelessly waving arms may *become* the arms that rule the world from the rostrum of parliament, and they may *become* the arms that pen great classics or fashion great art that lives on for generations, and they may *become* the arms that make earthshattering new inventions. (*Kaech'ŏkcha*, 395)[23]

"*Toeda*" projects onto the growth of an individual the ideology of progress and goals, which stands against the randomness of existence and the biological inevitability of its passing. Accordingly, it is a powerful modern system.[24] This is related to both the "adult-child" division and the educational system. On the one hand, through lines such as "Well, why would a young child get married? I'm going to study a bit more" (*Kaech'ŏkcha*, 389), and "We are children. . . . But from our failures we gain ability" (*Kaech'ŏkcha*, 400), the meaning of the temporality embodied by *Kaech'ŏkcha* is displayed. This temporality, which is also expressed in lines such as "For seven years Sŏngjae's lifelong friend had actually been this clock"; "That clock is a seven-year insurance policy, and this year is exactly seven years, so, as far as that clock's concerned, its life is over"; "But what do I have to show for being cooped up in this laboratory for more than seven years! I'm embarrassed to even look at that clock," takes the new "future-centered" values of history and progress and institutionalizes them in individuals' lives, and their breasts and wrists, in and on which watches now tick. This of course applies to Sŏngjae and Sŏngsun but it also reaches as far as the once "genius" now stuffed specimen who "wanders the streets without direction, looking into and looking into again the clocks along the road" or the "clock of Seoul Station,"[25] and inscribes clock time and progress upon all modern beings. Failing in this *"toeda"* means the deviation from time, that is to say madness or death. In fact, regarding the babbling of Chŏn'gyŏng in the quotation below, the work pronounces not only the judgment that "the people of that era all had a similar goal," but "long periods of suffering and disappointment piled atop each other to become the cause of madness" but also that this lead to death.

> You there, don't you know who I am? I am Kim Ch'amsŏ. I died a while ago, but Ham Sagwa is here to take you away. . . . Well, let us go visit the king of the underworld. (*Kaech'ŏkcha*, 362)[26]

In this light, Sŏngsun's suicide goes so far as to be in opposition to Chŏn'gyŏng's death. Unlike that of Chŏn'gyŏng, who talks of Ch'unhyang (the past) and spirits (the time of an other world), Sŏngsun's suicide takes place solely upon a unilinear (this world) time in which "the hour hand was between four and five, and the minute hand was between six and seven." That all the more represents a making of timetables that paradoxically actualized the future-oriented *"toeda."* As such, this also contrasts with Sŏngjae's being glad "like young children when they finally get something they have wanted" when he bought chemicals for his experiments with money from Sŏngsun's prospective husband, "Pyŏn *sŏbang*."[27] Contrary to the retrogression of Sŏngjae to "young child" when he deviated from modern ideology by denying the free love of his younger sister, Sŏngsun's suicide is a form of growth. Accordingly, the following deathbed scene is symbolic.

> I'm going. After I am gone, mother please be well, and *oppa* please succeed in your experiments no matter what. And our whole family should quickly forget the sadness of my death, and live in happiness. And our country should become civilized and prosper. Please become a country of justice, and freedom, and happiness, and love. (*Kaech'ŏkcha*, 457)

Even at the moment of her death, Sŏngsun does not think of the afterlife (or the next world, or nirvana). Instead she yearns for the progress of her family and nation. To her, suicide meant planning for the future.

THE SPACE-TIME OF FREE LOVE

The sort of temporality discussed above is also the essential form in which modern people relate to others and to society. Human relations as mediated by clock time at once suggest a removal from the universe (nature) and an ontological distance arising also between individual entities. Modern time itself arises from this distance. It is precisely the unbridgeable gap between person and person, between person and nature, that represents the historical horizon driving the train from starting point to ending point. This is expressed by the lines that Sŏngsun and Sŏngjae, "being two straight lines whose point of intersection had already passed," "even though their angle as brother and sister would not change, the distance between the two straight lines would gradually grow greater until finally it reached an infinite distance from which they could no longer even gaze at one another" (*Kaech'ŏkcha*, 407). Sŏngsun writes in her diary of "her mental fluctuation and trouble." In actuality, the magazine *Sonyŏn* (*The boys*), from the January 1910 issue, provided a supplement titled "Important Diaries since the Origin 4,213 Years ago,"[28] which was comprised of categories such as "cloudy or fair," "cold or warm," "epistles," "associations," "personal affairs," "worldly affairs," "new knowledge," "merits and demerits," and "abstracts," and this implies the modern meaning connoted by Sŏngsun's diary writing.

At this juncture, tTime that can not be calculated and surmounted lies among the various separate beings who write in their diaries self-centered events experienced and observed from different perspective than others`. No person, no hot or sweet relationship, can overcome the modern windowpane[29] known as the "diary." As seen below, through time spent together, people can only console themselves regarding the interstices.

"I have to go now."

"Yes, you must go. Hurry up and go."

After exchanging these words, they sat facing each other until, before they knew it, ten minutes, then twenty minutes had passed.

"Now I really have to go."

"Ah, it's late. Well, hurry up and go."

Even after both of them arose, they stood facing each other until, before they knew it, ten minutes, then twenty minutes had passed. Sŏngsun was supposed to be home by five-thirty, but they kept this up until it first became six, and then it became six-thirty, so there was no way the perceptive Sŏngjae was not going to be suspicious.

"This time, as soon as it turns five I'll go."

"Yes, please go as soon as it turns five."

Although they said the words, they were of course unable to do so. (*Kaech'ŏkcha*, 424)

The quotation depicts a scene in which the two lovers, while continually looking at the clock, are loath to part. *Kaech'ŏkcha*'s perception of time, in which time is ceaselessly measured, is observable even in scenes of free love. In this way, the meeting between Sŏngsun and Min, by being temporally pre-arranged or measured, transforms into a scene of modern frustration and restlessness. This frustration and restlessness, however, occur not only because the two lovers can only be together for a short time. Rather, they are inherent properties of free love. Free love is carried out on the premise that there are two separate individuals. *Kaech'ŏkcha* argues that "genuine love" is established based on "an understanding of each other's individuality, as well as the resultant passion of respect and affection" (*Kaech'ŏkcha*, 403). At this point, Min's words that "in all matters, in all operations, I have made 'we two' the nominative case" paradoxically express the objectivity of human beings as individual entities that move upon different timetables and write different diaries. By making one human being earnestly and wholly face another (the Other), free love embellishes, whether splendidly or gloomily, individual time and modern solitude. This emotion of love is different from the anxiety of the son-in-law protagonist who lives with his wife's family protesting "You're just using me. Why don't we complete the marriage ceremony!"[30] Accordingly, the "*you*" that appears below is quite significant.

"Yes, and then what do you intend to do?"
"I will follow *you*."[31]
Sŏngsun, for the first time, used the second person pronoun to refer to Min.
"Where to?"
"Anywhere!" (*Kaech'ŏkcha*, 428)

This suggests the coordinates of the location of those involved in free love, as well as of their relationships. Established between individuals, free love itself is both a modern system and time. This mediates (verifies) the insurmountable distance between individual entities. Just as Sŏngsun used the English "*you*," the Other is a foreign country. Free love is the genre of the individual free from engagements arranged between parents, or from predestined, transcendental, and organic human relations and integrated time that are realized through nidana. This is one device in the attempt at a new structuralization of relationships. In place of being insurmountable, the distance and time between modern beings are merely mediated. Together with systems and ideologies primarily formed in the West such as the individual, the nation, freedom, love, eugenics, education, Christianity, and progress, free love represents the most powerful mediating form. As such, it is natural that free love is primarily associated with time as a student,[32] during which one is liberated from the outmoded traditions of child labor and early marriage. This time is a gift, the gift of a preparatory period in order to become a bona fide constituent of modern society, which assigns labor to adults while assigning play and study to children. This derives from a new division called youth (The youth qua students are still one type of children), a new system of time. In point of fact, the time and environment necessary for free love inherently cannot exist for men and women in their late teens and early twenties who, through early marriage, are already parents providing for a family.

This gives rise to the issue of the solar calendar versus the lunar calendar presented in the work. Whereas to Sŏngjae's mother "holidays on the solar calendar still did not seem like holidays at all," Min and Sŏngsun, who assert the independence of the individual, make a date to meet on "Christmas night." This also stands in sharp opposition to the madness of Chŏn'gyŏng when he says, "I'm coming to get you on the eve of *Tongjinnal*"[33] (*Kaech'ŏkcha*, 414). The Christmas of free love defines and excludes *Tongjinnal* as madness. Free love, which is related to both the adoption of the solar (Western) calendar and to the "new thought of human rights" that "just recently came in from the West" (*Kaech'ŏkcha*, 388), is one aspect of the Western paradigm in full-scale operation.

This particularly brings to mind the Christian way of thinking, which places emphasis on love. In Christianity, the time of human beings is a time when they (must) love (or be loved by God). As such, human beings must serve in society, while their families must become "sweet homes." Free love, which occasionally takes on aspects of preference for the exotic, is an institutional device for realizing this sort of love through the youth. Ultimately, this is the decisive form for achieving "a room interior lit by a Western lamp" (*Kaech'ŏkcha*, 448). Free love as this sort of paradigm generates such thoughts and words of Sŏngsun as "How nice would it be to shake his hand in the Western style. Or a kiss . . ." (*Kaech'ŏkcha*, 382) and "I am already not *a girl*. I am *a woman*!"[34] (*Kaech'ŏkcha*, 433). In that sense as well free love is a translated idea.

In addition to the above, the work of establishing the plan of "*toeda*" operates in (on) space as well. Modern surveying, by partitioning space with no regard for the lives of those inhabiting the land—that is, the history, legends, and myths of the hometown, the reappropriation of which was representatively attempted in the poetry of Paek Sŏk—lays down railroads, assigns modern addresses, and establishes urban planning. In fact, Yi Kwangsu, "upon seeing the boundless highlands of Taegwangni, and seeing that most of it was virgin plains, fantasized about raising many cattle there to provide nutritious beef and milk to the people of Seoul, and even went so far as to compose a newspaper ad."[35]

This sort of alienated and estranged space formed relationships that were different from natural formations or from the inherent particularity entangled with the lives of human beings. And these came to occupy locations inside such modern projects as development of national territory or colonial policy. By way of comparison, just as Saussure defines the relationship between signifiant and signifié as arbitrary, place names and their existing peculiarity can no longer be inevitably linked. "Chin'gogae" can also be "Honmachi,"[36] while "Moraenae" or "Ch'ŏngnyangni" are just single dots on a bus line. The latter two places are no longer a peaceful streamside covered in white sand or a clear, cool hamlet.[37]

In this sense, free love, following the myth of modernity's having conquered nature, is no different from the "exploiting" of space-time, which had become an environment only of human beings (or, put another way, an environment alienated from humans). Modern people, through free love or new-style marriage, which are deeply related to modern systems, overcame the predestined positions of social status and ancestry and reorganized their social positions. This is suggested by lines such as "What could the son-in-law of a wealthy family have to worry about?" or "You really hit the jackpot."[38] Modern people rejected the unions their parents decided were inevitable and arbitrarily chose their partners at places like school and church. Hyŏngsik, who abandoned Yŏngch'ae and united with Sŏnghyŏng, would appear to be the Saussure of *Mujŏng*. Privately teaching English generated genuine social relations and the beginning of their endless slip.

This is also related to *ŏnmun ilch'i* (Jp., *genbun itchi*), or the correspondence between spoken and written language. Modern ideologies such as civilization and enlightenment, eugenics, and the *minjok* are at work in Hyŏngsik's arbitrary choice to become engaged to Sŏnhyŏng. In like fashion, *ŏnmun ilch'i*, despite the word "*ilch'i*" (correspondence), by dividing speech and writing through the mediation of plans for the country, the *minjok*, and the written language, actually arbitrarily united the two.[39] This, more than taking the existing Korean language and writing it in Korean rather than literary Chinese, through this entire process, arbitrarily created Korean language qua *minjok* language, while producing the subjects of that arbitrariness, *minjok* reason (national reason) and the modern individual. And the *minjok* language thus formed forcefully included its users inside itself, while generating an analogous relationship between the nation (*minjok*) and the individual. This is suggested, for example, by the sentence "Sŏnghun's wife, like Belgium or Switzerland, remained a neutral country without any connection to the shifting conditions of the world" (*Kaech'ŏkcha*, 410).

This being the case, *ŏnmun ilch'i* is yet another free love attempted between speaking and writing, language and subject, as well as the *minjok* and the individual. Sŏngsun's thoughts regarding the "manner of speaking" of Pyŏn, who held "Min in contempt and considered him undignified, even as he envied his speaking frankly and freely expressing his emotions," are related to this: "His speech was merely the grammatical organization of individual words; it did not seem like speech that came from a heart full of hot blood, full of life" (*Kaech'ŏkcha*, 374). Free love takes the distance and arbitrariness at work in individual or *minjok* relations and naturalizes them as "life" or "heart," thus making them into something self-evident. The individual, the *minjok*, and free love become things natural and inherent. This is the way in which free love acts as a grammar that modernly textualizes the relationship of space-time and subject(s). By reorganizing the individuals and the relationships of individuals in the new space-time called society, it was a form of ontological writing that translated them into something natural. As such, it is only natural that the "manner of speaking" known as "love" is criticized in the quotation below. This is due to the fact that "Auntie" could not understand the writing known as free love.

> "Oh dear, when we were young where would a gal go and use the word love. Gals today say love, love all the time—have they all up and become *kisaeng*? Have they become whores? Oh dear, where do they get off using such scandalous speech? Even between a married couple, the wife respects and honors her husband, and the husband looks after his wife's family, who uses words like love?"
>
> "Oh dear, you too Auntie. When you were young, Auntie, there wasn't any love yet, right? In today's world love is strewn all over the town like jawbreakers," Ŭlnam responded to the infuriated woman with a laugh and was done.[40]

THE MISUNDERSTANDING CALLED FORMULA

Yet another important issue is the fact that writing in the above sense is sometimes (or essentially) mistranslated. This arbitrary combination replete with modern meanings may carry with it misunderstandings such as that below.

> Aside from this, Sŏngsun has a spotted cat named *puppy* that she brought from a friend's house last spring. At the time, Sŏngsun was learning English and named it having misremembered the word *p'ŏp'i* (puppy) as meaning kitten, so that is what she calls it to this day. (*Kaech'ŏkcha*, 368)

In addition, in Sŏngjae's opinion, "Pyŏn," to whom Sŏngsun is betrothed, is also mired in a serious misunderstanding. Despite the fact that he studied philosophy and received "excellent marks," he took the modern knowledge that should have been used for the *minjok* and just "excreted all of it straight down like a dysentery patient." He thinks only of marrying Sŏngsun and "building a clean Western-style house, finely decorating the rooms, putting a piano inside, and telling Sŏngsun to play it" (*Kaech'ŏkcha*, 381). He is just another Elder Kim (*Mujŏng*) who understands and practices the life of a modern person only superficially. Accordingly, Sŏngjae's evaluation of Pyŏn has something in common with Sŏngsun's critical opinion of Pyŏn's manner of speaking.

In spite of this, however, the problem lies in the fact that Sŏngjae wants to marry Sŏngsun to Pyŏn. Driven by his lifelong goal of continuing his experiments and succeeding in invention, Sŏngjae falls into a contradiction. His intention in marrying off his younger sister negates both free love and the rights of the individual, both of which lie upon the same trajectory as his experiments. As a result, Sŏngjae's position in not only accepting Pyŏn's money but also proactively attempting to use it contrasts sharply with his attitude in the scene below where he goes so far as to decline the generous offer of a college professorship.

> In the fall of last year he received an offer from Seoul Engineering College, and in April of this year he received another from Yŏnhŭi College. In addition, the newly established Yŏnhŭi College even came to him bearing "courtesy and generous reward," but, stating that he was both lacking in ability and had no intention of becoming a professor, he refused the offer. Sŏngjae's intention was not focused on a monthly salary of 100 or 200 *wŏn*. (*Kaech'ŏkcha*, 331)

Of course, Sŏngjae's inconsistency originates from his financial condition and life difficulties. Sŏngjae's university classmates, who "while attending school in Tokyo, despite the fact that he was the youngest, asked him questions about math problems, and relied on him for translating Japanese to English and for writing essays" (*Kaech'ŏkcha*, 340), had all become "principals at secondary schools," "bank managers," "judges and prosecutors," and "lawyers." Unlike all of these "first-class personages" and "excellent gentlemen," however, Sŏngjae still went around wearing "cotton clothes" and "hempen sandals." In particular, the character Lee, who had borrowed and failed to repay money several times while they were studying abroad in Tokyo, had become a lawyer, then a judge, "acquiring the wealth of several hundred harvests," while, on the other hand, Sŏngjae had become a "lowly debtor" (*Kaech'ŏkcha*, 334). Sŏngjae fell into a situation in which he suffered provisional attachment over "a measly 3,000-something *wŏn*" at the hands of Ham Sagwa, who had risen from failure by opening a pawnshop with the 10,000 *nyang* given to him by Sŏngjae's father, Kim Ch'amsŏ. As a result, Sŏngjae, who had only "160 *wŏn* in his savings account at Hansŏng Bank," arrived at the following realization.

> There was no way the real world should enter into the laboratory, however, before abandoning the earth and flying up to the heavens, no matter where he

went, there was no place the hardships of the real world did not reach. If he opened a single windowpane, there was the real world; if he took over 10 steps, there were the streets of Chongno. Into Sŏngjae's laboratory as well, from morning to evening, the worry and agony of the real world came streaming in through the windows, through the walls. (*Kaech'ŏkcha*, 331)

The above quotation brings to mind Yi Sang's expression of capitalist society as "using those 'relationships' to burrow in through the walls."[41] But Sŏngjae's fall, which brought about this recognition, provides a few noteworthy points. First of all, his disdain regarding the success of his college classmates evokes the disappearance of stories that reward good and punish evil, that is to say the vanishing of "enjoyable novels recounting old tales,"[42] which can be likened to the inevitable combining of signifiant and signifié. Without fail, good people should be rewarded while bad people are punished, but, in Sŏngjae's view, his classmates and Ham Sagwa have succeeded despite their failing to be good in many respects. This sort of disconnect applies to Sŏngjae's case as well. On the contrary, he is an earnest person who continually helped them both academically and financially, yet he has not succeeded at all. Causal relations that reward good and punish evil have come to an end. Regarding this world ruled by arbitrariness, Yi Kwangsu posed the following question.

God is truly dead. Have they, as Son[43] stated, already concluded the funeral services for the first anniversary and the second anniversary of his death? Has it become a world where good people are trampled under the feet of bad, and evil people pick the figs they have planted among the thistles?[44]

Seen from this perspective, Sŏngjae, who is skeptical of those who have succeeded, seriously misunderstands the nature of modern society, which has moved beyond rewarding good and punishing evil, and come to be semiotic. Sŏngjae, who refuses the money guaranteed by a professorship in order to pursue experiments and inventions, is mired in the world of utility value. Unrelated to his ideas, however, the principle that guides modern society is exchange value, which, mediated by the market, arbitrarily combines things and value. Of course, this has no relation to the inevitability of rewarding good and punishing evil, but neither is it related to chemical inevitability. There is no inevitably determined owner of the chairman's swivel chair.

This is the core of what Min refers to as "reality." Faced with Sŏngsun's passion, expressed in the lines "I will follow *you*." "Anywhere!", Min responds with "Those words are nothing but ideals. First of all, people cannot live removed from economics" (*Kaech'ŏkcha*, 428). At this juncture, what completely affirm Min's words are "Shikishima" cigarettes (*Kaech'ŏkcha*, 341), "Lion Tooth Powder" (*Kaech'ŏkcha*, 405), and a Swiss watch. Brands, to a degree greater than can be imagined by the proper noun known as Sŏngsun, are the signs for "reality" and "economics," what truly synthesize the arbitrary combination and exchange value of signifiant and signifié. These represent the real "*yu*" (you) that Min and other modern people, in place of Sŏngsun who has committed suicide, must confront. These "*yu*"s will generate social position.

In this world of brands, Sŏngjae, who merely discusses "chemical elements he has dissolved naturally" but is incompetent when it comes to calculating money and interest, cannot help but be culled. Causal relations that reward good and punish evil are extinct, and their demise was partially led by Sŏngjae himself. On the other hand, the causal relations of the market, also known as contracts, operated accurately at all times. Sŏngjae was either unaware of that fact or ignored it. Moreover, his one and only hope, chemical causal relations, never yielded the desired result.

INVENTOR AND DEBTOR

In light of the above, Sŏngjae's situation is reminiscent of the failure of Dr. K, who was trapped in chemical formulae.

> "Doctor, it doesn't work that way. In the final analysis, no matter much you refine it, why wouldn't someone vomit after eating something made of shit? Because the world doesn't work according to formulas."
>
> "Formulas? No matter how much I think about it, it's your misunderstanding. It won't be like that."
>
> "Well then, why did they throw up?"
>
> "Well, there was no reaction, or was there. . . ."
>
> The simplistic doctor thought the only reason the patrons threw up was due to the particular smell of feces left by small remaining amounts of skatole and indole.[45]

Dr. K attempts to explain people's reactions to shit in terms of the chemical actions of skatole and indole. That is Dr. K's misunderstanding. This sort of misunderstanding was also at work in Sŏngjae's case. Sŏngjae, who requested an extension of the period for discharging his debt by appealing to outmoded "longstanding relationships between families" and "affection between friends," like Dr. K, mistakenly misapplied formulae and rules.

> "Yes, I went to Ham Sagwa, but he told me to come and talk to you. He said it was because you are in complete charge of this affair. And so. . . ."
>
> "That will be difficult. Hell, the deadline already passed over a month ago."

"Yes, it's been twenty-some days."

"Right, so do you expect the creditor to do nothing?"

"But with Ham Sagwa, our families have known each other for generations. . . ."

"Hah! There are no relationships between families anymore."

"Then are you telling me you have no affection for your friend?"

"Affection between friends is affection between friends, and a debt is a debt."

. . . .

At this point, an office worker politely entered.

"You have a call from the courthouse."

"Oh, do I need to appear?"

"Yes, Mr. Song said that court is now in session." (*Kaech'ŏkcha*, 342–43)

The passage depicts Mr. Lee—lawyer, former classmate, and agent of the creditor—getting rid of Sŏngjae, who is there to request an extension of the deadline for provisional attachment. Interesting here is that the line "There are no relationships between families anymore," brings to mind the scene below from *Konjiki yasha* (*The Gold Demon*, 1897). Thus, not only *Chaesaeng* (*Rebirth*, 1924) but *Kaech'ŏkcha* as well is deeply related to *Konjiki yasha*.

"Kamada is right. During high school we never ostracized or harmed you in any way, so, if only in remembrance of that affection, please grant our request."

"So, Hazama, what do you think?"

"Affection between friends is affection between friends, and money lent is money lent—two totally separate matters."[46]

In addition to this, Lee's using the time the courthouse opened as an excuse is also significant. Sŏngjae was not the only one who made timetables. Also worth noting is the fact that the life principles of Sŏngjae, who had previously acted completely according to a time plan, went completely unobserved with regard to his debt. Not only did Sŏngjae break his promise concerning the period of reimbursement, and request and extension, but he also encroached upon the time when Lee had to appear in court.

As a result, these episodes present the essence of modern time. Things like the discharge of debt or the calculation and fluctuation of interest are the practical aspects of capitalist time that form the contents of clock-time divisions. These are the central axis and the gears of the hour hand and minute hand that constitute and operate society. Modern time cannot be completely explained by things such as the individual, free love, growth, success, and progress. More than anything else, it is a graph of banks and markets that repeatedly changes over time. The dramatic unfolding of interest rates or stock prices replaces the rotation of the seasons and represents the contents of modern time that decide people's fates. The "bank game" that makes up the daily schedule of the lumpen Mansŏng in Yu Hangnim's *"Magwŏn* (Horse race ticket, 1936)" has this sort of situation as its backdrop.

> What suddenly popped into his head while he waited to cash a check at the bank was the bank game he had played as a child. He played by making paper bills, then depositing and withdrawing them. Taking a hint from there, he had put 50 *wŏn* in a special current account, and was on his way to make yet another deposit at the N Cooperative Credit Society when he ran into Chin'gyu. Chin'gyu's father also saw him. At the cooperative credit society he made an initial deposit of 20 *wŏn*, and from there went to the post office where he deposited another 20 *wŏn*, and received a new passbook. He thus spread out 90 *wŏn* over three places.
>
> The following day he took 10 *wŏn* out of both the credit society and the post office, and deposited them in the bank. And the day after that he withdrew 60 *wŏn* from the bank, and deposited it in the post office and the credit society. Having slept in late and then visited those three places, the day passed quite well without his having incurred any expenses.[47]

The humorously portrayed flow of capital in the quotation corresponds to the position of people who belong to modern society. Modern society is a world expressed by the rhetorical question, "Who said I would give my daughter to a 20-*wŏn* salaryman?" In this world that causes the lumpen Mansŏng to act busy, "checking the time for a third time during one round of miniature golf," things such as the natural divisions of the seasons as they relate to farming can possess no meaning. Also, as expressed in the line "Affection between friends is affection between friends, and a debt is a debt," the time of the bank (market) knows nothing of tolerance. But that does not mean it bears a grudge as did Suil, the protagonist of Cho Chunghwan's *Changhanmong (A long and sorrowful dream*, 1913) who failed in love and became a usurer, and, as a result, neither does it regret its mistakes. It merely coldly and accurately carries out exchanges and calculations according to the situation of the market. In principle, no one can be free from this total arena. Therefore, the true invention presented by *Kaech'ŏkcha* is this clock of exchange value that became the subject of social acts. Whether one suddenly becomes rich or goes broke, human beings scribe a graph, while having to adjust to the constantly ticking progress of the market. The opposite situation cannot exist. The passage below shows that even Kim Ch'amsŏ's corpse cannot sever relations with this progress.

> Still, Kim Ch'amsŏ was able to lie down on the warmest part of the floor in the large house he had worked so hard his entire life to attain. But had he delayed

only four or five days in dying, he would not even have been able to lie down on the floor of this house. (*Kaech'ŏkcha*, 359)

In short, what betrayed Sŏngjae's family to the point that it led to Kim Ch'amsŏ's death was not Ham Sagwa and his forgetting of the past "relationship between families" but modern time itself. Ham, rather than having orchestrated Sŏngjae's financial ruin, was merely the human trigger that mediated its decisive process. The true problem lies in the fact that while Ham and Lee succeeded and progressed, Sŏngjae was unable to do so. The core of the betrayal is this deviation in social positions. Up until An Pin discovers "Amorogen" and "Auramon" in the blood of Sŏk Sunok (*Sarang* [*Love*, 1939]), or Doctor Yi Wŏn'gu, who is associated with a university, is featured in the newspaper for inventing a "liquid fuel" to replace gasoline (*Kŭ tŭl ŭi sarang* [*Their love*, 1941]), Yi Kwangsu's protagonists, alienated from capital, remained at a standstill. Accordingly, Sŏngjae may even be the true betrayer. Just as Doctor K was unable to consider humanity's longstanding notions regarding shit, Sŏngjae was unable to measure the modern causal relations of social position and exchange value. In spite of his thorough making of timetables, Sŏngjae was unable to become an "excellent gentleman" who had succeeded at invention. Rather, he attempted to revive a temporality that had already gone, the "relations between families" and "affection between friends" of the past. But while human sympathy can at times briefly extend (or rarely cancel) the discharge of a debt, it cannot put an end to the system itself. In fact, appealing to sympathy over a contract that has already been agreed upon only generates more (or another kind of) debt. This is because one is dominating another's time plan (possession) by means of one's own timetable (possession). This amounts to interfering with the diary writing of another. It is what led to Sŏngsun's death, and it cannot serve as the grammar of the modern age. Or we would have to pay a tremendous amount of interest. *Konjiki yasha* satirized this sort of social situation as follows.

"Even if you strangle me, there will be no change to what I have already said. Hazama may kneel before the power of money, but he will not kneel before physical force. If you dislike me, strike my face with a wad of 500-*yen* bills."
"Won't gold coins work?"
"Gold coins, fine."
"Well then, it's gold coins!"[48]

Regarding the aspect of modernity that unfolds in the scene above, Sŏngjae was much more ignorant than was Pyŏn. Sŏngjae's true debt, which had snowballed, was ignorance and misunderstanding. This corresponds to the seven years of time he wasted on failed experiments with no tangible results.

It also, in that it will "seize" his social existence, which in the end was unable to achieve the state of "*toeda*," results in a death that is differentiated from Sŏngsun's suicide. Ironically, it was Sŏngjae's accurate laboratory, by being so formally disciplined by the clock that it exceeded the limit of the capital he possessed, that gave birth to his debt. By being isolated from and left behind by the complicated relationships of the "real world" and the speed of the market, which produce and exchange value, he actually invited capitalist relationships into his laboratory. His temporal compulsion notwithstanding, this eloquently attests to the fact that Sŏngjae's life was thoroughly unplanned and inefficient. (In this respect, Sŏngjae's timetable corresponds to Mansŏng's watching the clock while acting busy.) What is more, he intended to saddle his younger sister with the financial burden that resulted from his unproductivity.

In this regard, Sŏngjae's experiments were not a complete failure. This is because, through his own existence and actions, Sŏngjae was able to verify a sort of barbarism. Such things as isolation, which is not mediated by society (fixity=autism=primitive=social negligence); wasted time, which cannot be converted into products; inefficiency, which cannot lead the movement of capital; debt, which strips away singularity and self-reliance; lack of clarity in operating expenses, which is based on human relationships; and defaulting on contracts are precisely those dark parts of his own interior that Sŏngjae must pioneer and enlighten in the future. Owing to his unplanned life and inefficiency, his father and younger sister died, the family fortune was exhausted, while he himself was trapped inside "hempen sandals." The self-disciplined chemist Kim Sŏngjae, full of lofty principles, just as Chŏn'gyŏng who died of insanity, was a barbarian who could not help but make human sacrifice of himself and others. Of course, this was not only Sŏngjae's problem. This is due to the fact that rather than being the experiments' subject—the colonist/pioneer—he was in fact an experiment's object—the colonized.

This is how *Kaech'ŏkcha* presented aspects of the colonial practice that pioneered the subjective path of modern people by means of suicide. In addition, this novel confirmed barbarity as an object that required "pioneering," which is to say development, improvement, or colonization.[49] This corresponds to the colonial situation, and the existential horizons of the colonized, neither of which rise to the surface of the work. This, when compared to *Mujŏng*, which attempted through study abroad to present a macroscopic and optimistic outlook, represents the modern literary significance of *Kaech'ŏkcha*, which achieved a more microscopic and realistic perspective. This work succeeded in mediating modern subjectivity and barbarity by means of the contradiction(s) of the colonized.

NOTES

1. Yi Kwangsu, "*Aika?* (Is it love?)," trans. Kim Yunsik, in *Munhak sasang*, February 1981, 446.

2. Yi Injik, "*Hyŏl ŭi nu* (Tears of blood)," trans. W. E. Skillend, in *Korean Classical Literature: An Anthology*, ed. Chung Chong-wha (London: Keegan Paul International, 1989), 171.

3. Yi Injik, *Hyŏl ŭi nu*, 173.

4. Chŏn Yŏngt'aek's "*Hyesŏn ŭi sa* (The death of Hyesŏn)," in *Ch'angjo*, February 1919, 47.

5. Pak T'aewŏn, "*P'iro* (Fatigue)," in *Sosŏlga Kubo-ssi ŭi iril* (A day in the life of the novelist Kubo) (Seoul: Munjangsa, 1938), 73.

6. Kim Kirim, "*Han'gang indogyo* (Han river footbridge)," in *Kim Kirim chŏnjip* 1 (Seoul: Simsŏltang, 1988), 101.

7. Han Sŏrya, "*Maŭm ŭi hyangch'on* (Village of the heart)," in *Sinmun yŏnjae sosŏl chŏnjip* 2 (Seoul: Kip'ŭnsaem, 1999), 430.

Although the original is in Korean, the Japanese phrase "*Chotto matte kudasai*," which means "Please wait a moment," is not translated but merely transliterated into Korean.—Trans.

8. Yi Sang, "*Sirhwa* (Lost flowers)," in *Yi Sang munhak chŏnjip* 2, ed. Kim Yunsik (Seoul: Munhak sasangsa, 1991), 364.

9. Yŏm Sangsŏp, "*Chogŭman il* (A small matter)," in *P'yobonsil ŭi ch'ŏnggaeguri* (Seoul: Samjungdang, 1980), 97.

10. Yi Kwangsu, "*Kaech'ŏkcha* (The pioneer)," in *Yi Kwangsu chŏnjip* 1 (Seoul: Samjungdang, 1962), 392.

11. The original title is *XiaoJing* (孝經), and it is alternatively translated as the *Classic of Filial Piety*. The English translation is taken from the following source: http://www.chinapage.com/confucius/xiaojing-be.html

12. Yu Kilchun, *Sŏyu kyŏnmun* (*Things seen and heard in the West*), trans. Hŏ Kyŏngjin (Seoul: Hanyang ch'ulp'an, 1995), 306.

13. Kim Tongin, "*K paksa ŭi yŏn'gu* (Dr. K's research)," in *Kim Tongin chŏnjip* 2 (Seoul: Chosŏn ilbosa, 1988), 76.

14. *Symmetry* and *harmony* are placed in italics to denote that the original text uses Korean transliterations of the English words: "*ssimetŭri*" and "*hamoni*."—Trans.

15. Yi Kwangsu, "*Mujŏng* (The heartless)," in *Yi Kwangsu chŏnjip* 1 (Seoul: Samjungdang, 1962), 310.

16. Yanabu Akira, *Honyakugo seiritsu jijyō* (Circumstances of establishing translated language) (Tokyo: Iwanami shoten, 1998), 98.

"*Love*" is written in italics to denote that the original text uses Korean transliteration of the English word—"*rŏbŭ*"—in order both to mark it as distinct from "*yŏnae*" in the preceding sentence and to accentuate its modern, Western provenance.—Trans.

17. Na Hyesŏk, "*Isangchŏk puin* (The ideal woman)," in *Hak chi kwang*, Volume 3, December 1914, 13.

18. Kim Yunsik, *Kim Tongin yŏn'gu* (A study of Kim Tongin) (Seoul: Minŭmsa, 2000), 61.

19. In 1934, however, Yi wrote the following criticism of those who commit suicide due to failed love: "When one loves another, devoting one's life to that person represents a purity beyond reproach. When, however, that love is broken, immediately ending one's life represents an erroneous view of life. It is the unforgivable crime of ignoring the enormous obligation known as the individual's debt to society. The individual is not the individual's. The individual is the family's, the society's. Arbitrarily ending one's own life is nothing more than selfishness" ("*Yŏnae wa chasal* [Love and suicide]," in *Yi Kwangsu chŏnjip* 13 (Seoul: Samjungdang, 1962), 430).

20. Yi Kwangsu, "*Tonggyŏng chapsin* (Miscellaneous correspondence from Tokyo)," in *Yi Kwangsu chŏnjip* 17 (Seoul: Samjungdang, 1962), 476.

21. The Chongno curfew bell (*Chongno ŭi in'gyŏng*) was used during the Chosŏn dynasty (1392–1910), and indicates that Sŏngjae may have been born a bit too early ever to be truly "new" or "modern."—Trans.

22. Yi Chin'gyŏng, *Kŭndaejŏk si konggan ŭi t'ansaeng* (The birth of modern time and space) (Seoul: P'urŭnsup, 1997), 117.

23. Italics added to denote the verb "*toeda*" in the original text.—Trans.

24. For a discussion of this point, please refer to Yi Kyŏnghun, "*Tanbal, 'ahae' ŭi susahak* (Bobbed hair: the rhetoric of 'children')," in *Yi Sang Review*, September 2001, 97–137.

25. Yi Sang, "*Nalgae* (Wings)," in *Yi Sang munhak chŏnjip* 2, ed. Kim Yunsik (Seoul: Munhak sasangsa, 1991), 334.

26. Ch'amsŏ and Sagwa are not the given names of Kim and Ham but are official titles, albeit ones that are no longer valid under the Japanese.—Trans.

27. Although they are not married, the title "*sŏbang*," or son-in-law, is already being used by the family in an attempt to present Sŏngsun with a fait accompli.—Trans.

28. This number represents an ethnonationalist usage of the Tan'gun foundation myth found in the *Samguk yusa* (*Memorabilia of the Three Kingdoms*), as opposed to the imported Christian/Western system, to chronicle Korean history.—Trans.

29. For more on this, please refer to chapter 4: "The Fashion of *Mujŏng*."

30. Kim Yujŏng, "*Pom pom* (Spring)," in *Kim Yujŏng chŏnjip* (Seoul: Hyŏndae munhaksa, 1968), 44.

31. In the original, Sŏngsun uses the word "*yu*," a transliteration of the English "you" in the dialogue. For readers less versed in English, the author follows it with the parenthetical translation, "(*tangsin*)."—Trans.

32. For more on this, see Kim Tongsik, "*Yŏnae wa kŭndaesŏng* (Love and modernity)," in *Minjok munhaksa yŏn'gu*, Volume 18, June 2001, 299–326.

33. *Tongji* (冬至) is the winter solstice according to the lunar calendar. *Tongjinnal* is a combination of the Sino-Korean *Tongji* and the native Korean *nal* (day). It was left untranslated in order to reproduce the traditional, and hence paradoxically "foreign" to the young moderns, connotations it possesses in the original work.—Trans.

34. Here, quite uncharacteristically, actual English words are inserted in the text. The original reads "저는 벌써 a girl 이 아니에요. a woman 이에요."—Trans.

A nearly identical expression also appears in Yi's *Kŭ yŏja ŭi ilsaeng* (*That woman's life*, 1934): "Kŭmbong, looking upon his little sister whose nape, bosom, and appearance from behind were already no longer those of a *girl* but of a grown *woman*, sincerely apologized." In *Yi Kwangsu chŏnjip* 7 [Seoul: Samjungdang, 1966], 267.

35. Yi Kwangsu, "*Kŭmgangsan yugi* (Record of a journey to the Kŭmgang Mountains)," in *Yi Kwangsu chŏnjip* 18 (Seoul: Samjungdang, 1962), 11.

36. Chin'gogae is the old Korean name for the area between Chongno and Namsan, present day Ch'ungmuro and Myŏngdong. During the colonial period, the Japanese, and many Koreans, referred to it by its modern Japanese name, Honmachi.—Trans.

37. This sentence provides a literal translation of the Korean "Moraenae" and the Sino-Korean "Ch'ŏngnyangni," respectively.—Trans.

38. Yi, Kwangsu, *Mujŏng*, 199.

39. See Karatani Kojin, *Nihon kindai bungaku no kigen* (The origins of modern Japanese literature) (Tokyo: Iwanami shoten, 1980), 7–43.

40. Yi Kwangsu, *Kŭ yŏja ŭi ilsaeng*, 278–79.

41. Yi Sang, "*Chiju hoesi* (Two spiders meet a pig)," in *Yi Sang munhak chŏnjip* 2, ed. Kim Yunsik (Seoul: Munhak sasangsa, 1991), 312.

42. Yu Hangnim, "*Magwŏn* (Horse race ticket)," in *Tanch'ŭng*, April 1937, 96.

43. This is a Korean name, not a reference to Jesus.—Trans.

44. Yi Kwangsu, *Kŭ yŏja ŭi ilsaeng*, 236.

45. Kim Tongin, "*K paksa ŭi yŏn'gu*," 81.

46. Ozaki Kōyō, *Konjiki yasha* (The Gold Demon [Kŭmsaek yach'a]), trans. Sŏ Sŏgyŏn (Seoul: Pŏmusa, 1992), 138.

Although translated the same here ("affection between friends"), the Korean text uses the nouns *chŏng* (情) and *chŏngni* (情理), while the Japanese text uses *chŏngŭi* (情誼).—Trans.

47. Yu Hangnim, "*Magwŏn*," 86–87.

48. Ozaki Kōyō, "*Konjiki yasha*," 139.

49. The word *kaech'ŏk* (開拓), or pioneering, is taken from the title of the work, *Kaech'ŏkcha* (開拓者), and has multiple meanings according to context. The author plays with this fact here, and, in order to capture all the connotations of the word, the translation has included multiple glosses.—Trans.

Chapter 6

Rice Speculation, Hot Springs, English

THE LABORATORY AND THE RICE EXCHANGE

Time segmented by the clock represents an important novelistic device of Yi Kwangsu's *Mujŏng* (*The Heartless*, 1917). Yi Hyŏngsik, "having finished his two o'clock elementary English class," makes his way to the house of Elder Kim for a three o'clock private tutoring session. In addition, it is due to the late arrival of the streetcar bound for Ch'ŏngnyangni that he is unable to prevent Yŏngch'ae's rape. This also applies to his sending a telegram to the P'yŏngyang Police Station in order to find Yŏngch'ae. This is because Hyŏngsik predicts her spatiotemporal coordinates based on the train's arrival time.

Of course, his planning is frustrated by Yŏngch'ae's accompanying Pyŏnguk back to the latter's hometown. This turn, however, also arose owing to the intrusion of the school's timetable in the form of vacation. As such, Hyŏngsik and Yŏngch'ae's meeting again aboard a train taking them to study abroad was predictable. This is because the fact that Hyŏngsik and Sŏnhyŏng, Pyŏnguk and Yŏngch'ae took the same train on the same day means that they were all behaving according to the timetables of school and train. They all belong to an identical space-time in which the ideology and discourse of civilization and enlightenment operate. Accordingly, their meeting was neither coincidence nor "strange fate."[1] On the contrary, this evokes the inevitability of a new era standing in opposition to premodernity.

This issue, however, is not only important with respect to *Mujŏng*. It not only comprises the meaning of Yi's *Kaech'ŏkcha* (*The Pioneer*, 1917–1918) but also represents the crucial element for explaining the difference between *Kaech'ŏkcha* and *Chaesaeng* (*Rebirth*, 1924–1925). In *Kaech'ŏkcha*, Sŏngjae lives in his laboratory, cut off from society.

The hour hand of the octagonal clock was between four and five, and the minute hand was between six and seven. Sŏngsun thought to herself, "It's five minutes past four-thirty." Four-thirty was the time at which Sŏngjae stopped his experiments and for thirty minutes took a stroll or talked with Sŏngsun; for the past three years this had been an unwavering family rule. . . . When the octagonal clock chimed five times, he would say, "Well then, let's have dinner," and follow Sŏngsun to enter the living room he had left at eight in the morning for the first time in nine hours.[2]

As evident above, the clock is what formalizes Sŏngjae's life. His life and existence are nearly identified with the movement of the clock. But, like the Chŏng Chiyong poem that tells us "always sleeping at exactly the same time" is an "elegant expressionlessness,"[3] Sŏngjae's ordered life with the clock is expressionless. When viewed from the perspective that says, "They are people with jobs so they live a time life,"[4] Sŏngjae's life is actually not a "time life." As such, that the chemist Sŏngjae, whose seven years of faithfully executed research ended in failure, fell into debt and lost both his younger sister and his home is only natural. Far from "wringing the neck of babbling time," and despite having thoroughly lived according to a timetable,[5] this "elegant" unemployed Sŏngjae, by failing to repay his debt in the allotted time, broke the most essential time promise in capitalist society.[6] Sŏngjae, who exhausted his family fortune on experiments, was unable to move beyond the world of *Mujŏng*, which fundamentally did not problematize the "terrifying clock"[7] that is connected to money. On the one hand, Yi Hyŏngsik "mechanically (like a clock)" pursued, in addition to his desire for modern knowledge, an optimistic future based on the time of a school system that also presumed his graduation, while, on the other, he was haphazard and unrealistic when it came to using his salary or procuring funds for study abroad.

"Do you have any money? If you do, let me borrow about five *wŏn*."
　　Having said this, he thought he now had nowhere to get money. The school would give him his June salary, but he couldn't go pick it up, and from July Hyŏngsik and no income at all.
　　"What for?"
　　"I have to go and find Yŏngch'ae's corpse. Find it, and even if I have to carry it on my back, give it a proper burial."[8]

In light of the above, the following line from *Chaesaeng* is important: "When he looked at the people gathered here with the eyes he had viewed the world with four years earlier, Ponggu could not help but be surprised."[9] This indicates that the spatiotemporal reality that constitutes *Chaesaeng* has grown quite different from *Mujŏng* or *Kaech'ŏkcha*. Of course, the disappearance of the eyes that viewed the world four years earlier applies as well to Ponggu himself. Unlike Hyŏngsik's attempt to borrow money, Sin Ponggu resolves, "If I want to put together some money, I must borrow not so much as a spoonful of cold rice. If I intend to save money, I have to make my heart like that of a beast."[10] Also unlike Sŏngjae, who was so unconcerned with a "monthly salary" that he declined offers from both Seoul Engineering College and Yŏnhŭi College, which ended in his having to request an extension of the period for discharging his debt from Ham Sagwa, Ponggu, a student of Yŏnhŭi College,[11] compares himself to Hazama Kanichi of *Konjiki yasha* (*The Gold Demon*, 1897) and "marvels at the thought of how they could be so alike."[12] Ponggu, who loses Sunyŏng to Paek Yunhŭi, holder of such titles as director of the Hansŏng Bank, director of the Korean Commercial Bank, and president of the Taejŏng Trading Corporation, abandons all "thoughts of working for the nation, working for the world," and heads for Inch'ŏn. Also giving up on studying and the Christian faith, and harboring the "sole hope" of "doing nothing but earning money in order to exact a refreshing revenge upon Sunyŏng who betrayed me and Paek Yunhŭi who stole her," he "stoops to rice speculation, which he formerly considered no different from thieving." "With the objective of gathering the terrible sum of five million," he intends to become "the second Pan Pokch'ang."[13] Pan Pokch'ang is the "rice speculation king" of Inch'ŏn.

> Thus Pokch'ang chose money over school. Might he not have solemnly sworn to become a "*mammonist*," punish the world with gold, and avenge all his ill treatment and pent-up anger with "money"? In the end, the god of fate led him to that golden abode of demons, the rice exchange, so that the "Maruma" Store's Kwangt'aek Brokerage House became the place that raised him and brought him to greatness. Pokch'ang had never been able to go out into the world for study, but he was exceptionally intelligent and clever. In no time at all, his fluent Japanese could not be distinguished from that of a native speaker, and his daily life, like the appearance of his face, was so Japanized that the proprietor called him by the Japanese name "Jiro." Each passing day, with the exchange's opening bell, "Jiro"'s shouting of the market price grew more clear, accurate, and prompt. What he saw, heard, spoke, and thought was all rice exchange, all money. . . . Thus did a once poor and lowborn child obtain the great sum of five-hundred thousand *wŏn* in one fell swoop. According to one version, it was actually two million.[14]

Thus, Ponggu begins his life as an "order taker" answering the "continuous stream of phone calls from customers" at the Inch'ŏn Rice Exchange, which maintained mutual contact by telegraph with Osaka's "Dōjima" Exchange.[15] At this point a time unfolds before the Ponggu in Inch'ŏn that is different not only from the seven years Sŏngjae sacrificed to research but also from the two years and six months that Ponggu himself served in prison as a result of the "1919 riots incident."[16] It is a genuine capitalistic time operated at the risk of one's life to the point that Tuhwan in Ch'oe Sŏhae's *Hooe sidae* (*Age of the extra*, 1930–1931) would think regarding the death of Kang Sunch'ŏl, who had agreed to lend him 100 *wŏn*, "If you had to die, you should have died a few days later!", or a husband would demand his wife's "death postpone-ment" so that they might collect the money from their *kye* (mutual assistance society), as in Yi Pŏmsŏn's "*Samang poryu* (Death postponement, 1958)." In *Chaesaeng*, it takes the following form.

> "Please sell some, sir. Sell even just a little. The time is getting short."
>
> He said, pulling up his sleeve. . . .
>
> His watch already read eleven-fifty. Even if this watch were exactly the same as the exchange's clock, only five minutes remained. Ah, the dreaded needle of fortune made a ticking sound as it went around.
>
> As luck would have it, telephone calls came in from all over. They were orders to "Please sell!" But they were already out of time.
>
> "We're out of time. There are only two minutes left."
>
> While he answered like this, the noon gun rang out. The whole thing was over.
>
> At the exchange that day the rice speculators, their appetites whet by a rumor that the Japanese government would buy two-hundred thousand sacks of rice, competed to buy it all yelling me too, me too. In the process, with barely ten minutes remaining before noon, Maru Kim sold ten thousand sacks, after which the "Tsujiki" Company sold ten thousand more, sending the whole room into utter confusion. But with no time to do anything about it, noontime had already sounded.[17]

Ponggu, noontime sounding with no time to do anything about it, at this "noon where chaos reached its peak,"[18] emerges victorious. And, with this, he led the way for the time of "graph paper changed before it is even worn,"[19] or, going further, the time of Ch'ae Mansik's *T'angnyu* (*Muddy water*, 1937), in which it ruined Chŏng Chusa and his family, bringing him from "the salaried poor" to a "rice speculator," and "from a rice speculator back to a *habak-kun*."[20] Next, the genealogy of this sort of time introduces the stock investor Kim Kwangse of Kim Namch'ŏn's "*T ilbo sa* (The T daily newspaper com-pany, 1939)." He feels that "having money that is only a sum listed in your savings account book and a year passes, then two years pass, and nothing has happened is the same has having no money at all." He has "the guts to make one of two choices: to get rid of it all immediately and completely and restart from nothing, or, if not that, to drive the number recorded in the bank book like a locomotive."[21] And this led to the following result: "From the going price of '*yorizuki* (the opening quotation)' in the morning he pyramided. What he had sold at 162 *wŏn* over the last eighteen days was now at 146 *wŏn*, so it had plummeted 16 *wŏn* per share. A profit of 16,000 *wŏn*."[22]

As seen above, time and money walk in step with one another. Now the train qua world map of anthropogeography or source of modern knowledge takes on a new meaning, as depicted below.

> Yŏngjin spread the telegram atop the owner's desk so that he could see the message from London.
>
> . . .
>
> "If what that telegram says is true, it will have a big effect on the Japanese economy as well. In my opinion, I believe the *kabu* (stocks) will fall."
>
> "And if by chance Germany does not pay reparations to France, won't French government bonds fall sharply? If so, the British and American economies will also be shaken, and, as a result, the shock will reach Japan as well."[23]

School is no longer Ponggu's environment. "Speculation" (as rice trading) is *Chaesaeng*'s form of speculation (as contemplation). As he considers "ways to become extremely rich" like Min Yŏnghwi, Yi Wanyong, and Paek In'gi, Ponggu, who goes so far as to change his name to "Yŏngjin," lives only in the market. In fact, this was expected from the time Ponggu, saying "You can't trust that damned Ch'ŏngnyangni streetcar," hired a car and went to the train station. He is different from Yi Hyŏngsik who was vexed by the streetcar bound for Tongdaemun, which "seems to deliberately slow its pace," and merely imagined "racing like the wind in an automobile just like the Westerners in moving pictures."[24] Ponggu boldly rode in an expensive sleeping car to Wŏnsan. In order to win Sunyŏng back, he was willing to use unstintingly the 300 *wŏn* that was "at once both his tuition, the seed money for his whole life, and the provisions for his aged mother, now past 60."[25] He was a natural-born investor.

As evidenced above, automobiles and sleeping cars, viewed by Sunyŏng as "symbols of wealth," are different from the trains of civilization and enlightenment taken by Hyŏngsik and Yŏngch'ae. They, in place of the sound of the school bell, which not only accurately announced the "two o'clock elementary English class" but also, as in Yi T'aejun's "*Talbam* (Moonlit night, 1933)," occasionally rang too early, represent the indicators of the market, where, along with a plunge in prices, noontime sounds "with no time to do anything about it." In brief, as Yi Kiyŏng put it in his novel *Sin'gaeji* (*Newly opened land*, 1938), "From the time the trains came, the town developed in general, but, on the other hand, the traditional market gradually fell into decline." The scene depicted below also occurred with this sort of situation as backdrop.

When he got off the morning train he did not go straight to the bank. His reason for having sent the money just before closing time was to ensure that his transfer would be the final one of the day from the Iri branch to the Seoul headquarters. And he had chosen Friday to ensure that it would go up from Iri to Seoul on Saturday. Since on Saturdays banks only deal with office work in the morning, fortunately, if there were no wire transfer from Iri to Seoul on Saturday, meaning tomorrow, and since the day after tomorrow is Sunday, even if it were discovered by the appraiser to be a forged telegram, it would not happen until Monday. And by that time Tuhwan would have taken care of everything.[26]

If the protagonists of *Mujŏng* held a benefit concert to help the flood victims at Samnangjin, the junction of trains bound for Masan, then the protagonist of *Hooe sidae*, in order to elude a police dragnet, selects Iri, which lies along a "remote local line" where the rails branch off for Chŏlla province, as the place to commit financial fraud. The space-time of clocks and trains, rather than emblemizing the ideals of civilization and enlightenment, began to function as a criminal plot. As such, Sunyŏng's feeling "motion sick" is only natural, because, when she was a student living in her school dormitory, this was "a scene from a life she never could have imagined."

THE LURE OF THE SLEEPING CAR, THE DESIRE OF THE HOT SPRINGS HOTEL

In point of fact, however, for Sunyŏng, "the gilding she had received from school might fall away extremely easily." She thought of the crowds on Chongno as being like "a swarm of mayflies blocking the path of her automobile." Moreover, before the "crystal-clear windowpane" of the "automobile's silk-upholstered interior," she felt the "reddish color of excitement come over her face, and the multicolored flames of an unfathomable desire in her bosom." "Such a lofty and noble automobile, like the throne of a king or queen," made "a large enough impression to overcome all the moral lessons she had learned from Mrs. P in school." When Sunyŏng rode in a first-class sleeping car for the first time, lying atop the "velvet bed, snow-white blanket, and even whiter sheets," staring "vacantly at her lustrous hands and feet," she proclaimed, "This is how a person should live!",[27] and began to smile.

Thus the first-class car made a laughing stock of the notion that, by providing passengers with a technologically equal situation, the train would lead to social equality.[28] On the one hand, completely unrelated to beds themselves, which were from the nineteenth century onward viewed as a "hygienic precautionary measure" to individuate spaces for invalids, and which contributed to the formation of autonomy, personal/interior monologues, and the custom of enjoying personal pleasure,[29] sleeping cars became an arena for a desire of the sort that tickled Sunyŏng's body. The moment she lay atop the bed, Sunyŏng had become Paek Yunhŭi's "Madonna."[30] And, as consequence of this, in that she was infected with gonorrhea and syphilis, Sunyŏng's bed brought about a result diametrically opposed to a hygienic life.

This being the case, in the wake of the "market price" that Ponggu repeated growing ever more clear, accurate, and prompt, the train and the oratorical tone of Hyŏngsik as he screamed "What do we have to do to save them?" disappeared. And, as a result, this means that people such as Sŏnhyŏng and Pyŏnguk, who would support paupers like Hyŏngsik and Yŏngch'ae, also became extinct. In this regard, Chŏnggyu's cursing Son Myŏnggyu for offering to pay Kŭmbong's tuition is not unconvincing.

> Ha. He's going to pay your tuition? Why would that guy pay your tuition? Is he your paternal uncle? Is he your maternal uncle? That guy is black-hearted and has other things in mind. That's right, in today's world where are you going to find a Buddha who spends his own money on someone else's daughter's tuition? No matter how naïve a wench you are, how could you fall for it? Geez, a guy like that is the director of a school? That school is going to do just great.[31]

Chŏnggyu does curse the "wenches that go to school these days" as "all a bunch of bitches," and this also accords with the thoughts of Ponggu's mother who proclaimed "I guess those bitches with the shiny mugs can't see nothing but money with their peepers. That's why even all the gals that graduated school go off and become concubines."[32] As Sŏnju put it, there are no longer "people who fall to the life of a servant while chasing after love." Like Sunyŏng and Kŭmbong, who walked similar paths, women frequently became "concubines for money." Or, as Yi Kwangsu put it, "Even in today's world there are some people who speak of things such as love and fidelity, however, they are a group that sits in a waiting room whose lights have long since gone out, waiting for a train already passed, not knowing it has gone by their station and come out on the other side of that long tunnel called the past."[33]

With the advent of this "straightforward," "scientific and business-like love," quite the "opposite of the love of ten years ago referred to as sacred love," the ideologies of free love and civilization and enlightenment came to an end. By way of comparison, as opposed to Hyŏngsik, who along with Sŏnhyŏng was a senior at the University of Chicago, and "intended to return to his home country following his graduation in September and a subsequent tour of post-war Europe," Ŭn'gyo, who had intended to study English literature and Education at the University of Chicago graduate school from September of 1921, due to the betrayal of Ŭnhŭi who married the wealthy

Min Changsik, was unable to complete a "thesis titled 'Ethical Psychology,'" and set foot back in her "home country humiliated."³⁴ Madam Kang, who in the passage below is reminiscent of Yŏngch'ae in her transformation from *kisaeng* to student abroad, eventually became a member of the generation of dormitory housemothers who were "nothing but strict."

> She spent her youth as a *kisaeng*, but at some point entered the house of Kang Ch'amyŏng. After he died, she took the few thousand *wŏn* she left with, steeled herself for several years, and went to America. Within seven years of her leaving, she graduated and returned. So when people spoke of Madame Kang, she was held in high esteem by all as a model for women.³⁵

This means the advent of travel in a different sense from that of study abroad or pilgrimages to famous national sites. Ch'oe Namsŏn composed "*Kyŏngbu ch'yŏlto norae* (Song of the Seoul-Busan railway, 1908)," and, while serializing "*K'wae sonyŏn segye chuyu sibo* (Current news of a vigorous boy's trip around the world)" in his magazine *Sonyŏn*, intended to make "the cold winds of Siberia" and "the blistering rays of the Equator" a part of "*Uri undongjang* (Our Playing Field, 1908)." He is also famous, however, for having written more insular works such as "*Simch'un sullye* (Simch'un pilgrimage, 1925)," "*Paekdusan kŭnch'amgi* (Record of a visit to Mount Paekdu, 1926)," "*Kŭmgang yech'an* (In praise of the Kŭmgang Mountains, 1928)," and "*Chosŏn yuramga* (Song of sightseeing in Korea, 1928)." For Ch'oe, "the Korean territory" was "nature itself reflecting Korea's history and philosophy and poetry and spirit." This was "unwritten in letters and yet the most clear and accurate, as well as interesting record."³⁶ Yi Kwangsu, for his part, who wrote such travelogues as "*Kŭmgangsan yugi* (Record of a journey to the Kŭmgang Mountains, 1922)," "*Ch'ungmugong yujŏk sullye* (Pilgrimage to the sites of Admiral Yi Sunsin, 1930)," "*Tan'gun nŭng* (Tan'gun's Tomb, 1936)," and "*Haesamwi rosŏ* (To Vladivostok, 1915)," evaluated "Admiral Yi Sunsin as the great savior who gave his own life to sustain singlehandedly the fate of the national territory and *minjok*."³⁷ He also stated that he wandered Siberia in order to observe "in what manner, beginning with China and moving on to Vietnam, Persia, and Egypt, the countries of *minjok* that had fallen or were about to fall were planning for their independence."³⁸ He went on to state his opinion that "the express train from Busan bound for the plains of Manchuria, eyes wide open, flies like an arrow," while continuing, "It is a world of civilization, a world of science, and a world of competition. If we but utilize that grand means of transportation and all of the conveniences of civilization, we can be rich."³⁹ Thus, for Ch'oe and Yi, travel expressed the modern projects of *minjok chuŭi* (ethnonationalism) and *puguk kangbyŏng* (a rich country and strong army). With the Sino-Japanese War (1894–1895), which suggested the victory of international law, as backdrop, Ongnyŏn from Yi Injik's *Hyŏl ŭi nu* (*Tears of Blood*, 1906) pioneered the "travel of the *minjok*," while Yŏngch'ae from Yi Kwangsu's *Mujŏng* succeeded her.

By the time *Chaesaeng*'s Insun returns, however, "having received an M.A. degree from West Chicago University," she is no longer the work's protagonist. Now, far from emblematizing the ideal of the *minjok*, she is at best nothing more than an ancillary character mediating the jealousy of Sunyŏng. "We shall roam the various regions of China to our hearts content. . . . To India, to Asian Minor, to Egypt, to Europe, is there anywhere we cannot go? South America or North America, is there anywhere we cannot go?" When Doctor Kim, who has already returned from study abroad, offers the above, Sunyŏng follows with the thoughts below.

> Since Insun went to America, I'll go to France or Italy and learn music. . . . So I'll become a big musician. . . . Three years will be enough. . . . I am the best at music. . . . So I'll become a world-famous pianist—When that happens, why would I envy the likes of Insun?—When that happens, won't the people of Korea again come to laud me?[40]

To Sunyŏng, study abroad does not represent the ideology of civilization and enlightenment. In that it has become a symbol of jealousy and vanity, the study abroad she dreams of is no different than her experience of accompanying Paek Yunhŭi, with his offer of "Take this diamond ring," to the hot springs. Like the scene of "beating an egg and washing one's hair with it"[41] at a hot springs hotel, it is close to high-end consumption behavior. The tears shed by Sunyŏng as she claims "My entire life—till the day I die, I will love you (Ponggu) and stay by your side," had already become glasswork "worth 200,000 *wŏn*."[42] The observation that "a woman's tears are seldom genuine diamonds; they are mostly imitations"[43] had been confirmed as fact. Actually, during a previous encounter as well, Sunyŏng had retorted in her thoughts, "Body and mind? Can you live off of body and mind?"[44]

For Sunyŏng, study abroad and foreign travel are at once tourism and escape. That she resolves to "go to some far and distant land" is due to the fact that Ponggu, who blames her, "does not have enough money to follow them." This forms a pair with Ponggu's viewing himself as identical not to the aged student abroad Kim Kwanil of *Hyŏl ŭi nu*, but rather to the usurer Hazama Kanichi. Below is Sunyŏng's experience at the hot springs, which triggered all of these events.

> The following day they got off at Busan Station before eating, immediately had breakfast at the station hotel, then caught a car and headed up to Tongnae Hot Springs. . . .

"Tongnae Hotel is big, but the baths and food are not as good as the Myŏngho," he said as parked the car in front of the Myŏngho Inn.

Servants beautiful enough to be the wives of prominent houses or the daughters of certain families came out and bowed at the waist before prostrating themselves on the ground to receive the two guests. It was all a spectacle Sunyŏng was viewing for the first time. It was her first taste of luxury.

"This is how a person should live!" thought Sunyŏng, before smiling once again. She wondered how spacious and clean the rooms would be. . . .

Sunyŏng was extremely happy all through that day. Having taken a bath, she intended to take out a book to read, but books were the furthest things from her mind. That said, she also could not sit still, and so sat down then got back up, walked about, and looked out through the window. She then used tongs to cover the coals and expose them again, after which she put a branch covered in plum blossoms to her nose and sniffed its cool fragrance, and in other ways generally showed her heart to be excited.[45]

Thus did Sunyŏng feel happiness and fall into "excitement" in a "spacious and clean" room at the Tongnae Hot Springs' "Myŏngho Inn."[46] Due to "a branch covered in plum blossoms" she failed to notice her books. But, as is also apparent in the term "station hotel," this feeling of Sunyŏng's originates from tourism, an economic behavior in which the railroad and capitalism interact. In the case of Japan, it is said that from the late Meiji and up through the Taisho and Showa periods, with the completion of transportation networks and ensuing freedom of travel, the age of the popularization of hot springs began.[47] In like fashion, the railroads of colonial Korea were also closely connected with hot springs. Son Myŏnggyu's persistent attempts at seduction are interlinked with this situation.

"Next is Ch'ŏnan. Shall we get off at Ch'ŏnan, go over to Onyang Hot Springs, and continue on an early train tomorrow?" said Mr. Son as he checked for Kŭmbong's reaction. . . .

"Although we're getting off at night, there's no way to do any work at night. Let's get off at Taejŏn. You know Mount Kyeryong, right? We'll have a look around Mount Kyeryong and also grab a bath at Yusŏng Hot Springs, and then tomorrow—well, now it's already not tomorrow—a bit later we'll take the four p.m. train, and when we get to Busan it will be time for the night boat. All things considered, the night boat is better. . . ."

"There's still over an hour until the boat leaves, so we, uhm, should go to the station hotel for a bit of breakfast. On foot it's quite a ways, but if we go by car it's really quick. And only fifteen minutes to eat." . . .

Kŭmbong ate breakfast at the hotel, then, from inside a car speeding for Haeundae Hot Springs, looked out upon the scenery of Busan for the first time.[48]

As evident in the quoted passage, she was foolish to have thought "Now I am saved," as the train passed Ch'ŏnan. The Seoul-Busan Railway took care not only of Onyang Hot Springs but also of Yusŏng, Haeundae, and others. In spite of the fact that she had continually beat back the advances of Mr. Son, when Kŭmbong arrived at the end of the line Haeundae Hot Springs[49] was beckoning. And there, with her own naked body, Kŭmbong washed away the childhood tales "of her becoming the exotic heroine Madame Yagan (Jeanne D'Arc) or Madame Naran (Marie Jeanne Rolland) that she used to hear from adults like Yi Ch'amnyŏng." Ironically, at precisely this hot springs bath, the consciousness of Yi Kwangsu's novel *Nongch'on kyebal* (*Rural development*, 1916–1917), in which "a public bath" was built, sloughed off its dead skin. At this point, "the relationship between bathing and health" and "the subtle beauty of bathing"[50] came to take on entirely different meanings. Of course, this is also likely not unrelated to his insisting upon "Hongjewŏn bathing"[51] in his *"Ch'inilp'a ŭi pyŏn* (Excuses of a Japanese collaborator, 1948)." Returning to Yi's fiction, the decisive scene of *Kŭ yŏja ŭi ilsaeng* plays out below.

Suddenly, Kŭmbong discovered something strange, something she had been unable to see up until now. It was the beauty of her own body. Its soft, ruddy flesh, the lines of arms and legs and torso, the bulging breasts—for the first time in her life Kŭmbong discovered the beauty of her own body. . . . Kŭmbong's heart raced without reason. . . .

Kŭmbong finally stood up and attempted the various poses and movements she had been picturing in her head up till now. They were all beautiful and pleasurable. She also tried striking a pose in which, ashamed, she lowered her head and twisted her body, or she tried striking a pose in which she relaxed every muscle and sat absentmindedly.

"This beauty, who will see this beauty? This softness, who will touch this softness?" she thought as she softly closed her eyes. . . .

But in the following moment, she became aware of a pounding in her heart, and of the feeling that the blood throughout her body suddenly increased in temperature and speed. She became aware of the restlessness of wanting to meet then and there that person, "You." Kŭmbong next became aware of a gladness as if that person, a truly handsome, healthy, and strong man, were standing right in front of her. Then, as if distressed, she twisted her body and let out a long sigh.[52]

The above also shares something in common with the scene in Yi's *Sarang ŭi tagakhyŏng* (*The polygon of love*, 1930) in which "high-temperature water gushes out, and then licks Ŭnhŭi's beautiful skin." In addition, that Kŭmbong's heart pounds with "the restlessness of wanting to meet then and there that person, 'You,'" brings to mind Sunyŏng amid her excitement feeling "as if (she were) waiting for someone." The hot springs causes her to "think that there is no way one should be alone in this sort of place." And before Sunyŏng's very eyes, as she asks "Who could that person waiting over there be?", a whole throng of men stands arrayed.[53] At the hot springs, which permits both the free movements of and gaze at her naked body, she became aware of her own desire.

This causes us to think once again of the term "concubine for money." Money is endlessly exchanged. Money has no lawful wife. This symbolizes the coordinates of modern people. It means a market location that is slightly different from the anthropogeographic location of *Mujŏng*. Modern people are one indicator of the market. Their selves are expressed through capitalist desire. This is why Sunyŏng thinks the "painting of a nude beauty" hanging in Paek Yunhŭi's room "resembles her."

With the special selection for a prize at the Japanese Ministry of Culture's 10th Art Exhibition of the 1916 work "*Yūgure* (Nightfall)" by Kim Kwanho, who had graduated from Tokyo Art School at the top of his class, the painting of nudes in colonial Korea began. In accordance with this, colonial modern literature constructed the artistic context that allowed Sunmo gladly to serve as nude model for Chŏnghyŏn's graduation project at Ueno Art School in the Yi T'aejun novel *Sŏngmo* (*Holy mother*, 1935–1936). In a different sense from this, however, hot springs allowed the naked body, while the naked body stripped away desire. Meanwhile, colonial society also consumed books such as *Miin nach'e sajin* (*Photos of nude beauties*) and *Namnyŏ sangae saenggak taero hollinŭn pŏp* (*The mutual love of men and women: methods for temptation as you please*).[54]

And all of these processes were mediated by money. This is the meaning of hot springs. It announces the onset of hot springs tourism, which would for some time produce Sunyŏng and Kŭmbong's desire to set "a whole throng of men" to roaming. It would continue until Sunyŏng, leaving behind the final letter stamped with "the postal seal of Kŭmgang Mountain, Onjŏng (Hot Springs) Village," departed from Ponggu forever. Of course, then too she took a train.

> When the train was about to leave, Sunyŏng thrust her hand out the car window asking Ponggu for a handshake. Ponggu took Sunyŏng's hand. Sunyŏng squeezed Ponggu's hand with all her might—Sunyŏng's cold hand quivered—
> "Ponggu, please forgive me—Yes, please forgive me."[55]

TRANSLATED FATE, EXCHANGED SUBJECTIVITY

Yet another core of *Chaesaeng* is discovered in the following thoughts of Sunyŏng.

First, Paek was a dignified and polite person. How could he look so *"gentle,"* look so *"delicate"*? Sun'gi looks ugly, and Yun seems ugly and looks wicked, and Ch'oe is manly but a scatterbrain. Mr. Kim is a beanpole. He is also persistent and acts revoltingly. But Paek is *"round," "smooth,"* and truly *"aristocratic."* What's more, he's a *"millionaire."* He has such a nice house, and he also loves me.[56]

Sunyŏng comprehends Paek Yunhŭi through English words such as gentle, delicate, round, smooth, aristocratic, and millionaire. Perhaps due to the teachings that "the young people of Korea have an overly *'selfish'* temperament—the spirit of sacrificing oneself—*'self-sacrifice'* spirit is severely lacking. The idea of the *'sacrifice'* of oneself in order to *'serve'* God is severely lacking,"[57] Sunyŏng requests that "even if I have done some bad things, *'you'* please forgive them all." Sunyŏng is a character who has received an "English language-style education" that would be nearly unimaginable to the young Yang Chudong who, despite being "already well-read in the Four Books, the Five Classics, and in the works of all traditional philosophers and scholars," not only "had no way to understand the bizarre word *'saminch'ing'* (third person), which was merely a combination of three simple Chinese characters,"[58] but also had serious *"daubŭt'ŭ"* (doubts) about why "school" and "listen" were not pronounced *"sŭch'ul"* and *"risŭt'en."*[59] As such, she is "dissatisfied with Paek's Chinese language-style tone." At the same time, she also uses Korean language terms for "wicked," "scatterbrain," and "beanpole" when thinking of Sun'gi, Yun, Ch'oe, and Kim.

Of course, "English language-style education" that operates in this manner is not limited only to Sunyŏng. Exposure to English (or Japanese) is a characteristic that appears in the fiction of Yi Kwangsu in general. The "speeches and writings" of *Mujŏng's* Yi Hyŏngsik "mixed in a lot of English, quoted the names and words of many famous Westerners," and appeared "as if they were direct translations of those from the West." And Sŏnhyŏng thought that "if she came to be good at English, her qualifications would rise, and that others would also love her and respect her more than now." In *Kŭ yŏja ŭi ilsaeng*, Kwangjin, who "reads Western literature," judged his "fate" to be the "opening scene of a tragicomedy," as he recalled "English words" such as "Sin—Punishment—Curse—Catastrophe,"[60] while in *Sarang ŭi tagakhyŏng* Ŭn'gyo used English to refer to the gentle Kwinam as "Miss Modesty." In *"Hyŏngmyŏngga ŭi anae (A revolutionary's wife*, 1930)," Kongsan unfolded his thoughts through a mixture of Japanese, Korean, and English: *"Yasashī tega hoshī"* (I want women's tender hands); *"Irŏke mom i ap'ŭgo tayoriganai tokiniwa naniyorimo yasashī tega hoshī"* (When I am this ill, more than anything else, I want women's tender hands); *"Chungbyŏng i hyŏngmyŏngga rŭl ningen no jiganeni"* (This serious illness reduces a revolutionary to his true character); and "Reduce—*redyusŭ*—Soft—soft—tender—tender—tender—hand . . ." Going even further, about himself, Yi once admitted the following.

> Even though I didn't know how to read it, because my circumstances appeared so humble, with the pitiful thought that if I looked at an English-language newspaper I might rise up a bit, I gave a ten *chŏn* coin and bought a copy of the *China Press*, published this morning in Shanghai and said to be the most influential foreign paper in China, and just sat flipping through the advertisements and pictures, after which I stuck it into the pocket of my overcoat so about half remained showing and used this as an adornment.[61]

When Sŏngsun, referring to herself, claims that she is no longer "a girl" but rather "a woman," or when she mistakenly names her tabby cat "Puppy," the fashionization of English seen above serves as backdrop. This demands attention be paid to the genealogy of English usage, which once led to "interrogation" for "high treason" due to the sort of misunderstanding below.

> "It's an English dictionary called *Diamond*,"
> As he said this, he opened his writing box, pulled out a sheet of paper, and began to write a letter. The Miser, arranging some other books replied,
> "*Dy, Dy, Dynamite.* Aren't you going to buy anything else besides this?"
> T'aesun responded,
> "For now I'm not going to buy anything other than this book. Damn, I wrote it wrong. When you stood beside my saying *dynamite*, I wrote *dynamite* in my letter as well. If I write that I bought *dynamite*, people will think I'm one of the rebels. I'd better fix it."[62]

As seen above, the incorporation of English was frequently accompanied by misunderstandings, but this particular misunderstanding may actually have represented an accurate appraisal of the situation. This is because, whether at the hands of miners or of "rebels," dynamite always exploded due to diamonds (economic matters), while at that time the foreign language "dictionary" and the rebels collaborated with one another. The line from Ku Yŏnhak's *Sŏlchungmae* (Plum blossoms in the snow, 1908), "In the empires of the West as well, it is all the scholars who have been unable to succeed in the world who instigate things, organizing socialist parties for lower-class people and throwing society into disorder," as well as "Rosa" from Cho Myŏnghŭis's "*Naktonggang* (The Naktong River, 1927)" and the eponymous female protagonist of Yi Hyosŏk's "*Churiya* (Julia, 1933)" are all translated aspects of the "foreign ideology called revolution."[63] The Julia described below cannot be separated from the process of translation that went from the *Old Testament* to *Das Kapital*.

Julia's form tonight as she emerged naked from behind the black curtain covering the back of the room was a bit different from usual. She used to leap out from behind the curtain and appear in front of Chuhwa without so much as a single grape leaf covering her resplendent naked body, but today she appeared covering her front, not with a grape leaf but with a book. For some reason, she had suddenly felt ashamed in front of Chuhwa. The book she used in place of a grape leaf was a copy of *Das Kapital*.[64]

Of course, the scene above is also related to Naomi, that "modern Eve" who spoke of the "philosophy of the apple."[65] She asserted that eating apples on "the streets" befits the proletariat, while abstinence was not a proletarian virtue.

As a result of all this, "a Chinese character dictionary called *Diamond*" sparkles with symbolic meaning. Forming a pair with the diamond rings of Kim Chungbae and Paek Yunhŭi, it forms the origin of Yi Sang in Tokyo skipping meals in order to throw his "last twenty *chŏn*" into purchasing a "*Times 4,000 Word Everyday English*" vocabulary book.[66] Accordingly, in *Mujŏng*, Yi Hyŏngsik's thoughts regarding language are important: "nothing other than the type of speaking and writing" that resembles direct translation from Western languages "can express deep and detailed ideas."[67] This raises the issue of translation as it relates to the essence of colonial modernity. The modernity of colonial Korea began with translation. This is why the Kim Tongin protagonist K, on the death of his wife, recalls "in Tolstoy's *War and Peace*, that expression Andrei saw on the face of his dead wife."[68] Experiencing even his own personal sadness as "the sadness when sitting alone inside a fifteenth or sixteenth century-style palatial building reading a *romantic* ancient tale of a knight," K makes the following confession.

In order to find a novel with a story like mine, and from it derive some solace, I first read D'Annunzio's *Francesca*.[69] Paulo's lover Francesca, even though she did not want to, was married to Paulo's elder brother, after which she and Paulo committed lovers' suicide. From this I received not so much as a speck of relief from my anguish. After that I read Dostoyevsky's *Poor Folk*.[70]

This also appears in Songbin, the protagonist of Yi T'aejun's *Sasang ŭi wŏrya* (Moonlit Night of Thought, 1941–1942), referring to his lover Ŭnju by the name "Karete." She is an admixture of Katyusha (Tolstoy, *Resurrection*), Elena (Turgenev, *On the Eve*), and Lotte (Goethe, *The Sorrows of Young Werther*). In similar fashion, Kŭmbong, based on her experience of reading Shakespeare, thinks that "when ruined by tragedy, though ruined it is still nice to be the object of the audience's attention." And to her *oppa*'s command that she become a nun, she even asks, "Yeah, that's right, there's a bit like that in *Hamlet*. Did he say that to Ophelia?"[71] Thus, when Kŭmbong gives her child the name "Adam," it is not likely merely to express the "meaning of having no father." The name was decisive in the child's birth, while suggesting the historical meaning of the world that would govern its existence in the future as well. To borrow Yi Kwangsu's expression, unlike the past when "Confucius and Mencius sat" inside people, inside people now "Russeau and Voltaire have taken their place, or perhaps Marx and Lenin are sitting."[72] This, together with the operation of various modern systems, means that the reality of the new era is experienced, described, imagined, constituted, analyzed, and disciplined according to a Western paradigm and perspective. As such, it is symbolic that Sunmo in Yi T'aejun's *Sŏngmo* becomes aware of "birth control" while memorizing the English word "C—O—NT—R—O—L, control . . ."[73] In addition, it is only natural that Yang Chudong stated that through Western novels he "learned" not only "all sorts and conditions of emotion and thought and -ism" but also "love."[74] This would also lead to the sort of argument below.

> "Sunbok, well—what did Nora do? Already several decades ago what was it that Nora did?"
> "Who cares who did what? Nora is Nora, and I am me."
> "That's true. A cow is a cow, and a dog is a dog. But if you are a new woman, I mean aren't you ashamed when you think of Nora way back then?"[75]

Early on, in his 1924 "*Oppa ŭi pimil p'yŏnji (Oppa's secret letter)*," Yi Kiyŏng used a woman named "Maria" as protagonist to lampoon free love, and now, in *In'gan suŏp*, Hyŏnho, son of "Elizabeth," is criticizing his wife based on Ibsen's *A Doll's House*. Translation acts also as a behavioral norm. This is the reason the thoughts of Hyŏnho's wife, who is opposed to his suggestion that they live independently from his parents, are unfamiliar like a foreign language. In that sense, translation is Hyŏnho's mother tongue. This is also the fundamental reason that Kapchin in Yi Kwangsu's *Hŭlk* (*The soil*, 1932–1933) came to say that "things written only in Korean are exactly like looking at Greek," and "If you go to the library, it's filled with Japanese, English, and German newspapers, magazines, and books, and you're looking at that worthless Korean language?"[76] Finally, this recalls the scene in Futabatei Shimei's *Ukigumo* (*The drifting cloud*, 1897) where Ishida remarks that "when compared to English newspapers, Japanese newspapers are just like children's newspapers."[77] At this juncture, the following poem by Nakano Sigeharu reads symbolically.

Here is the West
Dogs use English[78]

By way of comparison, Japan's "Imperial Hotel" was constructed with English. Translation of course led the composition of objective reality, but it also led forms of subjectivity such as the self, national spirit, and the "Great Japanese Empire." Saying that *"kimch'i* is *national spirit (minjok chŏngsin)* among food"[79] relates exactly to this. This is because it specifies that *"minjok chŏngsin,"* which is identified with *kimch'i,* is a translation of "national spirit." English (Japanese) has seeped into the taste of *"kimch'i."* Together with the *"sandwich"* Pyŏnguk offered Yŏngch'ae in *Mujŏng,* the modern location of *"kimch'i"* was discovered.

This being the case, the *"minjok chŏngsin"* of Yi Kwangsu's *Hŭlk* originates not in Hŏ Sung's communal hometown village but rather in "national spirit." "The utilitarian view of fiction that it must serve to defend both civil rights and national rights"[80] was constructed through the pioneering role played by literature in translation. Translation did not stop at the "Japanese gilding, Western gilding"[81] pointed out by Mr. Han in *Hŭlk.* Rather it was more essentially and genuinely involved with the *minjok.* *"Yŏnae,"* which was to form new families and produce a new *minjok,* was a translation of "love," and the colony accepted it nearly unaltered. As such, the hometown was also a place as seen below.

Chwa Yahak's declaration of conversion
Moved by a youth who says, though he read it twenty times, he cannot understand it
I down three double shots though I can't drink[82]

The *"kohyang"* (hometown) and *"minjok chŏngsin,"* which were somewhat inebriated by the political conversion of Sano Manabu, leader of the Japanese Communist Party, cannot be explained solely by difficult-to-translate local collective nuances such as those of *"kaenippadi"* (dog tooth) in the Paek Sŏk poem *"Modakpul"* (Bonfire, 1936). Just as Im Hwa wrote in his poem *"Yahaengch'a sok"* (Inside a night train car, 1935) that "dialect is extremely difficult to understand," when the young Song Pin went to the village school his classmates' manners of speaking were all different so that he could not communicate with them, "just like foreigners."[83]

Modern national spirit/*minjok chŏngsin* is deeply related to the establishment of national or standard language. But national language does not only stand in opposition to foreign languages; in that it otherizes and disciplines dialects, it also shares something in common with foreign languages. It only becomes a "national language" standing shoulder to shoulder with foreign languages by translating and dominating its own various dialects. National language conspires with foreign languages. In fact, the shouts of *"Bansai!"* that "thundered throughout the second-class *cabin"* and the "southwestern dialect calling for a young child" in Im Hwa's poem *"Haehyŏp ŭi romaent'isijŭm* (Romanticism of the strait, 1938)" are not opposed on this same level. If the "thrill" and "threat" of *"Bansai!"* express the Japanese nation-state, the difficult-to-understand "southwestern dialect" shares something in common with "the fathers' sighs" beneath "the third-class cabins," or with "the painful, burning crying of young children who have lost their parents" in another Im poem, *"Hyŏnhaet'an* (The Korea strait, 1938)." They are close to unsegmented sounds. This is the language of those who cannot express themselves. Just as "for the ancient Greeks the *barbaros*, or barbarian, was literally one who babbled, who did not speak the language of civilized humanity,"[84] this expresses a kind of barbarism. The scream and the flesh are one. Dialect is yet another nature. Only through grammar (logic) and text do words become a language separate from the flesh. Accordingly, sound is naturally defeated by "languages from foreign lands." This is an inevitable scene that will arise between civilization and barbarity. This is also related to the "unknown words" chattered by "the men in suits," and to the meaning of "saying nothing and merely bowing at the waist" to the insult *"Baka!"* in *"Yahaengch'a sok."* All that can be heard is the "water sound" of the Naktong River, and the speaker of "dialect" cannot speak.

As a result of the above, linguistic opposition is established in the space between the Japanese empire's national language, which engenders a feeling of "threat," and the standard linguistic (textual) position of the speaker who finds dialect difficult to understand. Furthermore, the speaker sentimentalizes, and in so doing otherizes, dialect with the question "Why does it evoke my tears?" This is discipline and domination upside down. Paradoxically, standard language is yet another foreign language. It is a bit of a leap, but the "pure sound of Korea" was expressed by foreign musical instruments as in the scene below.

> Miss Sim Sullye is an artist who produces the pure sound of Korea from the keyboard of a piano, a Western musical instrument. Indeed, it is Miss Sim Sullye whom we should truly call the daughter of Korea, the artist of Korea.[85]

But this age of translation, which begins with "an English dictionary called *Diamond*" and draws a line all the way to Yi Sang's *"Times 4,000 Word Everyday English,"* does not seem to be adequately explained solely by the "transplantation" of which Im Hwa spoke. This is due to the fact that the botanical and organic trope of transplantation obscures the mutual interrelation of the complicated exchanges at work in translation. Despite their new location and environment, transplanted plants put down roots and grow in a single place. Here, growth brings to mind the process of education and learning. In addition, and more fundamentally, the trope of transplantation is premised upon permanent cropping of the kind that might have taken place in Paek Sŏk's hometown. It reduces the processes of relations and effects to the categories of subject and existence. But translation, the literary-historical original real significance of transplantation is closer to commerce and trade, or even nomadism or exchange, than it is to school or agriculture. It is the cultural form of the "crossroads," which is represented by the rice exchange or imperialism, and corresponds to the activity of capital. Capital does not remain in one place as an intrinsic substance. By way of example, Sunyŏng's English as she rode in the sleeper car was pronounced against the background of Ponggu's rice speculation and Paek Yunhŭi's wealth. And the "Ophelia"-esque fate Kŭmbong imagined was tangled up in Son Myŏnggyu's failed trade activities on stages in such places as Hong Kong, Shanghai, the South Seas, Singapore, and Australia. Just as the encyclopedic presentations of Western literary knowledge and internal confessions of diaries in "*Maŭm i yŏt'ŭn chayŏ*" were carried out simultaneously with the discoveries of P'yŏngyang's "T'aean Trading Company" or the "Singer Company dealer" established in Onjŏng Village in the Kŭmgang Mountains.

This indicates the meaning of a Hermes-like train, one different from the ideologically pursued train of civilization and enlightenment, which is to say different from linear travel of departure and arrival, or from the growth of a student. With neither start nor finish, it complexly vitalizes the market and relations. The national border is another name for the customs office. Accordingly, the words of Yi Kiyŏng as he heckled Yi Kwangsu, author of "*Hyŏngmyŏngga ŭi anae* (A revolutionary's wife, 1930)," are significant: "Now the nickname '*minjok*' brilliantly enjoys even more currency than his real name. This is equivalent to paper money's circulating more brilliantly than gold coins in our current society."[86] In *Chaesaeng* we also see something similar in the following conversation between Dr. Kim, who has studied abroad in America, and Sunyŏng.

> "*Wherever you are go, I'll go.*"
> He said this with a smile in search of agreement. . . .
> "*Come on! No hesitation! . . .*"
> "Sir, what will you do taking along a thing like me? I'll just be in the way."
> Sunyŏng finally came to speak these words.
> "*Oh never never mind. As long as you go with me, I can go anywhere and do anything. . . .*"
> "*Alright. I follow you. Yes.*"
> Thinking to herself whether she should respond like this, Sunyŏng demurely lowered her head.[87]

"*I follow you*" defines the structure of Sunyŏng's existence. Following money and a man, she intended to go abroad. And her intention was constituted in the English "I follow you." This suggests her subjectivity, which exchanged and translated rather than existed. To her, Paek Yunhŭi was not just a wealthy nobleman, but rather an "*aristocratic*" "*millionaire*" imagined in English. And Doctor Kim was a "*hypocrite.*"

In light of the above, she did not simply abandon Ponggu. By substituting Ponggu with Paek Yunhŭi, and Paek Yunhŭi with millionaire, she entrusted herself to the activity of capital—the hot springs and rice speculation—and to a relationship with the Other. This proves that her self, just like wage labor, could not avoid being exchanged and translated. Such is the extent to which Sunyŏng's national language, "worth 200,000 *wŏn*," was exchange and translation. For Sunyŏng, having become a "concubine for money" in order to use the money of a concubine, nothing outside of this could exist. Following various relationships (men), she existed only at the "crossroads" where customs was cleared. She was the exterior. Thus, when she departed from the context of all those "*I follow you*"s that caused the outside endlessly to unfold, and attempted to return to the interior of existence, the only thing she was able to do was commit suicide.

With this in mind, it may only have been natural that Kŭmbong, who walked a similar path to that of Sunyŏng, was considered "some sort of filthy carrier of infectious disease." This is because, quite separate from Yi Kwangsu's intentions as expressed in the word "*chaesaeng*" (rebirth), the form of the subject that comprised Sunyŏng or Kŭmbong was infection. For these protagonists, as Yi Sang put it in his poem "*P'ach'ŏp* (A torn memorandum, 1937)," "obscene foreign words writhed like so many germs." Thus translation is in many respects "treason." But through that very infection (translation), those women expressed the structure of the modern subject (particularly the colonial subject). It was regarding all this that people went on and on about "being deceived by love and in tears for money." Either that, or they scorned it as "betrayal."

NOTES

1. "Strange fate" is a translation of "*kiyŏn*" (奇緣), which can also be translated as "curious coincidence" or "irony of fate." This is the term Kim Tongin somewhat pejoratively used in his work *Ch'unwŏn yŏn'gu* (*A study of Yi Kwangsu*) (Seoul: Sin'gu munhwasa, 1956) to describe certain aspects of Yi's fiction that he deemed unrealistic.—Trans.

2. Yi Kwangsu, "*Kaech'ŏkcha* (The pioneer)," in *Yi Kwangsu chŏnjip* 1 (Seoul: Samjungdang, 1962), 323.

3. Chŏng Chiyong, "*Sigye rŭl chugim* (Killing the clock)," in *Chŏng Chiyong chŏnjip* 1 (Seoul: Minŭmsa, 1992), 104.

4. Ch'oe Sŏhae, *Hooe sidae* (*Age of the extra*) (Seoul: Munhak kwa chisŏngsa, 1994), 168.

5. This living completely according to a timetable also appears in the family that lives in the Western-style house in Kim Sŭngok's short story "*Yŏksa*" (The strongman, 1964).

6. For more on this, see the previous chapter, "Barbarian of the Laboratory."

7. Chŏng Chiyong, "*Sigye rŭl chugim*," 89.

8. Yi Kwangsu, "*Mujŏng* (The Heartless)," in *Yi Kwangsu chŏnjip* 1 (Seoul: Samjungdang, 1962), 195.

9. Yi Kwangsu, *Chaesaeng* (*Rebirth*), in *Yi Kwangsu chŏnjip* 2 (Seoul: Samjungdang, 1962), 25.

10. Yi Kwangsu, *Chaesaeng*, 138.

11. We are told that affixed to Ponggu's hat was "a tag on which sat three Cs" (Yi Kwangsu, *Chaesaeng*, 15). This is presumed to be the mark of Chosun Christian College, the forerunner of Yŏnhŭi College.

12. For more on the relationship between *Chaesaeng* and *Konjiki yasha*, see Kim Yunsik, *Yi Kwangsu wa kŭ ŭi sidae* (*Yi Kwangsu and His Times*) (Seoul: Han'gilsa, 1986), 821–29.

13. Yi Kwangsu, *Chaesaeng*, 131.

14. Ko Il, *Inch'ŏn sŏkkŭm* (*Inch'ŏn, past and present*) (Inch'ŏn: Kyŏnggi munhwasa, 1955), 181–82.

15. Ibid, 108. Another reference for the rice exchange is Han Suyŏng, "*Habakkun esŏ hwanggŭm kkaji*" (From habakkun to gold rusher), presented at the *Yŏnse taehakkyo kukhak yŏn'gudan simp'ojiŏm, singminji kŭndaehwa wa ilsang saenghwal* (Yonsei University Korean studies research symposium: colonial modernization and everyday life), November 8, 2002.

16. Yi Kwangsu, *Chaesaeng*, 193.

17. Ibid., 133–34.

18. Yi Sang, "*Nalgae* (Wings)," in *Yi Sang munhak chŏnjip* 2, ed. Kim Yunsik (Seoul: Munhak sasangsa, 1991), 344.

19. Yi Sang, "*Chiju hoesi* (Two spiders meet a pig)," in ibid., 303.

20. Ch'ae Mansik, "*T'angnyu* (*Muddy water*)," in *Ch'ae Mansik chŏnjip* 2 (Seoul: Ch'angjaksa, 1987), 15.

A *habakkun* is also a type of speculator, but one who, after having lost all of his money, continues to speculate without any capital.—Trans.

21. Kim Namch'ŏn, "*T ilbo sa* (The T daily newspaper company)," in *Inmun p'yŏngnon*, November 1939, 189–90.

22. Ibid, 200.

23. Yi Kwangsu, *Chaesaeng*, 132.

24. Yi Kwangsu, *Mujŏng*, 97.

25. Yi Kwangsu, *Chaesaeng*, 9.

26. Ch'oe Sŏhae, *Hooe sidae*, 329–30.

27. Yi Kwangsu, *Chaesaeng*, 70.

28. See Wolfgang Schivelbusch, *The Railway Journey: The Industrialization and Perception of Time and Space in the 19th Century* (Berkeley: The University of California Press, 1986), 70–73.

29. Philippe Ariès and Georges Duby, eds., *A History of Private Life*, Volume IV (Cambridge: Belknap Press of Harvard University Press, 1990). This is a translation into English of the French original: *Histoire de la vie privée*. The source used for the Korean version was the following translation: trans. Chŏn Suyŏn, *Sasaenghwal ŭi yŏksa* 4, (Seoul: Saemulgyŏl, 2002), 612.

30. "Madonna" is in quotation marks to denote its being used with reference to the Yi Sanghwa poem "*Na ŭi ch'imsillo*" (To my bedchamber, 1923).

31. Yi Kwangsu, "*Kŭ yŏja ŭi ilsaeng* (That woman's life)," in *Yi Kwangsu chŏnjip* 7 (Seoul: Samjungdang, 1966), 42.

32. Ibid., 24.

33. Yi Kwangsu, "*Hyŏngmyŏngga ŭi anae* (A revolutionary's wife)," in *Yi Kwangsu chŏnjip* 2 (Seoul: Samjungdang, 1966), 360.

34. Yi Kwangsu, "*Sarang ŭi tagakhyŏng* (*The polygon of love*)," in *Yi Kwangsu chŏnjip* 7 (Seoul: Samjungdang, 1962), 415.

35. Yi Kwangsu, *Chaesaeng*, 81.

36. Ch'oe Namsŏn, "*Simch'un sullye* (Simch'un pilgrimage)," in *Yuktang Ch'oe Namsŏn chŏnjip* 6 (Seoul: Hyŏnamsa, 1973), 259.

37. Yi Kwangsu, "*Ch'ungmugong yujŏk sullye* (Pilgrimage to the sites of Admiral Yi Sunsin)," in *Yi Kwangsu chŏnjip* 18 (Seoul: Samjungdang, 1962), 257.

38. Yi Kwangsu, "*Na ŭi kobaek* (My confession)," in *Yi Kwangsu chŏnjip* 13 (Seoul: Samjungdang, 1962), 208.

39. Yi Kwangsu, "*Odo tapp'a yŏhaeng* (Traveling through five provinces on foot)," in *Yi Kwangsu chŏnjip* 18 (Seoul: Samjungdang, 1962), 173.

40. Yi Kwangsu, *Chaesaeng*, 315.

41. Pak Hwasŏng "*Onch'ŏnjang ŭi pom* (Spring at a hot springs hotel)," in *Chungang*, July 1936, 118.

42. Yi Kwangsu, *Chaesaeng*, 49.

43. Natsume Sōseki, *Kōjin* (*The Wayfarer*, 1913), trans. Beongcheon Yu (Detroit: Wayne State University Press, 1967), 137.

44. Although not fully clear out of context, "*mom kwa maŭm* (body and mind)" here represent a complete love that is both physical and spiritual, perhaps closer to "body and soul." Sunyŏng's silent rhetorical question signals both her contempt for such conceptions of love and her sole focus on material concerns.—Trans.

45. Yi Kwangsu, *Chaesaeng*, 70–71.

46. In a guidebook published in 1923 by the *Chosŏn inswae chusik hoesa* (Korean Printing Corporation), which was operated by the Japanese Government General of Korea, titled *Chosŏn ch'ŏlto yŏhaeng p'yŏllam* (*A guide to rail travel in Korea*), Tongnae is mentioned as one of the places with "well-organized facilities such as hotels and restaurants, giving it the feeling of a true hot springs area," while also introducing among its lodgings the Tongnae Hotel, Yŏnyu Inn, Hwangjŏng Inn, Sizuno Family Inn, and the Myŏngho Inn.

47. *Nihon fūzokusi gakkai, Nihon fūzokusi jiten* (Dictionary of the history of Japanese customs) (Tokyo: Kōbundō, 1980), 80.

48. Yi Kwangsu, "*Kŭ yŏja ŭi ilsaeng*," 51–56.

49. Haeundae Hot Springs were discovered in 1897 by a Japanese medical doctor named Wada Nomo. There are over thirty geothermal wells, which from 1932

were run by a joint-stock company invested in by both Koreans and Japanese. See Naemubu (Korean Ministry of Home Affairs), *Onch'ŏnji* (*Hot springs areas*) (Seoul: Tongyang munhwa inswae chusik hoesa, 1983), 163.

50. Yi Kwangsu, "*Nongch'on kyebal* (Rural development)," in *Yi Kwangsu chŏnjip* 17 (Seoul: Samjungdang, 1962), 102.

51. Yi Kwangsu, "*Ch'inilp'a ŭi pyŏn* (Excuses of a Japanese collaborator)," in *Yi Kwangsu chŏnjip* 13 (Seoul: Samjungdang, 1962), 280.

"Hongjewŏn bathing" refers to a policy instituted by King Injo (r. 1623–1649) in order to solve the problem of the chastity of the unmarried women who had returned after having been taken away during the second Manchu invasion of Korea (1636–1637). He commanded that they bathe at Hongjewŏn before returning to Seoul, and that following this no further inquiries be made into the matter.

52. Yi Kwangsu, "*Kŭ yŏja ŭi ilsaeng*," 61–63.

53. Yi Kwangsu, *Chaesaeng*, 61–63. This is reminiscent of a scene at the baths of the Yusŏng Hot Springs in which Myŏngnye, despite the fact that she herself is no more than the concubine of an old man over fifty, feels sorry for the "girl" "living at the inn" who will have to service "numerous men." See Pak Hwasŏng, "*Onch'ŏnjang ŭi pom* (Spring at the hot springs hotel)," in *Hongsu chŏnhu* (Seoul: Paekyangdang, 1948), 83.

54. See Yi Kihun, "*Kŭndaejŏk toksŏ ŭi t'ansaeng* (The birth of modern reading)," in *Yŏksa pip'yŏng*, Volume 62, 2003, 352.

55. Yi Kwangsu, *Chaesaeng*, 341.

56. Ibid, 341.

All the italicized words are in transliterated English in the original. What sets them apart from other such instances, however, is that a parenthetical Korean translation is provided for each, which gives rise to several interesting questions about intended audience and effect/affect.—Trans.

57. Ibid, 255.

58. Yang Chudong, Munju pansaenggi (Record of half a life spent on literature and liquor) (Seoul: Sint'aeyangsa ch'ulp'an'guk, 1962), 28.

59. Ibid, 2.

60. Yi Kwangsu, *Kŭ yŏja ŭi ilsaeng*, 240–41.

61. Yi Kwangsu, "*Haech'amwi rosŏ* (To Vladivostok)," in *Ch'ŏngch'ŭn*, Volume 6, March 1915, 81.

62. Ku Yŏnhak, "*Sŏlchungmae* (Plum blossoms in the snow)," in *Han'guk sinsosŏl chŏnjip* 6 (Seoul: Ŭryu munhwasa, 1968), 28.

63. This phrase was coined by Isoda Kōichi in his work *Rokumeikan no keihu* (*The genealogy of the Rokumeikan*) (Tokyo: Bungei shunshū, 1984).

64. Yi Hyosŏk, "*Churiya* (Julia)," in *Yi Hyosŏk chŏnjip* 4 (Seoul: Ch'angmisa, 1990), 35.

65. Yi Hyosŏk, "*Orion kwa imgŭm* (Orion and the apple)," in *Yi Hyosŏk chŏnjip* 1 (Seoul: Ch'angmisa, 1990), 260.

66. Yi Sang, "*Sirhwa* (Lost Flower)," trans. Steven D. Capener, in *Acta Koreana*, Volume 13, Number 2, December 2010, 130.

67. Yi Kwangsu, *Mujŏng*, 182.

68. Kim Tongin, "*Maŭm i yŏt'ŭn chayŏ* (Oh, ye with faint hearts)," in *Ch'angjo*, Volume 3, December 1919, p. 35. (or *Chŏnjip* p. 149)

69. This refers to the play *Francesca da Ramini* written by Gabriele D'Annunzio. Although the publication date given is 1902, it was first performed on stage in December 1901.

70. Kim Tongin, "*Maŭm i yŏt'ŭn chayŏ,*" 70.

71. Yi Kwangsu, *Kŭ yŏja ŭi ilsaeng*, 218.

72. Ibid., 283.

73. Yi T'aejun, "*Sŏngmo*," 173.

74. Yang Chudong, *Munju pansaenggi*, 23.

75. Yi Kiyŏng, *In'gan suŏp* (*Human lessons*) (Seoul: Munu ch'ulp'ansa, 1948), 15.

76. Yi Kwangsu, *Hŭlk* (*The soil*), in *Yi Kwangsu chŏnjip* 6 (Seoul: Samjungdang, 1962), 40.

77. Futabatei Shimei, *Ukigumo* (*The drifting cloud*) (Tokyo: Iwanami bunko, 2000), 107.

78. Nakano Shigeharu, *Nakano Shigeharu shishyū* (*Collected poems of Nakano Shigeharu*) (Tokyo: Iwanami shoten, 1978), 82.

79. Yi Kwangsu, *Hŭlk*, 27.

As mentioned in chapter 3, "*national spirit*" is italicized to denote that it is transliterated in the original.—Trans.

80. Kim Pyŏngch'ŏl, Han'guk kŭndae pŏnyŏk munhaksa yŏn'gu (Research on the history of modern literature in translation in Korea) (Seoul: Ŭryu munhwasa, 1975), 169.

81. Yi Kwangsu, *Hŭlk*, 33.

82. Kim Kirim, "*Kohyang (Ta)* (Hometown [B])," in *Kim Kirim chŏnjip* 1 (Seoul: Simsŏltang, 1988), 361.

The word in the original for "converted" is *chŏnhyang* (Japanese, *tenkō*), which literally means to change direction. Here it refers to the renunciation, often coerced and later public, of communism/socialism. This poem recounts the shock felt in the poet's hometown (a Korean rural village) when this renowned Japanese communist leader renounced his views. Chwa Yahak (佐野學), the Korean pronunciation of Sano Manabu, literally means to help or encourage studying in rural areas, but is also homophonous in Korean with "leftist studying at night (左夜學)," which was another thing done by those who farmed or worked in factories by day.—Trans.

83. Yi T'aejun, "*Sasang ŭi wŏrya* (Moonlit night of thought)," in *Maeil sinbo*, March 11, 1941.

84. David Spurr, *The Rhetoric of Empire* (Durham: Duke University Press, 1993), 102.

85. Yi Kwangsu, *Hŭlk*, 439.

86. Yi Kiyŏng, "*Pyŏnjŏlcha wa kŭ ŭi anhae* (A turncoat and his wife)," in *Sin'gyedan*, May 1935, 103–04.

87. Yi Kwangsu, *Chaesaeng*, 313–14.

In the original, all italicized words are transliterated English, all of which are followed by parenthetical Korean translations. See endnote 55.—Trans.

Chapter 7

English Grammar, Sports, Cyborg

SPRING GARDEN'S ENGLISH GRAMMAR

Yi Kwangsu's discussions of marriage are widely known. Works such as *"Chohon ŭi aksŭp* (The vice of early marriage, 1916)" or *"Sonyŏn ŭi piae* (The sorrows of a boy, 1917)" criticize the abuses of early marriage, while in *Mujŏng* (*The Heartless*, 1917) Pyŏnguk poses a fundamental question regarding Yŏngch'ae's engagement, in which she merely obeys "the words of her father."[1] On the other hand, in pieces like *"Honin e taehan kwan'gyŏn* (Personal views on marriage, 1917)" and *"Honinnon* (On marriage, 1917)," Yi defines marriage as a contract. Marriage is a contract "to live together,"[2] and a "contractual act voluntarily undertaken by adult males and females."[3] And there can be no contract without conditions. As such, "conditions for marriage" such as health, mental strength, sufficient development, economic ability, love, and reason are indispensable. But these "conditions for marriage" at work in selecting a partner are also the various virtues of the modern subject. Furthermore, the contract is the essential form of relationship of modern subjects. In this sense, marriage is a thoroughly modern practice. This "contractual behavior" is carried out as follows.

"Yes, and then what do you intend to do?"
"I will follow *you*."
For the first time, Sŏngsun used the second person pronoun with Min.
"Where to?"
"Anywhere!"[4]

What is interesting in the quotation are the words "*you*" and "second person pronoun." A contract is undertaken between an equal and independent first person and second person. It is precisely the operation of this mutual subjectivity that comprises the structure of contracts concluded in the market. Early marriage is problematic because the subjects of the contract are not individuals. Modern marriage may actually be the projection onto the institution of marriage of a liberalistic order that takes individuals, rather than clans or families, as the subjects of possession and of contracts. This is similar to how free love, in which the choice of a partner is made according to an individual's ability and without regard for social status or the opinions of parents, displays homogeny with the economic system of free competition. In fact, Such'ŏl in Kim Tongin's short story "*Kudu* (Dress shoes, 1930)" prepares a pair of white dress shoes for Miss K in order to beat back the competitors for her affection. This suggests the position of "civilized humanity," who "conceive even of procreation, the purpose of the Creator, as their own purpose"[5] not as the Creator's purpose. This speaks eloquently of the appearance of the liberalistic and market economic individual.

> If, as biology teaches us, the objective of humanity (like other living creatures) is the preservation of the individual being and the preservation and development of the race,[6] then the center of the world is one's self, with the next most important being one's progeny, so that, excluding special cases, sacrificing one's self for others is evil, and, moreover, is not done according to one's free will, but rather as the slave of another.[7]

Both marriage and contracts are the domain of "free will" that establishes "one's self" as the "center of the world." This is why Sŏngsun put forth "an understanding of each other's individuality" as the condition for true love, while saying that "in all matters and all operations 'we two' have been the nominative case."[8]

In addition to the above, what also merits revisiting are terms like "*you*," "second person pronoun," and "nominative case." In Yi Kwangsu's case, the perspective from which he defined marriage or contracts was based on the grammatical divisions of foreign languages, particularly English. Different from the young Yang Chudong who, despite being "already well-read in the Four Books, the Five Classics, and in the works of all traditional philosophers and scholars," "had no way to understand the bizarre word '*saminch'ing*' (third person), which was merely a combination of three simple Chinese characters,"[9] the Yi Kwangsu who appeared in literary history, together with his fictional English instructor Yi Hyŏngsik in *Mujŏng*, interpreted the Chinese characters and literary Chinese passages related to marriage based on English grammar.

> Generally speaking, marriage is a contractual act voluntarily undertaken by adult males and females. Even though parents may provide considerable

guidance and support, "getting a man married" and "sending off a woman to be married" are not possible. A man marries; someone else does not get him married, and the same is true for a woman. The Chinese character *ch'wi* (娶) means a man marries; it does not mean someone else gets him married, while the Chinese character *ka* (嫁) means a woman marries; it does not mean she is sent off to be married. I am ignorant and do not have much knowledge of the classics, but even when the classics mention marriage it seems generally as if "the man marrying" and "the woman marrying" are in the nominative case. How shall we parse "*Samsip i yusil*" (三十而有室)? Is it "At 30, he was allowed (or caused) to have a wife."? Or is it "At 30, he had a wife."? If the former, it is transitive and causative; if the latter, it is intransitive. And for women, it is not that they are allowed (or caused) to put a pin in their hair at fifteen, it is that at fifteen they naturally have the ability to put up their hair with a pin.[10] "A man marries" is the proper saying. The term and custom of "getting a man married" only came into being after the institution of marriage had been corrupted and parents came to view children as their possessions.[11]

The crux of the above quotation is that marriage is not a transitive verbal activity of the parents in which children are taken to be objects, and that *ch'wi* (娶) and *ka* (嫁) are intransitive verbs carried out by children in the "nominative case." In this fashion, Yi, by appropriating (monopolizing=occupying) the structure and meaning of literary Chinese through the framework of English grammar, draws a conclusion regarding marriage that centers "on the primacy of children." Yi's views on marriage are carried out through a code of English grammatical interpretation and translation. At the risk of a slight exaggeration, the founding of the modern marriage system is no different than the establishment of the Western grammatical consciousness that made clear the distinction and renegotiated the relationship between subject and object, intransitive and transitive verb. And eventually this was to mediate the modern social order as a whole.

Of course, it is not only grammar and grammatical consciousness that are involved in this social interaction. In the case of Sŏngsun when she asserts that she is not "*a girl*" but "*a woman*," or, going further, as observed in the narration in *Mujŏng* that "the three young women, having held a benefit concert in the waiting room of Samnangjin Station, would now become fine *ladies*,"[12] this is also observable on the level of terms used to assign names, descriptions, and relationships to things and people. For example, that "Hyŏn," the female doctor in Yi Kwangsu's *Hŭlk* (*The soil*, 1932–33), although "not allowing her servants to use terms such as milady or ma'am," is referred to as "doctor"[13] is not unrelated to Sin Usŏn in *Mujŏng* referring to Yi Hyŏngsik as "*Mister Lee*." Sunyŏng, who in Yi Kwangsu's *Chaesaeng*

(*Rebirth*, 1924) requests that "Even if I have done some bad things, *you* please forgive them all," comprehends Paek Yunhŭi as below.

> First, Paek was a dignified and polite person. How could he look so "*gentle*," look so "*delicate*"? Sun'gi looks ugly, and Yun seems ugly and looks wicked, and Ch'oe is manly but a scatterbrain. Mr. Kim is a beanpole. He is also persistent and acts revoltingly. But Paek is "*round*," "*smooth*," and truly "*aristocratic*." What's more, he's a "*millionaire*." He has such a nice house, and he also loves me.[14]

Sunyŏng describes Paek's positive qualities in English, while she uses Korean for the negative aspects of Sun'gi, Yun, Ch'oe, and Kim. This is because she has received an "English language-style education," so much so that she is "dissatisfied with Paek's Chinese language-style tone." Accordingly, her primary existential coordinates appear to be translation. This also matches well with her location in comparing these various men. Of course, this sort of narrative attitude forms a pair with the historical process in Northeast Asia where "inspiration" (煙士披里純), "Montesquieu" (孟德斯鳩), "Lincoln" (林肯), and "Rousseau" (盧梭) all had to be transliterated using Chinese. Additionally, this brings to mind the case of Natsume Sōseki who preferred the "classical Chinese literary world" of a man and another man, that is to say a "symmetrical world" in which equal and mutual communication was possible, while detesting as "an English literary thing" the asymmetrical love between a man and a woman, as well as a woman's choosing of her own marriage partner.[15] In a word, Sunyŏng possesses tastes the opposite of Sōseki's.

We also discover aspects similar to those of Sunyŏng in the case of Yi Hyŏngsik, who dreams of writings in English. His speeches and writings "mixed in a lot of English, quoted the names and words of many famous Westerners," and appeared "as if they were direct translations of those from the West." But, from the standpoint of "*Mister Lee*" Hyŏngsik, with his "*engagement*" to Sŏnhyŏng, this was only natural. This is due to the fact that, just as Sunyŏng was immersed in "English language-style education," he believed that "nothing other than the type of speaking and writing" that resembles direct translation from Western languages "can express deep and detailed ideas."[16] As evidenced below, his thoughts too were "English language-style."

> Hyŏngsik theoretically considered Yŏngch'ae's acts to be wrong, however, emotionally he could not help but cry for her. But he considered her a "woman," or, to attach another adjective, an old-fashioned woman vehement about remaining pure. But Usŏn considered these acts of Yŏngch'ae to be absolutely good. One was English language-style, the other classical Chinese-style.[17]

This suggests that the English-language perspective that discovers, translates, and constitutes reality had taken effect, or, going a bit further, that the otherization of "classical Chinese-style" had begun to operate. At this juncture, the modern *"vision"* composed of English grammar and terms looked out upon the following scene.

> Then a *vision*[18] appeared before Ponggu's eyes. It was the vision of Jesus with bare feet and shabby clothes sitting at the edge of the sea in Galilee among the ignorant, simple fishermen and pitiful invalids he had gathered there, and on one side teaching, while on the other side healing sickness.[19]

That this *"vision,"* which is not only formed in English but also uses the English word to describe itself, is captured represents one scene of Christianity, which led the way for the modern age in colonial Korea. What the modern perspective looks out upon is only modernity. (Or by discovering modern scenes the modern perspective arises.) In like fashion, the nominative case children cannot help but dream of an intransitive verb marriage. They are the subjects of the *"vision"* and utterances that will choose, name (word), and constitute (grammar) their partners. They are also simultaneously the subjects of a contract carrying out an exchange. The significance of marriage as conceived of by Yi Kwangsu relates to this issue. The "nominative case" called groom and bride, through their acts and perspectives, will both constitute and observe modern reality. As a result, Yi's *"Honin e taehan kwan'gyŏn"* is not at all a modestly mentioned narrow opinion. It took the birth of the modern first person, that subject of various intransitive verb activities, and proclaimed it in the spring garden (Ch'unwŏn) of youth right on the verge of marriage.

PLAYING FIELD OF THE INTRANSITIVE VERB

One additional thing that should be discussed with regard to Yi Kwangsu is his views on the ultimate objective of marriage. As can be seen in the "conditions for marriage" he presented, marriage is designed for the production of physically and mentally healthy children. This view is deeply eugenic and evolutionary.

> A robust person should definitely produce a large number of robust children, so that, provided of course that there are no weaknesses in the maternal line, his descendants shall prosper in health for eternity. If this, however, is not the case, it is due to marrying imprudently and thereby bringing in the blood of an inferior maternal line. Furthermore, it has traditionally been said that the descendants of renowned ancestors will produce great men, and this too is the truth. If a hero of

the world may merely obtain a spouse with physical and mental strength equal
to his, then his descendants shall be intelligent and courageous generation after
generation.[20]

Of course, this sort of perspective is not only an attempt to make the genealogy flourish by planning for the prosperity of the family. Furthermore, it
does not stop at the pursuit of happiness in an individual's *"sweet home."*[21] As
eloquently expressed in opinions such as "good parents by no means think of
their children as 'my son,' but rather as 'a member of my race,'"[22] or "today,
when the competition among countries has reached maximum intensity, each
country considers its geniuses as important as life itself,"[23] this is the project
of a *minjok* (ethnonation) that fears it will die out as "a strain no different than
the 'Ainu' of Hokkaido."[24] This is the reason that Yi, while defining tuberculosis germs and syphilis germs as the "enemy of the *minjok*,"[25] had Kyehyang
in *Mujŏng* and Hŏyŏng in *Sarang* (*Love*, 1939) contract syphilis, and, going
even further, had Sunyŏng in *Chaesaeng* give birth do a blind daughter due to
congenital syphilis. Moreover, this is also the reason he criticizes the premodern view of chastity as embodied in the saying "a woman of virtue marries
but once," as well as the practice of "living as a widow."[26] Not permitting
remarriage not only caused individuals to "spend the flower of youth mired
in sad tears" but also brought about a "loss" that "prevented many millions of
the race's people who should have been born from appearing in the world."[27]
     Out of this conjoining through rational love, children who possessed the
best possible genetic factors, and, further, were healthy, having through such
projects as the permission of remarriage and education on hygiene defeated
all sorts of germs and "loss," would go on to take up arms for *minjok* and
country. This is because "all living animals have only one life," save for
human beings, who engage in social life and thus have "two lives,"[28] one
as an individual, and another as a member of the *minjok*. This means one
must think of "the group over the individual, that is consider public more
important than private, and service to society as one's life."[29] It is precisely at
this point, along with the categorical imperative "Youth of Korea, transcend
yourselves," that we arrive at the world of the "first person plural," the true
province of Yi's *minjok*-ist grammar.

> Truly the boys of Korea today are the destiny of the entire *minjok*, so that they
> must not use you and I, Kim and Yi, but only the first person plural "We."[30]

If it was modern marriage that realized concretely the first person singular
"I," then the *minjok*, mediated by the English grammar of "first person plural,"

was first born as "we." Thus the "*minjok*" is the "first person plural." And "independence" is the category that designates the intransitive verb activity of the first person plural in internalizing English grammar and English words. The intransitive verb practice of the *minjok* is established through the Other (transitive verb) known as English.

This brings to mind the fact that Yi Kwangsu, who stated "the remarkable trait of civilized people is that they possess emotions in common,"[31] and stressed "common emotions" and "sociality," brought up the national character and "free association" of the people of England in World War I who, by fighting as "volunteer soldiers," "sacrificed their individual freedom for the group."[32] This is the true origin of the provision that "*kimch'i* is national spirit (*minjok chŏngsin*) among food."[33] Ironically, "*minjok chŏngsin*" is a translation of "national spirit." English has seeped into the taste of "*kimch'i*." Division always begins from otherness. This is the structure of the modern arena called *minjok* (We). And it is in that arena, which includes eugenics, the struggle for existence, and often imperialism, the dialectic movement (sports) called history will begin to sweat. In that sense, the *minjok* is a genuine playing field. For example, the quotation below shows what "our playing field" was to Ch'oe Namsŏn.

1
Let us kick "*footballs*"
Let us run races
The quick energy generating
Let us bring it forth and unfurl it!
On the wide plains of that Oriental continent
Still waiting to meet its master
Let us
Let us
Le . . . et . . . us . . . !!!

2
Let us swim
Let us row
The limbs of young husbands and the bodies of young bachelors
Make them bronzed, make them firm!
On the great waters of that Pacific ocean !!
Desired as our playing field
Let us
Let us
Le . . . et . . . us . . . !!![34]

The reason An Ch'angho, while intending to give "the opportunity to cultivate the three forms of education—moral, physical, and intellectual—to the entire *minjok*,"[35] "prioritized physical education and moral education over intellectual education" was in order to activate playing fields like those above. The "*minjok*" was to implement a physical education that would "turn the wheel of a new world's era"[36] "with all their might" until they reached "the wide plains of that Oriental continent" and "the great waters of that Pacific ocean." In fact, on the "ideal base" in "Songt'ae, Taebo Village, Kangsŏ County, South P'yŏngan Province" that An Ch'ango himself designed, directed, built, and occupied, he intended to install playing fields and "children's playgrounds." By allowing the village "men and women, young and old, all to receive the benefits and pleasures of physical education," he planned to "improve the physiques of the *minjok* like they had in Sweden and Denmark, and to extend the average lifespan while enhancing activity efficiency."[37]

And this became Yi Kwangsu's standpoint as well. In "*Minjok kaejoron*" he proposed gaining a "healthy physique through a life in accord with the principles of hygiene and through regular exercise." Yi also advocated "reading three or more pages and exercising 30 or more minutes"[38] each day, as well as writing a poem titled "*Undong ŭi norae*" (Song of exercise), which appeared in the December 1, 1931, issue of the *Tonga ilbo*. In addition, in a 1933 piece, he opined that the "flourishing of *sports* such as baseball, tennis, soccer, basketball, and boxing is one of the best things that has happened recently."[39] Going even further, he wrote that "looking around on a beach, one can see just how inferior the physiques of Korean people are," while pointing out the fact that, due to the disappearance of the *hwarang*[40] spirit and the "universal conscription" of the early Chosŏn dynasty (1392–1910), present-day Koreans had become "a race effeminate enough to serve as a specimen in the history of humanity." Accordingly, Yi roundly criticized the "*yangban*," who held martial pursuits in contempt and considered horseback riding, hunting, wrestling, fighting, tug-of-war, sailing, and swimming "things done by lowborn people out in the hinterlands."[41] Not only did they, "with billowing sleeves and wide belts, burping from dyspepsia, walk around with the steps of one trying to catch a fly" but also, taking this further, forbade even "vivacious children" to run. In contrast to this, however, he described the appearance of the modernized Japanese as follows.

If one observes the looks of the Japanese, first of all, their piercing eyes are full of vigor, while their tightly closed lips express willpower, and this is the result of a long period of education, as well as of a long forging in the real world of intense struggle for existence. It is impossible to say that this is definitely an effect of physical education, however, try having a look at their naked bodies.

Are not their chests protruding, and the muscles of their arms developed rugged and hard like stone? Even though at first glance they may appear like weak scholars, they can easily travel on foot over more than100 *li* of rough trails, endure the blazing heat of the South Seas and the bitter cold of the North Continents, endure standing at attention for one or two hours and continuing hard work or research for four or five hours, and, if war breaks out, they immediately shoulder rifles and carry rucksacks, and endure protracted fierce battles while sleeping outdoors in a foreign land, so that this sort of physique has in fact been achieved through 50 years of school education and general physical education.[42]

As evidenced above, physical education and sports were an important modern project. Just as did marriage, they institutionalized the intransitive verb practice of the modern first person. For example, when Kim Namch'ŏn described the "great sports meet" in his novel *Taeha* (*Great river*, 1939), he related that in order to foster "thoughts on physical education and the improvement of health" even the women were made to watch the event. In addition, he describes that in places such as the early "enlightened" P'yŏngyang, not only did all students "die cotton cloth black and uniformly wear Western attire" but also that "because they even had a couple of buglers, their appearance, drilling, and conduct were all rather like an army." But, in opposition to this, some among the students of Tongmyŏng School did not even participate in sports meets held in their own village. They were the students who still had not cut their hair.[43] That is to say that *Taeha*, by presenting, along with those who did not participate in the sports meet, the wife of Pak Ch'ambong's telling the servant Ssangne to "address Pak Ch'ambong as his lordship, herself as milady, and their son as young master," presented the transitional period customs of around 1906, the time when the sports meet called the modern age had just begun. In spite of the *ch'angga*[44] that sang "Iron bones and stone muscles / Oh, young lad, / Do not forget / The spirit of civilization," the situation in *Taeha* had not arrived at the world of the modern first person, which forbade the appellation "milady," while vitalizing "*you*" and "*Mister Lee*." As such, that group of students at Tongmyŏng School who preserved their topknots and did not go to sports meets could become a laughingstock like the one below.

Hwong Ŭidon: There is a funny story about when tennis was first introduced.

Ko Hŭidong: Ah, that. They invited some high-ranking (Korean) officials to lunch at the British Legation, right? The minister maybe was named Jordan or something. Yes, after treating them (the Koreans) to a nice Western meal, the minister told his family to play tennis. Seeing this, I think a certain dignitary remarked, "What silly people indeed. That is no way for dignified people to behave. They should make their servants do it while they watch. Yes, going out there themselves and sweating profusely, what silly people." (Everybody laughs.)[45]

The essence of exercise and sports lies in that they are not activities people "should make their servants do (it) while they watch." One cannot exercise for another. It is accomplished and actualized only by sweating oneself. That sweat is not the painful and passive sweat shed by slaves or servants. Just as marriage is the intransitive verb practice of the first person nominative case, sports are the intransitive verb activity of the modern subject, and physically express the positive, progressive, and scientific qualities of existence and "self-maintenance." In that sense, the high-ranking officials of the Great Han Empire who failed to understand the tennis match of the British minister's family and the students of Tongmyŏng School who did not participate in the sports meet were living in the same world. They exist outside the playing field. They still have yet to enter the arena of practice in which the first person singular known as the individual is subjectively partitioned, and the first person plural known as the *minjok* is historicized (verbalized). No matter how imposing the *yangban* may have been, prostrated before their ancestral shrines, they were unable to exist by themselves and act by themselves in the modern world. As such, the perception of "Commander Kim," who had served as a "high official of the military" is extremely symbolic.

"Why were you late?"
"There was a soccer match at school so we went to cheer."
"Soccer match?"
"It's a bet where you kick a ball."
"Students should study. Why are they kicking balls?"
"It's exercise."
"Exercise? I don't know how to kick a ball, but that didn't keep me from serving as chief of training."[46]

MINJOK RECONSTRUCTION AND *MINJOK* CYBORG

But sweating oneself is of profound significance in another respect as well. Above all, it brings to mind the issue of occupation. Yi Kwangsu wrote on the matter as follows.

The group of people who are clothed and fed without shedding their own sweat is called *pulhandang* (hoodlums),[47] and *pulhandang* is another name for thieves. Since they plunder the gains of others' toil, how could they not be thieves? They are thieves of the society, thieves of the country, thieves of all humanity. The heavens, under the strictly impartial laws of survival of the fittest and natural selection, shall strip this group of their ability to reproduce and survive.[48]

The "*pulhandang*," who do not sweat themselves but exploit the labor and products of others, are akin to "thieves." The unemployed are "*pulhandang*," while *pulhandang* are thieves. "Unemployment" is "the root of all evil, the root of all misfortune."[49] It gives rise to all sorts of "vices" and "flaws" such as laziness. As embodied in the Cho Chunghwan play *Pyŏngja samin* (*The three invalids*, 1912), unemployment is a tremendous handicap, equivalent to illness or criminal offense. Unlike Hŭngbu whose status as Nolbu's kind younger brother was sufficient, or Dostoyevsky's *Notes from the Underground* in which the protagonist says, "'Sluggard'—Why, it is a calling and a vocation, it is a career,"[50] the *pulhandang* can possess absolutely no identity or property in a civil society composed of diverse professional lives. Moreover, Yi declared in his "*Minjok kaejoron*" that "those who do not work are criminals of a country or society." Accordingly, they are in danger of being "naturally selected." Regarding the more sentimental side of this equation, Baudelaire wrote the following.

To heal everything, misery, disease and melancholy, absolutely nothing is needed but the love of work.[51]

Occupation thus primarily defines the social system, as well as the individual's social location and identity. As one example, Pak Sŏgyun defined "life as a mission," while arguing that the accomplishment of that mission is the "first step" toward "self-reconstruction." He asserted that "only people who understand life as a mission are truly living,"[52] and "mission" here can be understood as meaning one's occupation. This is the reason Yi Kwangsu proposed in "*Minjok kaejoron*" "having standard learning, acquiring one or more specialized forms of knowledge or skill, and definitely possessing one or more occupations" as concrete provisions for "*minjok* reconstruction." As such, occupation and labor come to have a meaning identical to that of sports. Through intransitive verb activities in which people sweat themselves, occupation and sports socially establish the modern first person. Put another way, modern people play sports by means of marrying occupations. And in so doing, they become independent and "self-reliant." In fact, in the Kim Kyoje novel *Moktanhwa* (*Peony*, 1911), it was by taking on the occupation of teacher at Sŏhŭng School that Yi Chŏngsuk became a woman as a human being, and not as a sexual object quaking in fear of human trafficking.

In light of the above, that Yi Sang "limply took and held a pose of the twentieth century" in order not to disillusion those people who misunderstood him as a "*sportsman* of the twentieth century"[53] has its origins in his lumpen location from which he defined himself as a "beggarly existence."[54] Actually, Yi Sang's life, as symbolized in his phrase "two p.m. in the morning,"[55] squarely rejected Yi Kwangsu' position as embodied in his assertion that "life is change."[56] In this regard, Yi Sang's life of sloth possessed profound significance. Yi Kwangsu criticized Confucianism as a "fixed theory of life that denies evolution," while pointing out the "daydreams" and "empty theories" of the indolent Korean people. And, as will be seen below, he stressed the importance of "busyness."[57]

> As busyness is truly the insignia of civilized peoples, if a certain country is busy, that country is civilized, and if a certain person is busy, that person is civilized. The person who does not know that it is lamentable to waste even a minute of time cannot be called civilized, and so, belonging to this generation in which the intensity of the struggle for survival has reached its peak, an individual who does not compete for every minute, every second, will not be able to ensure his survival as an individual, nor will a *minjok* be able to ensure its survival as a *minjok*. If each member of a family is busy, that family will certainly prosper, and if each member of a *minjok* is busy, that *minjok* will certainly prosper, but the wages of the person who is not busy in this busy generation is ruin.[58]

It is from a perspective similar to that above that Yi also argued that a minute or second of Edison's time is more valuable than the entire hundreds and thousands of years of an "incompetent *minjok*," and that "one minute or one hour of civilized people is worth more than ten years or twenty years of uncivilized people."[59] He genuinely raised the issue of time and speed. Of course, emphasizing a busy life implies the social Darwinist will to reform fundamentally the "life that only looks backward," which was organized around ancestors and parents. The inability to be "busy" was a sign of barbarity. "Civilization" was to be achieved through a "life that only looks forward."[60]

What must be scrutinized here, however, is the metaphor at work in the phrase "life that only looks forward." Just as the well-regulated life of the chemist Kim Sŏngjae was thoroughly formalized according to clock time, or the "*Ch'ŏngnyŏn haguhoe haengboga* (Youth alumni association marching song, 1910)" expressed the movement of history as the turning of "the wheel of a new world's era," Yi Kwangsu presented a "diagram of the *minjok*'s fate" complete with calibrations and machines, while likening "*minjok* vitality" to the power of an engine. This was a natural expression for Yi, who in his *Mujŏng* pointed out the old man outside P'yŏngyang's Ch'ilsŏngmun (Gate) who "did not know of the railroad, did not know of the telegraph and telephone, and, moreover, had no way of knowing of submarines or torpedo boats," while going on to write that "Hyŏngsik and the old man were people of different countries totally unable to communicate in words or in writing."[61] In a non-fiction piece, Yi wrote the following.

> But (our) *minjok* vitality is like an engine that generates electricity whose fire, the source of its power, is about to go out. Hour by hour the roar of that engine grows more infrequent and weaker, so that this engine could easily stop its turning forever and the needle could freeze fixed in the direction of ruin.
>
> Build a fire! Burn some firewood, and throw in some coal! Truly time is short. No, the power to turn this engine lies only in those boys' heated devotion and boiling sweat. Their fat, their flesh, their bones. Boys, with one heart will you not throw all you have into that furnace to reverse the direction of that vibrating needle? With the roar of that engine will you not shake the entire land of Korea, and will you not take that wavering needle past prosperity, past wholeness, until it stands atop an infinite degree of boundless glory?[62]

This sort of rhetoric is also related to the deranged senses of *Mujŏng*'s Yi Hyŏngsik who felt as if the "sound of train wheels grinding on the rails" were "pleasant music," while he heard the "riotous sound when the train passed over an iron bridge or through a tunnel" as if it were "imposing martial music." He praised the "sounds of the city" given off by things such as street cars, rickshaws, wagon wheels, steam and electric engines, and iron carriages, while stating that, because "only when all of these sounds converge is resplendent civilization born," the "civilization of the modern age is a civilization of sounds." As a result, his position was that "Seoul too still does not have enough sounds."[63] This brings to mind Hyŏn Sangyun, who preached "powerism." Hyŏn defined the characteristic of modern civilization as lying in "steam" and "electricity." And he asserted that "until we replace hand-operated looms with steam-powered spinning machines," and "engine-using iron works drive out hand-hammering blacksmiths, not one ray of civilization will be able to shine through."[64] The "meaning of sounds" mentioned by Yi Hyŏngsik speaks of these "poweristic" achievements. The "sound of iron hammers" ringing from every corner of the land was the sensation of the civilization and enlightenment ideals of Yi Kwangsu—who once screamed "more than anything else, to the people of Korea we must first give science"—concretized and incarnalized as machines.

In actuality, however, "the train wheels grinding on the rails" and "the blood circulating in his (Yi Hyŏngsik's) body" formed a pair. In addition, the clamorous noise of the city, "so loud that standing in Chongno or Namdaemun people could not hear each other speak,"[65] was based upon the "sound of cells whispering." That is, the true origin of the noise that suggested a high level of technology was science, including such fields as astronomy, biology, anatomy, physics, and engineering. Only through these things was the "sound of *ether* molecules flowing" analyzed and amplified. Regarding these sounds of civilization, Yi Kwangsu wrote the following.

> In Hyŏngsik's ear could be heard the sound of trains' moving and the sound of the world turning. He also heard the sound of star and star colliding in the infinitely distant sky, as well as the sound of infinitely small *"ether"* molecules flowing. The rustling sound of grasses and trees striving to grow through the night in the hills and fields, and the sound of blood circulating in his body, and of cells whispering in enjoyment at receiving that blood could all be heard.[66]

The "engine" of *"minjok* vitality" was manufactured by internalizing this sort of modern discourse of scientific technology. Thus the act of viewing human history as identical to the rotation of a machine, or the taking of the "sweat" and flesh, even their entire lives, of "boys" as the power of an engine was justified. This is because the scientific, analytical, and systematic understanding of the world and of life was to give birth to a bio-mechanistic imagination that judged "whether the body of a man or the body of an animal, they are all like machines that make warmth."[67] This is also the reason Yi Kwangsu stressed "scientific knowledge and systematic training," while presenting diverse statistical data in his *Nongch'on kyebal* (Rural development, 1916–1917). In relation to this, Kōsaka Masāki once said the following.

> Thus, the demand for anthropocentricity, and as a result for the domination of nature, made machines, and the natural sciences developed in tandem with them. Machines were not made by observing nature. Machines were assembled by dominating nature. And together with them, at least in thought experiments, the entirety of nature also became something to be assembled as a machine. The simple observation of nature will rather cause nature to be understood as an organism. The demand that nature must be understood as an enormous machine arose from human beings' themselves making machines. And the result, insofar as the human beings who made machines were themselves a part of nature, was a reversal that reached the point where human beings were understood as machines, as so-called human machines. This is the logic that validates the theory of human machines. In simple nature things like simple mechanical devices are nowhere to be found. It is simply that only humans were able to abstract and structure from nature the most rational machines, pure machines. And in so doing the entirety of nature first began to be understood according to this pure mechanical model. The basis of mechanism was if anything anthropocentrism.[68]

At the same time, this bio-mechanistic imagination was also related to the essence of *"minjok* reconstruction," which sought through hygiene and exercise to "improve the physique of the *minjok*, and extend the average lifespan, while enhancing activity efficiency." Among these, "systematic training" and "enhancing activity efficiency" in particular were to mass produce skilled workers, who simultaneously represented both a civilized identity to overcome the barbarity of "*pulhandang*" and "empty theories," and a social minimal unit. They were equipped with enough knowledge and health to assimilate fully their assigned tasks, and scrupulously carried out their work, thereby allowing the enormous structure called society and the engine of history to operate smoothly. They were both the motor momentum and the motor impetus of society and history. Moreover, they were at once autonomous parts and single cells allowing "*minjok* vitality" to circulate almost like an organism.

Due to the above, Yi Kwangsu defined Sŏnhyŏng as being "like a machine that has never once been used but only stored in a shed." She merely existed as Elder Kim's daughter, "as she was chemically combined and physiologically composed."[69] She was not shedding sweat to turn the engine of "*minjok* vitality." She had failed to attain an "independent" social identity as one momentum of the structure. In fact, regarding Sŏnhyŏng, so like a "machine" stored in a shed, Yi Kwangsu wrote that she was "not yet a person," and it is precisely this phrase that connotes the core of the modern first person. The modern first person as defined by Yi operated with smooth "self-action," like a machine oiled by sweat, in the social arena outside the dark "shed." This activity, which was accomplished through skilled occupations, represented the "intransitive verb" that both combined marriage and sports, and was the most genuinely civil. Through this process, the first person was to shed its rusty barbarity and rough marginalization, and adjust itself inside the whole called society. This was what Yi Kwangsu referred to as "*kusil*" or "role." Through this "self-reliant" activity that externalized the self, human beings became positive and progressive modern subjects. Therefore, Yi leveled the command to "consider your occupation your art," while also stressing the "artistic freedom and joy of an occupation."[70] Below is one concrete example of enjoying that sort of freedom.

> Doctors seemed to be people who had only eyes and hands, while nurses seemed to have only ears and eyes. At a single glance or word from a doctor, they moved here, moved there, like a well-oiled machine.
> "No mistakes. Quickly."
> Aside from these, they had no other thoughts.
> "Thud."
> With this strange sound, Chŏngsŏn's leg dropped. The leg was still warm, still supple. The nurse, as if lifting a piece of wood, took the fallen leg and placed it atop something that looked like a large metal plate. . . .

The doctor took his forceps and returned the displaced flesh and skin to cover the severed bone, then quickly sewed it up using a crescent moon shaped needle and white silk thread.[71]

The scene above displays the core of civil professional activity. The doctor and nurse have not only escaped from caste passivity and slavelike drudgery but also, by voluntarily internalizing education and discipline, have overcome the fear and mental shock of bloody human vivisection. As such, the excerpt's likening of the doctor and nurse to "a well-oiled machine" is convincing. This is because they carried out their work as proficiently and accurately as if they only had eyes and hands. In addition, the surgical act itself of cutting off and stitching up a leg is behavior that views the human body as a type of machine. The work of the doctor and nurse relates to the cyborg (cybernetic organism) in many respects.

And when it reached this "self-acting" cyborg existence, the modern first person as designed by Yi was completed. Educated and trained mentally and physically, completely blocking out invasion from germs and viruses, it would, scribing a regular and efficient line of movement, organically follow both all of the tasks inside the social factory, and the first person plural ideals of the *minjok* community.

It was a type of robot that operated a "capital machine." This was the concrete appearance of a member of Yi Kwangsu's "reconstructed" *minjok.* "*Minjok kaejoron*" was just another name for a cyborg project.

IN LIEU OF A CONCLUSION

In the real world, however, the first person plural was not easily obtained. For example, in the Yokomitsu Riichi short story "*Kikai* (The machine, 1930)," whose plot unfolds in a nameplate factory, the characters "I," "Karube," and "Yashiki" suspected one another and eventually came to blows over the technology leakage of a "special red coloring process using amorphous selenium." "I" and Yashiki teamed up to beat on Karube, after which Karube and Yashiki teamed up to beat on "I." They unfolded a three-person struggle among three people. This was the reality of the world of free competitive occupations. Of course, they also got drunk together when the owner lost all their money. But on that very day, like the *I-ching* line "if three people travel together, one person will be lost," Yashiki drank ammonium dichromate from what he mistook as a water bottle and died. He was, so to speak, "selected." This is suspected of being a murder. The murderer could be "I," and it could be Karube. Or it may have been that "I" and Karube teamed up to kill Yashiki. Regarding this, however, "I" was unable to render a clear judgment. The only thing certain was the fact that "some mechanism that we could not see, a machine which was unceasingly making calculations about us and which then directed our actions according to the light of these calculations."[72] As such, the work ends with the following lines.

> And hadn't my head at some time or other been taken over already by the iron chloride, reduced to the same state as that of the boss? I have reached the point where I no longer understand myself. All I feel is that there is the sharp point of some machine coming slowly toward me, getting closer and closer to me. Let somebody take my place and judge me. For if you are to ask me what I have done, how can I be expected to know?[73]

As seen above, "I" was suspect. Not even an individual's interior was established with a single voice. It served as its own Other, while also being "hell." But it may be precisely this sort of state that represented the true structure of the "nominative case" first person. As such, a *minjok* that spoke with one voice while also "sympathizing" was an illusion. On the contrary, it is what drove Ch'oe Sŏk to Siberia "fussing and fighting over a tiny bit of thought, an iota of conscience, and a two-bit ideal."[74] The conflict between Ch'oe and his wife was also far from the ideal of *minjok*. The world of *Yujŏng* (*Kindheartedness*, 1933) proves the *"mujŏng"* (heartlessness) of Korean civil society.

Thus, Yi Kwangsu was either naively optimistic or overly pessimistic regarding of course the oneness of the first person singular with itself, and also the first person plural's true nature, as well has his own relationship to them. Ch'oe Sŏk was viewed as identical to the *minjok*. And when that could no longer be the case, he was completely eliminated. In all cases, the first person singular imagined its own oneness, and was adjusted so that this could be repeated with respect to the first person plural as well. But in so firmly believing in the "nominative case," eventually the first person singular returned to "he" or "it." The "he" before the mirror did not see "I" but "we" (*minjok*). Thus self-alienation originated from imagined oneness. This was the true appearance of the reconstructed cyborg.

In actuality, this was a thoroughly predictable situation. From the outset, the first person singular and first person plural were primarily configured only grammatically. As such, the complex circumstances and practical "conditions" by which various "I"s and "we"s established relationships were never really considered. As discussed above, Yi Kwangsu stipulated financial ability and several other exacting "conditions for marriage," the very institution that gives birth to the family relationship closest to the first person plural. That is to say he acknowledged the circumstances at work in the following lines from Baudelaire.

When I would come home penniless
Her cries tore me apart.[75]

Yi displayed a different position, however, with regard to the relationship between individual and society, individual and *minjok*. In his "*Choson minjongnon* (On the Korean *minjok*, 1933)" he wrote that the "*minjok* is destiny," while in his "*Yŏ ŭi chagak han insaeng* (My self-awakened life, 1910)" he likened it to "solid and strong bonds" from which the individual cannot escape. Without any sort of contractual conditions, the relationship between individual and *minjok* was transcendentalized as something a priori and inevitable. And its transcendence and one-sidedness were projected onto the internal principles of the *minjok*. Those principles were "sympathy" and "unity" centered upon a "leader." The cold contract was to yield its place to hot solidarity. This formed a pair with the process of self-expansion, which endlessly excluded the Other.

Of course, the proposition that *minjok* equaled destiny would be particularly justified through bloodline. Yi Kwangsu emphasized "bloodline" as the "essential element of *minjok*." Viewed in this manner, the relationship between *minjok* and individual was close to that of parent and child. The *minjok* was the family. And, of course, one must follow leaders who are like parents. The rhetoric of "Japan and Korea as one body" or "newborn babies of the Emperor"[76] was based on tropes that viewed the parent and ruler as identical. But as long as bloodline was stressed, the *minjok* would remain an endless genre of the second generation, that is to say a grammar of brother (son)s' and sister (daughter)s'. The minjok was indeed "centered upon children" and evolutionary. Parents each had a different bloodline. Different bloodlines were the first condition for marriage. Children were the only ones who shared the same bloodline. But children too would go on to marry spouses (at times Japanese spouses as encouraged by the policy of Japanese-Korean intermarriage)[77] with different bloodlines. Furthermore, as Yi himself revealed, it was the parents who carried out these contractual relations.

Bloodline, therefore, rather than being the *minjok*'s origin that ensures self-sameness, is the result of a contract made with the Other. The *minjok* is an eternally postponed future. Indefinite, it is futile. Due to this futility, "tradition" is devised. As such, tradition is turned upside down, and *minjok* may not be the destiny of "I." Rather, it is "you." In fact, "*I*" exists through "*am*" or "*was*," but "*We*" exists through "*are*" and "*were*." Accordingly, the "*We*" called *minjok* is closer to "*You*" than to "*I*." This is because "*You*" also exists through "*are*" and "*were*."

But, like a cyborg standing before a mirror, "We" may still be discussing "destiny." If this is the case, the "We" who so frequently criticize the pro-Japanese activities of Yi Kwangsu, and the "We" who, like this sentence, cannot throw away "We" are all Yi Kwangsu.

NOTES

1. "Spring Garden" is the literal translation of Yi Kwangsu's penname, Ch'unwŏn (春園).—Trans.

2. Yi Kwangsu, "*Honin e taehan kwan'gyŏn* (Personal views on marriage)," in *Yi Kwangsu chŏnjip* 17 (Seoul: Samjungdang, 1962), 61.

3. Yi Kwangsu, "*Honinnon* (On marriage)," in ibid., 141.

4. Yi Kwangsu, "*Kaech'ŏkcha* (*The pioneer*)," in *Yi Kwangsu ŭi chŏnjip* 1 (Seoul: Samjungdang, 1962), 428.

5. Yi Kwangsu, "Honin e taehan kwan'gyŏn," 53.

6. The term from "race" in the original is *chongjok* (種族). It has several possible meanings, among them being tribe, clan, species, ethnicity, and strain. Tribe or clan may have been appropriate in certain earlier writings, but by the early twentieth century nationalism and attendant theories of race had taken hold in Korea. Add this to Korea's colonial situation—there was no Korean nation-state, only a Korean race within the Japanese empire—and the preservation and strengthening of the Korean race becomes an all the more urgent project for many intellectuals, Yi Kwangsu being foremost among them.—Trans.

7. Yi Kwangsu, "*Chanyŏ chungsimnon* (On the primacy of children)," in *Yi Kwangsu chŏnjip* 17 (Seoul: Samjungdang, 1962), 42.

8. Yi Kwangsu, *Kaech'ŏkcha*, 469.

9. Yang Chudong, *Munju pansaenggi* (*Record of half a life spent on literature and liquor*) (Seoul: Sint'aeyangsa ch'ulp'an'guk, 1962), 28.

10. Both of these examples are taken from the *Liji* (*Book of Rites*) chapter titled "*Nei Ze* (The patterns of the family)." The second has to do with a woman's becoming an adult and the attendant change in hairstyle. The original reads, "*Sipyuonyŏn i kye*" (十有五年而笄), most commonly translated as "At fifteen, she assumed the hairpin." See http://ctext.org/liji/nei-ze.—Trans.

11. Yi Kwangsu, "*Honinnon*," 141–42.

12. Yi Kwangsu, "*Mujŏng* (*The Heartless*)," in *Yi Kwangsu chŏnjip* 1, (Seoul: Samjungdang, 1962), 317.

Simple italics will be used to denote English words transliterated into Korean. Italics and underlining denotes when actual English words are inserted directly into the text.—Trans.

13. The term in the original is *sŏnsaengnim*. It is most often used for teachers but also a common modern form of address for doctors.—Trans.

14. Ibid., 341.

All the italicized words are in transliterated English in the original. What sets them apart from other such instances, however, is that a parenthetical Korean translation is provided for each, which gives rise to several interesting questions about intended audience and effect/affect.—Trans.

15. Komori Yōichi, *Sōseki o yominaosu* (*Rereading Sōseki*) (Tokyo: Chikuma syobō, 1995), 178.

16. Yi Kwangsu, *Mujŏng*, 182.

17. Ibid., 140.

18. This *"vision"* is actually written *"pijyun"* in a seemingly deliberately poor approximation of the original pronunciation with a parenthetical Korean definition, *kwanggyŏng*, following it for clarity. The second "vision" is simply a translation of the Korean original, again *kwanggyŏng*.—Trans.

19. Yi Kwangsu, "*Chaesaeng* (Rebirth)," in *Yi Kwangsu chŏnjip* 2 (Seoul: Samjungdang, 1962), 292.

20. Yi Kwangsu, "*Kyoyukka chessi ege* (To the Esteemed Educators)," in *Yi Kwangsu chŏnjip* 17 (Seoul: Samjungdang, 1962), 78.

21. "Sweet home" (*sŭwit'ŭhom*) appears to be a shortened transliteration of the English "home sweet home" and was used in the first decades of the twentieth century to signify a modern Western-style house, theoretically occupied by a young, modern nuclear family.—Trans.

22. Yi Kwangsu, "*Chanyŏ chungsimnon*," 44.

23. Yi Kwangsu, "*Ch'ŏnjaeya! ch'ŏnjaeya!* (Oh, genius! oh, genius!)," in *Yi Kwangsu chŏnjip* 17 (Seoul: Samjungdang, 1962), 51.

24. Yi Kwangsu, *Mujŏng*, 606.

25. Yi Kwangsu, "*Munsa wa suyang* (The writer and cultivation)," in *Ch'angjo* Volume 8, January 1921, 16.

26. Chinese characters are provided in the original in order to accentuate the premodern origins of these beliefs and practices. They are *pulgyŏng ibu* (不更二夫) and *sujŏl* (守節), respectively.—Trans.

27. Yi Kwangsu, "Honin e taehan kwan'gyŏn," 60.

28. Yi Kwangsu, "*Kyoyukka chessi ege*," 79.

29. Yi Kwangsu, "*Minjok kaejoron* (On national reconstruction)," in *Yi Kwangsu chŏnjip* 17 (Seoul: Samjungdang, 1962), 201.

30. Yi Kwangsu, "*Sonyŏn ege* (To the boys)," in ibid., 240.

31. Yi Kwangsu, "*Nongch'on kyebal* (Rural development)," in ibid., 131.

32. Yi Kwangsu, *Minjok kaejoron*, 198.

33. Yi Kwangsu, "*Hŭlk* (*The soil*)," in *Yi Kwangsu chŏnjip* 6 (Seoul: Samjungdang, 1962), 27.

34. Ch'oe Namsŏn, "*Uri ŭi undongjang* (Our playing field)," in *Sonyŏn*, December 1908, 32–33.

35. Yi Kwangsu, "*Tosan An Ch'angho* (Tosan An Ch'angho)," in *Yi Kwangsu chŏnjip* 13, (Seoul: Samjungdang, 1962), 141.

36. "*Ch'ŏngnyŏn haguhoe haengboga* (Youth alumni association marching song)," in *Sonyŏn*, Volume 17, May 1910, 77.

37. Yi Kwangsu, "*Tosan An Ch'angho*," 158.

38. Yi Kwangsu, "*Kaein ŭi ilsang saenghwal ŭi hyŏksin i minjokchŏk palhŭng ŭi kŭnbon ida* (Reform of the daily lives of individuals is the basis for the rise of the *minjok*)," in *Yi Kwangsu chŏnjip* 17, 447.

39. Yi Kwangsu, "*Sŭp'ooch'ŭ yŏl* (The sports boom)," in *Yi Kwangsu chŏnjip* 13, (Seoul: Samjungdang, 1962), 398.

40. Although he facilely overlooks many salient differences between the two groups, Yi Kwangsu uses the *hwarang* here as a sort of analog to the samurai of Japan.—Trans.

41. Yi Kwangsu, "*Sinsaenghwallon* (On a new life)," in in *Yi Kwangsu chŏnjip* 17, 535.

42. Yi Kwangsu, "*Tonggyŏng chapsin* (Miscellaneous correspondence from Tokyo)," in *Yi Kwangsu chŏnjip* 17, 485.

43. Kim Namch'ŏn, *Taeha (Great river)* (Seoul: Inmunsa, 1939), 357–60.

44. *Ch'angga* (唱歌) refers to a type of song popular following the Kabo Reforms (1894–1895) that set Korean lyrics to Western music.

45. *Chwadamhoe* (Symposium), "*Sinmunhwa tŭrŏodŏn ttae* (When the new culture entered)," in *Chogwang*, June 1941, 131.

46. Yi T'aejun, "*Sasang ŭi wŏrya* (Moonlight of thought)," in *Maeil sinbo*, June 8, 1941.

47. Although the dictionary glosses *pulhandang* as "hoodlum" or "hooligan," the actual etymology of this Sino-Korean term is related to Yi's argument regarding sweat. The Chinese characters making up the word are 不汗黨, literally meaning "the group that does not sweat."—Trans.

48. Yi Kwangsu, "*Tonggyŏng chapsin*," 498.

49. Yi Kwangsu, "*Nongch'on kyebal* (Rural development)," in *Yi Kwangsu chŏnjip* 17, 89.

50. Fyodor Dostoyevsky, *Notes from the Underground* (Rockville: Serenity Publishers, 2008), 22.

51. Charles Baudelaire, *Baudelaire: His Prose and Poetry*, ed. T. R. Smith (New York: Boni and Liveright, 1919), 245. (http://archive.org/details/baudelairehispro00b audiala).

52. Pak Sŏgyun, "'*Chagi' ŭi kaejo* (Reconstructing 'oneself')," in *Hak chi kwang*, Volume 20, July 1920, 15.

53. Yi Sang, "*Sasin* 7 (Private correspondence 7)," in *Yi Sang munhak chŏnjip* 3 (Seoul: Munhak sasangsa, 1993), 235.

54. Yi Sang, "*Choch'un chŏmmyo* (Early spring sketches)," in *Yi Sang munhak chŏnjip* 3, 42.

55. The original is contained in the work "*Hyuŏp kwa sajŏng*" (Closures and circumstances, 1932), and reads "*ach'im ohu tu si*" (아침 오후 두 시). This is a deliberate subversion by Yi of readers' common conceptions regarding time. He clarifies by explaining that because he (the autobiographical protagonist Posan) most often does not awake until 2:00 pm, for him it is the morning.—Trans.

56. Yi Kwangsu, "*Sinsaenghwallon*," 516.

57. The words translated here as "busyness" and "busy" are *ch'ongmang* (忽忙) and *ch'ongmang hada* (忽忙하다), respectively, and can also mean (to be in) a great hurry or (to make) great haste.—Trans.

58. Yi Kwangsu, "*Tonggyŏng chapsin*," 488.

59. Ibid., 487.

60. Yi Kwangsu, "*Chanyŏ chungsimnon*," 46.

61. Yi Kwangsu, *Mujŏng*, 165.

62. Yi Kwangsu, "*Sonyŏn ege*," 240.

63. Yi Kwangsu, *Mujŏng*, 264.

64. Hyŏn Sangyun, "*Kangnyŏk chuŭi wa Chosŏn ch'ŏngnyŏn* (Powerism and the youth of Korea)," in *Hak chi kwang*, Volume 6, July 1915, 48.

65. Yi Kwangsu, *Mujŏng*, 264.

66. Ibid., 69–70.

67. Pin T'on, "*Saram mada almyŏn chyohŭl il* (Things everyone should know)," in *Tae Chyosyŏn tongnip hyŏbhoe hoebo*, Volume 4, January 1896, 9.

68. Hiromatsu Wataru, *Kindai no chokoku ron* (*On overcoming modernity*) (Tokyo: Kodansha, 1991), 42–43.

69. Yi Kwangsu, *Mujŏng*, 72.

70. Yi Kwangsu, "*Yesul kwa insaeng* (Art and life)," in *Yi Kwangsu chŏnjip* 16 (Seoul: Samjungdang, 1962), 38.

71. Yi Kwangsu, "*Hŭlk* (The Soil)," in *Yi Kwangsu chŏnjip* 6 (Seoul: Samjungdang, 1962), 318–19.

72. Yokomitsu Riichi, "*Kikai* (The Machine)," in "*Love*" *and Other Stories of Yokomitsu Riichi*, tr. Dennis Keene (Tokyo: University of Tokyo Press, 1974), 177.

73. Ibid., 180.

74. Yi Kwangsu, "*Yujŏng* (Kindheartedness)," in *Yi Kwangsu chŏnjip* 8 (Seoul: Samjungdang, 1962), 79.

75. Charles Baudelaire, "*Le Vin de l'assassin* (The Assassin's Wine)," in *The Flowers of Evil*, tr., Keith Waldrop (Middletown: Wesleyan University Press, 2006), 142.

76. These are respective translations of *Naisen ittai* (Kor., *Naesŏn ilch'e* 內鮮一體), a Japanese colonial slogan and policy geared toward assimilation, and *Tennō no sekishi* (K. *Ch'ŏnhwang ŭi chŏkcha* 天皇 の 赤子), the newborn babies of the emperor who share race, language, and culture with the Japanese people.—Trans.

77. The policy was called *Nissen tsūgon* (Kor., *Ilsŏn t'onghon* 日鮮通婚).—Trans.

Chapter 8

The Flesh, Yi Sang's Windowpane

A METHOD FOR DISPOSING OF THE FLESH

Yi Sang once referred to himself as "a bastard on the verge of blacking out, jammed in the crack between the nineteenth century and the twentieth century." Unlike people's misunderstanding of him, Yi was not a "*sportsman* of the 20th century." In an attempt not to "disappoint" and "disillusion" people, he merely "limply took and held a pose of the twentieth century."[1] In a word, he was unable to brandish powerfully "the burly arms of the young heroes of this *generation* who run carrying *rugby* balls."[2] Rather, having undergone the regression of a "stuffed specimen" lost in playing with a magnifying glass, in the end Yi Sang became at once a "skeleton whose knees are above its ears" and "your distant ancestor."[3] By "becoming my father" and "becoming the father of my father," he put into practice both a "*yŏkdobyŏng*" (disease of arriving in reverse) that concluded with an evolution into apes,[4] and a "eugenics of the stuffed specimen."[5] In this sense, he did not "develop" or "progress." Instead, as below, he experienced "rage."

I do not develop and I do not progress.
This is rage.[6]

By means of this "rage," Yi Sang "sentimentalized a method for disposing of the flesh." His self was no longer naïve or simple; however, "reproduction" too was impossible. At this juncture, with this whiskered "despair," all he could do was paint a "self-portrait" like the one below.

Grass at the North Pole that did not reach puberty, these whiskers recognize despair and do not reproduce.[7]

185

What should be paid attention to here is the phrase "method for disposing of the flesh." This suggests the historical location of Yi Sang's literature. What can first be pointed out in regard to this is the anatomical perspective discovered in Yi Sang. Lines such as "The whereabouts of the heart are unknown. Some say in the stomach, others in the chest. The two theories are divergent and cannot be controlled,"[8] "SS emerged carrying his young daughter in the space between his bouldery chest and stomach—inside his body this would correspond to the area around his diaphragm,"[9] and "One of his suit jackets fell off. At the same time, his eyes, his mouth, his brain, his fingers, overcoat, and breeches all together fell off,"[10] serve as but a few examples. In addition, the poem "*Ogamdosi che-6 ho* (Crow's eye view, poem number 6)" describes dissection. This indicates the location of "Yi Sang, the doctor in charge" who in "*Ogamdosi che-4 ho* (Crow's eye view, poem number 4)" "diagnoses" the "problem of the patient's condition." He is a modern person with the authority to "dispose of" the flesh.

This being the case, it is not that Yi Sang was not twentieth century man. This is because in the wake of works such as Kim Tongin's "*Moksum* (Life, 1921)" and Yŏm Sangsŏp's "*P'yobonsi lŭi ch'ŏnggaeguri* (Green frog of the specimen room, 1921)," at least in colonial Korea, the doctors in charge who carried out surgeries and dissections would have been more twentieth century than anyone. In his essay "*Munhak ŭl pŏrigo munhwa rŭl sangsanghalsuŏpta* (Without literature, there is no imagining culture, 1936)," Yi Sang expressed that "for the mere reason that life is life I am already prescribed an intravenous injection of three grams of Pantopon,"[11] while in his poem "*Ijŏna kagyaku hannō* (A strange reversible reaction, 1931)" he wrote that "beneath the microscope, artificiality developed exactly the same as nature." Going even further, as seen below, with the analysis of "bone fragments" of "Pithecanthropus," he oriented himself to the historical coordinates of "degeneration" = "progress."

From a mere four or five bone fragments of Pithecanthropus, we can first of all observe, resulting either from rainstorms or an enemy's attack, the very first example of dark, misanthropic thought, and that, having gradually become larger, degenerating and progressing until mankind learned how to commit suicide, although the day this was carried out on earth for the very first time is shrouded in legend, from the time the notion of human beings came into being to the time they sat leaning against a wall spattered with the bloodstains of bedbugs while listening to the voice of Johann Strauss, it is precisely the various sufferings of all things in the universe over which we rat on one another that is the eternal brand that began with the mistake of Adam and Eve, it is nothing to lament as if it were the original sin assigned only to this land for being this land.[12]

But Yi Sang's protagonist was not merely a doctor in charge taking the bone fragments of Pithecanthropus as an object of scientific observation. He "did not resemble (in the least) any among all the healthy people of this world"[13] and was a tuberculosis and syphilis patient who "self-diagnosed the disease(s) in photographs from his youth."[14] To Yi Sang, who "secretly insisted on the monism of spermatozoa, and succeeded in separation experiments on the organic matter of spermatozoa,"[15] the doctor in charge and the patient were from the beginning indistinguishable. This is the reason he confessed, "I possess the least of 'Dr. Jekyll' and far more of 'Mr. Hyde.'"[16] Metaphorically speaking, Yi Sang was sentenced to the "brand"[17] "over which we rat on one another." What is more, at "a certain university hospital" he visited due to "an affliction not so honorable, but, then again, not so very dishonorable,"[18] he even became the laboratory animal for a clinical lecture. A similar situation is expressed in his novel *12 wŏl 12 il* (*December 12th*).

Absorbed in conversation, he had briefly forgotten about his left leg, which now still, even more than before, ached and throbbed and numbed. From outside his clothes, he downwardly stroked the leg, while suddenly making an "Ouch" sound and gulping down a mouthful of saliva. The spit was exceedingly sticky, making him feel as if he were swallowing *"condensed milk"* or taffy. The gentleman, three small furrows laying vertically between his eyebrows, sat looking for a long while upon the scene, then suddenly changed to a cheerful tone and opened his mouth.

"Certainly bizarre when it's the doctor's leg that hurts!"
"Yeah, he thought his shit don't stink!"[19]

Thus, the liminal location of Yi Sang, who depicts himself as always simultaneously both doctor in charge (Dr. Jekyll) and laboratory animal (Mr. Hyde), also matches well with the design of "*ka oe ka*" (街外街),[20] in which his wife is a prostitute. Even as he advocated carrying out "the eugenics of great decisive judgment," "the simultaneous massacre of all human beings who were not worthy of living,"[21] it was in fact Yi Sang himself who was a "beggarly existence," the target of eugenics. Yi Sang himself was outraged at becoming a laboratory animal, but, on the other hand, while providing as examples Dr. Noguchi's[22] falling to yellow fever, and a certain researcher's voluntarily ingesting cholera bacteria for the progress of medical science, wrote that "compared to cases such as these, merely having ones private parts briefly exposed to a bunch of students can hardly qualify as worthy of petulance. On the contrary, I should be honored and rejoice that my brief endurance of pain and shame provided a modicum of assistance to serious research." He is saying that if there were "the establishment of a new moral sense and the dissemination of a new emotional custom," then, after saying "It appears a certain sort of affliction has arisen on my private parts, but I have never before seen nor heard of it. In any case, it is my hope that several scholars and students will gather and research it," "some admirable personage might very well make an appearance."[23]

Such is the degree to which Yi Sang was both doctor in charge and laboratory animal. And, as if affirming this sort of position, Yi, as an "aggrieved skeleton appearing in an academic paper,"[24] sentimentally commanded a "method for disposing of the flesh" with which he vivisected and "sacrificed" himself. As such, might not this have been the true meaning of "a bastard on the verge of blacking out, jammed in the crack between the nineteenth century and the twentieth century." And might not "Pithecanthropus" have been another name for Yi Sang, prescribed and ascribed to himself by Kim Haegyŏng who had evolved into an "ape" of "biological second-class standing"? Adding credence to this is the fact that Yi Sang served as an official of the empire while simultaneously remaining a barbarian of the colony. He was that "whiskered despair."

THE MUSEUM AND PITHECANTHROPUS

Yi Sang mentions the bone fragments of Pithecanthropus in some of his other works as well. Significantly, Pithecanthropus appears during a discussion of antiques in the series of essays "*Choch'un chŏmmyo* (Early spring sketches, 1936)."

> When attempting to ascertain such things as the way of life, folklore, and folk art of a certain age, only then does the position of antiques become critical, which is to say that if antiques do not exist in tandem with museums that gather only antiques, not only does their raison d'etre cease to exist but also they fail to play any "role" whatsoever. By gathering things of the same age and of the same tendency together in a single place, truly concrete historical knowledge becomes obtainable—that is why of course the more the better—without this, one isolated shard, like a single bone fragment of Java man, "Pithecanthropus," is far too impoverished for any assumptions. The antiquarianism of the present age in which people take a single urn or a couple of plates and display them by their bedsides, and, worrying that someone might find out, even secretly tuck away the finer pieces is, first of all, detestable in the archaeological sense mentioned above, and, secondly, that despicably miserly concept of private ownership is hateful.[25]

Important in the passage above is the fact that Yi Sang mentions "museums" (or "archaeology"). This is because following King Sunjong's setting up a royal museum on the grounds of Ch'anggyŏng Palace in September of 1908, or following the colonial government general's construction of a museum, the museum began to embody the modern windowpane, which was equal to the show window.[26] Just as the modern person—the subject of observation, science, hygiene, and development—came into being by putting nature on the other side of the microscope, and just as capitalist desire (the future) is generated by putting products on the other side of the show window, the museum is an institution that dynamically forms modernity and the modern person by putting the past and barbarity on the other side of the windowpane in the name of civilization and progress. By projecting the past and barbarity onto a different *minjok* beyond the windowpane, the historical present and future of the civilized person is established. The rationality of the West confining the East inside the museum windowpane of "Asian stagnation" is not unrelated to this. It is one form that emblematizes modern history. This is the reason the modernist Yi Sang denied the value of antiques themselves that were not displayed in museum exhibit halls. From beyond the museums' windowpanes installed in all sorts of places, the modern person was born as the subject of studies such as folklore, anthropology, phrenology, archaeology, history, and geography. And things like antiques, remains, and customs would be appropriated as objects of observation of that modern (or imperialist) perspective.

On the other hand, even as the past and barbarity became a sort of colony, exhibits, through the rhetoric of beauty and the reproduction system of the invention of tradition, were also sublated into *minjok* identity. The Great Han Empire's Office of the Royal Palace Grounds once placed an "announcement of purchasing items for display" in a newspaper.

At this time, the museum division of this office is purchasing for display those items from among this country's art and artistic crafts that are old and excellent or historically referenced, etc. Those wishing to sell may bring their items every Thursday from 10:00 a.m. to 2:00 p.m. to the government office building in front of Changnyewŏn outside the Kŭmho Gate of Ch'angdŏk Palace where an employee dispatched from this office will, after inspection, be making purchases.

In addition, items made in Japan and China are also being purchased.[27]

Thus, the museum was an arena of raison d'état that *minjok*-istically mediated past and present, barbarity and civilization. It essentially carried out domination and mobilization. The museum was filled not only with relics of the past. Having internalized exclusion, ranking, and consolidation, that place was also rife with political meanings. This makes understandable both the new conception of world history known as the "Greater East Asia Co-Prosperity Sphere" and the reason Yi Kwangsu, who went along with "overcoming modernity," appears so agitated below.

> In spite of the fact that we Asians and the British/Americans have such irrec-
> oncilable views of life and views of the nation, in the past, for about a century,
> East Asians unavoidably followed behind them. Certain East Asians, mimicking
> the scholars of Britain/America, even dared to look upon the ideals and culture
> of our ancestors with archaeological interest. Like museum employees search-
> ing for the dead and buried remains of a primitive *minjok*, they explored the
> scriptures and remains of our sacred ancestors.[28]

The modern world is not only a laboratory or a department store but also one big museum. In that sense, the comments regarding Pithecanthropus are important. This, by distinguishing between subject (gaze) and Other (object), present and past, suggests the operation of the modern windowpane that sharply and coldly makes inevitable the historical and social meeting and conflict between the two. As a result, in relation to this, the lines in Yi Sang's essay "*Ch'udŭn gchapp'il* (Miscellaneous writings by autumn lamplight, 1936)" that discuss the "discourteous" gazes of Westerners merit attention.

> Allowing them to view the spectacular things in this land is completely different
> from the mind of a bear or a wolf in a zoo making a spectacle of its own body.
> This is because our intention is to introduce and boast of places that are in every
> respect as good as theirs, of places they do not have, and of places better than
> theirs—
>   Their attitude sitting atop the rickshaws pointing with the tips of their canes
> is certainly similar to that of viewing the spectacle of a zoo. As such, it is a
> discourtesy, and the ultimate insult.
>   It would be proper for the state to institute laws forbidding them to ride in
> rickshaws even in the remotest of areas.
>   . . . .
>   Some years ago in a certain park I witnessed a white man, after making a
> charitable contribution of a fifty *chŏn* coin to a beggar, begin to play with his
> camera when a most martial young man who was passing by stopped and gave
> him a beating. There is no doubt that this behavior too arose from this youth's
> laudable pride in his own land.[29]

The crux of the quotation above is that a person of "his own land" became the spectacle of a "white man" who may have been a "world-renowned geographer."[30] The "beggar" of his own land who, like a bear in a zoo, had become the subject of the camera's lens, is no different from the bone fragments of Pithecanthropus. In addition, he is also similar to products on the other side a show window or a laboratory animal used for dissection. From the white man's perspective, he is an object (barbarity, Other) that can be exchanged for fifty *chŏn* and observed (dissected). With words such as "boast" and "pride," this is what Yi Sang finds problematic. This is because Yi himself is the subject of a gaze that can "witness" a white man's being beaten. In fact, to the extent that he wrote of "horrifying green" and "stupid nature," Yi Sang was in the location of a "civilized person" playing with a camera.

Therefore, it may only be natural that Yi Sang asserted state "supervision" was necessary in order to prevent the situation above. For it is precisely the imperialist state that represents the civilized focus and magnification at work in the camera lens pointed by the white man. Accordingly, the only mutual subjectivity he could put forth regarding this was the blueprint of yet another state: "rather than merely agonizing over attracting groups of tourists, the 'Tourist Bureau' must also devote its attention to a variety of internal conditions in order to forestall these sorts of mistakes."[31] This sort of position reveals Yi's doctor-in-charge aspect. He also was unable to avoid being a civilized person who saw things through the eyes of the state or the *minjok*. At least following discussions like the one from Fukuzawa Yukichi below, even the colonist Yi Sang accepted "civilization" as "a unified nation."

> Hence the term civilization in English. It derives from the Latin *civitas*, which means "nation." Civilization thus describes the process by which society gradually changes for the better and takes on a definite shape. It is a concept of a unified nation in contrast to a state of primitive isolation and lawlessness.[32]

But the "unified nation" that ensures "civilization," that is to say Yi Sang's nation-state that he demands spare him "from viewing this revolting procession of rickshaws not only on the streets of Tokyo but on those of Seoul as well,"[33] is "the Great Japanese Empire." This in turn is related to the social meanings implied by the episode in Pak T'aewŏn's novel *Ch'ŏnbyŏn p'unggyŏng* (*Scenes from Ch'ŏnggye Stream*, 1938) in which Chaebong "feels no ennui whatsoever" during his observation of the scenes "on the other side of the well-washed windowpane of the barbershop."

> "He's only the second boss. But do you know where he is headed?"
> "How would I know?"
> "Now watch," announced the boy proudly,
> "he's going to go to the store by the stream."

"Let's see. . . . You're right, he is about to go into the store. Do you suppose he wants to buy cigarettes?"

"Just wait and see. He will come out without buying anything. Look, isn't he returning this way?"

"Yes. Where is the fellow going now I wonder."

"Now he is headed for the tavern along the stream."

"Oh, yes, he really is. But I am sure he must have bought something at the store. I see no reason why he would go there for nothing."

"I can tell you why. He often goes under the bridge to collect money from the beggars there, some ten *chŏn* or twenty *chŏn*. He uses the money to go to the tavern, and gets some food. But, as you know, beggars beg for pennies, so the twenty or thirty *chŏn* are all in pennies. This man never goes to the tavern with all those pennies. That's why he always goes to the store first, to exchange the pennies for ten-*chŏn* bills."[34]

Chaebong's gaze observes and remembers (records) in great detail not only every move of the "boss of beggars" but also the logic behind the actions. This seems to correspond to the perspectival appropriation of the imperialist state, which operates diverse systems of surveillance and mobilization such as the police, the military, hospitals, and schools. At this juncture, Chaebong's perspective possesses a dual meaning. Firstly, it implies and internalizes the eyes of the imperialist state, which extend to even the most microsopic aspects. At the same time, however, through both the subject and objects of that gaze, it secondly testifies to the vivid yet essentially haphazard daily lives of the colonists. Amid the parallel and repetitive presentation of life endlessly filtered through various exchange values, that detailed description reaches the point of being sentimental. As shown in extreme form through the existence and behavior of the "boss of beggars," who, excluded from genuine exchange and production, can do no better than to trade the coins he has begged for paper money, the lives of the streamside colonists are incoherent and inconsistent. They are nothing more than the objects of the state's grand blueprints for "Greater East Asia" and "*Ōdōrakudo*" (Asian Arcadia ruled by virtue of royal justice), or of the plan (plot) to cover Seoul's Ch'ŏnggye Stream (Chapter 17) in the name of hygiene. From long before the "downfall" of the "shoe store owner," "a loser in the battle of survival in the big city,"[35] the narrative of the old shoe store had been ruined. In that regard, the description in *Ch'ŏnbyŏn p'unggyŏng* rivals Yi Sang's "sentimentalizing a method for disposing of the flesh." This also developed into the structural characteristic of *Ch'ŏnbyŏn p'unggyŏng*.

One additional important point is the fact that this sort of "novel-of-manners" description, by being carried out through the eyes of colonists who had internalized the imperialist perspective, involutely novelizes the museumesque perspective of the colonial modern subject. This is the true meaning connoted by the novelist Kubo's "modernology," which was just an imitation of KonWajirō's. The camera-lens description of the novel of manners expresses novelistically the essential contradiction and aporia of the colonial subject (as represented by Yi Kwangsu) who, even as he self-internalized the imperialist perspective that otherized himself as barbarian, could at best mock the topknot-wearing "*yobo*," but could never possess his own project. It is from here that the sentimentalism of *Ch'ŏnbyŏn p'unggyŏng* originates.

And this sentimentalism may just be related to the "fatigue" that Kobayashi Hideo felt in front of Sŏkkuram.[36] Regarding this, Kim Yunsik wrote the following.

That he admitted no blame lay with Sŏkkuram once again confirms that he is first-rate, however, it was also a fact that upon viewing Sŏkkuram he became fatigued. What is the concrete meaning of that feeling of fatigue's coming from his own lack of "Buddha"? . . . The "Buddha" of Sŏkkuram can be viewed in the end as his inability to feel the past as an object of belief. This is due to the fact that in the end it was impossible for him to take Silla as an object of belief. . . . He is known to have had an interest in ancient art, and to have first encountered Chosŏn white porcelain. Even if, however, he viewed this not merely as an antique but rather understood it as a kind of beauty, and if Chosŏn white porcelain were true beauty, it still would have been unrelated to the fact that the poor ancestors of the common people of the colony had created it, and no different from a Grecian urn. When viewing a Greek statue as well he would have rightly been fatigued. Because he did not possess Greek mythology.[37]

That Kobayashi was fatigued in front of Sŏkkuram was due to the operation of the imperialist perspective that confined colonial Korea inside a museum. The beauty commanded by Sŏkkuram, however, was not completely appropriated by that perspective. Rather, it evoked the existence of yet another gaze. That gaze, which created Sŏkkuram, was looking upon Kobayashi.

But the "first-rate" Kobayashi did not adopt the flippant attitude expressed by some Japanese: "I know Yi Sunsin to be a person of Japanese blood. None but a member of the *Kuroshio minzoku* could become such a resourceful general, great commander, and brave admiral of the sea."[38] He experienced his confusion honestly. It may have been he who was on display. Fatigue was natural. Of course, this would likely have been the same before a "Greek statue." Because Western civilization, which is emblematized by the "Greek" statue, was looking at the Koreans, of course, and the Japanese as well from the other side of the museum's (zoo's) windowpane.

Pak T'aewŏn's observation forms a pair with this gaze of Kobayashi's. And in that sense Pak's modernological description also compares to the topography of Dublin in Joyce's *Ulysses*, which satirizes British imperialism (civilization) as "syphilization." In addition, this is also related to Yi Sang's "*Nalgae* (Wings, 1936)," in which the narrator observes himself as a "stuffed specimen." Actually, unlike the Greek hero Odysseus who was on the road home, to the colonists of Seoul's Honmachi, who were essentially no different from the bone fragments of Pithecanthropus on display in the museum, the yearned-for hometown (Ithaca) and chaste wife (Penelope) urging them to tie fast their own bodies with rational subjectivity[39] and thereby overcome the temptation of the Sirens did not exist. Instead, the streets teemed with all sorts of products and flashing neon signs and women. Accordingly, "*Nalgae*," which not only fails to bind itself or block its ears to avoid the Sirens but, along with its itching armpits, goes so far as to scream "wings, sprout once more," is the anti-heroic epic poem of a colony-produced Odysseus that is commanded by a "stuffed specimen" who on the other side of his playing with a magnifying glass witnessed his own being displayed side by side with the bone fragments of Pithecanthropus. This is the reason X, the protagonist of *12 wŏl 12 il* (*December 12*), defines himself as "a worthless antique, stripped of most of life, decayed, dented, and covered with scars."[40] The "skeleton whose knees are above its ears" who, with neither wife nor home to return to, wanders the mise-en-scène-like streets and licensed quarters of colonial Seoul was a museum's Pithecanthropus helplessly ensnared by the siren song of "the Great Japanese Empire." He was an "aggrieved skeleton appearing in an academic paper." As seen below, he was an Odysseus native to the colony.

> But now the only difficult thing for me to decide was whether I should trudge back to my wife. Should I go? And if so, where?
>
>   At that moment, the noon siren wailed: *Tuu—u—!* People extended their four limbs and flapped around like chickens, while all sorts of glass, steel, marble, money, and ink seemed to rumble and boil up—right then, the noon reached the zenith of its dazzling splendor.[41]

THE ONTOLOGY OF *KUDU*

Thus did the Pithecanthropus of the colony "get out of the rickshaw at the gateway to the city, and always leisurely stroll along this street."[42] At this point, the "*Hombura*"[43]-esque ambulation of the native Odysseus, who has been caught by the capitalistic siren so like a "sticky, invisible web,"[44] takes on a fateful character. This suggests the directionlessness of the native Odysseus who, having viewed the "sight of adult dress shoes and adult dress shoes bumping into each other," cannot distinguish whether it is right or not to go back to his wife. For this "child" who rushes through the "streets" not caring whether they are open alleys or blind alleys, plans and calculations are impossible.[45] He can only express himself as in the excerpts below.

> On that day I wrote my own obituary and inserted it in my autobiography. From then on, my body was not in that sort of hometown.[46]

> Atop the blank page, in pencil he blurrily composed a draft of one person's fate. Is it this wishy-washy. Leaving money and the past there, he tries to write his body into the throng.[47]

The cores of these quotations are the phrases "wrote my own obituary and inserted it" and "write his body into the throng." As seen in the line "in pencil he blurrily composed a draft of one person's fate," the speaker translates his own existence and actions into sentences. This is yet another directionality/directivity that replaces the native Odysseus' directionlessness. The divining of fate, no, fate is expressed only as sentences and text. The divination sign, even while it is not life itself, from a transcendental location preempts and describes life. At times it even places a "*period* announcing the return home of (my) runaway wife."[48] It is an "artful document." When viewed in this way, the meaning of the poem below becomes clearer.

> I cough. I strain myself surrounded by air to spit out air. The street I stiflingly walk is my story; the boring air massages and soothes the punctuation I cough out. When I have walked a full chapter and come to cross the railway, then there is someone treading my path. Pain is slashed by a dagger while it commingles with the railway to form a cross. I collapse and thereby shed my cough. The sound of laughter roars, and then a toxic ink is poured atop a self-deprecating expression. The cough just flops down upon thought and chatters. I am utterly dumbfounded.[49]

The above poem compares the speaker's life "path" to a "story." Life is sentences and text. Noteworthy here is the expression "the punctuation I cough out." This can be interpreted as worsening health, as evidenced by coughing, putting a stop ("*p'eriodŭ*" = period = punctuation mark) to a certain kind of walking. Or it can be understood as saying, just as he coughed (disease), he continued to walk with dress shoes on ("the street I stiflingly walk" = prostitution) "to cross the railway (derailment=deviation)." That is to say, "*kudu* (punctuation)" exchanges meaning with the "*kudu* (dress shoes)" below.

But for me voluntarily avoiding entering through this door may rather be utterly impossible.

Before long, my eyes bloodshot with hatred spot a pair of dress shoes.

Dress shoes! It was a pair of dress shoes that had rusted like bone while long lying there in a corner of my thoughts. Upon their inwardly-turned noses overflowed vestiges of the chaos of stomping through brambles. . . .

Timber hewn beneath the glow of the poisonous primeval forest harbors blood.

My pathetic figure—look at these feet. . . .

Oh all *Member* present in the room, well, I (from now on) wear those dress shoes. Please record (from now on) all language of resentment on my feet— Here is the bill.[50]

Established here is the following equivalent relation: "dress shoes = sexual organ = prostitution = walking = disease = punctuation mark = sentence." This forms the diagram of the "LOVE PARADE" written out in Yi's short story *"Chido ŭi amsil* (Darkroom of the Map, 1932)": "He continued to walk in place, but the *pavement* fluttered like fluttering chocolate slipperily sliding out from beneath the soles of his dress shoes, and was the cause that made him walk in place more and more." This, while exchanging meanings with "the live alley is a dead (-end) alley, the dead (-end) alley is a live alley"[51] or "13 children rush down a street / (A dead end alley is suitable),"[52] suggests the meaning of the "map" of which Yi Sang wrote. The "map" metaphorizes the perspectives of modernology and of the detective novel, which, like bugs crawling at ground level, explore every nook and cranny of the city. The description "right in the middle of the city, this time atop a newly-appeared grave, the laughter of every country stained on a beetle is disseminated and gathered" is related to this. Accordingly, this establishes yet another bug's perspective different from the bug's-eye view (*ch'unggwando*蟲觀圖), which is the opposite of the bird's-eye view (*chogamdo*鳥瞰圖). This is one of the meanings of *"kudu"* (Western dress shoes as opposed to Korean straw shoes or leather shoes).

The meaning of "the punctuation I cough out," however, does not stop here. Going further, it embodies the bird's-eye-view desire to look upon from a transcendental perspective the diseased flesh of the colonist who turns "pages from which my hopes and ambition were erased"[53] while continuing to wander. The following excerpt serves as a general reference in relation to this.

And the combination or accumulation of bugs' eyes, through a figuration, view a unique possibility arising from the fact that they give birth even to a bird's-eye imagination. That is to say, "details" or "macrosituations" of which we usually are not conscious, and, as a result, have never even been measured, go about being displayed in pictures mediated by a measurement of reality. Even without flying through the sky, even without shrinking the body, we are able to constitute a bird's-eye perspective or a bug's-eye experience from among the manipulations of records. That is the process of defamiliarization. This is because, through the maximization and minimization of those sorts of perspectival experiences, daily impressions themselves come to be examined one more time.[54]

Of course, Yi Sang's bug-like point of view embodied in *"Chido ŭi amsil"* does not continue into a bird's-eye view. The bird's-eye-view location that marks punctuation is premised upon a point of view outside the work's sentences and space. That is the location that describes history and constitutes buildings. Metaphorically speaking, it is the point of view that draws a world map in place of the *"arae a"*[55] ("-" = sky = celestial realm), which fell out of use beginning with the modern age. This leads such things as observation, division, logic, design, constitution, and progress. But Yi Sang's *"kudu"* is "the *kudu* (punctuation) I cough out." Word spacing—together with *ŏnmun ilch'i* (Jp. *genbun itchi*), a standard language, the draft for a unified spelling system, and national language—embodied in orthography such things as modern grammatical consciousness, rationality, and raison d'état. This represents a self-consciousness that writes sentences while simultaneously analyzing them. It operates, together with the *"haetta"* style, as yet another modern windowpane. Segmented into all sorts of grammatical categories, structures, rules, functions, differences, and distinctions, it visualizes atop the page a basic and stable framework with which to recognize the world rationally.

It is this word spacing that Yi Sang deliberately ignored. Yi strove to maintain to the end this bug's point of view that draws maps (or crawls around atop maps) using *kudu* (dress shoes). Therefore, it is precisely this that corresponds not to marking *kudu* (punctuation) with a pen (ink) but to marking *kudu* (punctuation) with a cough (blood).[56] If organized sentence structure, which is viewed as identical to the modern rational subject, corresponds to general punctuation marks, then the location of the endings and beginnings of sentences whose word spacing has been destroyed by the bug's point of view shall be displayed solely through diseased flesh, that is through "the punctuation I cough out." As a result, and unrelated to the fate of the Korean language itself coming to hang by a thread due to such policies as *"kokugojōyō,"*[57] these sorts of sentences convert history into "destiny." And the appearance of that destiny is apparent below.

Iamtwentythreeyearsold—itisMarch—itishemoptysis.[58]

The sentence above, which is written without word spacing but with two coughs (punctuation marks = "—"), suggests a breakthrough from a different angle by a speaker who has lost the direction of rationally planned progress yet has risked his life to soar. The speaker, rather than planning (bird's-eye view) life, punctuated the hectic "*story*" of destiny with his coughs. Truly this represents one of the meanings of "*Ogamdo* (Crow's-eye view, 1934)" that set the "children" to running. It mediated the bug's point of view and the bird's point of view by means of the fear of falling. At this juncture, by the speaker who is at once doctor in charge and laboratory animal writing his own body in, the path of the destiny that came to appear in an academic paper takes on a reflective character. As evidenced in the quotation below, the text of destiny that replaced a plan of life was the "I inside the mirror," the "opposite of me."

> The I inside the mirror is really the opposite of me, but
> Also quite similar
> Unable to worry for or examine the I inside the mirror, I am awfully sad.[59]

Such was the extent to which the mirror served as Yi Sang's windowpane placed between the doctor in charge (bird's point of view) and the laboratory animal (bug's point of view). The doctor in charge looked at the laboratory animal on the other side of the windowpane, but the laboratory animal was the doctor in charge himself. The windowpane was the mirror. In front of the "windowpane = mirror" ("open alley" = "blind alley") of "*Ogamdo*" that combined the bird's point of view and the bug's point of view, he looked out toward the inside or looked in toward the outside. No, by means of the diseased flesh of the native Odysseus, who was also the same as Pithecanthropus, Yi Sang's speaker himself became "windowpane = mirror."

As such, that Yi Sang defined himself as "a bastard on the verge of blacking out, jammed in the crack between the nineteenth century and the twentieth century" is of profound significance. On the streets of colonial Seoul where history ceased to exist, he stood precisely atop the threshold. Until the diseased flesh became the windowpane (mirror), until the "sense of touch (feeler) diagrammed this sort of scene,"[60] he made his own punctuation marks atop the modern boundary between doctor in charge and laboratory animal.

NOTES

1. Yi Sang, "*Sasin* 7 (Private correspondence 7)," in *Yi Sang munhak chŏnjip* 3, ed. Kim Yunsik (Seoul: Munhak sasangsa, 1993), 235.

2. Yi Sang, "*Sanch'onyŏjŏng* (Lingering impressions of a mountain village)," trans. John M. Frankl, in *Azalea: Journal of Korean Literature & Culture*, Volume 2, 2008, 336.

3. Yi Sang, "*Chongsaenggi* (Record of a life)," in *Yi Sang munhak chŏnjip* 2, ed. Kim Yunsik (Seoul: Munhak sasangsa, 1991), 388.

4. Yi Sang "*Ch'ulp'anbŏp* (Publication law)," in *Yi Sang munhak chŏnjip* 1, ed. Yi Sŭnghun (Seoul: Munhak sasangsa, 1989), 175.

5. For a more detailed discussion, see Yi Kyŏnghun, "*Tanbal, 'ahae' ŭi susahak* (The bob, the rhetoric of 'children')," in *Yi Sang Review*, September 2001, 97–137.

6. Yi Sang, "*Ijōna kagyaku hannō* (A strange reversible reaction)," in *Chosen to kenchiku*, July 1931, 15.

7. Yi Sang "*Chasang* (Self-portrait)," in *Yi Sang munhak chŏnjip* 1, ed. Yi Sŭnghun, 175.

8. Yi Sang, "*1931 nyŏn* (1931)," in ibid, 238.

9. Yi Sang, "*Hyuŏp kwa sajŏng* (Closures and circumstances)," in *Yi Sang munhak chŏnjip* 2, ed. Kim Yunsik (Seoul: Munhak sasangsa, 1991), 154.

For a more detailed discussion of "*Hyuŏp kwa sajŏng*," see Yi Kyŏnghun, "*Asŭp'irin kwa Adallin* (Aspirin and Adalin)," in *Yi Sang munhak chŏnjip* 5, ed. Kim Yunsik (Seoul: Munhak sasangsa, 2001), 157–87.

10. Yi Sang, "*Chido ŭ iamsil* (Darkroom of the map)," in *Yi Sang munhak chŏnjip* 2, ed. Kim Yunsik (Seoul: Munhak sasangsa, 1991), 170

11. Pantopon is the brand name of an F. Hoffmann La Roche painkiller made from opium.—Trans.

12. Yi Sang, "*Munhak ŭ lpŏrigo munhwa rŭl sangsanghalsuŏpta* (Without literature, there Is no imagining culture)," in *Yi Sang munhak chŏnjip* 3, ed. Kim Yunsik (Seoul: Munhak sasangsa, 1993), 249.

13. Yi Sang, "*Ŏrisogŭn sŏkban* (A foolish supper)," in *Yi Sang munhak chŏnjip* 3, ed. Kim Yunsik, 126.

14. Yi Sang, "*Kakhyŏl ŭ iach'im* (Morning of hemoptysis)," in ibid, 327.

15. Yi Sang, "*1931 nyŏn* (1931)," in *Yi Sang munhak chŏnjip* 2, ed. Kim Yunsik, 237.

16. Yi Sang, "*Hyŏlsŏ samt'ae* (Three forms of writing in blood)," in *Yi Sang munhak chŏnjip* 3, ed. Kim Yunsik, 23.

17. "Brand," here and in the excerpt above, is a translation of *nakhyŏng* (烙刑), or branding with a hot iron as a form of criminal punishment.—Trans.

18. Yi Sang, "*Ch'udŭn gchapp'il* (Miscellaneous writings by autumn lamplight)," in *Yi Sang munhak chŏnjip* 3, ed. Kim Yunsik, 83.

19. Yi Sang, 12 wŏl 12 il (December 12th), in Yi Sang munhak chŏnjip 2, ed. Kim Yunsik, 81.

20. For more on "*ka oe ka*" see Yi Kyŏnghun, Yi Sang, *ch'ŏlch'ŏn ŭi susahak* (Yi Sang, *the piercing rhetoric*) (Seoul: Somyŏngch'ulp'an, 2000).

21. Yi Sang, "*Choch'un chŏmmyo* (Early spring sketches)," in *Yi Sang munhak chŏnjip* 3, ed. Kim Yunsik, 41.

22. http://en.wikipedia.org/wiki/Hideyo_Noguchi

23. Yi Sang, "*Ch'udŭngchapp'il*," 84–85.

24. Yi Sang, "*Kŭmje* (Taboo)," in *Yi Sang munhak chŏnjip* 1, ed. Yi Sŭnghun, 75.

25. Yi Sang, "*Choch'un chŏmmyo*," 48.

26. For more on the modern meaning of "glass," see chapter 4, "The Fashion of *Mujŏng*."

27. *Taehan minbo*, February, 10, 1910.

28. Yi Kwangsu, "*Taitoa bungaku no michi* (The path of greater East Asian literature)," in *Kungmin munhak*, January 1945, 24–27.

This was originally published in Japanese. The Korean translation is quoted from *Ch'unwŏn ŭi ch'inilmunhak chŏnjip* 2, ed. Yi Kyŏnghun (Seoul: P'yŏngminsa, 1995), 455.

29. Yi Sang, "*Ch'udŭng chapp'il*," 86–87.

30. The word in the original is *hyangt'o* (鄕土) and can be glossed as locality, own land, or country depending on context. In this particular essay, Yi uses different words such as *kukka* (國家) to refer to the nation-state as a political entity, which at the time was part of the Japanese empire, and thus by definition not "his own land."—Trans.

31. Yi Sang, "*Ch'udŭng chapp'il*," 87.

32. Fukuzawa Yukichi, *Bunmeiron no gairyaku* (*An Outline of a Theory of Civilization*), trans. David A. Dilworth and G. Cameron Hurst III (New York: Columbia University Press, 2008), 45–46. "English words employed by Fukuzawa in the original Japanese text are shown by the use of bold face."

33. Yi Sang, "*Ch'udŭng chapp'il*," 87.

34. Pak T'aewŏn, *Ch'ŏnbyŏn p'unggyŏng* (*Scenes from Ch'ŏnggye Stream*), trans. Ok Young Kim Chang (Singapore: Stallion Press, 2011), 22.

The "ten-*chŏn* coins" at the end of this excerpt appear to be a mistranslation. At the time, and in the novel, ten-*chŏn* bills were used.—Trans.

35. Ibid., 58.

36. Sŏkkuram (石窟庵) is a grotto hermitage and part of the Pulguksa temple complex in Kyŏngju. It dates from the early years of the Unified Silla dynasty (668–935). It was obviously already a popular tourist destination when Kobayashi toured Korea in support of the war in 1940. In 1962, it was designated the twenty-fourth national treasure of Korea, and in 1995 it was added to the UNESCO World Heritage List.—Trans.

37. Kim Yunsik, *Han'guk kŭndae munhak sasangsa* (*History of modern Korean literary thought*) (Seoul: Han'gilsa, 1984), 377.

38. These words were spoken to Yi Kwangsu by one Captain Kuroki of the Seoul Naval Military Office. Ironically, Yi Sunsin was Korea's greatest admiral and is best known for his repeatedly defeating the Japanese during the Hideyoshi Invasions (1592–98). The term *Kuroshio minzoku* (Kor. *Hŭkcho minjok* 黑潮民族) is used here to refer to the Japanese race. It literally means the "race of the black tide," but "black tide" is also translated as "The Japan Stream." What may also be significant here is the fact that the *Kuroshio* flows only on the eastern side of Japan, not on its west in the seas shared with Korea.—Trans.

39. For more on this, see Max Horkheimer and Theodor W. Adorno, *The Dialectic of Enlightenment*, ed. Gunzelin Schmid Noerr, trans. Edmund Jephcott (Stanford: Stanford University Press, 2002).

40. Yi Sang, *12 wŏl 12 il*, 52.

41. Yi Sang, "*Nalgae* (Wings)," trans. Walter K. Lew and Youngju Ryu, in *Modern Korean Fiction: An Anthology*, eds. Bruce Fulton and Youngmin Kwon (New York: Columbia University Press, 2005), 83.

As will be seen below in the section on *kudu* (the word for both "dress shoes [no Chinese characters]" and "punctuation [句讀]"), the sheer volume of homophones in the Korean language provides an ample source not only for puns and double entendres but also for ambiguities and misreadings. This is particularly true where Chinese characters exist but are not provided, as is the case with the word *hyŏllan*, parsed as "dazzling splendor" (絢爛) in this excerpt from "*Nalgae*." Given the context, however, *hyŏllan* (眩亂) seems more appropriate and is translated earlier in this work as "chaos" in the phrase "noon where chaos reached its peak."—Trans.

42. Yi Sang, "*P'ach'ŏp* (A torn memorandum)," in *Yi Sang munhakchŏnjip* 1, ed. Yi Sŭnghun, 207.

43. For more on "*Hombura*," see Yi Kyŏnghun, "*Missŭk'osi, kŭndae ŭi syowindou*" (Mitsukoshi, show window of the modern age), in *Hyŏndae munhak ŭi yŏn'gu*, Volume 15, 2000, 107–47.

44. Yi Sang, "*Nalgae*," 83.

45. This sentence makes reference to one of Yi Sang's best known poems, "*Ogamdo, siche 1 ho*" (Crow's-eye view, poem number 1).

46. Yi Sang, "*1933. 6. 1* (June 1, 1933)," in *Yi Sang munhak chŏnjip* 1, ed. Yi Sŭnghun, 186.

47. Yi Sang, "*Yŏktan* (Divining by the *Book of Changes*)," in ibid, 61.

48. Yi Sang, "*Muje* (Untitled)," in *Yi Sang munhak chŏnjip* 1, ed. Kim Yunsik, 213.

49. Yi Sang, "*Haengno* (Path)," in *Yi Sang munhak chŏnjip* 1, ed. Yi Sŭnghun, 63.

50. Yi Sang, "*Kudu* (Dress shoes)," in *Yi Sang munhak chŏnjip* 3, ed. Kim Yunsik (Seoul: Munhaksasangsa, 1993), 302–03.

51. Yi Sang, "*Chido ŭi amsil*," 170.

The original line is written completely in Chinese characters: "活胡同是死胡同死胡同是活胡同." "Live" here corresponds to a through alley, while "dead" obviously overlaps with the English "dead-end."

52. Yi Sang, "*Ogamdo, siche 1 ho* (Crow's-eye view, poem number 1)," trans. Walter K. Lew, in *Modern Korean Fiction: An Anthology*, 65.

The original translation reads "13ChildrenRushdownaStreet. / (AdeadendalleyisSuitable.)" Standard capitalization and spacing between words have been added for clarity.—Trans.

53. Ibid., 83.

54. Satō Genji, *Hūkei no seisanhūkei no kaihō* (The production of landscape, the liberation of landscape) (Tokyo: Kōdansha, 1994), 107.

55. The "*arae a*" is a Korean vowel represented by a single dot beneath a consonant, or vertically between two consonants, thus retaining its "beneath" orientation

(*arae* means beneath). It is no longer in use in modern Korean, although it can occasionally be seen for dramatic effect in advertising and brand names.—Trans.

56. Yi Sang suffered from tuberculosis marked by sever bouts of hemoptysis.

57. The literal meaning of the phrase is the seemingly benign "common use of the national language." In practical terms, however, it referred to an increasingly strict and unforgiving insistence on Japanese at the expense of Korean, and was representative of the overall mood of the wartime Japanese empire, which increasingly demanded a total mobilization and assimilation that had not existed up to the late 1930s.—Trans.

58. Yi Sang, "*Pongbyŏlgi* (Record of meeting and parting)," in *Yi Sang munhak chŏnjip* 2, ed. Kim Yunsik (Seoul: Munhaksasangsa, 1991), 348.

59. Yi Sang, "*Kŏul* (Mirror)," in *Yi Sang munhak chŏnjip* 1, ed. Yi Sŭnghun, 187.

60. Yi Sang, "*Tonghae* (Child's skeleton)," in *Yi Sang munhak chŏnjip* 2, ed. Kim Yunsik, 259.

Chapter 9

The Humor of an Empty Stomach

A POOR MEAL

"The irony of devouring the dishes you dislike most"[1] is the most impressive line in Yi Sang's "*Nalgae* (Wings, 1936)." This, together with the scene atop the Mitsukoshi Department Store, represents the core of "*Nalgae*." As such, Yi also elaborated in his short story "*Tanbal* (The bob, 1939)" that "eating the foods one dislikes most without grimacing, and thus refusing to stop until one has found the 'taste' that is the 'taste' in these things, this is, so to speak, a '*paradox.*'"[2]

"*Wit* and *paradox*" thus defined provide a viewpoint for the rereading of "*Nalgae.*" From the words "(w)henever nicotine sinks into the worm-ridden coil of my intestines, a clean sheet of paper is ready in my head,"[3] to the line "I realized that I too would have to drag this body along, disintegrating from hunger and exhaustion, and dissolve into the grimy flow,"[4] "*Nalgae*" consistently describes its protagonist's physiological and physical states. And representative among them are an empty stomach and malnutrition.

These are not related only to the protagonist's ancillary actions as observed in his taking in the "(v)arious smells" of "(g)rilled herring, *T'angodoran*[5] foundation, rice rinsings, soap . . ." or noticing "the residents don't come out to the gate to get their bean curd: they just slide their doors open and buy it right in their rooms."[6] Much more, they are linked to those events that comprise the framework of the story. In contrast to the wife's ordering out for food while cavorting with her "guests," the emaciated husband dines alone on food unappetizing to the point of cruelty. Precisely this represents the essential situation of "*Nalgae.*" Accordingly, the quotations below portray decisive scenes that rival in importance the spatial division of the couple's rooms.

> My wife's guests don't seem to know that I'm on the other side of the paper door. They don't hesitate to indulge with her in the kinds of games that even I would find difficult to attempt. However, one could see that a few of her visitors were relatively well mannered; on the whole, they didn't stay much past midnight. But there were others of very shallow cultivation, the type who usually ordered food. Replenished by the food, they continued to enjoy themselves, generally without incident.[7]

> I always ate and slept alone in the inner room. The food was terrible, the side dishes skimpy. Like a chicken or puppy dog, I silently gulped down what she gave me, although not always without resentment. I grew completely pale and began to waste away. My strength dwindled visibly with each passing day. Due to lack of nourishment, my bones began to stick out all over. They ached so much that I had to change position dozens of times each night.[8]

The first quotation relates to a slightly later description: "My wife should be able to see that I am hungry. Still, she never gives me leftovers from the outer room. No doubt this is out of her deep respect for me."[9] While the second quotation is connected to a pair of slightly earlier lines: "I've never seen her cook but she delivers meals to my room every morning and evening," and "it is clear that she is the one who prepares these meals."[10] Thus these situations physically mediate the daily life of the protagonist with his wife.

The protagonist of "*Nalgae,*" who, "like a chicken or puppy dog," "silently gulped down what she gave," even as he is tormented by bedbugs, scratching "the itching bites until they bleed,"[11] is hungry enough to investigate "the kinds of dishes served in the outer room."[12] But his meals taste horrible and the side dishes are skimpy. The meals his wife prepares for him are no different from those purchased at the "peaceful restaurant" in Yi's 1931 poem "LE URINE": "a lunch long since cold, no doubt the joint fatigue of the upper limbs and lower limbs."[13] Just as he wrote that "(w)ings collapsed in exhaustion the butterfly eats the meager dew that collects glistening from my exhaled breath,"[14] on his table "pickled garlic, soybean paste, and unripe peppers lie arranged like the law of inertia."[15] With his "hungry face,"[16] Yi always had "poor meals"[17] "as dried out as old man Amundsen's."[18]

In light of the above, the line "(a)t around 3 or 4 at night, I usually go to the outhouse"[19] is interesting. This is because Yi Sang's protagonist, who had once been a "constipation sufferer,"[20] deposited in the toilet not excrement but his piggy bank. The child in Sŏngch'ŏn who had become the "foul loser" in the "final improvisation game"[21] of taking a shit was also Yi Sang himself.

A STRANGE DINNER

Thus this life of malnutrition, veins "skinny as a whistle,"[22] caused Yi Sang to "want to eat a single warm, freshly laid egg."[23] This suggests Yi Sang's true living conditions. For example, Cho Yongman once described Yi's "making do for both breakfast and lunch with a bowl of *sŏllŏngt'ang*."[24] Chŏng Int'aek provided considerably more detail.

> With the money his wife had earned, Yi Sang roamed the streets deep into the night, drinking booze and babbling away. The both of them were out so late at night that even when morning came they never got out of bed before noon, and even when they supposedly got up even in the middle of the day the room was as dark as night. So with only a single bowl of tofu stew haphazardly thrown together with some red pepper paste, while also chewing on some dried pollack, they shoveled down a few servings of rice not knowing whether it was for lunch or for breakfast. After this they again fell right back down for a nap, and around the time the electric lamps came on, when his wife washed her face, got dolled up, and went out, Yi Sang too, cutting a plodding and unsavory figure, went out into the streets to a bar or to wherever and wandered around until his wife returned home.[25]

The line "a single bowl of tofu stew haphazardly thrown together with some red pepper paste" seems to symbolize the relationship between the protagonist and his wife that constitutes the essence of *"Nalgae."* As evidenced in the protagonist's saying "my wife has never called me over to her room,"[26] they normally do not sit across from one another and share food. Or there were even times when "as if in derision, the very socks my wife had taken off" wore the "expression of an empty stomach like me."[27] To the degree that he would confess "because I only take in the scent of nutrition through my nose, I continually grow more haggard,"[28] his wife is not at home. In the end, and in spite of the tuberculosis patient's "sadness at going hungry last night,"[29] this leads to the revealing of his dissatisfaction in the line "as I do not want to eat, you had better place your slipper atop the gramophone."[30]

In fact, however, this language expresses the desire to eat "those peach-colored calves, looking ever so much tastier than any other sort of fruit"[31] or "a red apple all the way to its core."[32] As appears in *"Kongp'o ŭi kirok* (Record of fear, 1937)," due to his "empty stomach—the desperate emptiness" of his wife's unknown whereabouts, the protagonist "like a ghost, roamed the streets in agitation." He "acted solely in order to fill the single strand of empty stomach."[33] The protagonist who "tripped over *restaurants*"[34] and "swallowed colors,"[35] "finding that he had no bag of crackers in his right hand / had now retraced some five *li* of dead-end street in order to find the bag of crackers he held in his left hand."[36] But for all that, never mind sweet "lump sugar,"[37] he was unable to eat anything other than the "frighteningly" salty food below.

> Picking up some sterilized chopsticks, I pick up a pitch-black burdock root. It looks sticky and sweet as if soaked in tar. My mouth awaits it.
> It's frighteningly salty. My eyeballs are about to pop out. A woman enters. I am unable to greet her entrance. Because my entire face is salty.[38]

Unlike Yi Sang who, after she had run away only to return two months later, filled Kŭmhong's stomach with beer, goldfish crackers, and beef soup with rice from the restaurant Taech'angok,[39] the wife in "*Nalgae*," after her husband spends a single night out, "tore wildly at my flesh with her teeth," and "rails at me: 'What do you do all night? Run around robbing people? Drop in on whores?'"[40] It was not only bedbugs that bit the protagonist. Furthermore, as defined in "*Chijuhoesi* (Two spiders meet a pig, 1936)," she is also a spider. No, in the end, in that he lives off the money his wife earns, it is actually the protagonist who is both bedbug and spider. Regarding such aspects as planting "red peppers confused with food,"[41] while sucking each other dry, "*Chijuhoesi*" narrates the following.

> Spider—clearly he himself was a spider. Realize you yourself are the spider that sucks from his wife who grows gaunt as a root in water. A mouth that smells of blood. No, then does that mean that his wife does not suck anything from him? Just look—the pale five-o'clock shadow—hollow eyes—thinly spread nutrition with neither substance nor shadow—look. The wife is the wife. She cannot not be the wife. Are spider and spider's spider and spider? Do they suck from each other? Where do they go? What is the reason they both grow gaunt? On what morning shall the bones tear through the skin to emerge[42]

At this point, the lines "The wife is the wife. She cannot not be the wife" exchange meaning with "(t)he irony of devouring the dishes you dislike most," while summarizing the situations of "*Nalgae*" and "*Chijuhoesi*." This expresses the fact that the wife is not the wife in terms of both food and sex, and that the home is a place of dining out and prostitution where they both suck the life from one another. This is the concrete content of "*ka oe ka*" (街外街) in which "lips that must eat to live, atop a spitefully wrinkled mire, furtively imitate dining."[43] Expressed in Yi Sangian fashion, the protagonist is a "ragged man resembling Christ," while the wife is a "frigid Maria" "atop a bar."[44]

When viewed in this way, we are able to constitute newly the entire plot of "*Nalgae*" centered on the protagonist's act of eating. Returning home with "hollow eyes," the protagonist gives his wife five *wŏn* and sleeps in her room for the first time. But the following day, when he returns, unable to endure his wife's provocative scent, to his own room, its floor covering burned the "color of sponge cake,"[45] the "meal" his wife has prepared is right there. And the feel of that "feed" "long since cold" is "frigid as cold ashes," so much so that it makes the hungry protagonist put down his spoon and crawl under his covers. Like the "exotic, sensual fragrance" of her cosmetics, the table set by his wife merely fans the flames of his empty stomach. Accordingly, he writes in a poem "Who first ate an eel? Who first ate an egg? In any case, he must have been very hungry."[46] Finally, the protagonist, having not eaten for two days and returned home from his second outing, gives his wife two *wŏn* and again sleeps in her room, only after which he experiences his first and "Last Supper" facing his wife who had theretofore "not even once deigned to peck at a grain of rice."[47] Below is the scene in which they eat that "strange dinner."

> Yielding to her wishes, I allowed myself to be dragged into her room. A humble dinner was waiting for us there. It suddenly struck me that I hadn't eaten for two days. Just a few moments ago, I had been lolling about, not even sure if I felt hungry.
>
> It was clear to me now. Even if a bolt of lightning were to strike me the moment I finished this Last Supper, I would have no regrets. Human society is so uninteresting that I couldn't have stood it much longer anyway. Everything is a nuisance, but sudden calamity is a joy!
>
> My mind thus at ease, I sat across from my wife and shared the bizarre dinner. The two of us didn't chat. We never do. After finishing the meal, I just got up and went over to my room without saying a word. My wife did not detain me. Back in my room, I waited, leaning against the wall with a cigarette dangling between my lips, thinking to myself all the while that if lightning is going to strike, let it strike now![48]

Judging from the above, the line from "*Tonghae* (A child's skeleton, 1937)," "before my mouth began to water, dropless tears began to well up in my eyes like dew clinging to a cold cup,"[49] also represents the situation in "*Nalgae*." Not only did the protagonist sleep in his wife's room for the first time after giving her five *wŏn* but also he was able to eat together with her in her room only after paying her two *wŏn*. This again brings to mind the lines from Baudelaire: "When I would come home penniless / Her cries tore me apart."[50]

In reality, Kŭmhong had criticized Yi Sang, calling him both a "retard without a single useful thing to his name," and a "moron incapable of earning
money."[51]

Thus, when considered in relation to this sort of landscape, the real "feed"
his wife gives him is "some warm water and four white tablets."[52] Unrelated
to curing his cold, the wife feeds the protagonist Adalin for a full month. This
represents a sort of punishment for having seen "what my wife would prefer
me not to see."[53] This appears to be "too harsh" even for the protagonist who
possesses an "appetite" as "simple as a linear equation."[54]

In spite of this, however, when viewed from the standpoint of the protagonist
who muses, "(t)o devise a counterfeit of myself would also be worthwhile,"[55]
aspirin could also become Adalin. Paying two *wŏn* and eating a "Last Supper,"
and taking Adalin confused for aspirin are both due to the irony and paradox
of forever "devouring the dishes you dislike most," even as you expect some
"unforeseen accident" like "lightning." In addition, this evokes the humor
of the masochist who "stands guilt on its head by making punishment into a
condition that makes possible the forbidden pleasure."[56] This being the case,
it is only natural that the protagonist, because he was "tired of thinking about
it" and "cross," "chewed up" and swallowed the remaining six pills of Adalin
while feeling "(t)here was a funny taste to them."[57]

At this juncture, having deceived the protagonist, Kŭmhong is revealed
as having been the active supporter and assistant of a "*Nalgae*"-esque
"humor (*iksal*)" and *irony* that move beyond the binary opposition of
aspirin and Adalin. Unlike his opinion that "(m)y wife and I are a pair
of cripples destined to be out of step with each other,"[58] the protagonist's
plan to "draw up plans for life with a woman"[59] proved a complete success. With the Adalin given to him by Kŭmhong, the "strange dinner" was
complete. In that regard, Kŭmhong, who may also have been an "enormous stone,"[60] was Yi Sang's true partner. This is because, as evidenced
in the line "my empty stomach resonates with the sound,"[61] an "empty
stomach" was the artistic fountainhead of Yi Sang who was "eating *concrete*" in "Broad Daylight."[62]

In light of the above, Yi Sang is close to Arthur Rimbaud who had only
a "taste for eating earth and stones" rather than for the "one piece of French
bread"[63] recommended by Victor Hugo. Just as Rimbaud wrote, "When I
feed, I feed on air, Rocks and coals and iron ore,"[64] Yi forever accomplished
his meals "without even the coarse and miserable food" of the "*concrete*
countryside."[65] Paradoxically, the meal prepared by Kŭmhong gave birth to
one of the monumental scenes of Korean colonial period literature. He wrote
that "I too would have to drag this body along, disintegrating from hunger
and exhaustion, and dissolve into the grimy flow."[66] He was writing that "my
empty stomach alone was able to direct me."[67]

THE TASTE OF FRAGRANT MJB

Yet another aspect of *"Nalgae"* that merits our attention is that the protagonist is continually either drinking or intending to drink coffee. In fact,
buying coffee is nearly the only social act practiced by the protagonist who
appeared to have "already lost any capacity for spending money."[68] "Sitting
in a booth across from no one at all"[69] in the hall of Kyŏngsŏng (Seoul)
Station,[70] he drinks a well-brewed cup of coffee. Additionally, he goes to
Kyŏngsŏng Station in order to "rinse from his mouth" the "utterly bitter
taste" of Adalin, but, suddenly realizing he has not a cent in his pocket, is
at a total loss like a "man who has lost his mind."[71] In that sense, drinking
coffee, in contrast to taking Adalin or "(t)he irony of devouring the dishes
you dislike most," represents the protagonist's true taste. These lines by Yi
Sang are relevant here: "Tokyo's coffee must be better than Seoul's *coffee*, right? And it's impressive that you drank twelve cups throughout the
day with Yun. But when you come back, this time let's have twenty-four
cups each."[72] Regarding the daily lives of Yi Sang and Pak T'aewŏn, Cho
Yongman wrote the following.

> They might go into a room and talk for a while, but eventually the two young
> men would appear on the main thoroughfare of Chongno and head for what at
> the time was called Honmachi, that is to say Chin'gogae, which has now become
> Ch'ungmuro. The two young men would stop by the tearoom Kŭmgangsan or
> the Meiji Bakery and each drink a cup of *coffee*; they praised the taste of the
> brew at these two places as the best in Seoul.[73]

In both Yi Sang's life and literature, coffee has an important meaning.
The opening line of his essay *"Sanch'on yŏjŏng* (Lingering Impressions of
a Mountain Village, 1935)" speaks eloquently of this: "More than twenty
days have passed since I last savored my fragrant MJB."[74] Like Yu Yŏngsŏp,
the character in the Ŏm Hŭngsŏp short story *"Insaeng samak* (A life desert,
1940–41)" who receives the following criticism, "So, you came back from
studying in *America* and all you can do is manage this *tearoom*? Why you're
just a guy who would fry tempura in shit water!", Yi Sang, a graduate of
Keijō Industrial High School,[75] himself owned and managed a series of tearooms cum bars including *Chebi* (The Swallow). In a letter to Kim Kirim
he also wrote, "Today is the lunar New Year's Eve. Homesickness is on the
rise. I am on my way back from having *kōhi*[76] with O, a Japanese university
student." Moreover, while writing the essay *"Tonggyŏng* (Tokyo, 1936),"
he announced that "at 'French Mansion' we had a cup of 'coffee' that had
already been mixed with milk," while in the short story *"Sirhwa* (Lost flower,
1936)," he narrated the following.

Jean Arthur enjoyed a cup of coffee in ADVENTURE IN MANHATTAN. If
you drink it with cream, said the novelist Kubo—it smells like rat piss.
    But since I was able to enjoy it as much as Joel McCrea.[77]

So much so that he longed for "the taste of fragrant MJB" even from
bucolic Sŏngch'ŏn, or that he wrote "from a few years after my 60th birth-
day, for as long as I am able to stand, I want to take my grandchildren who
will look like a bunch of grapes carved from *oak* lumber and go to a coffee
shop,"[78] for Yi Sang coffee was not a simple item of favorite food. Following
the scene in Yi Injik's *Moranbong* (*Peony peak*, 1913) in which Ongnyŏn
calls the hotel's "*ppoi* (boy)" and orders "*coffee* and *brandy* and cookies" for
Ku Wansŏ,[79] it came to symbolize the modern lifestyle that lumpen colonial
intellectuals were able to enjoy as a thing of their own. As can be surmised
from various articles—"Nangnang, a place that has long been loved by the
intelligentsia of Seoul, has a vast *record collection*," or the Korean intelligentsia gathers in old tearooms such as *Mexico* and *Bon Ami*, but since
some among them order one cup of coffee and sit there for half a day, the
"tearoom neologism *pyŏkhwa* (mural) came into being"—the act of drinking
coffee may have almost been equivalent to modernity itself. This brings to
mind the Kanagaki Robun novel *Aguranabe* (*The Beefeater*, 1871–1872),
which introduced men who "liked the West," men who "liked newspapers,"
and *geisha* in Yokohama who, by catering to foreigners, became addicted to
beef, while also describing *gyūnabe* (beef stew) being viewed as identical to
Japan's civilization and enlightenment.[80]
    In this sense, the taste for coffee was not limited to Yi Sang alone. The
tearoom pilgrimage of the novelist Kubo, during which he observed people
"each taking a seat in front of a table of their liking and enjoying a cup of
tea or a cup of *coffee*," or "a happy young man accompanying his young and
beautiful wife while appreciating a *lemon tea* or something like that,"[81] is
also related to this. Certain lines from the poems of Kim Kirim are also not
unrelated.

Oh—my lover
You are a piece of "*choux a la crème*."
You are a cup of "*coffee*."[82]

Mouths without whiskers
From a "*coffee*" cup of "*Brazil*" coffee shop
Soaked in blue steam
Drink the sky blue of the Mediterranean Sea.[83]

Yi Hyosŏk, for his part, wrote, "After eating some *hotcakes* with *coffee*, I have no appetite at all in the evening. *Coffee* on an empty stomach is dangerous, but when I tried drinking black tea it was like scentless rice rinsings that stuck inside me, and I thought about drinking *lemon squash*, but it's overly luxurious for an everyday beverage."[84] Or, on the recommendation of a "friend who had grown fat on the taste of *coffee*," he wrote the following about the Nanam tearoom *"Don"* that had come to serve "three distinct types of *mocha java mixed*."

> It was about ten *li* from Kyŏngsŏng to Nanam, but I came to frequent Nanam as if it were right in front of my door. This was because, while I loved the village of Kyŏngsŏng, I also grew fond of the streets of Nanam. I traveled by train, and rushed by bus, and, at times, even went over the hill on foot. Before I had been going there a month, I had placed a clear map of the life on its streets inside my head. I knew the lay of the land: for bread, *Kaneko* was the best; among bookstores, Pukkwanggwan was not so bad; for tea, Palchinok had everything; and for coffee, *"Don"* was the real deal. There were times I plodded ten *li* just to buy a pound of bread, and there were times I wobbled on the bus just to have a cup of *coffee*.[85]

Yi Hyosŏk's exotic taste in food is famous.[86] It carries on the genealogy of the *"samp'anju* (champagne)" and *"raisŭk'al* (curry rice)" that added to the flavor of Cho Chunghwan's *Changhanmong* (*A long and sorrowful dream*, 1913), and, going further, the genealogy of the *sandwich* that Pyŏnguk pulled out in front of Yŏngch'ae in Yi Kwangsu's *Mujŏng* (*The Heartless*, 1917). Returning to Yi Hyosŏk, in his novel *Hwabun* (*Pollen*, 1939), when Hyŏnma and his party are going on a summer vacation to escape the heat, along with Korean soybean paste, they prepare things like *jam, sausage, butter*, and canned goods. In addition, in his short story *"Chihyŏp ŭi kaŭl* (Autumn of the isthmus, 1935)," he describes a table topped not only with "wild grape *jam* and pure honey" but also with milk and bread crumbs. The novel *Pyŏkkong muhan* (*Endless blue sky*, 1940) narrates the holding of a dinner with "a basket of flowers atop the white dining table, and a bottle of *champagne* emerging at an angle from the ice in a small bucket"[87] for the Russian woman Nadia or the making of *whiskey tea* for Hun. This sort of tendency is also quite apparent in the following scene from the short story *"P'urip* (Leaves of grass, 1942)" that depicts the consumption of the butter left by the missionaries who had departed following the outbreak of the Pacific War.

> As she drank coffee from the full glass cup, Sil's large eyes again began to shine with hope.

"When I come next time, I'll bring you some *butter*. I bought more than ten *pounds* from the American missionaries when they left. I think there are still five or six of the huge two-*pound* tins in my elder sister's refrigerator. I'll bring it so you can spread it on in lumps and eat it. So you quickly get as fat as me."[88]

Similar to the examples above, Yi Sang wrote that "(t)he scent of Wrigley's Chewing Gum" is "more pleasingly warm than actual peppermint."[89] Also, even on his deathbed, he requested "French-style coupé bread"[90] and a "melon from Sembikiya."[91] This is the reason Yi Sang, particularly in his writings set in Tokyo, came to bring up coffee so often. It expresses a hunger and thirst for the modern. That he "somehow felt as if 5 *rin* were greater than 9 *sen* and 5 *rin*"[92] while drinking a "10 *sen*" cup of coffee in Tokyo's Shinjuku ultimately corresponds to his having cast his "last twenty *sen*"[93] to buy a "*4,000 Word Everyday English*"[94] book even as he went hungry. This orientation, which was also expressed as "wanting to live according to ideals, even should that mean collapsing in the wilderness and becoming food for ravens,"[95] gives rise to yet another empty stomach, one different from the "strange dinner" of devouring the dishes you dislike most. This is why the Yi Sang of Tokyo, who grew penniless drinking coffee and buying foreign language books, was still saying, "With a foreign language vast as the ocean clamped in my armpit, I cannot rashly become hungry. Ah, I am full."[96] And this had already begun in the following scene in the hall of Kyŏngsŏng (Seoul) Station where he felt the "occasional whistle of a train . . . was closer to my heart than even the music of Mozart."

I read many times over, backward and forward, the names of the few dishes scrawled on the menu. They became jumbled and vague, like the names of my childhood friends.[97]

Yi Sang's hometown was the modern. His hometown was either a foreign country (the West) or the relationship with a foreign country. As such, Yi Sang deplored the "miserable tradition, lacking both luster and leisure," of ancestors who "demand repayment of the original cost of serum."[98] In addition, he wrote, "beginning with the hatred for his family, just how much had he hated the *minjok*."[99] This is the reason he moves beyond the "national language like a gramophone"[100] and feels the names of foreign dishes on the menu "like the names of my childhood friends." Thus, when "as a rejection of daily life," he "played the gramophone's record upside down,"[101] the names of his friends pronounced through the "'cocoa' lips" were "Imi," who came carrying "sponge cake and goat's milk wrapped in a kerchief,"[102] the "performance angel"[103] and the "madwoman," who prepared a feast of chocolate while bidding an "ADIEU like humming,"[104] and the "daughter of the *oden* stand, who was as beautiful as Käthe von Nagy."[105] These are "MADEMOISELLE NASHI"[106] who are comparable to the "Italian girl in Shinmachi" with whom Kapchin spent a night in *Hŭlk*,[107] or the Russian woman "Yura" whom Yi Hyosŏk's protagonist met at the "Fantasia Cabaret."

This is a palate fundamentally different from the enlightening and national literary taste of Yi Kwangsu. Yi wrote that "*kimch'i* is national spirit (*minjok chŏngsin*) among food," and that "the energy to broil and gnaw on ribs is the one and only energy that remains to the people of Korea."[108] Moreover, he did not stop at this but criticized a modern literature that had been forced upon the national public in the name of true high art when it was actually a "literature that smelled of butter" and was not suited to "our stomachs."[109] He was claiming "(w)e must exchange tea room-esque sentiments for a spirit as lofty as if it sat atop the peak of Mt. Fuji."[110]

When compared to these views of Yi Kwangsu, for Yi Sang—who thundered, "Do we simply plan to sit idly as we fall several decades behind others!"[111]—Adalin and coffee function identically. In the sense that they form the background and wellspring that gave birth to certain of Yi Sang's works, both of them converge in the modernity and the modern art of which he dreamt. What birthed the genre of irony and humor in which he "devours the dishes he dislikes most," while simultaneously being unable to "rashly become hungry" is the interrelation of aspirin and Adalin, Adalin and coffee. As such, the taste of the coffee he drank "sitting in a booth across from no one at all" in Kyŏngsŏng Station with its "plaintive atmosphere," and the funny taste of the Adalin he chewed up and swallowed both stand in direct opposition to Yi Kwangsu's nationalistic taste that attempted to exclude the smell of butter. Just as the "alleys" of "*Ogamdosi che-1 ho* (Crow's eye view, poem number 1)," whether blind or open, are spaces completely different from the "Greater East Asia" asserted by Imperial Japan.

A FOOLISH SUPPER

But Yi Sang's "alley"-dashing palate was opposed not only to the exclusionary taste of Yi Kwangsu but also to Paek Sŏk's palate of rural community, which had him, holed up in a "Storeroom" in "Fox-Born Village," together with his cousin, "stealthily drink a tart brew," or "yummily down pumpkin rice cakes."[112] For Paek, the act of eating food represents the warmest form of relationship one can form with an Other. Much more so than any other sort of metaphor, eating physically and chemically unites things and existence. What's more, these are hometown dishes shared with family. Through local food and dialect, Paek moves beyond both the brutal imperialist order of survival of the fittest and modern alienation, and embodies a kind of world of pre-alienated totality and fellowship in which elements such as hometown, family, friends, ancestors, spirits, play, and nature are all mutually intertwined.[113] Only in such a world can snow come tumbling down just because "Impoverished I / Love beautiful Natasha."[114] Food eaten with the family on the "*arŭgut*[115] boiling hot" or the "toasty floor"[116] mediates this interiority (hometown). As seen below, the exterior (foreign land) is, more than anything else, a place that lacks familiar food.

> Today is *Chŏngwŏl porŭm*[117]
> The first full moon holiday, but
> I am far from my hometown, my lot the lonesome weariness of a traveler in another's land
> In days long past, the poets of this country like Du Fu and Li Bai
> Must also have spent this day in strange and distant lands
> Today were I at my house in my hometown
> I would wear new clothes, put on new shoes, and gorge myself on rice cakes and meat, and
> Gather together with kinfolk and pass the time in joy and laughter, but
> I, today, in worn, grimy clothes and with one piece of dried fish
> Alone and lonely sit thinking lonesome thoughts of this and that[118]

But unlike Paek Sŏk who aspires toward the hometown, Yi Sang is located in the alley of "*ka oe ka*" that hovers between inside and outside, or the inner room of "No. 33," with its floors seared the "color of sponge cake." In addition, as was the case with Im Hwa, for Yi Sang "dialect is extremely difficult to understand."[119] This corresponds to Yi Sang's discussions of, along with an "arrogant belch that reeked of garlic," primarily the tastelessness of food, or the pain of a "full stomach." Going even further, for Yi the act of eating food also represents foolishness. In his first novel, he wrote, "We ordered and ate all sorts of delicious foods. . . . This party was very liable to be foolish.[120] He followed this with descriptions such as "By asking each other 'Have you eaten?' we create a segue for the foolish, useless chatter that invariably follows."[121] In addition, he is not so positive regarding the natural phenomenon of hunger. Yi Sang wrote things such as "I finish breakfast. There is nothing to do"[122] or "When I stop to think about it, I seem to be hungry. If this is true, then why am I hungry? What have I done to cause hunger?"[123] For him, being hungry is at once a scandalous physiological phenomenon" and a pathetic and "shameful affair."[124]

Therefore, Yi Sang, rather than eating himself, describes a "daughter-in-law again taking in peaches and wild grapes, their cool juices fully permeating her mouth, while she chews them with enthusiastic sound effects."[125] Like the "certain white man" who "played with his camera"[126] after having given a beggar a

50-*chŏn* coin, Yi takes the act of eating as an object for vision and description. This can also be compared to Pak T'aewŏn's indicating in his novel *Ch'ŏnbyŏn p'unggyŏng* (*Scenes from Ch'ŏnggye Stream*, 1938) that the price of an order of sweet and sour pork with a half-liter of Chinese liquor and some soybean paste noodles was 2 *wŏn*, or pointing out a 15-*chŏn* plate of curry rice in his short story "*P'iro* (Fatigue, 1938)." The source of Yi Sang's visual description is the distance between food and Yi himself. And what leads and controls this distance is money. Things such as the tastelessness of food, the pain of a full stomach, and the foolishness of eating all arise from this distance. But food is essential for "maintaining life." Due to this fact, its taste becomes even more inadequate. Accordingly, as evidenced below, Yi Sang commands a humor and wit that bear a "respectful regard" for tasteless meals.

> The state of a full stomach is quite close to pain. I ate garlic and chicken. In addition, I ate *fukujinzuke* that held complete disregard for human beings, and tofu like a rubber eraser, and boiled napa cabbage with no crushed red pepper in it that was like a death mask,[127] and some boiled eggs for which, other than salty, no taste at all could be sensed. All of the side dishes are completely salty. They are no more than races similar to salt that had already taken on various outward appearances. This is none other than a completely pleasant act that has its objective in maintaining life. Toward this sort of meal, I already now bear a respectful regard.[128]

This is the extent to which Yi Sang, "(a)ble to forego even the pleasures of appetite," was "the greatest animal ennuiite(s) on Earth."[129] Thus, the protagonist of "*Chijuhoesi*," with expressions such as "turkey—ham—sausage—fatty meat—Western pig," negatively perceives the "fat owner of R café" and his "Western pig"-like patrons, while the protagonist of "*Hyuŏp kwa sajŏng* (Closures and circumstances, 1932)," confirms that "the brain of the fatso SS must be tremendously bad." For Yi, who wanted to "Cast off putrid body weight and / To the Parthenon, to the Parthenon, fly,"[130] body weight was forever "body weight like a stone monument."[131] To Yi, who had difficulty "coping even with one body," and, even as he vomited up what he had eaten upon the skirt and stockings of Chŏnghŭi as she sat in a "dark and secluded room in Hŭngch'ŏn Temple," still proclaimed to the end "I possessed" "a sort of power of wisdom" so that even "taking in only one spoonful of cold rice and one mouthful of cold water, I could amply overawe a generation,"[132] body weight was death, while food was the enemy of art. This is why he remarked to Yun T'aeyŏng, upon the latter's suggestion they eat dinner before going out, that "(f)rom days of old, artists have not filled their stomachs with food, rather they have filled them with feelings. For only then do masterpieces emerge."[133]

Thus what Yi Sang, who both described "the sound of water like popping open Champagne,"[134] and said "booze shines in my body like perfume,"[135] "dropped the *knife*" to pursue was an aesthetic sense qualitatively abstracted and conceptualized toward the modern. And through this an empty stomach and tastelessness made the leap into that realm of art and literature known as *irony* and *paradox*. Thus, to Yi, the "aesthetic subject"[136] who sculpted a portrait of "Jesus of Golgotha"[137] upon his own face so like a "skeleton whose knees are above its ears," being preoccupied with food went so far as to be "filthy." Likening burdock root to "a young child's poop,"[138] and "pest,"[139] he worried as follows.

> Someone is eating a meal. It's an awfully filthy sight.
> Yes. Clearly there is no doubt that eating a meal is filthy.
> But
> If that character called someone turns out to be none other than myself, what then?[140]

Thus, for Yi Sang, things such as the "savory stew enjoyed with liquor" "boiled by adding ox blood to a soup of dried radish greens and tofu" in Paek Sŏk's poem "*Kujangno* (The playing field road, 1939)," the *sŏllŏngt'ang* beef soup Kim Ch'ŏmji bought for his wife in the Hyŏn Chin'gŏn short story "*Unsu choŭn nal* (A Lucky Day, 1924)," the "orange peels" of Mr. Pak's wife in Ch'oe Sŏhae's short story "*T'alch'ulgi* (Record of an escape, 1925)," and "those days of poverty when our frozen rice mad us cry" in the Im Hwa poem "*Negŏri ŭi Suni* (Suni at the crossroads, 1929)," likely held little meaning. The same was likely true of the "tale of a rice cake that had eaten a person" told by Kim Yujŏng. This is because the following scene, which brings the young girl Ok to nearly a death completely different from the "sacrosanct and brilliant love suicide" of which Yi Sang dreamt, merely evokes issues of quantity such as poverty and social distribution.

> Ok, making great haste, snatched it up instantly. This rice, this rice. The amount would be enough to make one fine meal even for an adult. . . . She goes in front of the cupboard when a palm-sized rice cake filled with red beans appears. Accepting it, she again quickly swallowed it up. . . . She was probably stuffed to the gills with food. One strange thing was found by her. Again a rice cake appeared, but, upon examination, it was not filled with red beans but was a steamed white rice cake with chestnuts and jujubes sticking out all over it. It looked like if you took a big bite it would just melt in your mouth. . . . Of course, she courageously began eating. At first she ate quickly. After a while, she ate slowly. But soon, unable to finish it all, leaving about half, she gave it back to the young mistress, then turned her head to the side. Not only is it

a miracle that Ok had eaten the steamed white rice cake with that stomach but that she gave back the uneaten portion must also be called a miracle. . . . When she was asked "Anyway, what about these?" Ok took the *chuwak* cakes without the least bit of hesitation. And then she picked one up with her fingers, sucked the honey out of it, then stuck it in her mouth. After chewing on that honey for a good while she tries gulping it down. But she just feels pain in her chest; the rice cake immediately comes back up. She chews again. Bending her shoulders and head forward, straining, she once again tries swallowing it. These are not considered the actions of a person at all. But what must be paid attention to is the mistake of intestines that have long known only starvation in daily life.[141]

MUNG BEAN FRITTERS AND COUPÉ BREAD

And, at the end of all these discussions, we come face to face with the honest "physiological" "nostalgia of hunger and thirst" that Yi Sang confronted. Yi Sang in Tokyo, who complained to Kim Kirim that "no matter where I go there is nothing that whets my appetite," having returned home after drinking coffee, amid the loneliness of a lunar New Year's Eve, finally admitted the following to An Hoenam.

> I will live honestly. While fighting with loneliness, that is the one and only thing I am thinking of. Today is New Year's Eve according to the lunar calendar. Mung bean fritters, persimmon punch, clear rice wine, and seasoned slices of roast—the nostalgia of hunger and thirst for all of these tortures me. It is physiological. I cannot overcome it.[142]

In contrast to his stated plan to lie even in his last will and testament, the Yi Sang of February 10, 1937, no longer speaks of committing "a perfectly calm error of approximately one character in a single line of poetry composed of five Chinese characters."[143] Just prior to the first day of the lunar new year, when "the rustic spirits of our departed patriarchs return,"[144] now, rather than "resembling Li Bai" as the "member of a magnificent race," Yi, as in Paek Sŏk's poem *"Tu Bo na Yi Paek kach'i* (Like Du Fu and Li Bai, 1941)," spending the holiday in a "strange and distant land" "with one piece of dried fish," "sit(s) thinking lonesome thoughts of this and that." On this day, approximately two months before his death, he finally became Kim Haegyŏng of the Kangnŭng Kim clan.

If it is the case, for hungry Yi Sang who at last had become unable to overcome his nostalgia for mung bean fritters, persimmon punch, and seasoned slices of roast, was the desire for "the taste of fragrant MJB" then nothing more than an insincere pose? When he wrote to An Hoenam that he was "envious of my brother's (An's) health," had he failed to achieve the level of "the irony of devouring the dishes you dislike most"? Were the "Ennui" and "Fatigue" of Yi Sang, to borrow Kim Namch'ŏn's words, the result of "his complete ruin" to the extent that "upstairs they ate Western food, but when they came downstairs it was *kkakdugi* (spicy pickled radish) with chopsticks"?[145]

If, however, the Yi Sang who wrote a poem that asked "Is not the clock younger than I?"[146] truly were, so much so that he would lament, "Oh moon, once companion to Li Po! Wouldn't it have been much nicer if you too had perished along with the 19th century?"[147] "a bastard on the verge of blacking out, jammed in the crack between the nineteenth century and the twentieth century,"[148] or a "purebred Korean"[149] unable to forget the holidays of the lunar calendar, then the true "physiology" of that purebred who simultaneously resembled both Li Bai (Li Po) and Jupiter, while also paying homage to Akutagawa Ryunosuke should have been unable to overcome the hunger and thirst not only for mung bean fritters, persimmon punch, and seasoned slices of roast but also for "the taste of fragrant MJB," as well as for "sponge cake" and "*oden.*" This is because, at least for Yi Sang, the purebred who craves only mung bean fritters and persimmon punch, rice wine and seasoned slices of roast meant death and absence. In fact, it is precisely the taste at the end of the Japanese colonial period as expressed below that rather attempted to annihilate the "purebred."

> No matter how long she stayed there, her simple and honest personality was not assimilated to the cheerful Yankees but rather wanted to return to her home-town, sleep on a heated *ondol* floor, and eat rice wrapped in lettuce and loaded with red pepper paste.[150]

Indeed, however, Yi Sang was the master of a rhetoric that could make "orange(-colored) bitter melons ripen" even atop a "millet stalk fence."[151] He was no Master Yun, bewildered in Ch'ae Mansik's *T'aep'yŏng ch'ŏnha* (*Peace Under Heaven*, 1938) by the "*nantchi*" (lunch) in a department store restaurant. Yi Sang, who wanted "melons/lemons" and coupé bread, with a palate that at once tasted Western food and *kkakdugi*, restored the irony of aspirin and Adalin. To the end, rising above the opposition between Adalin and coffee (or aspirin), or rising above the confusion between melons and lemons, he flapped the wings of a humor that gazed down upon all things. He maintained what Baudelaire termed the "strength to be simultaneously self and Other."[152] In fact, even on his deathbed, not only did he express his irritation regarding the authenticity of the coupé bread Kim Soun, "sweating profusely,"[153] brought him but he also "could not swallow"[154] the melon his wife Pyŏn Tongnim bought for him.

Thus, he overcame Kim Haegyŏng, who craved mung bean fritters and persimmon punch and rice wine and seasoned slices of roast, and died as "Yi Sang," who was, like the citron he once described, a "humorous figure, neither vegetable nor fruit."[155] It appears his last supper, replete with coupé bread and melon, was a "final improvisational game"[156] to rival the pooping of the children in Sŏngch'ŏn. Such was the extent to which he was a "healthy talker."[157] The man who wrote that "(a) person with no secrets is as poor and empty as one with no belongings"[158] was thorough in "saving emotional energy,"[159] which is the essence of humor. As a result, this purebred (mongrel) *"hutei Senjin"* (不逞鮮人), Yi Sang, while measuring "Ginza 8-*chome*" as being a "set-like street" of "approximately two and a half feet," in a solemn "underground public toilet" in the capital of the great Japanese empire, the city that bore the tremendous expression of Greater East Asian Co-Prosperity, carried out a "simple excretion" in which he abolished himself.[160] Just as he had thrown his piggy bank into the toilet, he shitted out his self.

It may even be that the above forms a pair with the following.

Thus, that night, for the first time in six years, he met with Noritake in Kyŏngsŏng, and they started drinking like the old days, got drunk, then, no sooner had they come down from a dining establishment in Ukchŏng (Hoehyŏn-dong) to the square in front of the Bank of Chosen, the mischief of the old days arose in Kyōkichi's thoughts. Thus, in a fully contemptuous tone, Kyōkichi blurted out to Noritake, "Look here, there's no way a coward like you could take a shit in the middle of this square." Immediately Noritake, who on that night was so drunk his face was deathly pale, began to show off while screaming "Fine, then I'll give those guys a taste of my ass," after which he climbed up onto the fountain in the middle of the square, which hadn't seen any water since the war began, squatted down on one end of it, and actually began to pull his zipper down. The plaza in front of the Bank of Chosen corresponds to the entrance to Ponjŏngt'ong (Ch'ungmuro), which is called the Ginza of Kyŏngsŏng, and is also the place in Kyŏngsŏng with the most people coming and going. That was also one of the things Kyōkichi was counting on, however, Noritake was also a part-time employee of an odd group known as the Anti-Communist Federation, which was part of the Government General Office of Police Administration's Department of Security. So if such behavior was discovered by a police officer, there was ample danger of his being dismissed. But the dare was so pleasing that the two were of a pathological mood just like that of six years hence. . . .

"Whoa, there are Japanese people here. Hey you Japanese, lick my ass!"[161]

As such, both the sorrowful Mun Chonghyŏk, who defined himself as a "guilty friend," while disclosing regarding Yi Sang's "poor" health, "My heart aches so terribly that I can write no more,"[162] and even Kim Kirim, who was forever ashamed of "every morning being unable to forget Danish calisthenics,"[163] were most likely unable to understand Yi Sang's tremendous health and wealth. In addition, they also likely completely failed to grasp Yi Sang's final "humor," which was written with the pen of Kim Soun. That is the humor below giggling as it looks upon the line Yi Sang alive had written: "I am a corpse."[164]

> Even looking at his corpse lying in the mortuary, for some reason I did not yet really feel he was dead. He was such a sly and humorous fellow that it truly seemed he would, wearing that peculiar wry smile of his, sit up at any moment.[165]

NOTES

1. Yi Sang, "*Nalgae* (Wings)," trans. Walter K. Lew and Youngju Ryu, in *Modern Korean Fiction: An Anthology*, eds. Bruce Fulton and Youngmin Kwon (New York: Columbia University Press, 2005), 66

2. Yi Sang, "*Tanbal* (The bob)," in *Yi Sang munhak chŏnjip* 2, ed. Kim Yunsik (Seoul: Munhak sasangsa, 1991), 250.

3. Yi Sang, "*Nalgae*," 66.

4. Ibid., 83.

5. The translation reads "dark *Tango* foundation," but the original is "*T'angodoran* (탕고도—란)," which was actually the brand name of a cosmetic product at the time. "*T'ango*" is thought to come from the Japanese pronunciation of the characters 丹紅 (Kor. *tanhong*), which signify a cosmetic product akin to contemporary cheek rouge, while "*doran*" likely has its origins in the German cosmetic company Dohran. In any case, in both Korea and Japan, putting on stage makeup was referred to as "applying *dorang*."—Trans.

6. Ibid., 67.

7. Ibid., 71.

8. Ibid., 71–72.

9. Ibid., 72.

10. Ibid., 71.

11. Ibid., 70.

12. Ibid., 72.

13. Yi Sang, "LE URINE," in *Yi Sang munhak chŏnjip* 1, ed. Yi Sŭnghun (Seoul: Munhak sasangsa, 1989), 124.

14. Yi Sang, "*Ogamdo si che 10 ho nabi* (Crow's-eye view poem number 10 butterfly)," trans. Walter K. Lew, in *The Columbia Anthology of Modern Korean Poetry*, ed. David R. McCann (New York: Columbia University, 2004), 67.

15. Yi Sang, "*Kwŏnt'ae* (Ennui)," trans. John M. Frankl, in *Azalea: Journal of Korean Literature & Culture*, 2011, 273.

16. Yi Sang, "*Ŏlgul* (Face)," in *Yi Sang munhak chŏnjip* 1, ed. Yi Sŭnghun, 129.

17. Yi Sang, "*Chongsaenggi* (Record of a life)," in in *Yi Sang munhak chŏnjip* 2, ed. Kim Yunsik, 379.

18. Yi Sang, "*Hwang* (A dog)," in *Yi Sang munhak chŏnjip* 3, ed. Kim Yunsik (Seoul: Munhak sasangsa, 1993), 311.

This appears to be a reference to Roald Amundsen, the leader of the first expedition to reach the South Pole in December 1911. Pemmican comprised a substantial portion of the team's diet.—Trans.

19. Yi Sang, "*Nalgae*," 70.

20. Yi Sang, "*Ijōna kagyaku hannō* (A strange reversible reaction)," in *Chosen to kenchiku*, July 1931, 15.

21. Yi Sang, "*Kwŏnt'ae*," 273.

22. Yi Sang, "*Kakhyŏl ŭi ach'im* (Morning of hemoptysis)," in *Yi Sang munhak chŏnjip* 3, ed. Kim Yunsik, 328.

23. Yi Sang, "*Ŏrisŏgŭn sŏkban* (A foolish supper)," in ibid., 126.

24. Cho Yongman, "*Yi Sang kwa Pak T'aewŏn* (Yi Sang and Pak T'aewŏn)," in *Yi Sang ŭi piryŏn* (Seoul: Kip'ŭnsaem, 1991), 8.

Sŏllŏngt'ang is a type of beef soup made from boiling cow bones for broth and actually contains very little beef.

25. Chŏng Int'aek, "*Pulsanghan Yi Sang* (Pitiful Yi Sang)," in *Chogwang*, December 1939, 309.

26. Yi Sang, "*Nalgae*," 71.

27. Yi Sang, "*Chibi* (Paper monument)," in *Yi Sang munhak chŏnjip* 1, ed. Yi Sŭnghun, 199.

28. Yi Sang, "I Wed a Toy Bride," in ibid., 201.

29. Yi Sang, "*Munhak ŭl pŏrigo munhwa rŭl sangsanghalsuŏpta* (Without literature, there is no imagining culture)," in *Yi Sang munhak chŏnjip* 3, ed. Kim Yunsik, 250.

30. Yi Sang "Le Urine," 124.

31. Yi Sang, "*Sanch'aek ŭi kaŭl* (Autumn of the promenade)," in *Yi Sang munhak chŏnjip* 3, ed. Kim Yunsik, 29.

32. Yi Sang, "*Kakhyŏl ŭi ach'im*," 327.

33. Yi Sang, "*Kongp'o ŭi kirok: sŏjang* (Record of fear: preface)," in ibid., 332.

34. Yi Sang, "*Chido ŭi amsil* (Darkroom of the map)," in *Yi Sang munhak chŏnjip* 2, ed. Kim Yunsik, 173.

35. Yi Sang, "*Hwang ŭi ki* (Record of a dog)," in *Yi Sang munhak chŏnjip* 3, ed. Kim Yunsik, 319.

36. Yi Sang, "*Kongbok* (Empty stomach)," in *Yi Sang munhak chŏnjip* 1, ed. Yi Sŭnghun, 114.

37. Yi Sang, "*Au Magasin De Nouveautes* (at the Department store of novelties)," in ibid., 167.

38. Yi Sang, "*Aeya* (A sad night)," in *Yi Sang munhak chŏnjip* 3, ed. Kim Yunsik, 309.

39. Song Minho and Yun T'aeyŏng, *Chŏlmang ŭn kigyo rŭl natko* (*Despair gave rise to virtuosity*) (Seoul: Kyohaksa, 1968), 41.

Taech'angok is the name of a restaurant in Chongno at the time.

40. Yi Sang, "*Nalgae*," 82.

41. Yi Sang, "*Kongp'o ŭi sŏngch'ae* (Fortress of fear)," in *Yi Sang munhak chŏnjip* 3, ed. Kim Yunsik, 337.

42. Yi Sang, "*Chijuhoesi* (Two spiders meet a pig)," in *Yi Sang munhak chŏnjip* 2, ed. Kim Yunsik, 301.

43. Yi Sang, "*Ka oe ka chŏn*" (The story of a street outside a street), *Yi Sang munhak chŏnjip* 1, ed. Kim Yunsik, 64.

44. For more on this, see Yi Kyŏnghun, *Yi Sang, ch'ŏlch'ŏn ŭi susahak* (*Yi Sang, the piercing rhetoric*), Somyŏngch'ulp'an, 2000.

45. Yi Sang, "*Kongp'o ŭ ikirok* (Record of fear)," in *Yi Sang munhak chŏnjip* 2, ed. Kim Yunsik (Seoul: Munhak sasangsa, 1991), 203.

46. Yi Sang, "Tsukihara Tōichirō," in *Yi Sang munhak chŏnjip* 1, ed. Yi Sŭnghun, 247.

47. Yi Sang, "*Chibi* (Paper monument)," in ibid., 198.

48. Yi Sang, "*Nalgae*," 77.

49. Yi Sang, "*Tonghae*" (Child's skeleton), in *Yi Sang munhak chŏnjip* 3, ed. Kim Yunsik, 282.

50. Charles Baudelaire, "*Le Vin de l'assassin* (The Assassin's Wine)," in *The Flowers of Evil*, trans. tr., Keith Waldrop (Middletown: Wesleyan University Press, 2006), 142.

51. Ko Ŭn, *Yi Sang p'yŏngjŏn* (*A critical biography of Yi Sang*) (Seoul: Minŭmsa, 1975), 255.

52. Yi Sang, "*Nalgae*," 79.

53. Ibid.

54. Yi Sang, "*Hwang ŭi ki*," 319.

55. Yi Sang, "*Nalgae*," 66.
The translation actually reads "counterfeit of yourself."—Trans.

56. See Gilles Deleuze, "Coldness and Cruelty," in *Masochism:*
Coldness and Cruelty & Venus in Furs, trans. Jean McNeil and Aude Willm (Cambridge: Zone Books, 1991), 81–91.

57. Yi Sang, "*Nalgae*," 81.
It should be clarified here that the word used for "funny" in the original is *iksal matta*. Although in English "funny taste" more readily brings to mind a strange or unexpected flavor, the original is clearly referring to the taste of the pills being humorous, comical, or even farcical.—Trans.

58. Ibid., 83.

59. Ibid., 66.

60. Yi Sang, "*Irŏnsi* (This sort of poem)," in *Yi Sang munhak chŏnjip* 1, ed. Yi Sŭnghun, 184.

61. Yi Sang, "*Hwang ŭi ki*," 319.

62. "Broad Daylight" is the translation of one of Yi's poems originally written in Japanese with the title "*Mahiru* (眞晝)." The title of the Korean translation is "*Daenat*" (대낮), which can mean both "broad daylight" and "in the middle of the day." For an English translation of the poem, the title rendered as "Noon," see "Noon—A

Certain," trans. Edward Mack, in *The Columbia Anthology of Modern Korean Poetry*, ed. David McCann (New York: Columbia University, 2004), 77.

63. Yi Sang, *"Nalgae* (Wings)," in *Yi Sang munhak chŏnjip*2, ed. Kim Yunsik, 319. This is related to lines from both *Les Misérables* and Akutagawa Ryunosuke's *"Shuju no kotoba"* (Words of a dwarf, 1925) Akutagawa remarked that Hugo was a chunk of bread that covered the entirety of France, and, the more he thought about it, one not very generously covered in butter.—Trans.

64. Arthur Rimbaud, "Hunger."
    http://www.poemhunter.com/best-poems/arthur-rimbaud/hunger-42

65. Yi Sang, *"P'ach'ŏp* (A torn memorandum)," in *Yi Sang munhak chŏnjip* 1, ed. Yi Sŭnghun, 207.

66. Yi Sang, *"Nalgae,"* 83.

67. Yi Sang, *"Kongp'o ŭi kirok* (Record of fear)," in *Yi Sang munhak chŏnjip* 3, ed. Kim Yunsik, 201.

68. Yi Sang, *"Nalgae,"* 73.

69. Ibid., 78.

70. Actually, the official name of the city was Keijō (京城), making Keijō Station the official name of the central train station. As the story was written in Korean, however, Kyŏngsŏng, the Korean pronunciation of the Chinese characters was used, and so will be used here.—Trans.

71. Yi Sang, *"Nalgae,"* 342.

72. Song Minho and Yun Taeyŏng, *Chŏlmang ŭn kigyo rŭl natko,* 86.

73. Cho Yongman, "Yi Sang kwa Pak T'aewŏn," 8.

74. Yi Sang, *"Sanch'onyŏjŏng* (Lingering Impressions of a Mountain Village)," trans. John M. Frankl, in *Azalea: Journal of Korean Literature & Culture* Volume 2, 2008, 331.

75. Yi Sang studied architecture at this very prestigious state institution, which is now essentially Seoul National University's College of Engineering. He was one of only two Koreans in a class of sixteen, but that did not prevent him from graduating top in his class and gaining immediate special employment at the Japanese Government General.—Trans.

76. In his personal letters, Yi often mixes Korean and Japanese. Here, in a sentence otherwise written in Korean, Yi elected to write *kōhi* (coffee) in Japanese.—Trans.

77. Yi Sang, *"Sirhwa* (Lost flower)," in *Yi Sang munhak chŏnjip* 3, ed. Kim Yunsik, 366.

78. Yi Sang, *"Tonghae,"* 279.

79. Yi Injik, *"Moranbong* (Peony peak)," in *Han'guk sinsosŏ lchŏnjip* (Seoul: Ŭryumunhwasa, 1968), 62.

80. For a brief description of and excerpt from this work, see *Modern Japanese Literature: An Anthology*, ed. Donald Keene (New York: Grove Press, 1956), 31–33.

81. Pak T'aewŏn, *"Sup'unggŭm* (Accordian)," in *Pak T'aewŏn tanp'yŏnjip* (Seoul, Hagyesa, 1939), 163.

82. Kim Kirim,"'*K'ŏp'i' chan ŭl tŭlgo* (Holding a coffee cup)," in *Kim Kirim chŏnjip* 1, (Seoul: Simsŏldang, 1988), 43.

83. Kim Kirim, *"Hot'el"* (Hotel)," in *Ssinema p'unggyŏng* (*Cinema scenery*), in ibid., 83.

84. Yi Hyosŏk, *"Nangnang tabanggi* (Record of Nangnang Tearoom)," in *Yi Hyosŏk chŏnjip* 7 (Seoul: Ch'angmisa, 1990), 205.

85. Yi Hyosŏk, *"Koyohan 'Don' ŭi pam* (The silent night of *'Don'*)," in ibid., 111.

86. For more on this topic, see the chapter *"Yi Hyosŏkkwa 'palgyŏn'toen hyangt'o* (Yi Hyosŏk and 'discovered' locality)," in Sin Hyŏnggi, *Minjo kiyagi rŭ lnŏmŏsŏ* (Seoul: Samin, 2003), 108–35.

87. Yi Hyosŏk, *"Pyŏkkong muhan* (Endless blue sky)," in *Yi Hyosŏk chŏnjip* 5 (Seoul: Ch'angmisa, 1990), 122.

88. Yi Hyosŏk, *"Purip* (Leaves of grass)," in *Yi Hyosŏk chŏnjip* 3 (Seoul: Ch'angmisa, 1990), 217.

89. Yi Sang, *"Sanch'on yŏjŏng,"* 336.

90. Kim Soun, *Hanŭlkkŭt e sarado* (*Even living at the edge of the sky*) (Seoul: Tonghwa ch'ulp'an kongsa, 1968), 299.

91. Kim Hyangan, *"Ije Yi Sang ŭi chinsil ŭl alligo sipta* (Now I want to tell the truth about Yi Sang)," in *Munhaksasang*, May 1986, 62.

Kim Hyangan is the name taken by Yi Sang's wife, PyŏnTongnim, when she remarried. Sembikiya is, by its own description, a "venerable fruit shop" operating in Nihonbashi, Tokyo, since 1834. It modeled itself after fruit shops in Europe and sold imported as well as domestic fruits.—Trans.

92. Yi Sang, *"Tonggyŏng* (Tokyo)," trans. John M. Frankl, in *Azalea: Journal of Korean Literature & Culture*, Volume 5, 2012, 340.

93. Yi Sang, *"Sirhwa,"* 365.

94. Yi Sang, *"Sirhwa* (Lost Flower)," trans. Steven D. Capener, in *Acta Koreana*, Vol. 13, No. 2, December 2010, 130.

95. Yi Sang, *"Tongsaeng Okhŭi poara* (To my younger sister Okhŭi)," in *Yi Sang munhak chŏnjip* 3, ed. Kim Yunsik, 217.

96. Yi Sang, *"Sirhwa,"* 365.

97. Yi Sang, *"Nalgae,"* 78–79.

98. Yi Sang, *"Munbŏl* (Lineage)," in *Yi Sang munhak chŏnjip* 1, ed. Yi Sŭnghun, 83.

99. Yi Sang, *"Kongp'o ŭi sŏngch'ae* (Fortress of fear)," in ibid., 334.

100. Yi Sang, *"Chido ŭ iamsil,"* 174.

101. Yi Sang, *"Muje 1* (Untitled 1)," in *Yi Sang munhak chŏnjip* 3, ed. Kim Yunsik, 297.

102. Yi Sang, *"Tonghae,"* 267.

103. Yi Sang, *"Hŭnghaengmul ch'ŏnsa* (Performance angel)," in *Yi Sang munhak chŏnjip* 1, ed. Yi Sŭnghun, 142.

104. Yi Sang, *"Kwangnyŏ ŭi kobaek* (Confessions of a madwoman)," in ibid., 136.

105. Yi Sang, *"Pulhaenghan kyesŭng"* (Unfortunate succession)," in *Yi Sang munhak chŏnjip* 3, ed. Kim Yunsik, 210.

106. Yi Sang, *"Hwang* (A dog)," in ibid., 311.

107. Yi Kwangsu, *"Hŭlk (The soil),"* in *Yi Kwangsu chŏnjip* 6 (Seoul: Samjungdang, 1962), 182.

108. Ibid., 27.

109. Yi Kwangsu, *"Bungaku no kokuminsei* (The nationality of literature),"* in *Kyŏngsŏng ilbo*, November 14, 1939. (The quotation originally appeared in *Ch'unwŏn Yi Kwangsu ch'inil munhak chŏnjip* 2, ed., trans. Yi Kyŏnghun [Seoul: P'yŏngminsa, 1995], 55.)

110. Ibid., 58.

111. Yi Sang, *"Sanmukchip* (Collection of scattered ink),"* *Yi Sang munhak chŏnjip* 3, ed. Kim Yunsik, 353.

112. Paek Sŏk, *"Yŏu nan kol"* (Fox-born village),"* in *Chŏngbon Paek Sŏk sijip*, ed. Ko Hyŏngjin (Seoul: Munhak tongne, 2007), 218.

113. For more on this, see Yi Kyŏnghun, *"Minjok ŭi mal, minjok ŭi mat: cheguk chuŭi ŭi muhanhan ch'ogŭk* (The *minjok*'s language, the *minjok*'s taste: the endless overcoming of imperialism),"* in *Ŏttŏn paengnyŏn, chŭlgŏun sinsaeng* (Seoul: Hanŭl yŏnmot, 1999), 11–21.

114. Paek Sŏk, *"Na wa Natasha wa hŭin tangnagwi* (I and Natasha and a white donkey),"* in *Chŏngbon Paek Sŏk sijip*, 242.

115. This is another word for *araenmok*, the warmest portion of an *ondol* floor.—Trans.

116. Paek Sŏk, *"Kujangno* (The playing field street),"* in *Chŏngbon Paek Sŏk sijip*, 262.

117. *Chŏngwŏl porŭm*, the fifteenth day of the first lunar month, is a traditional holiday to celebrate the first full moon of a new year.—Trans.

118. Paek Sŏk, *"Tu Bo na Yi Paek kach'i* (Like Du Fu and Li Bai),"* in *Chŏngbon Paek Sŏk sijip*, 136.

119. Im Hwa, *"Yahaengch'a sok* (Inside a night train car),"* in *Hyŏnhaet'an* (Seoul: Tonggwangdang sŏjŏm 1939), 136.

120. Yi Sang, 12 wŏl 12 il (December 12), in Yi Sang munhak chŏnjip 2, ed. Kim Yunsik,86.

121. Yi Sang, *"Ŏrisŏgŭn sŏkban,"*122.

122. Yi Sang, *"Kwŏnt'ae,"* 262.

123. Ibid., 273.

124. Yi Sang, *"Chijuhoesi,"* 313.

125. Yi Sang *"Mosaek* (Evening twilight),"* in *Yi Sang munhak chŏnjip* 3, ed. Kim Yunsik, 134.

126. Yi Sang, *"Ch'udŭng chapp'il* (Miscellaneous writings by autumn lamplight),"* in ibid., 87.

127. The original word is *"tettomasu"* (뗏도마수). The author, Yi Kyŏnghun, interprets this as a misprint of "death mask."—Trans.

128. Yi Sang, *"Ŏrisŏgŭn sŏkban,"*122.

129. Yi Sang, *"Kwŏnt'ae,"* 270.

130. Kim Kirim, *"Chyup'it'ŏ ch'ubang* (Jupiter exile),"* in *Kim Kirim chŏnjip* 1, 209.

131. Yi Sang, *"Aeya,"* 307.

132. Yi Sang, "*Chongsaenggi,*"385.

133. Song Minho and Yun T'aeyŏng, *Chŏlmang ŭn kigyo rŭl natko*, 54.

134. Yi Sang, "*Ch'ŏtpŏntchae pangnang* (The first wandering)," in *Yi Sang munhak chŏnjip* 3, ed. Kim Yunsik, 169.

135. Song Minho and Yun T'aeyŏng, *Chŏlmang ŭn kigyo rŭl natko*, 27.

136. For more on this, see Sŏ Yŏngch'ae, "*Han'guk kŭndaesosŏl e nat'anan sarang ŭi yangsang kwa ŭimi e kwanhan yŏn'gu*" (A study of the aspects and meanings of love in early modern Korean fiction), PhD diss. (Seoul National University, 2002). The author discusses an aesthetic subject, represented by Yi Sang, who appeared as a rejection of the patriotic subject of Yi Kwangsu and the artisanal subject of Yŏm Sangsŏp.

137. Kim Kirim, "*Ko Yi Sang ŭi ch'uŏk* (Memories of the late Yi Sang)," in *Chogwang*, June 1937, 313.

138. Yi Sang, "*Aeya*," 305.

139. Ibid., 307.

140. Yi Sang, "*Muje (na)* [Untitled (b)]," in *Yi Sang munhak chŏnjip* 3, ed. Kim Yunsik, 349.

141. Kim Yujŏng, "*Ttŏk* (Rice cake)," in *Kim Yujŏng chŏnjip* (Seoul: Hyŏndae munhaksa, 1968), 209–11.

142. Yi Sang, "*Sasin 9* (Private correspondence 9)," in *Yi Sang munhak chŏnjip* 3, ed. Kim Yunsik, 242.

143. Yi Sang, "*Chongsaenggi*," 386.

144. Yi Sang, "*Sanch'on yŏjŏng*," 336.

145. Kim Namch'ŏn, "*Maek* (Barley)," in *Maek* (Seoul: Ŭryumunhwasa, 1947), 228.

146. Yi Sang, "*Undong* (Movement)," in *Yi Sang munhak chŏnjip* 1, ed. Yi Sŭnghun, 132.

147. Yi Sang, "*Tongyŏng*," 344.

148. Yi Sang, "*Sasin 7* (Private correspondence 7)," in *Yi Sang munhak chŏnjip* 3, ed. Kim Yunsik, 235.

149. Kim Yunsik, "*Remon ŭi hyanggi wa mellon ŭi mat* (The scent of lemon and the taste of melon)," in *Munhak sasang*, June 1986, 160.

150. Chang Tŏkcho, "*P'amanent'ŭ* (Permanent)," in *Chogwang*, August 1939, 320.

151. Yi Sang, "*Sanch'on yŏjŏng*," 335.

152. This quotation was taken from Karatani Kojin, *Yumoatoshite no yuibutsuron* (*Materialism as Humor*) (Tokyo: Kodansha, 1999), 142.

153. Kim Soun, *Hanŭlkkŭt e sarado*, 300.

154. Kim Hyangan, "*Ije Yi Sang ŭi jinsil ŭl alligo sipta.*" This citation is from *Kŭriun kŭ irŭm Yi Sang* (*The nostalgic name, Yi Sang*), eds. Kim Yujung and Kim Juhyŏn (Seoul: Chisik sanŏpsa, 2004), 186.

155. Yi Sang, "*Sanch'on yŏjŏng*," 337. It should be noted here that the original word in quotation marks can be read either as "Yi Sang" or "*isang*" (ideals). As such, the sentence provides two possible readings, the latter being something like "Thus he overcame Kim Haegyŏng, who craved mung bean fritters and persimmon punch and rice wine and seasoned slices of roast, and died according to his humorous

'ideals' like the citron he described as a 'humorous figure, neither vegetable nor fruit.'"—Trans.

156. Yi Sang, *"Kwŏnt'ae,"* 273.

157. Yun T'aeyŏng, *"Chasin i kŏndamga radon* Yi Sang (Yi Sang, the self-styled healthy talker)," in *Hyŏndae munhak*, December 1962, 247.

158. Yi Sang, *"Sirhwa,"* 125.

159. Sigmund Freud, *Jokes and Their Relation to the Unconscious* (*Nongdam kwa muŭisik ŭi kwan'gye*), trans. Im Inju (Seoul: Yŏllin ch'aektŭl, 1997), 300.

160. Yi Sang, *"Tonggyŏng,"* 342. The phrase "simple excretion" is a direct translation of *"kandanhan paesŏl."* In the published translation of the essay, however, the line reads "(w)hile casually relieving myself in an underground toilet near Kyōbashi . . ."

161. Tanaka Hidemitsu, *Yoidore fune* (*The drunkards' boat*), trans. Im Chongguk (Seoul: P'yŏnghwa ch'ulp'ansa, 1978), 6–7.

162. Mun Chonghyŏk, *"Simsim sanch'ŏn e mudŏjuo"* (Please bury me deep in nature)," in *Yŏwŏn*, April 1964, 241.

163. Kim Kirim, *"Ko Yi Sang ŭi ch'uŏk,"* 314.

164. Yi Sang, *"Chongsaenggi,"* 397.

165. Kim Soun, *Hanŭlkkŭt e sarado*, 300.

Chapter 10

Manchuria and Pro-Japanese Romanticism

HUMAN LESSONS: THE STARTING POINT OF LIQUIDATION AND AFFIRMATION

In'gan suŏp (*Human lessons*, 1936) is a novel Yi Kiyŏng serially published in the *Chosŏn chungang ilbo* newspaper following his release from prison after having been arrested in the second roundup of KAPF members. In so much as Yi is on record as saying that he took his creative inspiration from *Don Qixote*, while also defining this work as "the first test of a humorous novel in Korea,"[1] its protagonist, Hyŏnho, displays comedic characteristics rivaling Don Quixote. Both the son of a wealthy family and a man with a history of mental illness, Hyŏnho reflects on having lived "until now like a parasitic animal, relying on the strength of others," while "vowing to take life by the horns and move forward"[2] with his own strength. He thus "leaves his home, leaves his fortune, leaves his parents, wife, and children, and strikes out, a naked body stripped of everything, searching for all sorts of hardships, with a *bento* box as if he were a wandering poor laborer"[3] to begin "human lessons."[4]

The "great life" of this philosopher of human lessons begins with his going out into the streets, clad in the garb of a Chosŏn dynasty scholar together with a headband displaying a slogan, to awaken those who are napping. With his "farsighted ideals" and "plans," Hyŏnho on the one hand publishes the philosophy journal *Chagi ch'angjo* (*Self-creation*) and discusses *samsul chuŭi* (三術主義, the doctrine of three skills),[5] while on the other hand he throws himself into physical labor as a porter or a worker on road construction sites. This is because he espouses a "manual philosophy"[6] that stresses labor. In his view, like the Earth that "day and night, with great speed, is running a marathon around the Sun," "there are no objects in the world that do not

229

move," and "nothing that does not labor." He thinks that this labor "creates the life"[7] of human beings who have escaped from barbarity. In addition, he argues that, "due to the division of physical labor and mental labor," an "extreme prejudice" has arisen among humans, while elucidating that "uniting and harmonizing the opposition between these two sides, we must break new ground from which a new life can begin."[8] He argues that "through a unification of labor that jointly uses the hands and the head," "self-creation"[9] can be achieved, and this is the process of making the "individual self" and the "social self" identical. This type of thought, when Hyŏnho directly experiences "the group labor of many people" making "a fine mountain road in a mere week" by carving up a rugged, steep mountain slope where it was thought "there will probably never be a road," grows into the conclusion that "all truth lies in labor."[10]

Of course, the thoughts of Kim Ch'ŏnsik, the second Sancho Panza, differ from this. Having come up from the countryside, and following Hyŏnho around in order to become the manager of a factory that produces foodstuffs from air, he protests, "Sir! Are you not aware that because from a tender age I engaged in those sorts of human lessons until I was sick and tired of them I haven't the slightest need to do them once again?" At this, however, Hyŏnho rebukes, "Mr. Kim, no matter how much labor you performed in the countryside, working like a slave without knowing the real meaning and discovering the philosophical significance and doing it voluntarily have completely different meanings."

Hyŏnho's thoughts in stressing voluntary labor bring to mind the assertion of the Yi Kiyŏng short story "*Saengmyŏngsŏn* (Lifeline, 1941)" that the "lifeline of farmers" lies in the soil. This is because the core of this work, defined as "contemporary fiction," lies in the words "(w)e must become not the slaves of the soil but truly its masters."[11] Kwŏn Hyŏngt'ae, a worker in the press's editing department who considered Seoul the "seedbed of success," intended to actualize through literature "his own personal ideals,"[12] making them unified both physically and spiritually. As soon as that dream is shattered, however, he comes to consider the city and its "fierce struggle for survival" as a "hotbed of sin."[13] For him, urban life is an "unnatural life like that of a flower trapped in a flowerpot." "True happiness" lies in the "development of life," but a flower in a flowerpot cannot do much to develop its life. As a result, Hyŏngt'ae returns home, "longing for the soil" and for "true life." As a citizen of the city he was estranged from his wife due to poverty and gained nothing but illness. Thus, in order to grow his "inner person," he abandons copying (*p'ilgyŏng*, 筆耕) and chooses farming (*nonggyŏng*, 農耕) to become a "new rural man."

For Hyŏngt'ae there can be no "slavish labor" that condones even thievery or gambling on the grounds of poverty and survival. "We farm every year, but we run out of provisions before the new year begins. Every year only our debt increases." "If we can steal, let's do it! Then let's do a bit of gambling!"[14] This is precisely the sort of self-abandonment that represents the actions of a slave. The "master of the soil," rather than cursing poverty while rationalizing gambling, through labor not only overcomes his slavish state but also wholly and organically actualizes his self and life. Kwŏn Hyŏngt'ae states the following.

> Everybody! Please don't misunderstand. When I say now we must become masters of the soil that does not mean that each of us should become landlords. What I'm saying is that even if we become tenant farmers, each of us must thoroughly realize that we are farmers, and at the same time we must strive for farming improvements and use every ounce of strength we have for rural development till the day we die. So what I'm saying is that we need to consider farming as a calling.[15]

The quotation stresses the need to "thoroughly realize that we are farmers," and the recognition of farming not as a *ch'ŏnjik* (賤職, base occupation) but as a *ch'ŏnjik* (天職, calling). Of course, this sort of assertion is also related to the overall situation in which this work was published alongside an array of "rural field reports" such as Pak T'aewŏn's "*Ch'ungnam nongch'on chŏmmyo* (A sketch of rural South Chungcheong province)," An Hoenam's "*Non e kadŭkhan mul, mul hŭlk ŭi chidoja kunsang* (Paddies filled with water, leaders of the water and soil)," and Kim Namch'ŏn's "*Kangwŏndo tonghaean ŭi pada wa san kwa tŭl* (The sea, mountains, and fields along the east coast of Gangwon province)."[16] This also relates to the "back-to-earth movement of culture" spoken of by Ch'oe Chaesŏ, and Im Hwa's "theory of totalitarian literature." Im Hwa wrote that the "urban spirit" is "different from that of farmers, is 'bohemian' with no attachment to the local, and is one-hundred percent opportunistic regarding the environment." He claimed it was at once the "spirit of the bourgeois" and the "temperament of the merchant," in which "profit and loss governed all things."[17] Moving forward, this recalls the assertions of Yi Kwangsu. He discussed the phrase from the "Doctrine of the Mean (Ch., Zhongyong 中庸)" "without sincerity there would be nothing (不誠無物)," while stating that through "labor" based on sincerity "(t)he possessor of sincerity does not merely accomplish the self-completion of himself. With this quality he completes other men and things also (誠者非自成己而已也. 所以成物也)," "and this is the way by which a union is effected of the external and internal (合內外之道也)." [18] It is in this way that "calling" overcomes slavish labor and the profit-and-loss relations of the city. And this mediates the postmodern human type.

THE IDEA OF CALLING

But this "theory of calling" that says not to be dissatisfied with tenant farming also represents the philosophical conclusion arrived at by Hyŏnho, who in *In'gan suŏp* defines wealth as "the accumulation of labor," learning as "the fruition of mental labor," art as "the perversion of labor," life as "the continuation of labor," love as "the coupling of labor," politics as "the policy of labor," and philosophy as "the systemization of labor." He insists, "We were not put on this earth to play but rather for self-creation," while continuing, "If we are to possess any pleasure, it will be found while carrying out our calling." Accordingly, this calling also corresponds to the "contentment,"[19] "role," "duty," and "profession" (業) of Yi Kwangsu, who wrote "there is the position (職) of cabinet minister, and there is the designation (分) of sanitation worker, but both duties (職分) are necessary for the nation." Regarding "true occupations" in which one can demonstrate one's spontaneous, functional, and organic "natural calling," Hyŏnho provides the following comments.

> I consider it a great trouble that so many people in this world are unable to find an "occupation" that is right for them, and, additionally, that regarding their occupations they misunderstand, in today's parlance. They think occupation naturally means only earning money, so that, even if it does not fit with their inherent talents, if it is something that will make them a lot of money they consider it a good occupation. That is why people have the self-discrepancy of appearing to be alive only to eke out a living.
>
> But I'm telling you a true occupation is not at all like that. You can never find human happiness in that sort of occupation. Only an occupation in which they can display their natural abilities and expand their lives can be called a calling.[20]

In light of the above, the rural community of "*Saengmyŏngsŏn*," having overcome the comedic abstractness of *In'gan suŏp*, which did not move past a "menial labor" unfamiliar to its Seoul setting, represents a space of concrete ideals and life that allows the attainment of true calling. And this is also the context of "*Kwangsanch'on* (Mining town, 1943)" in which we find the following lines: "Of course, that's how professionalism must be. Isn't that why when a person has a profession that's right for him it's known as a calling?"[21] The mines of Gangwon Province, where the draftee Hyŏnggyu earnestly works, represent the space in which the philosophical conclusion of *In'gan suŏp* is concretely practiced.

Hyŏnggyu, through his year of living as a miner, comes to possess an "interest in mining." This differs from "daydreaming about striking it rich." Rather, this relates to a "joy of life"[22] that has "transcended such material concerns."[23] "Joy of life" is gained through the blooming of "the flowers of the lives of people faithful to the occupations each has taken on, just as flowers of every color bloom in a contest to boast of their own appearances."[24] That is what "gives them the actual feeling that comes from the fierce struggle with nature, as well as a confidence that is full of fight."[25] What is more, "the pride of conquering nature with the strength of humans more than offsets the hardships of labor."[26] For the trained laborer Hyŏnggyu, who has the skills to manage "machines as if they were slaves"[27] while "going into the ground, the heart of nature, laying open its internal organs, and extracting treasures," the miner is like a "brave soldier on the front line charging the enemy's position."[28] No longer are human beings slaves. Only machines are slaves.

This labor, which is also expressed in the phrase "decisive battle of the workplace,"[29] is the process for revealing the "inner person"[30] to "bring the character to fruition." Here the phenomenon of the alienation of labor cannot exist. Accordingly, Hyŏnggyu, who has found fun in work, falls into a "state of self-surrender (忘我之境)"[31] that ranks with Yi Kwangsu's "human training (人間修行)" through the "artistic reconstruction of life" or the "state of complete concentration on work (勤勞三昧境)."[32] A "magnificent industrial warrior," he reveals the following regarding "pride in one's occupation" and "understanding of one's occupation."

> Of course, among them there are some people who consider the life of a miner as simply nothing more than that of a wage laborer. Such people calculate profit and loss solely according to the relationship of capital and labor, which leads to an inferiority complex that they are nothing more than worthless coolies. Yes, they began from a self-abandoned mental corruption and wasted their matter and mind on debauchery, idling their lives away until their wretched final days.
>
> But these are the dregs of idiotic and outdated thought.
>
> The miner is a calling by no means inferior to the farmer. First of all, aren't they equal in confronting nature in order to engage in production?[33]

The core of the above quotation lies is the portion that defines thinking of the life of a miner solely in terms of the relationship of capital and labor as "idiotic and outdated thought." This also corresponds to the lines from *"Saengmyŏngsŏn"* that read, "What I'm saying is that even if we become tenant farmers, each of us must thoroughly realize that we are farmers, and at the same time we must strive for farming improvements and use every ounce of strength we have for rural development till the day we die." For instance, it is actually Tolsoe from the short story *"Sŏhwa* (Fire play, 1937),"* with his affirmation of gambling on the pretense of poverty, who has fallen into "mental corruption."

This eloquently puts forth the basic position of the "novel of production" in which "relations of production are disregarded and only the development of productivity is an issue."[34] As evident also in the words "equal in confronting nature in order to engage in production," this substitutes the capital-labor relationship with the calling(labor)-nature relationship. Furthermore, it disavows the shallow modern attitude that "considers mouth and stomach as heavenly important things."[35] Farmers or laborers are not Otherized existences with an "inferiority complex" and exploited by landlords and capitalists. Overcoming the "realm of hungry ghosts (餓鬼道)" and "realm of beasts (畜生道)"[36] of modern society, which, "thinking that even government officials or people in the teaching profession were in it for the monthly paycheck," did not hesitate "even to go on strike if it was an issue related to wages,"[37] they leap forward to become "masters of the soil" who take nature as the object of conquest and development. In addition, mediated by calling versus nature, the schema of modernity versus premodernity=the West versus the East is converted into the East versus the West. At this point, the tenancy disputes or strikes seen in works such as Yi Kiyŏng's *Kohyang* (*Hometown*, 1933–1934) will discard their progressive tinge. They are nothing more than "the dregs of idiotic and outdated thought" that arose in the West. What must now be battled are not capitalists or landlords but nature. As such, the title of Kanno Masao's work, *Tsuchi to tatakau* (*Fighting against the soil*, 1939)[38]—a memoir of his life at the training camp of the "Manchurian Development Youth Volunteer Army" that was evaluated as a "classic of literature originating from the new frontier"—is symbolic.

Of course, this emphasis on "masters of the soil" has as its background the general tendency of the time. For instance, what An Hamgwang wrote in his short story "*Nongmin, Chiksami* (Chiksam the farmer, 1942)" is a representative example of this. Chiksam is a character who, carrying on the work of his grandfather and father, "selflessly devotes" himself to "research on the improvement of rice seeds." For developing the "Sŏnorang ear," named after his father, he receives a special medal of honor and a monetary prize from the Meiji Emperor at the 1882 Tokyo Agricultural Exposition. In addition, *Changhanmong* (*A long and sorrowful dream*, 1913) and *Pyŏngja samin* (*The three invalids*, 1912) author Cho Ilchae's discussing of "benevolent acts" or introducing of the late-Edo agriculturalist Ninomiya Sontoku, who "cultivated wilderness into fertile fields,"[39] is also related to this. These sorts of discussions represent the origins that gave birth to Ch'anho, the agricultural teacher in An Sugil's "*Mokch'ukgi* (A record of stock farming, 1943)," a work that mediates individual and state through a labor in which workers become "masters of the soil." He is different from the "orators" who fled to Manchuria around the time of the March 1, 1919, Independence Movement. "Without a single word of impassioned eloquence to light a fire in the hearts of students, he silently digs the earth with pick and hoe." He also admires the "thorough and perfect life of Rou Sung," a laborer who specializes in pig farming, "who has turned himself into a pig."[40] This sort of conversion forms a pair with the son of a bourgeois family Hyŏnho's autonomously becoming an urban manual laborer. Yi Kiyŏng, by comedically depicting Hyŏnho, who voluntarily disavows his own class and capitalistic individuality (=property), settles the problems of production relations, class, and the individual. Both the poor (Kwŏn Hyŏngt'ae in *"Saengmyŏngsŏn"*) and the rich (Hyŏnho in *In'gan suŏp*) abandon their respective class positions.

This being the case, *In'gan suŏp*, which thus mediates settlement and affirmation, represents a decisive moment for Yi Kiyŏng's literature. This is because it expresses the leap to overcome modernity and its attendant frustration through the comic story of the lunatic Hyŏnho. Expressed in the words of Yu Hangnim, this is the behavior of throwing away "rubles that are useless as currency" while screaming "the future lies only in madness."[41] With the situation of the late 1930s, in which, following the dismantling of KAPF, things such as capitalist modernity and the death of bourgeois literature were discussed in earnest, as backdrop, it novelized the logic of this "transition period." As such, the following quotation is quite significant.

Mankind has seen struggles between tribe and tribe, however, on the other hand, there is also the struggle between mankind and nature. Since ancient times, nations have risen and fallen in war, but each time the struggle with nature always ends in the victory of mankind.

This is because science is more developed than before.

Even as war means destruction, it simultaneously brings construction. Even as it is a tremendous expense, it simultaneously provides enormous productivity. Consequently, the larger the scale of a war, the more concentrated all the strength of a nation becomes. As with the present Greater East Asia War, it means the total mobilization of one hundred million national subjects.

Therefore, although they say that the end of the war will bring a peaceful era, in a peaceful era as well the struggle with nature continues. In a word, this is because science ceaselessly develops. This is because science confronts nature and divulges its secrets.[42]

In this way, *In'gan suŏp*, in the name of science (productivity) pitted in a "struggle with nature," was the first step toward affirming the totalitarian activities known as the "Greater East Asia War." This was the origin of the pro-Japanese novel of production.

THE TRACKS OF PROSPECT: FROM
REVOLUTION TO SPORTS

In addition to the above, Yi Kiyŏng writes, "If we could cultivate all of the boundless plains and wilderness of east, south, and north Manchuria making them into fertile land and paddy fields, what a truly amazing sight that would be." Moreover, he discusses the "revolution of nature" and the "great creativity as a pioneer."[43] This is important because it emphasizes the new and bright spectacle Manchuria provided in place of the prospect of history that had been lost. Unlike Yi Sang's "*Ogamdo* (Crow's-eye view, 1931)," which had lost its pupil and, by making his body into a windowpane=mirror, arrived at the "tentacle's (sense of touch's) diagramming these emotional landscapes,"[44] Yi Kiyŏng's vision discovered the nature of Manchuria as an object of cultivation that could replace the struggle against capitalists. Through Manchuria, which combined farming village ("*Saengmyŏngsŏn*") and mining town ("*Kwangsanch'on*"), while also appearing simultaneously as a place and a method for actualizing "calling" and "ideals," the abstractness of Hyŏnho, the "taker of human lessons" who had been stuck between "before" and "after," was completely solved. Like Yi Kwangsu's Sambongi ("*Sambongi ne chip* [Sambongi's house, 1930–31])" who "developed" his "territory" while warring against the "sedge roots," amid the total system of representation of Imperial Japan that had appropriated the spectacle of Manchuria, the runaway Hyŏnho would return as a "*Sŏnnong* (Jp., *Sennō*)," or Korean farmer.

At this juncture, in step with the various policies of a Japanese state shouting for "Greater East Asian Co-Prosperity" and "*Ōdō rakudo*" (Asian Arcadia ruled by virtue of royal justice, Kor., *Wangdo nakt'o*, 王道樂土), Manchuria becomes the stage for a genuine commitment, upon which both gaze and productivity will be concentrated. Beyond the end of history, the space called Manchuria begins to appear. The vast spectacle of Manchuria is precisely the concrete reality that will be "surveyed" by photographs and described by maps and rails. Thus, history begins anew.

In a place like Manchuria for which there were not yet any detailed maps, one could not simply haphazardly set up surveying instruments in the rugged mountains, or amidst the forests where one place was indistinguishable from the next. Therefore, in such places, before actual surveying was begun, photographic surveying was undertaken from an airplane. Based on photographic surveying, which was accomplished by commissioning an airline company, they made a "1:10,000" map, and upon this they drew for the first time the estimated lines for the railroad using the shortest distances possible, and then took this with them to commence surveying the actual locations. The cartography in which

Kwangho was presently engaged entailed the task of precisely calculating the results of photographic surveying and transferring them to a "1:10,000" reduced map. . . .

Tiny streams appeared then grew into great rivers, and those flowed toward the sea. Wide plains were tightly walled in, bisected by towering mountains. Ocean-wide forests, atop the map, appeared exactly like lovely lawns. Through all this, the railroad, taking the shortest distance possible, while avoiding difficult construction projects, crossed bridges, went through "tunnels," and made a mark like a personal seal for the station at the destination point. Wherever the locomotive took him, while drawing "image" and "illusion" atop the drafting table, he felt the natural features of Manchuria.[45]

The above work explains a "method for the direct liquefaction of coal," a way to make artificial oil, while also describing such things as the "ceaseless superhuman efforts of scientists" and the "founding of 'Jilin Artificial Oil' with a capital of one hundred million *wŏn (yen)* as one portion of the second five-year industrial plan." But the lines that integrate all of these elements are "I am utterly infatuated with that process by which technology, time after time, went on to conquer nature," and "The technician does not bother to ask where the oil will be used."[46] Productivity merely romantically idealizes the technology that "conquers nature"—it appears indifferent regarding all other matters. This brings to mind the words of Engineer K who defined as "sentimentalism" the "humanism" that concerned itself with things such as the conditions of the workers' lives, while going on to opine that "feeling humanity amidst the cold numbers or printing type of formulae and equations and postulates and theorems was an all the more noble and beautiful thing."[47]

This is also intimately related to the emphasis on disciplining the body in place of ideology or worldview. Training the body is indispensable for carrying out the "fierce struggle against nature" that accompanies the process of production. It is also a virtue of the soldier. In fact, Hyŏnggyu sees the "brave soldier on the front line charging the enemy's position" and the miner as identical. This suggests a "political anatomy" that "imposed upon them a relation of docility-utility," and carried out a "calculated manipulation" of the body.[48] The term "decisive battle of the workplace" synthesizes all of these. And, when viewed in this way, the following scene from *In'gan suŏp*, which discusses "construction" while mentioning a "new understanding of sports," proves immensely suggestive.

"So in the future we're planning to build a park here. Well, I guess it'll be next spring before anything concrete happens, but we've already drafted a general plan. . . . First of all, in the front we're going to make a playing field . . ."

"Playing field . . ."

He was struck by the rather odd idea of a philosopher preparing the ground for a playing field.

"What, a playing field, have you taken an interest in sports?"

"No, in the past I had no connection with sports, but let's just say that in as much as a philosopher is also a human being, I recently gained a new understanding of sports as something that doesn't have to be kept at such a distance."

"Ah—is that so?"

"Look here! As you also well know—And can't the great development of Greece be seen as lying in the fact that they greatly trained the bodies of their citizens?—there is also a Western proverb that says a sound mind resides in a sound body!"[49]

In fact, from the time he stated that, like the Earth that "with great speed, is running a marathon around the Sun," "there are no objects in the world that do not move" and "nothing that does not labor," Hyŏnho was viewing labor and sports as identical. In addition, the formula sports=labor is also what gave birth to the "sound mind" that overcomes the "unclean atmosphere of the era." This is also related to the discussion in "*Kwangsanch'on*" of the "increased production week" being "not only for work in the mines" but also "establishing a norm for private lives as well in order to begin a self-discipline movement." For increased production in the mines, the miners are instructed to "reduce consumption and forge spiritual culture and physical strength,"[50] and this is supposed to convert the laborers' class consciousness that befits slaves into a calling consciousness that befits masters. This is the meaning of the "marathon" spoken of by Hyŏnho. It is sports as a physical activity that overcomes nature according to a totalitarian plan. What is more, the production competition itself that arises as a result of the increased production week takes on the aspects of a sort of sports meet. This situation is described in the scene below.

> At this mine, from this year, the last week of each month was designated an increased production week, and each workshop strained to raise performance.
>
> It was a sort of competition. As such, each department formed a single unit, and the various groups each competed in their work.[51]

Thus, the emphasizing of a productivity that conquers nature takes sports as its equivalent. These replace revolution and struggle, forms of movement that raise questions regarding the contradictions in the relations of production. The shift from relations of production to productivity corresponds to the march from revolutionary activities to sporting activities. These are the tracks of prospect and *undong* (movement, sport) depicted by Yi Kiyŏng at the end of the Japanese colonial period.

For reference, if we look at the case of Japan, the word *undo* (Kor. *undong*, 運動) contains the dual meanings of movement as physical exercise, and political movement for a given objective. The *undokai* (sports meet, athletic meet [Kor. *undonghoe*]) was a form of activity of the *"sōshi,"* a political group of the Meiji period. The largest distinguishing characteristics of these *undokai* lay in the "manifestation of physical activity and movement qua political practice as perfect equivalents," and in the "practice for achieving political demands being embodied in the physical exercise of the *undokai*."[52] Thus, the physical exercise of the *undokai* exteriorized such things as "will and (fighting) spirit, the primary principles of the *sōshi* movement,"[53] or "morale, mind, and sincerity, the formless sorts of political practice." Political practice was "sublimated into movement of the body."[54]

At this juncture, those spectators who had not previously participated in the ideology of political movement, the moment they began the physical exercise along with the *"sōshi,"* "turned away from the outsiders, and, together with activists, constituted 'politics=movement.'" They came to take on a "political disposition that was homogeneously distributed based not on a political position proportional to ideology or subjectivity but rather on the equality of their actions themselves, of moving their bodies, being in a 'movement' together."[55]

As a result, these *undokai* (athletic meets), which had become a custom of the age, were satirized as *udonkai* (noodle meets). The following is a scene from Futabatei Shimei's novel *Ukigumo* (*The Drifting Cloud*, 1887–1889).

> "Be quiet. You don't know anything about this. As I was saying, we weren't in the house, so I gave him 50 *sen* and he said that wasn't enough. He wanted 1 *yen*. I decided that there would be no end to it if I gave in this time so I put my foot down. He took the 50 *sen* grudgingly enough and then said that day after tomorrow there's to be an outing at Asukayama—an *udonkai* or something."
>
> Osei laughed in genuine mirth. Noboru nodded eagerly. *"Undokai,"* he said.
>
> *"Undokai* or *sobakai* or whatever—he wanted 50 *sen* more. I told him to come tomorrow to get the money, but he wouldn't listen and insisted on taking it right away. Even that wouldn't have been so bad but he said something terrible. When I asked him if he'd come by tomorrow, he said 'I got the money already so I don't have to. I'll come to see you when I run short again.'"
>
> "Mother, even if there is a charge for an *undokai*, it isn't more than 10 or 20 *sen*."[56]

Of course, this sort of custom is not unrelated to the meaning of the *undonghoe* as described in Kim Namch'ŏn's novel *Taeha* (*The great river*, 1939). These *undonghoe*, as "enlightened gatherings," unlike traditional wrestling tournaments that "didn't have a single woman spectator," specially prepared "women's seats" and not only publicized the "need for a philosophy of physical education and the promotion of health" but also "made the goal of encouraging women to take the lead in sending their children to school and making them study new knowledge the main point of the tournaments."[57] At the same time, however, the practicing of "mass gymnastics" or "mock cavalry battles," in which they "repeated several times the scene of rapidly finishing with 'Attention, right dress! Drop down, number, right face!', and changing from marching in a column of fours to marching in line,"[58] also showed aspects of military training.

That in June 1916 the Korean students in Tokyo organized a "student union soccer team" and traveled to Korea but "disbanded without even once receiving government approval,"[59] and that the government general, citing reasons such as the "excessive issuance's of *undonghoe* hindering students' education" or that "students could be influenced depending on the ideology of the sponsoring organization,"[60] came to carry out "sports regulation" are all due to the above-mentioned meanings of *undong*. Yi Kwangsu, on the other hand, criticized the authorities by asserting that in "Korea where sports were immature" the excessive issuance of *undonghoe* was actually a good thing, while rhetorically asking, "In this conflation of sports and ideology it appears as if the authorities have heard talk of Czechoslovakia's Sokol movement, but don't they possess the power to allow us fully and happily to enjoy sports as sports while dealing with ideology however they please?"[61]

When viewed in relation to this characteristic of *undonghoe*, the scene in Yi T'aejun's *Sŏngmo* (*Holy mother*, 1935–1936) where Sunmo places on the head of her son Ch'ŏlchin, a member of an underground organization who is fleeing abroad, an "old cap" in place of a school hat proves extremely significant. Moreover, Ch'ŏlchin, in order to put Sunmo's mind at ease, says, "Mother? Please be happy as if your son were an athlete going to the Olympics."[62] In short, Yi Kwangsu's description below relating to "the strike of students" does not stop at mere wordplay.

> He said, "Chongnyŏl, but this is not good. Regardless of the reason, a student 'strike' against the school cannot be good."
> Kim Chongnyŏl was uncertain of the exact meaning of the word "strike," but judging from the fact that there was a "strike" in "baseball" he thought it must generally mean attacking the school.[63]

In light of the above, it stands to reason that Hyŏnho, who had acquired a new politics that stressed struggle against nature, gains a "new under-standing" of sports. By means of sports and labor he must transform his "opium addict" face. People like Kyŏngho in Kim Namch'ŏn's "*Yojigyŏng* (Kaleidoscope, 1938)" who sees his "heart's fortress" crumbling, or opium addicts like Hyŏnhyŏk in Ch'oe Myŏngik's "*Simmun* (Pattern of the mind,

1939)," who have been frustrated by the modern project of Marxism, must now all throw away the "frivolity of those who have only brains but in their entire lives have never experienced living,"[64] and be rehabilitated through "living." Or, like the gold mine king Sangmun, they must become "athletes of the era"[65] who carry out Imperial Japan's gold mining policies. He is not a mad prospector looking to strike it rich. Rather, while cultivating nature, he "cultivates" his own "life." And what intensifies all of this practice is "Manchuria," propagandized as a space of "*Ōdō rakudo*" and "*gozoku kyōwa* (harmony among five ethnicities, Kor., *ojok hyŏphwa*, 五族協和)." In that place, *undong* stands in opposition to opium, while increased production stands in opposition to smuggling. Hyŏn Kyŏngjun's writing of "*Milsu* (Smuggling, 1938)" or "*Bentto bakko sok ŭi kŭmkoe* (The gold bar inside a bento box, 1938)" is connected with these sorts of meanings. In "*Yumaeng*" Hyŏn depicts the following.

> The village was constructed eight months ago, in the twelfth year of Showa—since that would be the eleventh month and XX day of the fourth year of Kangde's reign in Manchukuo it was right after that historic abolition of extraterritorial rights.
>
> After having been processed at the consular police station, the traffickers and addicts who had been rounded up from all over Manchukuo were placed at five spots around the country and organized into collective villages, but that intention to shine a new hope and light onto these people who had lost the light was by no means as easy as simply sitting down and eating the fruit one had picked. . . .
>
> In the newly emerging state they gritted their teeth and struggled to salvage even one person and turn him into an upstanding citizen. . . .
>
> Even though they may have failed, there was a time when they all held ideals and strove toward a glorious future.
>
> Among them there were technicians and political activists, there were artists and religious men and medical men and educators, and every title was represented.
>
> In terms of linguistics, it goes without saying there were people proficient in the national language (Japanese) and Manchurian, as well as in English, Russian, and even German.
>
> Thus it was perfectly natural that the political authorities came to value these talented people.
>
> But dragging those who had already once derailed from the tracks of life back onto the proper path was a truly difficult task. More than anything else, the opium addicts were a problem.[66]

In this sort of space, sports as *undong* that excluded ideology and politics once again recovers its politics. This is because, together with things such as the "General Principles of the Youth Volunteer Corps for the Development of Manchuria and Mongolia,"[67] *undong* comes to be indistinguishable from the national policies that aim at the health and rehabilitation of the "*kokumin* (Kor. *kungmin*, 國民)," or national subjects. As suggested in the Yi Kiyŏng novel *Sin'gaeji* (*Newly opened land*, 1938), this also shares something in common with "cultivating the wilderness of the mind" through the "joy of production." Namely, *Sin'gaeji*, which emphasizes a "reclamation project inside the mind," interprets "not desiring the small profit right before one's eyes but rather taking in the whole situation as the duty of the common people." As a result, the *undonghoe* is no different from the "*puhŭnghoe* (復興會, revival)" and "*pŏnyŏnghoe* (繁榮會, cooperative)" satirized below.

> "Huh, what kind of *hoe*?—*Puŏnghoe* (owl meeting). . . . Even if I heard it day and night I'd forget that damn word!"
>
> "It's not a *pungŏhoe* (crucian meeting, crucian sashimi) but a *puŏnghoe* (owl meeting), ha ha ha."
>
> Kim Sŏnyŏ, Sunok, Tŏgin, and Ilsŏng—the people of the village sat together in a single place eating lunch while looking out at and chattering about the townspeople abundantly enjoying themselves across the way.
>
> "Then what sort of *hoe* is it? I truly have no idea whether it is an *ingŏhoe* (carp meeting, carp sashimi) or a *sungŏhoe* (mullet meeting, mullet sashimi), ha ha . . ."
>
> Thinking she had become the laughingstock of several people, Sunok's face blushed as she looked around embarrassedly.
>
> "It's a *pŏnyŏnghoe* (cooperative). *Pŏnyŏnghoe*!"[68]

The reason Sunnam goes to Manchuria in *Sin'gaeji* is in order to bring about a "*puhŭnghoe*" (revival), in this sense of the word, because Manchuria was a space of rehabilitation. Her migration to Manchuria shares something in common with Ch'ansu, who in the An Sugil short story "*Pyŏ* (Rice, 1940)" emigrates to Manchuria in order to "break through mental suffocation while simultaneously constructing a new life."[69] At this point all people must strive in the sport of "cultivation" upon the playing field known as Manchuria. "(S) olitude trivial as a germ"[70] can no longer exist.

RICE AND PADDIES: THE ELDEST
SON OF MANCHURIA

As seen above, Manchuria unfolded as a space of reclamation and, simultaneously, as a space of rehabilitation. This "reclamation" and "rehabilitation," which substituted for liberation from colonial rule, likely gave rise to a fantasy of "Manchurian utopianism" accompanied by a "pseudo feeling of liberation and a pose as a para imperialist."[71] Here, the "Japan/ Korea" dichotomy based on the formula "modern/premodern=West/ East" fails to bear any meaning. This is because, amid the new dichotomy of "East/West" and noisy slogans such as "Greater East Asian Co-Prosperity," it was sublated into *"naisen ittai* (Japan and Korea as one body, Kor. *naesŏn ilch'e*, 內鮮一體)" or *"gozoku kyōwa."* The description that "today, after a period of six years has passed since the founding of Manchukuo, the phrase going to Manchuria has come to mean 'going in order to work and to find hope'"[72] has this entire situation as its backdrop. Toward a "Chŏlla province lass just about to cry but never crying" "in a North Manchurian tavern lacking both reliable walls and neighbors" the words "pink ribbon fluttering behind, shy lest it be tainted by touch/go back for a while to your own country"[73] can no longer be uttered. This is because Manchuria was appropriated by the ideal of a nation and was a romantic space cheerfully represented/embellished by the rhetoric of "advance" known as Greater East Asian Co-Prosperity.

This being the case, as pointed out by one Japanese writer, in the end the emphasizing of "reclamation (settler) literature" represents a "way of thinking directly connected to such things as 'conquering modern literature' or 'overcoming modernity.'"[74] Yi Kiyŏng`s novel *Taeji ŭi adŭl* (*Son of the earth*, 1940) clearly shows this way of thinking. One example of this is Kang Chusa's claim that "it is not merely to fill our bellies that we came to these desolate Manchurian plains. Much more than that, in order to become honest farmers we will fulfill our mission as pioneers (settlers), as one element of the Manchurian national subjects who will develop this East Asian continent."[75] As such, Manchuria is not merely a natural space. It will mediate a history that is different from what came before.

By interpreting ancient history to make "Manchuria our native land,"[76] or by novelizing the painful "history of cultivating paddies" through such works as Yi T'aejun's "*Nonggun* (Farm laborers, 1939)" or Chŏng Int'aek's "*Kŏmŭn hulk kwa hŭin ŏlgul* (Black soil and white faces, 1942)," the time and space of Manchuria are appropriated into both the past history and the actually remembered life history of the Korean people. (Of course, the Japanese state is operating behind the scenes.) That is, Manchuria neutralized and dehistoricized as a wilderness or natural space obtains a new temporality through the "reclamation" of "native land." In fact, this view of Manchuria had deep roots. For example, one writer in the journal *Hak chi kwang* (*The light of learning*), dividing Korean history into two periods, stating that "the first was the 3,300 year period during which they rose to power on the Manchurian continent" and "the second was a 1,000 year period during which they retrogressed on the Korean peninsula."[77] This is also related to the following passage from the 1910 novel *Sogŭmgang* (*The Small Diamond*).

Long ago the place called western Manchuria was our country's territory, but the kings of old revered only culture while remaining indifferent to military defensive preparations, so that they were only able to keep (the territory) within the Yalu River and because they were neglectful of (the territory) outside it, in the end it fell into the domain of China. But because China is originally a country famous the world over for the vastness of its land, even without cultivating this wilderness it did not lack fertile soil. Accordingly, although it did put Manchuria inside its territory with rapacious greed, because until now it neglectfully left it alone, farmers from our country who lived on the banks of the Yalu River in frontier counties such as Ch'osan crossed over one and two at a time and farmed the vast plains as they wished, and because that land is fertile if they planted a *toe* (of seeds) a *sŏm* of grain grew.[78] Thus, hearing such rumors, landless people gathered in ever greater numbers, sometimes two or three households and other times three or four households lived relying on each other, not studying at all, they lived only farming millet and potatoes. At first they cultivated the utterly wide wilderness as their hearts saw fit and as their strength allowed, but soon the nearby Chinese were overcome by an enormous greed, and they ran about the flat plains and drove in signposts making the land their property and sold it for a price to the newly arrived people from our country so that the rights to a livelihood fell completely into the hands of the Chinese. Several tens of thousands of our country's people crossed over after wandering here and there, but since there were no officials from our country to regulate and protect them it became, in a word, a world ruled by the fist. There was utterly no distinction between men and women, and no etiquette between the old and the young, making it resemble a barbarian village. And those ignorant people had absolutely no thought of their own country, and thinking only of following the power that presently held sway they scrambled to register themselves as citizens of China. It is sad. Who knew that unawares we would lose so many of our country's people?[79]

While overcoming situations like the one above, "reclamation (settler) history" at once neutralized and rehistoricized Manchuria. In fact, while *Taeji ŭi adŭl* describes the July 7, 1934, incident in which a group of Manchurian vigilantes murdered nineteen Koreans at Sahotun (沙虎屯), Namjŏnja (南甸子), Datun (大屯), it asserts "it is in no way conceit to state that by historically displaying their ample aspirations and abilities" "our predecessors came to occupy the honorable position of being the first to cultivate paddies in Manchuria." And it repeats similar comments many times over. Below are three examples of this.

Amidst suffering these innumerable persecutions, even after several people were ultimately offered up as sacrificial victims, by day they were so scared that they only continued construction work in the evenings and at night so that it wasn't until late spring of the following year that they just barely finished the (irrigation) canals. The history of cultivating paddies—as that is what we have in common all over Manchuria, this farm at Kaeyangtun (開陽屯) was a record soaked in blood that cannot be separated from previous instances.[80]

In addition, in the time before the Manchurian Incident when they were unable to maintain public peace and order, they really couldn't even farm free of worry. In years of bountiful harvest, bandits rushed in to plunder, and even when this was not the case they suffered floods every other year.[81]

Moreover, as I told you earlier as well, prior to the Manchurian Incident for a long history of 100 years our emigrant countrymen suffered every imaginable sadness and cruelty and carnage at the hands of the natives of this place while cultivating the paddies, and when we think of that history of tears of blood how could we waste even a single grain of rice?[82]

Important in the above quotations are the account of suffering "every imaginable sadness and cruelty and carnage at the hands of the natives of this place while cultivating the paddies" and words such as "public peace and order," "bandits," and "floods." For example, after having been captured by "bandits" and barely making it out alive, some (Koreans) joined with the (Japanese) punitive forces to stamp out the bandits. The term "bandits" stands in opposition to the expansion of public peace and order following the Manchurian Incident. Manchuria was simultaneously a boundless "great nature" to activate productivity, while also being a place of barbarism that, far from recompensing Koreans for "cultivating the windswept Manchurian plains from a wilderness into fertile land while enduring the sadness of step-children," demanded of them a "hellish life" in which "they shed blood, had their property confiscated, and had their maidens stolen."[83] As suggested by the line "The yellow waves of the Songhua River and the black tile-roofed houses of the Manchurians seemed to be eternally interconnected like some sort of fate," the "natives" of Manchuria were "barbarians."

Actually, when viewed through the eyes of the empire that made pad-dies by applying the scientific agricultural methods supplied by the South Manchurian Railway Company, which operated an "agricultural testing facility," or the Manchurian Development Company, the aborigines' farm land would have appeared close to a wilderness, while their farming methods could have been demeaned as a sort of hunting and gathering. The position of Kang Chusa, the village head, and Kŏno who, regarding "the Manchurians' ritual to pray for rain," while also considering "other methods," rhetorically asked "what use is there in a ritual to pray for rain,"[84] combined with their attitude when bringing up "the Manchurians' mood with regard to lunar New Year's Day" while also criticizing as lamentable their "Korean countrymen" for, like the Manchurians, "being too fixated on the lunar New Year's Day, which leads to the abuse of celebrating the new year twice, and thereby living a life that is behind the times" is no different from the point of view of the Japanese state manifested through Koreans.

In a word, the Koreans in Manchuria no longer displayed the attitude seen in the poetic lines "Wiping away tears, with a blossom of the lily of the valley / the faint shadow of the Ainu being driven off!"[85] Furthermore, they had forgotten the fact that they once thought "because it is utterly ignorant and bigoted to lack a sympathetic mind and to ridicule the behavior of a stranger with especially different ethics and customs for not being the same as their own," endeavoring to "put oneself in another's position" and "to the extent possible generously tolerate" is the "true quality of a (Confucian) gentleman."[86] By locating Manchurians solely in barbarity, they attempted to recover lost prospect and passion. It may have been that Koreans, by being reborn as imperialistic quasi-Japanese, hoped to restore the failed dreams of the Great Korean Empire and the students abroad who saw Manchuria as "our country's territory in days of old." Such a state of affairs would surely have been attractive. But it is precisely the inability to break free from this attraction that demands painful reflection.

This is also related to the customs depicted below.

When I showed an album and explained to the Manchurian farmers who did not even know what a photograph was that if I took their picture their faces too would appear atop the photograph exactly as they were, turning their heads to the left then to the right, they first considered me like a conjurer, then, when I told them the price was more than one *wŏn*, they likewise feared me as a magician and fled. So I went to an emigrant village and took a few pictures, but not only was I unable to receive a decent price but also I couldn't afford even to eat as much of their cheap food as I wanted, which made me grow tired of the countryside.[87]

The scene above shows the custom of the camera, as an implement of civilization, visually and capitalistically otherizing and appropriating the Manchurians. This is how domination becomes institutionalized in everyday life. This coincides with the activities of Sŏ Ch'idal, the student of theology and of agriculture who lectures from the *Reader on Improving Paddy Farming* in order to increase productivity. In the case of Kŏno's son Tŏksŏng, after having graduated at the top of his class, shining "clearly like the sun" among the flags of all nations at the graduation venue, he goes on to enter an agricultural and forestry school. This too is no different from taking photographs of the Manchurians. Sŏ Ch'idal and Tŏksŏng are a sort of camera that symbolizes the active operation of "civilization" (masters of the soil), which will unilaterally operate upon "barbarity" (slaves of the soil) of Manchuria, which is in turn the photographic subject that "did not even know what a photograph was." In this way, productivity (technology) is civilization. And each will justify and strengthen the other. In contrast to the barbarity of Manchuria, Sŏ Ch'idal's gospel as elucidated at an "evangelical rally" is that of civilization. It can be seen below.

> But as we consider this place a second hometown and reside here permanently generation after generation, how nice would it be if we were to become "sons of the earth" and while admirably cultivating the land simultaneously construct a Heaven in every farming village? If we are to do this, it is my opinion that all of you must first believe in Jesus and then struggle and strive both physically and spiritually. Before I think I told you that ignorance is scarier than a tiger. But tyranny is even scarier than that. Prior to the Manchurian Incident—beneath the tyranny of the northeastern regime the lives of our emigrant countryman were extremely miserable. At that time no matter how hard they tried to live well it was impossible, but now that what is called *Wangdo nakt'o* (*Ōdō rakudo*) has been established, if all of you work hard I believe it will not be so difficult to construct a Heaven in this village as well.[88]

The quotation emphasizes taking Manchuria as "a second hometown" and residing there "permanently generation after generation" in order to become "sons of the earth." When this occurs, a *Wangdo nakt'o* (*Ōdō rakudo*) that has destroyed the "ignorance" and "tyranny" that existed prior to the Incident will be "constructed" in Manchuria. These sorts of ideas are also repeated in the words of Kang Chusa who states, "I believe that we must have a grand purpose so that even our descendants may flourish on this land. That is we must become sons of the earth and seek a second hometown in this land."[89] In addition to this having been expressed in terms such as "*chohyangsim* (造鄉心, the will to create a hometown)"[90] and "*pukhyang chŏngsin*(北鄉精神, northern hometown spirit),"[91] becoming "masters of the soil" by means of a calling that overcomes alienation and barbarity as well as manifests a life concludes in becoming the owners of Manchuria who take Manchuria as their "hometown." This is the reason those Koreans who cultivated "the windswept Manchurian plains from a wilderness into fertile land while enduring the sadness of stepchildren" considered the Manchurian paddies as welcome as "people from their hometown."

And this "hometown" is another name for "the East." This place is the site that overcomes Western modernity, which is based on the consciousness of homogenous space that considers the world as one big market or one city.

There the Koreans shall escape from the slavelike position of "stepchildren" to occupy Manchuria as "sons of the earth" for generations to come. Furthermore, unlike the aborigines who neglected this vast land as a "bog" allowing only "weeds" to grow or, at best, "knew only how to grow corn and sorghum" in dry fields, the Koreans accomplished the "miracle" and "grand project" of cultivating paddies and farming rice. Thus, based on their healthy bodies, the Koreans, who took "the soul of rice (稻魂)"[92] to be the "spiritual pillar of the cultivation of Manchuria,"[93] would have to take the position of eldest son. This is because by producing rice, which, when "compared to sorghum and corn," could be none other than the "eldest son," they gave birth to the legitimate line of descent among the five ethnicities that were to be harmonized. Thus the Koreans could not help but be the legitimate children of the Emperor. As such, the following quotation is decisive.

> In fact, that jade-like rice grew in this land that had previously only known how to plant corn and sorghum was an astonishing miracle. It is certainly the son of the earth. When compared to sorghum or corn, rice is not just a son. Rather, it can be called the eldest son. Thus, if we turn this entire land into paddies, how many farms could we reclaim? And by whose hand shall this grand project be constructed! The mere thought of it makes the heart full and overflowing.[94]

The quotation sums up the core of the patriarchal and macro narrative of "Manchurian romanticism" that "makes the heart full and overflowing." This is the ultimate meaning of Manchuria as depicted by Yi Kiyŏng. In this way, together with the "impression of a grand alternation"[95] that changed the "brown sea of grasses" into paddies, or together with the energy of the era that attempted to convert the formula "premodern/modern=West/East=Japan/Korea" into "East/West→Japan=Korea," Manchuria cast the people adrift amid the storm and gale called "Pro-Japanese Romanticism."

NOTES

1. Yi Kiyŏng, *Chosŏn chungang ilbo* (The Korean central daily), December 28, 1935.
2. Yi Kiyŏng, *In'gan suŏp* (*Human lessons*) (Seoul: Munu ch'ulp'ansa, 1948), 25.
3. Ibid., 194–95.
4. Ibid., 45.
5. Ibid., 181.
6. Ibid., 29.
7. Ibid., 368.
8. Ibid., 316.

9. Ibid., 173.

10. Ibid., 438.

11. Yi Kiyŏng, "*Saengmyŏngsŏn* (Lifeline)," in *Pando chi kwang*, August, 1941, 41–42.

12. Ibid., 47.

13. Ibid., 40.

14. Yi Kiyŏng, "*Sŏhwa* (Fire play)," in *Sŏhwa* (Seoul: Tonggwangdang sŏjŏm, 1937), 70.

15. Yi Kiyŏng, "*Saengmyŏngsŏn*," 41–42.

16. These works appeared in the June, July, and August 1941 issues of *Pando chi kwang*, respectively.

17. Im Hwa, "*Chŏnch'e chuŭi ŭi munhangnon* (Theory of totalitarian literature)," in *Munhak ŭi nolli* (Seoul: Hagyesa, 1940), 764–65.

18. English translations of "The Doctrine of the Mean" are taken from the following site:
    http://classics.mit.edu/Confucius/doctmean.html

19. Yi Kwangsu, "*Kŭllo wa munhwa 3—Ilbonin ŭi kŭllo e taehaya* (Labor and culture 3—on the labor of the Japanese)," in *Maeil sinbo*, July 1, 1941.

20. Yi Kiyŏng, *In'gan suŏp*, 342.

21. Yi Kiyŏng, "*Kwangsanch'on* (Mining town)," in *Kwangsanch'on* (Seoul: Sŏngmundang, 1944), 5.

22. Ibid., 48.

23. Ibid., 38.

24. Ibid., 48.

25. Ibid., 42.

26. Ibid., 95.

27. Ibid., 41.

28. Ibid., 40.

29. Ibid., 48.

30. Ibid., 74.

31. Ibid., 98.

32. Yi Kwangsu, "*Yesul kwa insaeng* (Art and life)," in *Kaebyŏk*, Volume 19, January 1922, 6.

33. Yi Kiyŏng, "*Kwangsanch'on*," 42–43.

34. Yi Sanggyŏng, *Yi Kiyŏng: sidae wa munhak* (*Yi Kiyŏng: his times and literature*) (Seoul: P'ulbit, 1994), 286.

35. Yi Kwangsu, "*Yesul ŭi kŭmil myŏngil* (The today and tomorrow of art)," in *Maeil sinbo*, August 6, 1940.

36. Yi Kwangsu, "*Sensō to bungaku* (War and literature)," in *Sinsidae*, August, 1944 (Translated in *Yi Kwangsu ch'inil munhak chŏnjip* 2, ed. Yi Kyŏnghun [Seoul: P'yŏngminsa, 1995], 443).

37. Yi Kwangsu, "*Taedonga chŏnjaeng ŭi kyohun* (The lessons of the Great Pacific War)," in *Yi Kwangsu ch'inil munhak chŏnjip* 2, 411.)

38. Kawamura Minato (川村湊), *Ikyō no Showa bungaku* (*Showa literature of foreign lands*), (Tokyo: Iwanami shoten, 1990), 46.

39. Cho wrote about Ninomiya in *Katei no tomo* (*Friend of the family*), a monthly journal published in Seoul, from June 1940 to January 1941. See Aramata Hiroshi, *Daitōa kagaku kidan* (*Witty talk of the great Asian science*) (Tokyo: Chikuma bunko, 1999), 320–22.

40. An Sugil, "*Mokch'ukgi* (A record of stock farming)," in *Han'guk taep'yo myŏngjak ch'ongsŏ* 10 *An Sugil*, ed. Kim Yunsik (Seoul: Pyŏkho, 1993), 77.

41. Yu Hangnim, "*Magwŏn* (Horse race ticket)," in *Tanch'ŭng*, April 1937, 96.

42. Yi Kiyŏng, "*Kwangsanch'on*," 97–98.

43. Yi Kiyŏng, "*Manju wa nongmin munhak* (Manchuria and agrarian literature)," in *Inmun p'yŏngnon*, November 1939, 22.

44. Yi Sang, "*Tonghae* (Child's skeleton)," in *Yi Sang munhak chŏnjip* 2, ed. Kim Yunsik (Seoul: Munhak sasangsa, 1991), 259.

45. Kim Namch'ŏn, *Sarang ŭi sujokkwan* (*Aquarium of love*) (Seoul: Inmunsa, 1940), 325.

46. Ibid., 485.

47. Kim Namch'ŏn, "*Kil uesŏ* (Upon the road)," in *Munjang*, July 1939, 238.

48. See Michel Foucault, *Surveiller et punir: naissance de prison* (*Discipline and Punish: The Birth of the Prison*), 2nd ed., tr. Alan Sheridan (New York: Vintage Books, 1995), 137–38.

49. Yi Kiyŏng, *In'gan suŏp*, 139.

50. Yi Kiyŏng, "*Kwangsanch'on*," 99.

51. Ibid., 91.

52. Kimura Naoe, *Seinen no tanjō* (*The birth of youth*) (Tokyo: Shinyōsha, 2001), 75.

53. Ibid., 66.

54. Ibid., 75.

55. Ibid., 78.

56. Futabatei Shimei, "*Ukigumo* (The Drifting Cloud)," in *Futabatei Shimei zenshū*, 3rd ed. (Tokyo: Kadokawa shoten, 1981), 116.

The English translation is taken from Marleigh Grayer Ryan, *Japan's First Modern Novel "Ukigumo" of Futabatei Shimei* (Ann Arbor: Center for Japanese Studies, University of Michigan, 1990), 272. Although the terms "*undokai*," "*udonkai*," and "*sobakai*" (buckwheat noodle meet) have been left in the original in order to preserve the puns on which the argument is based. The translation skillfully handles these by using the terms "athletic," "ascetic," and "aesthetic," respectively.

57. Kim Namch'ŏn, *Taeha* (*The great river*) (Seoul: Inmunsa, 1939), 357.

58. Ibid., 155.

59. "*Uri sosik* (Our news)," in *Hak chi kwang*, Volume 10, September 1916, 59.

60. Yi Kwangsu, "*Sŭp'ooch'ŭ t'ongje* (Sports regulation)," in *Yi Kwangsu chŏnjip* 13 (Seoul: Samjungdang, 1962), 410.

61. Ibid.

62. Yi T'aejun, "*Sŏngmo* (Holy mother)," in *Sinmun yŏnjae sosŏl chŏnjip* 4 (Seoul: Kip'ŭnsaem, 1999), 256.

63. Yi Kwangsu, *Mujong* (*The Heartless*), 6th ed. (Seoul: Hoedong sŏgwan, 1925), 82.

64. Im Hwa, "*Chakka ŭi nun wa munhak ŭi segye* (The writer's eye and the world of literature)," in *Munhak ŭi nolli (The logic of literature)* (Seoul: Sŏŭm ch'ulp'ansa, 1989), 175.

65. Ch'ae Mansik, "*Kŭm ŭi chŏngyŏl*" (The passion of gold), in *Ch'ae Mansik chŏnjip* 3 (Seoul: Ch'angjak kwa pip'yŏngsa, 1987), 220.

66. Hyŏn Kyŏngjun, "*Yumaeng* (Nomads)," in *Inmun p'yŏngnon*, July 1940, 123–24.

67. Its contents were as follows: "1. We hereby pledge to support the Imperial dynasty's grand plan, to push forward with one mind, to devote our bodies to the sacred work of founding Manchukuo, before the gods we swear to abide unfailingly by the great mind of His Majesty the Emperor. 2. We hereby pledge with our bodies, united in virtue and in mind, to carry out the ideal of harmony among ethnicities and to become the cornerstones of the establishment of a moral world." Yun Sanghŭi, "*Chosŏnin Manju kaech'ŏk ch'ŏngnyŏn ŭiyongdae e taehayŏ* (On the Korean youth volunteer corps for the development of Manchuria)," in *Pando chi kwang*, July 1941, 14. The author worked as an administrative official for the government general.

68. Yi Kiyŏng, *Sin'gaeji (Newly opened land)* (Seoul: Sammunsa, 1938), 321.

69. An Sugil, *Pugwŏn (The northern plains)* (Seoul: Yemundang, 1944), 257.

70. Yi Sang, "*Kwŏnt'ae* (Ennui)," tr. John M. Frankl, in *Azalea: Journal of Korean Literature & Culture*, 2011, 270.

71. Kim Ch'ŏl, "*Mollak hanŭn sinsaeng* (Collapsing rebirth)," in *Sanghŏ hakbo*, Volume 9, August, 2002, 156.

72. Ham Taehun, "*Nambuk Manju p'yŏndapki* (A record of travels in south and north Manchuria)," in *Chogwang*, July 1939, 72.

73. Yi Yongak, "*Chŏllado kasinae* (Chŏlla Province lass)," in *Orangk'aekkot* (Seoul: Amun'gak, 1947), 63.

74. Kawamura Minato, *Ikyō no Showa bungaku*, 45.

75. Yi Kiyŏng, "*Taeji ŭi adŭl*" (Son of the earth), in *Han'guk kŭndae changp'yŏn sosŏl taegye 14* (Seoul: T'aehaksa, 1988), 115.

76. Yi Sŏn'gŭn, "*Manju wa Chosŏn* (Manchuria and Korea)," in *Chogwang*, July 1939, 58.

77. Ch'ŏn oe cha, "*China chibang e Chosŏn yujŏk* (Korean historic sites in Chinese territories)," in *Hak chi kwang*, Volume 10, September 1916, 35.

78. A *toe* is equal to 1.8 liters, while a *sŏm* is 180 liters. It means that if they planted a certain amount of seeds they harvested 100 times that amount in grain. Thus, this represents a figurative if somewhat hyperbolic way to represent the land's fertility.

79. Pinghŏja, *Sogŭmgang (The Small Diamond)*, in *Taehan minbo*, February 16–17, 1910.

80. Ibid., 50.

81. Ibid., 51.

82. Ibid., 91.

83. Ibid., 87.

84. Ibid., 154.

85. No Chayŏng, "*Pukhaedo ŭi chŏngjo* (The atmosphere of Hokkaido)," in *Nae hon i pult'al ttae* (Seoul: Ch'ŏngjosa, 1928), 4.

86. Yi Kwangsu, "*Tongjŏng* (Sympathy)," in *Ch'ŏngch'un*, Volume 3, December 1914, 63.

87. Pak Yŏngjun, "*Chungdokcha* (The addict)," in *Minu Pak Yŏngjun chŏnjip* 1 (Seoul: Tongyŏn, 2002), 231.

88. Yi Kiyŏng, *Taeji ŭi adŭl*, 90.

89. Ibid., 115.

90. Yi Kwangsu, "*Aehyangsim, chohyangsim* (Love for the hometown, will to create a hometown)," in *Yi Kwangsu chonjip* 13 (Seoul: Samjungdang, 1962), 533–34.

91. An Sugil, *Pukhyangbo* (*Record of a northern hometown*) (Seoul: Munhak ch'ulp'an kongsa, 1987), 36, 201, and 206.

92. Ibid., 251.

93. An Sugil, *Pukhyangbo*, 251.

94. Yi Kiyŏng, *Taeji ŭi adŭl*, 201.

95. Yi Hyosŏk, "*Habibin* (Harbin)," in *Munjang*, October 1940, 3.

Afterword

Fashion, Custom, and Modern Korean Literature

Janet Poole

"Fashion . . . does not mean merely modern costume. Rather it metaphorically expresses the various devices and phenomena that sensitize, embody, and symbolize the essence of social organizations."

Toward the beginning of his wide-ranging cultural history of Korean literature, covering the first decades of the twentieth century, Kyounghoon Lee describes his own methodology. His aim, he writes, is to examine customs as they appear in fiction during the early decades of modernity, a period that coincides with the beginnings of modern literature. Lee's attention passes over a huge range of fictional objects: from food to trademarks, eugenics to speculation, English grammar to sports, and free love to the romance of production. To turn to such customs involves exploring aspects of texts that have previously been ignored and deemed insignificant. In a literary archive that appears scattered with novel ideas, products, and practices, Lee takes snippets of objects that are often considered mere background content, setting the scene as it were and supplementary to the important work of each text occurring elsewhere. But in Lee's rearrangement these objects become the embodiment of new customs, whose necessary interconnection offers up important insights into modernity in Korea. No longer passed over as background detail, these customs rewrite our understanding of Korea's modern literature. Lee's expansive conceptualization of the notion of "fashion" in many ways acts as a microcosm for his methodology: fashion, normally associated with objects or apparel that herald novelty and style, is mobilized here as a custom in order to probe into the very essence of social organization. Just as we arrange items of clothing on our bodies to produce an outfit, Lee rearranges customs to produce a new meaning for the whole: the novel, modern literature and, ultimately, modernity in Korea.

   To readers unfamiliar with Korean intellectual history, the cultural analysis of fashion might call to mind Roland Barthes's semiotic study of the language describing women's clothing in fashion magazines as the "fashion system," or the class-based sociological research of Georg Simmel. But Lee is invoking an alternative genealogy here, which returns us to the work of cultural analysts in the Japanese empire in the 1920s and 1930s, and so to the contemporaries of the writers whose work is examined in Lee's book. In the case of Korea, this cultural analysis is most frequently associated with the fiction writer, Marxist critic and political activist Kim Namch'ŏn (1911–1953). It is worth spending some time with Kim, whose advocacy of custom as a method of thought aimed to penetrate the very nature of society. Kim's cultural analysis was itself a product of a particular arrangement of historical forces. By the mid-1930s Kim, along with other leftist activists, was feeling the heat of surveillance and suppression by the Higher Police, whose focus on "thought criminals" aimed to crush the vibrant communist movement and the threat it posed to the colonial occupation. With the imperial state's manufacture of the Manchurian Incident in 1931 and founding of Manchukuo the following year, the Korean peninsula had assumed ever more strategic importance at the heart of the empire. Kim Namch'ŏn was caught up in a major crackdown on the leaders of KAPF (Korea Artista Proleta Federacio) in 1931 and imprisoned for two years. Although he escaped a prison sentence in the second major round up of KAPF activists in 1934, Kim was one of three KAPF leaders who walked into a police station in May of 1935 to declare the formal dissolution of the organized leftist arts movement. This suppression of a socialist vision for the future hovers over Kim's subsequent, and extensive, fictional output and his emergence as a major literary critic in the latter half of the decade.

   Kim Namch'ŏn turned to the concept of custom in the course of his reflections upon the reasons for the perceived failure of the leftist arts movement. A debate on the state of the contemporary novel and prose narrative in the Korean language provided the occasion to work through his ideas, and his fellow former KAPF leader, poet and critic Im Hwa (1908–1953) an important interlocutor. Along with other Korean writers of the time, Kim had come under attack from Im for writing fiction that was deemed too personal and too focused on the individual, who seemed impotent and unable to effect change in society. Where Im criticized such fiction as defeatist, Kim countered that the failure of KAPF had stemmed in part from an idealism that had insufficiently accounted for the concrete situation in Korea. Only by becoming more "concrete"—a term Kim invoked constantly—could fiction begin to describe the reality of life in the colony. For Kim, the narration of personal experience offered one way of doing so. The problem, of course, was whether experience was sufficient as the grounds to both understand and narrate the forces governing society. Ultimately, the success or failure of the novel would depend upon the way in which individual experience was embedded in social experience in the fictional setting.

It was at this point that Kim invoked the concept of morality and its "concretization" in the form of custom. Kyounghoon Lee quotes directly from Kim's 1938 essay on morality that "the essence of social organizations is completely incarnated only after it reaches the status of custom" (43). For Kim, as for Lee, custom, that is repeated habits and practices, provides the surface points which embody the moral essence of the larger social organization. What might appear to some as mere surface phenomena—forms of dressing, practices of love and gender relations, the organization of family life, or even the food that we eat—are to Kim and Lee the very objects through which we can understand the broader moral forces of society. As Lee writes, "It is precisely the extremely superficial-seeming microscopic phenomena themselves causing the core of social structures and ideologies to open itself up for inspection" (44). Yet, custom is not only an object but also a method of analysis: it is the way in which these objects are arranged that promises to unlock the deeper meanings of something bigger than each individual object. Thus, Lee promises to arrange materials in a fashion that will produce "important meanings within the whole," just as we choose clothes to wear as an ensemble (44).

When Kim Namch'ŏn wrote about custom he was reading his contemporary, Japanese philosopher Tosaka Jun (1900–1945), who argued that the actual reality of a society "appears by and large in the form of custom."[1] Tosaka had turned to the concept of custom in the course of his inquiry into the nature of Japanese fascism, examining the mode of reproduction of reality and custom in media such as film with its capacity to produce a sense of satisfaction for the masses. Clearly mass culture was on Tosaka's mind as he sought to understand the attraction of fascism and its ability to mobilize the masses, even or especially in the cause of war. For Kim, however, custom was still a question of the individual body, as the title of his essay "Morality and the Truth of the Body" suggests. Kim thought the meaning of literature lay in this seeking of bodily truth. As he wrote: "The object of science is truth. In relation to this, literature takes the truth of one body as its object. The truth of one body means that scientific concepts have been rendered as subjects."[2] Where Im Hwa had called for the "rebuilding" of the impotent subject, Kim sought to understand the enfolding of the subject into the historical social formation.

Kim's focus on the body should be understood in the context of a clear trend in the late 1930s toward fiction concerning the supposed intimate realm of the writer. As one critic had noted—or lamented?—in a monthly review

of published fiction in 1940, "almost all the stories in this issue deal with
either the writer's own private world or a world which could be compared
to his private world."³ Such stories had become associated with Japanese-
language fiction of the Taishō period (1912–1926). A special term had even
been coined to refer to such fiction, which whether written in the first or the
third person was presumed by readers to tell stories from the writer's own
life. Subsequently the *shishōsetsu* (commonly translated as "I-novel") was
discussed by many critics and understood alternately to represent a form
of decadent or deformed individualism, or occasionally even celebrated
as a uniquely "Japanese" form of narration, placed in comparison with the
supposedly European novel. The proliferation of such literature around the
empire during the mass mobilization era of the 1930s and 1940s seemed
increasingly to herald the absorption of social conflict into the personal realm
in fiction. Kim's attempt to ground the often rambling psychological drama
of the *shishōsetsu* in bodily experience seems to be an attempt to explore this
social conflict at the level of the individual. This was, however, hard for critics such as Im Hwa to accept, as this personal absorption seemed to displace
any possibility of collective action toward a different political future.

In fact, in his criticism if not always in his fictional practice, Kim himself
was soon to shift his attention away from experience and toward observation,
and concurrently a move away from the personal narrative to the multi-char-
acter novel. Custom remained at the conceptual heart of his work, however,
in the form of the novel of manners. Kim's celebrated 1939 novel *Taeha*
(literally, a great river, but published in English translation as *Scenes from
the Enlightenment: A Novel of Manners*) is a mosaic-like panorama through
which Kim unwinds the entangled love interests of three brothers, set against
the backdrop of social change in rural Korea in the 1910s.⁴ The retitling of the
translation works well as the reader is indeed provided with scenes from the
enlightenment: in the descriptions of the arrival of the first bicycle in a small
town, the passing through of Japanese surveyors in the wake of the imposition
of colonial rule, and the excitement of the first athletics meet to be held in
conjunction with the traditional summer Dano Festival, along with not a few
love scenes and love triangles. It seems that Kim ultimately considered this
novel of manners a failure, but we see in it, and in a series of essays he wrote
at the time on Balzac, the intention behind the move toward an omniscient
narrator attempting to describe the forces motivating an entire community at
a historical moment of great transformation.

These two literary tendencies—of psychological depth and surface
description—were famously singled out by the critic Ch'oe Chaesŏ (1908–
1964) in the mid-1930s and heralded as the forms in which Korean literature
became contemporary with literature from around the (capitalist) world. In an
essay titled "The Expansion and Deepening of Realism," Ch'oe had noted a

deepening of the inner-directed observation of the psychological subject and a panorama-like expansive observation of the surface environment, represented by the fiction of Yi Sang (1910–1937) and Pak T'aewǒn (1909–1986), respectively. In fact, if Yi Sang's work recalled the *shishōsetsu*, he had also, together with his friend Pak, openly advocated "modernology," a term coined for the cultural analysis of urban customs popularized by the Japanese ethnographer Kon Wajirō (1888–1973). In the 1920s Kon had taken to the streets of Tokyo to conduct statistical analysis of customs, drawing up charts and figures that recorded observed phenomena, such as the clothes worn by pedestrians analyzed according to a variety of factors of gender, cost, and perceived origin, among others. In Ch'oe's opinion too, the two apparently disparate literary tendencies had more in common than not. Ch'oe praised both Yi and Pak's writing as advancing the capacity for scientific observation and realism in the Korean language. Whereas Yi had, he wrote, turned the observing gaze inward onto the subject, Pak had extended his watch over the urban environment. For Ch'oe, the new realism was built upon the alienation of the psychological subject, who could observe both himself and his environment with detachment and a finer grain of detail. In a suggestion of the modern technology behind this new form of visuality, Ch'oe argued that the writer had now to become a camera. Ch'oe's only criticism was that Pak's writing sometimes lacked the thread of a whole running through it, so that surface phenomena remained as scattered details and failed to bring together a sense of a complete reality. This returns us to Kim Namch'ǒn and his attempts to allow the surface object to speak a deeper truth and to Kyounghoon Lee's return to custom at a distance of more than half a century.

Kyounghoon Lee's own work notably begins with the body too; not the trustworthy body of experience but the body in pieces as the object of scientific analysis. Lee's opening discussion of the tale of Nolbu sets the stage for the cultural history of literature to follow, where the discovery of the physical body begins the removal of the individual from the spiritual world and ends the narrative reward of good over evil, attesting to the age of science and objectivity, modernity and disenchantment. Like Ch'oe, Lee charts the alienation of the observing subject, but he weaves it into a constellation of customs and material objects in an attempt to arrive at a "physical" reading of modern Korean literature. The body is dissected into pieces and subject to experiment, but also cultivated as a complete machine, the subject of sports. It is preened and cured through trademarked medicine and foodstuffs but also starved in the colonial economy. The alienated gaze looks through a glass windowpane to discover a landscape; a train window enables a glimpse of a horizon but prevents the intimacy of touch. Temporally, Lee's argument arcs from the rejection of the world of the parents through the rise of the sister and brother and the drama of free love in the modern nation.

Yet, perhaps it is Lee's port of arrival that most reveals the ethical force of his work. Lee's history comes to an end in the plains of Manchuria and the Japanese puppet state of Manchukuo, where Korean farmers and visiting intellectuals alike attempt to forge new Korean communities in the imperial diaspora. Manchuria becomes the spatial focus for a romance of production, which offers up a false promise to return the body to the earth, bringing about the end of landscape, and overcoming the foundational alienation of modernity. It is, of course, wartime and the real bodies in the earth were those of soldiers. At the heart of Lee's depiction of Korea's early modern literature lies the argument that fascism emerged from enlightenment, a fascism in which Japan's colonial subjects also played their part, not only on the ground but also in the intellectual and literary realms. Lee's work aligns itself with other recent histories by South Korean scholars, who have worked to define Japanese imperialism, including its Korean participants and agents, as one consequence of this alienated regime of seeing, rather than a resulting anomaly. This is why Lee's exhilarating book speaks to the global history of modernity, at the same time that it elucidates the most seemingly trivial and superficial phenomena of everyday life in Korea under colonial occupation.

NOTES

1. Ken C. Kawashima et al., *Tosaka Jun: A Critical Reader* (Ithaca: Cornell East Asia Series, 2014), 109.
2. Chŏng Houng and Son Chŏngsu eds., *Kim Namch'ŏn chŏnjip I* [Collected works of Kim Namch'ŏn] (Seoul: Tosŏ ch'ulp'an Pak Ijŏng), 354.
3. Paek Ch'ŏl, "*Hyŏnsil kwa ŭimi, kŭrigo chakcha ŭi sasegye*" [Reality and meaning, and the private world of the writer], *Munjang* 2, no. 8 (October 1940), 171.
4. Kim Namcheon, *Scenes from the Enlightenment: A Novel of Manners*, trans. Charles LaShure (Champaign: Dalkey Archive Press, 2014).

Selected Bibliography

SHORT STORIES AND NOVELS

An Hoenam, "Kich'a (The train)," in An Hoenam tanp'yŏnjip (Seoul: Hagyesa, 1939).

———, "Kigye (Machine)," in An Hoenam tanp'yŏnjip.

An Sŏgyŏng, "Modŏn kkŏl (Modern girl)," in Chogwang (May 1937).

An Sugil, "Pugwŏn (The northern plains)" (Seoul: Yemundang, 1944).

Ch'ae Mansik, "Irŏn nammae (This type of brother and sister)," in Ch'ae Mansik chŏnjip 7 (Seoul: Ch'angjak kwa pip'yŏngsa, 1987).

———, "Kŭm ŭi chŏngyŏl (The passion of gold)," in Ch'ae Mansik chŏnjip 3 (Seoul: Ch'angjak kwa pip'yŏngsa, 1987).

———, "T'angnyu (Muddy water)," in Ch'ae Mansik chŏnjip 2 (Seoul: Ch'angjak kwa pip'yŏngsa, 1987).

Chang Tŏkcho, "P'amanent'ŭ (Permanent)," in Chogwang (August 1939).

Cho Ilchae, "Changhanmong (A long and sorrowful dream)," in Han'guk sinsosŏl chŏnjip (Seoul: Ŭryu munhwasa, 1968).

Ch'oe Ch'ansik, "Ch'uwŏlsaek (Autumn moon colors)," in Han'guk sinsosŏl chŏnjip 4 (Seoul: Ŭlyu munhwasa, 1968).

Ch'oe Sŏhae, "Hooe sidae (Age of the extra)" (Seoul: Munhak kwa chisŏngsa, 1994).

Chŏn Yŏngt'aek, "Ch'ŏnch'i? ch'ŏnjae? (Idiot? genius?)," in Ch'angjo (March 1919).

———, "Hyesŏn ŭi sa (The death of Hyesŏn)," in Ch'angjo (February 1919).

———, "K wa kŭ ŏmŏni ŭi chugŭm (K and his mother's death)," in Ch'angjo (May 1921).

———, "Nammae (Brother and sister)," in Munjang (November 1939).

Han Int'aek, "Oppa (Older brother)," in Sindonga (May 1936).

Han Sŏrya, "Inyŏng (Mire)," in Munjang (May 1939).

———, "Maŭm ŭi hyangch'on (Village of the heart)," in Sinmun yŏnjae sosŏl chŏnjip 2 (Seoul: Kip'ŭnsaem, 1999).

————, "T'aeyang ŭn pyŏng tŭlda (The sun grows ill)," in Han Sŏrya tanp'yŏn sŏnjip 2 Kwihyang, ed. Kim Oegŏn (Seoul: T'aehaksa, 1989).

————, "Yujŏn (Vicissitudes)," in Han Sŏrya tanp'yŏn sŏnjip 3 sukmyŏng, ed. Kim Oegŏn (Seoul: T'aehaksa, 1989).

Hyŏn Chin'gŏn, "Chŏkdo (The equator)" (Seoul: Munhak kwa pip'yŏngsa, 1988).

————, "Kohyang (Hometown)," in Han'guk sosŏl munhak taegye 7 (Seoul: Tusan donga, 1997).

————, "Sul kwŏnhanŭn sahoe (A society that drives you to drink)," in Hyŏn Chin'gŏn chŏnjip 4 (Seoul: Munhak kwa pip'yŏngsa, 1988).

Hyŏn Kyŏngjun, "Yumaeng (Nomads)," in Inmun p'yŏngnon (July 1940).

Kim Namch'ŏn, "Kil uesŏ (Upon the road)," in Munjang (July 1939).

————, "Maek (Barley)," in Maek (Seoul: Ŭryumunhwasa, 1947).

————, "Odŭi (Mulberry)," in Munjang (April 1944).

————, "Sarang ŭi sujokkwan (Aquarium of love)" (Seoul: Inmunsa, 1940).

————, "Taeha (The great river)" (Seoul: Inmunsa, 1939).

————, "T ilbosa (The T daily news)," in Inmun p'yŏngnon (November 1939).

————, "Tŭngbul (Lamplight)," in Kungmin munhak (March 1942).

Kim Tongin, "K paksa ŭi yŏn'gu (Doctor K's research)," in Kim Tongin chŏnjip 2 (Seoul: Chosŏn ilbosa, 1988).

————, "Maŭm i yŏt'ŭn chayŏ (Oh, ye with faint hearts)," in Ch'angjo, Volume 3 (December 1919).

————, "Munŭngja ŭi anhae (The incompetent's wife)," in Kim Tongin chŏnjip 2.

————, "Sigol Hwang sŏbang (Country Mr. Hwang)," in Kim Tongin chŏnjip 1 (Seoul: Chosŏn ilbosa, 1987).

————, "Sup'yŏngsŏn nŏmŏro (Over the horizon)," in Kim Tongin chŏnjip 7 (Seoul: Chosŏn ilbosa, 1988).

————, "Ŭmak kongbu (The study of music)," in Ch'angjo (January 1921).

————, "Yakhanja ŭi sŭlp'ŭm (Sadness of the weak)," in Ch'angjo, Volume 1 (February 1919).

Kim Tongni, "Onui (Brother and sister)," in Kim Tongni chŏnjip 1 (Seoul: Minŭmsa, 1995).

Kim Yujŏng, "Pom pom (Spring, spring)," in Kim Yujŏng chŏnjip (Seoul: Hyŏndae munhaksa, 1968).

————, "Ttŏk (Rice cake)," in Kim Yujŏng chŏnjip.

Ku Yŏnhak, "Sŏlchungmae (Plum blossoms in the snow)," in Han'guk sinsosŏl chŏnjip 6 (Seoul: Ŭryu munhwasa, 1968).

No Chayŏng, "Insaeng t'ŭkkŭp (Life special express)," in Sinmun yŏnjae sosŏl chŏnjip 4 (Seoul: Kip'ŭnsaem, 1999).

Pak Hwasŏng "Onch'ŏnjang ŭi pom (Spring at a hot springs hotel)," in Chungang (July 1936).

Pak T'aewŏn, "Ch'ŏnbyŏn p'unggyŏng (Streamside scenes)" (Seoul: Pangmun ch'ulp'ansa, 1947).

————, "P'iro (Fatigue)," in Sosŏlga Kubo-ssi ŭi iril (A day in the life of the novelist Kubo) (Seoul: Munjangsa, 1938).

————, "Sosŏlga Kubo-ssi ŭi iril (A day in the life of the novelist Kubo)," in Sosŏlga Kubo-ssi ŭi iril.

————, "Sup'unggŭm (Accordian)," in Pak T'aewŏn tanp'yŏnjip (Seoul: Hagyesa, 1939).

Pak Yŏngjun, "Chungdokcha (The addict)," in Minu Pak Yŏngjun chŏnjip 1 (Seoul: Tongyŏn, 2002).

Pang In'gŭn, "Nun onŭn pam (A snowy evening)," in Ch'angjo, Volume 6 (May 1920).

Sim Hun, "Yŏngwŏn ŭi miso (Eternal smile)," in Han'guk munhak chŏnjip 17 (Seoul: Minjung sŏgwan, 1959).

Yi Hyosŏk, "Churiya (Julia)," in Yi Hyosŏk chŏnjip 4 (Seoul: Ch'angmisa, 1990).

————, "Habibin (Harbin)," in Munjang (October 1940).

————, "Orion kwa imgŭm (Orion and the apple)," in Yi Hyosŏk chŏnjip 1 (Seoul: Ch'angmisa, 1990).

————, "Purip (Leaves of grass)," in Yi Hyosŏk chŏnjip 3 (Seoul: Ch'angmisa, 1990).

————, "Pyŏkkong muhan (Endless blue sky)" (Seoul: Ch'unjosa, 1959).

Yi Injik, "Hyŏl ŭi nu (Tears of blood)," in Sinsosŏl, Pŏnan (yŏk) sosŏl che-1 kwŏn (New novels, adapted (translated) novels, volume 1) (Seoul: Asea munhwasa, 1978).

————, "Moranbong (Peony peak)," in Han'guk sinsosŏl chŏnjip (Seoul: Ŭlyu munhwasa, 1968).

Yi Kiyŏng, "In'gan suŏp (Human lessons)" (Seoul: Munu ch'ulp'ansa, 1948).

————, "Kwangsanch'on (Mining town)," in Kwangsanch'on (Seoul: Sŏngmundang, 1944).

————, "Oegyowŏn kwa chŏndo puin (The salesman and the missionary woman)," in Minch'on (Seoul: Kŏnsŏl ch'ulp'ansa, 1946).

————, "Oppa ŭi pimil p'yŏnji (Oppa's secret letter)," in Kaebyŏk (July 1924).

————, "Pyŏnjŏlcha wa kŭ ŭi anhae (A turncoat and his wife)," in Sin'gyedan (May 1935).

————, "Saengmyŏngsŏn (Lifeline)," in Pando chi kwang (August 1941).

————, "Sin'gaeji (Newly-opened land)" (Seoul: Sammunsa, 1938).

————, "Sŏhwa (Fire play)," in Sŏhwa (Seoul: Tonggwangdang sŏjŏm, 1937).

————, "Taeji ŭi adŭl (Son of the earth)," in Han'guk kŭndae changp'yŏn sosŏl taegye 14 (Seoul: T'aehaksa, 1988).

Yi Kwangsu, "Aika (Is it love?)," trans. Kim Yunsik, Munhak sasang (February 1981).

————, "Chaesaeng (Rebirth)," in Yi Kwangsu chŏnjip 2.

————, "Hŭlk (The soil)," in Yi Kwangsu chŏnjip 6 (Seoul: Samjungdang, 1962).

————, "Hyŏngmyŏngga ŭi anae (A revolutionary's wife)," in Yi Kwangsu chŏnjip 2 (Seoul: Samjungdang, 1966).

————, "Kaech'ŏkcha (Pioneer)," in Yi Kwangsu ŭi chŏnjip 1 (Seoul: Samjungdang, 1962).

————, "Kŭ ŭi chasŏjŏn (His autobiography)," in Yi Kwangsu chŏnjip 9 (Seoul: Samjungdang, 1962).

————, "Kŭ yŏja ŭi ilsaeng (That woman's life)," in Yi Kwangsu chŏnjip 7 (Seoul: Samjungdang, 1966).

————, "Mujŏng (The Heartless)," (Seoul: Hoedong sŏgwan, 1925).

————, "Nongch'on kyebal (Rural development)," in Yi Kwangsu chŏnjip 17 (Seoul: Samjungdang, 1963).

————, "Sarang ŭi tagakhyŏng (The polygon of love)," in Yi Kwangsu chŏnjip 7.

————, "Sŏndoja (The leader)," in Yi Kwangsu chŏnjip 4 (Seoul: Samjungdang, 1962).

————, "Sonyŏn ŭi piae (The sorrows of a boy)," in Yi Kwangsu chŏnjip 14 (Seoul: Samjungdang, 1962).

————, "Yujŏng (Kindheartedness)," in Yi Kwangsu chŏnjip 8 (Seoul: Samjungdang, 1962).

Yi Sang, "Chido ŭ iamsil (Darkroom of the map)," in Yi Sang munhak chŏnjip 2, ed. Kim Yunsik (Seoul: Munhak sasangsa, 1991).

————, "Chiju hoesi (Two spiders meet a pig)," in Yi Sang munhak chŏnjip 2.

————, "Chongsaenggi (Record of a life)," in Yi Sang munhak chŏnjip 2.

————, "Hyuŏp kwa sajŏng (Closures and circumstances)," in Yi Sang munhak chŏnjip 2.

————, "Kongp'o ŭ ikirok (Record of fear)," in Yi Sang munhak chŏnjip 2.

————, "Nalgae (Wings)," in Yi Sang munhak chŏnjip 2.

————, "Pongbyŏlgi (Record of meeting and parting)," in Yi Sang munhak chŏnjip 2.

————, "Sirhwa (Lost flowers)," in Yi Sang munhak chŏnjip 2.

————, "Tanbal (The bob)," in Yi Sang munhak chŏnjip 2.

————, "Tonghae (Child's skeleton)," in Yi Sang munhak chŏnjip 2.

————, "12 wŏl 12 il (December 12)," in Yi Sang munhak chŏnjip 2.

Yi Sangch'un, "Kiro (Crossroads)," in Ch'ŏngch'un Volume 11 (November 1917).

Yi Sŏnhŭi, "Yŏin myŏngnyŏng (The female command)," in Sinmun yŏnjae sosŏl chŏnjip 4 (Seoul: Kip'ŭnsaem, 1999).

Yi T'aejun, "Kkamagwi (The crow)," in Chogwang (January 1936).

————, "Sasang ŭi wŏrya (Moonlit night of thought)," in Maeil sinbo (March 11, 1941).

————, "Sŏngmo (The Virgin Mary)," in Sinmun yŏnjae sosŏl chŏnjip 4, 2nd ed. (Seoul: Kip'ŭnsaem, 1999).

Yŏm Sangsŏp, "Mansejŏn (On the eve of the uprising)," in Yŏm Sangsŏp chŏnjip 1 (Seoul: Minŭmsa, 1987).

————, "P'yobonsil ŭi ch'ŏnggaeguri (Green frog of the specimen room)," in Yŏm Sangsŏp chŏnjip 9 (Seoul: Minŭmsa, 1987).

————, "Ttong p'ari wa kŭ ŭi anhae (Shit fly and his wife)," in Yŏm Sangsŏp chŏnjip 9.

Yu Chino, "Hwasangbo (Mellifluous score)," in Sinmun yŏnjae sosŏl chŏnjip 3, 2nd ed. (Seoul: Kip'ŭnsaem, 1999).

Yu Hangnim, "Magwŏn (Horse race ticket)," in Tanch'ŭng (April 1937).

POETRY

Ch'oe Namsŏn, "Kyŏngbu ch'yŏlto norae (Song of the Seoul-Busan railway)" (Seoul: Sinmungwan, 1908).

———, "Uri ŭi undongjang (Our playing field)," in Sonyŏn (December 1908).

Chŏng Chiyong, "Haehyŏp (The straight)," in Chŏng Chiyong chŏnjip 1, 2nd ed. (Seoul: Minŭmsa, 1992).

———, "Sigye rŭl chugim (Killing the clock)," in Chŏng Chiyong chŏnjip 1.

———, "Yurich'ang 1 (Windowpane 1)," in Chŏng Chiyong chŏnjip 1.

———, "Yurich'ang 2 (Windowpane 2)," in Chŏng Chiyong chŏnjip 1.

Im Hwa, "Han chan p'odoju rŭl (A glass of wine)," in Ch'an'ga (Seoul: Paegyangdang, 1947).

———, "Hwangmuji (Wasteland)," in Hyŏnhaet'an (Seoul: Tonggwangdang sŏjŏm, 1939).

———, "Negŏri ŭi Suni (Suni at the crossroads)," in Chosŏn chi kwang (January 1929).

———, "Ŏmŏni (Mother)," in Chosŏn chi kwang (April 1929).

———, "Uri oppa wa hwaro (My oppa and the brazier)," in K'apŭ siinjip (Seoul: Chipdansa, 1931).

———, "Yahaengch'a sok (Inside a night train car)," in Hyŏnhaet'an.

Kim Hyŏngwŏn, "Chujŏnggun (A bad drunk)," in Kaebyŏk (March 1922).

Kim Kirim, "Chyup'it'ŏ ch'ubang (Jupiter exile)," in Kim Kirim chŏnjip 1 (Seoul: Simsŏldang, 1988).

———, "Han'gang indogyo (Han river footbridge)," in Kim Kirim chŏnjip 1.

———, "Hot'el (Hotel)," in Ssinema p'unggyŏng (Cinema scenery), in Kim Kirim chŏnjip 1.

———, "'K'ŏp'i' chan ŭl tŭlgo (Holding a coffee cup)," in Kim Kirim chŏnjip 1.

———, "Pada ŭi hyangsu (Longing for the ocean)," in Kim Kirim chŏnjip 1.

———, "Pom ŭn chŏnbo to an ch'igo (Spring, without sending so much as a telegram)," in T'aeyang ŭi p'ungsok (Seoul: Hagyesa: 1939).

———, "Sanggong undonghoe (The sports meet of commerce and industry)," in Kim Kirim chŏnjip 1.

———, "Ssinema p'unggyŏng hot'el (Cinema view hotel)," in Kim Kirim chŏnjip 1.

Paek Sŏk, "Kujangno (The playing field street)," in Chŏngbon Paek Sŏk sijip, ed. Ko Hyŏngjin (Seoul: Munhak tongne, 2007).

———, "Kuksu (Noodles)," in Paek Sŏk chŏnjip, ed. Kim Chaeyong (Seoul: Silch'ŏn munhaksa, 1997).

———, "Na wa Natasha wa hŭin tangnagwi (I and Natasha and a white donkey)," in Chŏngbon Paek Sŏk sijip.

———, "Sŏnusa (Poem of good friends)," in Paek Sŏk chŏnjip.

———, "Tu Bo na Yi Paek kach'i (Like Du Fu and Li Bai)," in Chŏngbon Paek Sŏk sijip.

———, "Yŏu nan kol (Fox-born village)," in Chŏngbon Paek Sŏk sijip.

Yi Kwangsu, "Kich'a (Train)," in Chosŏn mundan (March 1925).

Yi Sang, "Au Magasin De Nouveautes (At the department store of novelties)," in Yi Sang munhak chŏnjip 1.

———, "Chasang (Self-portrait)," in Yi Sang munhak chŏnjip 1.

———, "Chibi (Paper monument)," in Yi Sang munhak chŏnjip 1.

———, "Ch'ulp'anbŏp (Publication law)," in Yi Sang munhak chŏnjip 1, ed. Yi Sŭnghun (Seoul: Munhak sasangsa, 1989).

———, "Haengno (Path)," in Yi Sang munhak chŏnjip 1.

———, "Hŭnghaengmul ch'ŏnsa (Performance angel)," in Yi Sang munhak chŏnjip 1.

———, "Ijō na kagyaku hannō (A strange reversible reaction)," in Chosen to kenchiku (July 1931).

———, "Irŏnsi (This sort of poem)," in Yi Sang munhak chŏnjip 1.

———, "Ka oe ka chŏn (The story of a street outside a street)," in Yi Sang munhak chŏnjip 1.

———, "Kongbok (Empty stomach)," in Yi Sang munhak chŏnjip 1.

———, "Kŏul (Mirror)," in Yi Sang munhak chŏnjip 1.

———, "Kŭmje (Taboo)," in Yi Sang munhak chŏnjip 1.

———, "Le urine," in Yi Sang munhak chŏnjip 1.

———, "Muje (Untitled)," in Yi Sang munhak chŏnjip 1.

———, "Munbŏl (Lineage)," in Yi Sang munhak chŏnjip 1

———, "Ogamdo, si che 1 ho (Crow's-eye view, poem number 1)," in Yi Sang munhak chŏnjip 1

———, "Ŏlgul (Face)," in Yi Sang munhak chŏnjip 1.

———, "P'ach'ŏp (A torn memorandum)," in Yi Sang munhakchŏnjip 1

———, "Yŏktan (Divining by the book of changes)," in Yi Sang munhak chŏnjip 1.

———, "1931 nyŏn (1931)," in Yi Sang munhak chŏnjip 1.

———, "1933. 6. 1 (June 1, 1933)," in Yi Sang munhak chŏnjip 1.

Yi Yongak, "Chŏllado kasinae (Chŏlla province lass)," in Orangk'aekkot (Seoul: Amun'gak, 1947).

ESSAYS AND OTHER TEXTS

Ch'oe Namsŏn, "Simch'un sullye (Simch'un pilgrimage)," in Yuktang Ch'oe Namsŏn chŏnjip 6 (Seoul: Hyŏnamsa, 1973).

Ch'oe Sŭngman, "Na ŭi hoegorok (My memoirs)" (Inchŏn: Inha taehakkyo ch'ulp'anbu, 1985).

Chŏn Yŏngt'aek, "Togŏrok (Record of a monologue)," in Hak chi kwang, Volume 10 (May 1916).

Chŏng Int'aek, "Pulsanghan Yi Sang (Pitiful Yi Sang)," in Chogwang (December 1939).

Ham Taehun, "Nambuk Manju p'yŏndapki (A record of travels in south and north Manchuria)," in Chogwang (July 1939).

Hyŏn Sangyun, "Kangnyŏk chuŭi wa Chosŏn ch'ŏngnyŏn (Powerism and the youth of Korea)," in Hak chi kwang, Volume 6 (July 1915).

Im Hwa, "Chŏnch'e chuŭi ŭi munhangnon (Theory of totalitarian literature)," in Munhak ŭi nolli (Seoul: Hagyesa, 1940).

Kim Kirim, "Chosŏn munhak e ŭi pansŏng (Reflections on Korean literature)," in Inmun p'yŏngnon (October 1940).

———, "Ko Yi Sang ŭi ch'uŏk (Memories of the late Yi Sang)," in Chogwang (June 1937).

Kim Namch'ŏn, "Ilsinsang ŭi chilli wa moral (Personal truth and morals)," in Chosŏn ilbo (April 22, 1938).

———, "Set'ae p'ungsok myosa kit'a (The description etc. of social conditions and customs)," in Kim Namch'ŏn chŏnjip 1, ed. Chŏng Houng (Seoul: Pagijŏng, 2000).

Kim Soun, "Hanŭlkkŭt e sarado (Even living at the edge of the sky)" (Seoul: Tonghwa ch'ulp'an kongsa, 1968).

Kim Yŏp, "Kangho esŏ Tongjŏngho kkaji (From Edo to Dongting Lake)," in Ch'angjo, Volume 3 (December 1919).

Ko Il, "Inch'ŏn sŏkkŭm (Inch'ŏn, past and present)" (Inch'ŏn: Kyŏnggi munhwasa, 1955).

Mun Chonghyŏk, "Simsim sanch'ŏn e mudŏjuo (Please bury me deep in nature)," in Yŏwŏn (April 1964).

Na Hyesŏk, "Isangchŏk puin (The ideal woman)," Hak chi kwang Volume 3 (December 1914).

No Chayŏng, "Pukhaedo ŭi chŏngjo (The atmosphere of Hokkaido)," in Nae hon i pult'al ttae (Seoul: Ch'ŏngjosa, 1928).

———, "Yŏsŏng undong ŭi cheil inja Ellen K'ei (Ellen Key, the leader of the women's movement)," in Kaebyŏk (February 1921).

Pak Sŏgyun, "Chagi ŭi kaejo (Reconstructing 'oneself')," in Hak chi kwang, Volume 20 (July 1920).

Yang Chudong, "Munju pansaenggi (Record of half a life spent on literature and liquor)," in Reprint (Seoul: Sint'aeyangsa ch'ulp'an'guk, 1962).

Yi Hyosŏk, "Koyohan 'Don' ŭi pam (The silent night of 'Don')," in Yi Hyosŏk chŏnjip 7 (Seoul: Ch'angmisa, 1990).

———, "Nangnang tabanggi (Record of Nangnang Tearoom)," in Yi Hyosŏk chŏnjip 7.

Yi Kiyŏng, "Manju wa nongmin munhak (Manchuria and agrarian literature)," in Inmun p'yŏngnon (November 1939).

Yi Kwangsu, "Bungaku no kokuminsei (The nationality of literature)," in Kyŏngsŏng ilbo (November 14, 1939).

———, "Chanyŏ chungsimnon (On the primacy of children)," in Ch'ŏngch'un (September 1918).

———, "Ch'inilp'a ŭi pyŏn (Excuses of a Japanese collaborator)," in Yi Kwangsu chŏnjip 13 (Seoul: Samjungdang, 1962).

———, "Ch'ŏnjaeya! ch'ŏnjaeya! (Oh, genius! oh, genius!)," in Yi Kwangsu chŏnjip 17 (Seoul: Samjungdang, 1962).

———, "Ch'ungmugong yujŏk sullye (Pilgrimage to the sites of Admiral Yi Sunsin)," in Yi Kwangsu chŏnjip 18 (Seoul: Samjungdang, 1962).

———, "Haesamwi rosŏ (To Vladivostok)," in Ch'ŏngch'ŭn (March 1915).

————, "Honin e taehan kwan'gyŏn (Personal views on marriage)," in Yi Kwangsu chŏnjip 17.

————, "Honinnon (On marriage)," in Yi Kwangsu chŏnjip 17.

————, "Kŭllo wa munhwa 3—Ilbonin ŭi kŭllo e taehaya (Labor and culture 3—On the labor of the Japanese)," in Maeil sinbo (July 1, 1941).

————, "Kŭmgangsan yugi (Record of a journey to the Kŭmgang Mountains)," in Yi Kwangsu chŏnjip 18.

————, "Kyoyukka chessi ege (To the esteemed educators)," in Yi Kwangsu chŏnjip.

————, "Minjok kaejoron (On national reconstruction)," in Yi Kwangsu chŏnjip 17.

————, "Munsa wa suyang (The writer and cultivation)," in Ch'angjo (January 1921).

————, "Na ŭi kobaek (My confession)," in Yi Kwangsu chŏnjip 13.

————, "Odo tapp'a yŏhaeng (Traveling through five provinces on foot)," in Yi Kwangsu chŏnjip 18.

————, "Sensō to bungaku (War and literature)," in Sinsidae (August 1944).

————, "Sinsaenghwallon (On a new life)," in Yi Kwangsu chŏnjip 17.

————, "Sonyŏn ege (To the boys)," in Yi Kwangsu chŏnjip 17.

————, "Sŭp'ooch'ŭ t'ongje (Sports regulation)," in Yi Kwangsu chŏnjip.

————, "Sŭp'ooch'ŭ yŏl (The sports boom)," in Yi Kwangsu chŏnjip 13.

————, "Taegu esŏ (From Daegu)," in Yi Kwangsu chŏnjip 18.

————, "Taitoa bungaku no michi (The path of greater East Asian literature)," in Kungmin munhak (January 1945).

————, "Tonggyŏng chapsin (Miscellaneous correspondence from Tokyo)," in Yi Kwangsu chŏnjip 17.

————, "Tongjŏng (Sympathy)," in Ch'ŏngch'un (December 1914).

————, "Tosan An Ch'angho (Tosan An Ch'angho)," in Yi Kwangsu chŏnjip 13.

————, "Yesul kwa insaeng (Art and life)," in Yi Kwangsu chŏnjip 16 (Seoul: Samjungdang, 1962).

————, "Yesul ŭi kŭmil myŏngil (The today and tomorrow of art)," in Maeil sinbo (August 6, 1940).

————, "Yŏnae wa chasal (Love and suicide)," in Yi Kwangsu chŏnjip 13.

Yi Sang, "Aeya (A sad night)," in Yi Sang munhak chŏnjip 3.

————, "Choch'un chŏmmyo (Early spring sketches)," in Yi Sang munhak chŏnjip.

————, "Ch'ŏtpŏntchae pangnang (The first wandering)," in Yi Sang munhak chŏnjip 3.

————, "Ch'udŭn gchapp'il (Miscellaneous writings by autumn lamplight)," in Yi Sang munhak chŏnjip 3.

————, "Hwang (A dog)," in Yi Sang munhak chŏnjip 3.

————, "Hwang ŭi ki (Record of a dog)," in Yi Sang munhak chŏnjip 3.

————, "Hyŏlsŏ samt'ae (Three forms of writing in blood)," in Yi Sang munhak chŏnjip 3.

————, "Kakhyŏl ŭi ach'im (Morning of hemoptysis)," in Yi Sang munhak chŏnjip 3.

————, "Kongp'o ŭi sŏngch'ae (Fortress of fear)," in Yi Sang munhak chŏnjip 3.

————, "Kudu (Dress shoes)," in Yi Sang munhak chŏnjip 3.

————, "Kwŏnt'ae (Ennui)," in Yi Sang munhak chŏnjip 3.

————, "Mosaek (Evening twilight)," in Yi Sang munhak chŏnjip 3, ed. Kim Yunsik (Seoul: Munhak sasangsa, 1993).

————, "Ŏrisogŭn sŏkban (A foolish supper)," in Yi Sang munhak chŏnjip 3.

————, "Pulhaenghan kyesŭng (Unfortunate succession)," in Yi Sang munhak chŏnjip 3.

————, "Sanch'aek ŭi kaŭl (Autumn of the promenade)," in Yi Sang munhak chŏnjip 3.

————, "Sanch'on yŏjŏng (Lingering impressions of a mountain village)," in Azalea: Journal of Korean Literature & Culture Volume 2, trans. John M. Frankl (Harvard University, 2008).

————, "Sanmukchip (Collection of scattered ink)," in Yi Sang munhak chŏnjip 3.

————, "Sasin 7 (Private correspondence 7)," in Yi Sang munhak chŏnjip 3.

————, "Sasin 9 (Private correspondence 9)," in Yi Sang munhak chŏnjip 3.

————, "Tonggyŏng (Tokyo)," in Yi Sang munhak chŏnjip 3.

Yi Sŏn'gŭn, "Manju wa Chosŏn (Manchuria and Korea)," in Chogwang (July 1939).

Yu Kilchun, "Sŏyu kyŏnmun (Things seen and heard in the West)," trans. Hŏ Kyŏngjin (Seoul: Hanyang ch'ulp'an, 1995).

Index

About the Contributors

Janet Poole is an associate professor in the Department of East Asian Studies at the University of Toronto. Her research and teaching interests lie in aesthetics in the broad context of colonialism and modernity, in history and theories of translation, and in the creative practice of literary translation. Her book *When the Future Disappears: The Modernist Imagination in Late Colonial Korea* writes the creative works of Korea's writers into the history of global modernism, and colonialism into the history of fascism, through an exploration of the writings of poets, essay writers, fiction writers, and philosophers from the final years of the Japanese empire. It won the Modernist Studies Association Book Prize (2015) and Honorable Mention for the Association of Asian Studies James B. Palais Prize (2016).

https://www.eas.utoronto.ca/people/directories/all-faculty/janet-poole

John M. Frankl is professor of Korean and comparative literature at Underwood College at Yonsei University. Frankl completed a BA at the University of California, Berkeley, in East Asian languages, after which he earned an MA at Yonsei University in the Department of Korean Language and Literature. Following Yonsei, he attended Harvard University, earning an AM in regional studies: East Asia and a PhD in East Asian languages and civilizations in 2003. He then returned to UC Berkeley to spend the following year as a postdoctoral fellow, after which he returned to Korea and Yonsei. He is the author of the book, *Han'guk munhak-e nat'anan oeguk ŭŭ ŭŭim* (Images of "The Foreign" in Korean Literature and Culture) published in Seoul by Somyŏng in 2008, as well as several articles on Yi Sang, the most recent— "Distance as Anti-Nostalgia: Distorted Memories of Rural Korea in Yi Sang's 'Ennui'"—appearing in *The Journal of Korean Studies*, Spring 2012.

https://www.harvard-yenching.org/person/john-mark-frankl/

Kyounghoon Lee is a professor in the Department of Korean Language and Literature at Yonsei University. He is widely considered to be one of the most highly regarded commentators on modernism and colonial literature and it is the penetration of his insights that have won him so wide an audience. His research and teaching interests have focused on everyday life, modernity, mass culture, and urban space, with special interest in wartime fascism and *chin-il* (pro-Japanese) literary works. His scholarship has contributed greatly to a variety of related fields whose work relates to such things as Japanese colonialism/imperialism; interactions among Japan, Korea, and Manchuria; the circulation of texts and culture in early twentieth-century Northeast Asia; and the reception of Western (often American) culture and language in Korea and Japan. A prodigious scholar, Lee is the author of seven monographs, including, *A Study on the Pro-Japanese Literature of Yi Kwangsu* (1998), *A Certain 100 Years, A Pleasurable New Life* (1999), *Yi Sang, The Piercing Rhetoric* (2000), *The Birth of Oppa* (2003), *Dictionary of Manners and Customs in Early Modern Korean Literature* (2006), *Memories of the Waiting Room* (2007), and *The Sunday of History, The Sunday after History: The Modern Literature of Colony* (2018). He has also edited several important volumes as well as written numerous essays on colonial writers such as Yi Sang, Pak Taewŏn, and Yŏm Sang-sŏp, which have appeared in such journals as *SAI, Hyŏndae munhak ŭi yŏn'gu, Munhak kwa sahoe, Sahoe wa yŏksa*, and *Sanghŏ hakbo*. He has also translated a number of Japanese and English works into Korean by Karatani Kojin, Takahashi Fujitani, Tomi Suzuki, Michael Ryan, among others.

Theodore Jun Yoo is a professor of Korean language and literature at Yonsei University. He has authored three books, all with University of California Press. His first, *The Politics of Gender in Colonial Korea: Education, Labor, and Health, 1910–1945* (2008), was followed by *It's Madness: The Politics of Mental Health in Colonial Korea* (2016) and, most recently, *The Koreas: The Birth of Two Nations Divided* (2020). His next book *#Seoul* is under contract, also with UC Press, and explores the city through time and space: "a place of crucial bearers of cultural memories and a vast archive of stories."
https://tableau.uchicago.edu/articles/2021/04/microhistory-making

www.ingramcontent.com/pod-product-compliance
Lightning Source LLC
Chambersburg PA
CBHW022303280326

41932CB00010B/969